State of the Clinical Trials Industry

A Sourcebook of Charts and Statistics

2006

THOMSON
CENTERWATCH

22 Thomson Place · Boston, MA 02210
Phone (617) 856-5900 · Fax (617) 856-5901
www.centerwatch.com

THOMSON
CENTERWATCH

State of the Clinical Trials Industry

Editor
Mary Jo Lamberti, Ph.D.

Contributors
Paul Dewberry
Stephen DeSantis
Jody Kalt
Sara Gambrill
Steve Zisson

Design
Paul C. Gualdoni, Jr.

ISBN 1-930624-50-6

Table of Contents

List of Figures and Tables

FOREWORD

Thank you for purchasing a copy of *State of the Clinical Trials Industry—2006*, the highly anticipated second edition of our top selling industry sourcebook. In our 2005 edition we took some of the most useful aspects of our long running An Industry in Evolution sourcebook and combined them with the latest market intelligence data, news briefs and editorial features to create a truly unique and comprehensive picture of the clinical trials marketplace. The result was our top-selling publication of 2005 and our top-selling sourcebook of all time. I can't tell you how much we appreciate your purchase and continued business. Many customers shared stories with us about business plans and presentations in which they incorporated data from the book and we helped a number of customers by developing custom reports to address their specific needs or expand upon a particular data set.

State of the Clinical Trials Industry—2006 builds on this momentum, by adding the following new features:

- Over one-hundred fifty new slides, many featuring proprietary CenterWatch data
- Hundreds of updated slides
- Ninety additional pages of material
- Twelve disease profiles with pipeline information
- 2005 Year-in-Review Article
- Top stories from The CenterWatch Monthly newsletter

- Reorganized to be more topical and useful, with an index, an expanded table of contents and list of figures

I am truly pleased with this edition of the sourcebook and I am confident that you will feel the same. I'd also like to thank all the members of our Market Intelligence and Editorial teams, especially Paul Dewberry and Dr. Mary Jo Lamberti who worked so hard over the past year to bring this product to you.

Our goal is to continue providing you with unique information and insights that you can't find anywhere and that you've come to expect from Thomson CenterWatch. Should you find that your specific needs exceed the contents of the book in some way, please contact our Market Intelligence group directly and speak with them about a custom report. Thank you for your continued business and best wishes for a safe and happy year.

Dan McDonald, Vice President
Thomson CenterWatch

INTRODUCTION
2005 in Review

The Year of Surprising Data

By Sara Gambrill and Steve Zisson
Published January 2006

Sometimes even the most hardened industry observers get taken aback by a surprising development or new revelation about the clinical trials industry. 2005 was a year for a number of unexpected new trends in this industry. Some developments didn't seem to fit with the conventional wisdom.

Maybe the most talked about reversal, and top story for the year, was revealed in the Thomson CenterWatch 2005 Survey of Investigative Sites in the U.S. which found that most sites rate the contract and budget negotiation and approval process as the number one factor most often causing study delays—edging out the oft-cited patient recruitment and enrollment process.

Of course, delays in the contract and budget negotiation and approval process can have broad implications for the drug development process, including holding up the patient recruitment and enrollment process. Sites' attempts to speed the process before signing a contract by completing regulatory packets without receiving an upfront fee often backfire, costing sponsors and sites time and money. Accepting unfavorable terms can lead to a site cutting corners on the informed consent process or to investigative site insolvency.

Investigative sites have been trying to address the problem areas—low fees, rotating and/or ill-informed sponsor contract personnel, no industry-wide standardized contract and indemnification clauses—for years, but for some they have only gotten worse, in fact, the worst problem for sites in terms of study delay.

The clinical research industry has focused for so long on time reductions in the patient recruitment and enrollment process, according to industry insiders, that it has lost sight of the fact that the unnecessarily difficult and protracted contract and budget negotiation and approval process causes major delays in the patient recruitment and enrollment process. But, investigative sites see ways to improve the contract and budget negotiation and approval process with efforts such as a standardized contract. This, in turn, could improve cycle times for the patient recruitment and enrollment process.

Given this unexpected turn of events in the site arena, CenterWatch will study the progress that sponsor companies have made in its next Survey of U.S. Sites and continue to monitor new attempts to streamline the vexing problem of the contract and budget negotiation and approval process, both in CenterWatch's upcoming Survey of Investigative Sites in Europe this year and in the next iteration of the Survey of Investigative Sites in the U.S. next year.

Clinical Trials Transparency

The push for more clinical trials transparency has been growing the past 18 months, and CenterWatch data revealed that pharmaceutical companies, under growing pressure to provide more information about clinical research on new drugs and to restore public trust in the industry, have taken significant steps towards clinical trials transparency. They spent about $90 million in 2005 to disclose clinical trials information.

A CenterWatch analysis found that 100% of the top 15 biopharmaceutical companies are posting their active clinical trials online in some capacity. Specifically, 93% of the companies registered their studies on clinicaltrials.gov, while 60% of the drug companies posted their information on commercial registries such as centerwatch.com and 33% posted on their own web sites. In the past 18 months alone, the top 15 biopharmaceutical companies have posted more than 1,300 trials.

At a time when big pharma is under pressure to keep down headcount, on average, major biopharmaceutical companies have dedicated about 40 full-time equivalents (FTEs), depending on the retrospective work required, to clinical transparency efforts. To produce and maintain registries, personnel are needed in areas such as project management, web development, data entry, medical writing, regulatory and legal. Once the backlog of trial data has been processed and systems established, large pharmaceutical companies will require somewhere between five and 10 FTEs to maintain the registries depending on the volume of research. GlaxoSmithKline, for one, has dedicated about 40 FTEs to work on summaries and databases for its clinical trial results register.

While many companies have expended significant resources, there is still much work to be done. Efforts to post trial results lag behind the progress made in registering active clinical trials. CenterWatch analysis found that currently about 87% of the top 15 companies are posting trial results online; most companies are posting results to the new PhRMA site (clinicalstudyresults.org).

Pharmaceutical companies must continue to explain to the public what all the clinical trial information available on web sites really means. And more regulatory bodies will want more information. The state of Maine, for example, recently passed a law requiring drug manufacturers who do business in the state to disclose clinical trial data, including adverse impacts, on a publicly accessible web site approved by the Maine Department of Health and Human Services. At least nine states this year introduced legislation

that would require public registry and disclosure of clinical drug trials. Multiple web sites, with differing data requirements, present a problem for biopharmaceutical companies.

Negative Press

The clinical trials industry continues to be under assault from a mainstream media that often doesn't understand how the industry functions. Thomson CenterWatch recently completed a survey of how the top daily newspapers in the United States report on clinical trials and found that their reporting for the most part failed to discuss potential risks and benefits for patients. This surprising study found both successes and failures in the discussion of clinical trials in the print media, which point to consistent trends in the public discourse surrounding drug development and trial participation. The reporting of basic information and context were deemed largely successful, supporting a strong public awareness of many types of drug development efforts. Unfortunately, there were shortcomings noted regarding the inclusion of information on the intrinsic risks and potential benefits of trial participation, and insufficient attention was paid to the role of regulatory and monitoring authorities. This lack of discourse supports a lack of understanding in the public about clinical research, which bears important implications for CROs, sites and sponsors conducting clinical trials.

The most extreme example of negative press came when SFBC International, a CRO, was hammered by a series of reports by Bloomberg that questioned, among a number of issues, its recruitment of poor immigrants at its Miami facility. While the series of stories in November and December focused mainly on SFBC, it also called into question industry practices. While one can debate the merits of reporting in the article, the fact is that public stock market is merciless. SFBC's share price plunged to around $12 a share, almost one-quarter the value of its 52-week high. These stories will be talked about for awhile.

While the questions about SFBC piqued Congress's interest about how the industry operates, Wall Street's lack of confidence in SFBC has not spread to other public CROs. Most of the top CROs, such as PPD, Parexel, PRA, Covance and ICON, are at least within shouting distance of healthy 52-week highs.

Volunteers Satisfied

Despite public perception of clinical trials possibly at an all time low, another counterintuitive Thomson CenterWatch report finds that a vast majority of those who participate in clinical studies are satisfied with their overall quality of care and would not only volunteer for another study but would recommend a friend or family member to a clinical study.

The survey also found that participants were cognizant of clinical studies as a treatment option, indicating that the industry has improved its efforts to get the word out about clinical trials, and showed that nearly half of the study volunteers had participated in two or more trials. Those involved in clinical research at the investigative site level say the report's conclusions reflect what they see in caring for study volunteers. In particular, during an era when primary care doctors are under pressure to keep patient visits short, industry experts say the survey results indicate that those who participate in clinical trials feel they get more attention from clinical research investigators and clinical research coordinators, a more robust battery of exams and tests, and benefit from study staff who take time to educate volunteers.

Emerging Markets

One of the biggest surprises for 2005 is how quickly some global markets are developing. Center-Watch focused its coverage on these disparate markets and found many differences—and similarities. Among those markets are:

China

Increasingly, large pharmaceutical companies are shifting the way they treat China in the context of their global drug development programs. Instead of an outsourcing opportunity, China has—within the past five years—become a place where the top pharmaceutical companies are establishing a clinical research unit. In some cases, pharmaceutical companies are shifting from an emerging market model in China to a developed market model. AstraZeneca has been a leader in China but other global biopharmaceutical companies are following AstraZeneca there.

Singapore

The clinical trials market in Singapore has doubled in size since the country adopted ICH-GCP in 1998. Bolstered by well-developed technology and hospital infrastructures, strict adherence to international standards, considerable investment by multinational pharmaceutical, biotech companies and CROs, and a well-educated English-speaking population, Singapore has become an attractive place to conduct clinical trials. In addition, the country's pro-business policies have helped make Singapore an important hub for companies' pan-Asian strategy for clinical trials

South Africa and Africa

Growth of the clinical trials industry in South Africa stems from recent legislative changes, a favorable exchange rate, wider public awareness about clinical trials and the need for doctors to find alternative revenue streams. Underlying it all is the production of consistent quality data. Further growth should result from South Africa's role as a gateway to the rest of Africa.

India

CROs and SMOs continue to move headlong into the Indian market. Two years ago, about a dozen CROs and a couple of site management organizations (SMOs) had set up shop in India, the second largest pharmaceutical market in Asia. Now those numbers have doubled from both CROs and SMOs. Broad regulatory reforms combined with highly attractive professional and patient populations make India a very compelling region for conducting global clinical trials. Intellectual property issues are still giving some pharmaceutical companies pause in India although Pfizer and Glaxo-SmithKline are making concerted efforts there.

In 2006, the Latin American clinical trials market is expected to be en fuego.

Looking to 2006

A number of sponsors and CROs will be watching the success Wyeth and RPS had last year and see if they can duplicate it. Results from the 2005 Thomson CenterWatch survey of 612 investigative sites in the United States showed that the quality of sponsor-site relationships has improved across the board. Wyeth, which was rated highly in the CenterWatch survey, was faced with an enviable problem of having more than 200 new and ongoing studies and a new compound entering development each month for the next four years. So it wanted a new way to meet its growing regional field operation needs. The sponsor didn't see the value in paying hourly rates for monitors from $110 to $150, or about $300,000 a year. So Wyeth forged a strategic partnership with RPS. In the first year alone, the initiative shifted Wyeth's outsourcing model from 80% use of CROs to 20%. In years to come, Wyeth expects to continue this dramatic outsourcing shift.

With sponsors under increasing pressure to cut costs and, at the same time refill drug pipelines, the key area where they can make improvements—and show results—is in clinical development. Wyeth clearly needed to leap forward—and it did.

Wyeth's and RPS efforts will extend to Canada and Latin America. We will continue to watch those hot clinical trials markets, and others, for new trends that could cut drug development cycles.

INDUSTRY BRIEFS

CROs

January

Kentucky-based **Omnicare**, a provider of pharmaceutical care for the elderly, has acquired **Clinimetrics Research Associates**, a privately held contract research organization (CRO) headquartered in San Jose, Calif. It is the first CRO acquisition for Omnicare since 1998 when it bought IBAH. The addition of Clinimetrics would boost Omnicare's CRO business to about $160 million in annual revenue, according to Cheryl Hodges, spokeswoman for Omnicare. Before buying IBAH, Omnicare purchased another CRO Coromed in 1997. Founded in 1988, Clinimetrics is a 300-employee CRO with about $40 million in annual revenue. The CRO has a backlog of $85 million.

PPD, a contract research organization and specialty pharmaceutical company, has agreed to acquire biomarker business assets from privately held biotechnology company **SurroMed**. PPD and SurroMed have worked together for a number of years. PPD sold its genomics business in 2003 and took an equity stake in the biotech company. The acquisition will expand PPD's business by adding biomarker discovery and patient sample analysis services. Biomarkers are particular components of bodily fluids that indicate the progression or presence of a disease. SurroMed's technology allows clients to analyze patient samples for novel or known biomarkers, in the presence or absence of a drug. The changes in the biomarker profile of a patient can assist in the evaluation of the efficacy of a drug.

Cincinnati-based **Kendle** continues to stake its claim as a global contract research organization by opening offices in growing clinical trials markets, India and South Africa. In South Africa, Kendle is establishing a new office in Johannesburg, which will expand its access to patients across a number of therapeutic areas such as HIV/AIDS, cancer, diabetes, infectious diseases (tuberculosis, malaria and pneumonia) and neurological disorders. In India, Kendle is opening an office in New Delhi, joining more than a dozen global CROs that have set up shop in India. From its offices in India and South Africa, Kendle will provide phase I through IV clinical development services.

The **Association of Clinical Research Organizations** (**ACRO**), which represents the clinical outsourcing industry to regulators, biopharmaceutical customers and policy makers in the U.S. and worldwide, recently elected officers for 2005. Josef von Ricken-bach, chairman and chief executive officer of Parexel International, was elected chairman of ACRO. Candace Kendle, chairman and CEO of Kendle, will serve as treasurer.

Icon reported that its second quarter revenues increased 9% as its project cancellation rate improved dramatically, but earnings declined as expected by 7%. Even as its prospects improved, Icon said it cut its fiscal 2005 guidance to between

$1.68 to $1.70 a share. The company's cancellation rate plunged from 51% of gross business awards to 2%.

Australia-based **Bionomics Limited,** a genomics company that is developing therapeutics and diagnostics for central nervous system (CNS) disorders and cancer, has agreed to acquire the French contract research organization (CRO), Neurofit.

Februrary

Contract research organizations (CROs) continue to find Central and Eastern Europe to be fertile ground for expansion. Stamford, Conn.-based **AbCRO** continued its expansion into Southeastern Europe by opening a new office in Belgrade, Serbia. Founded in 1999, AbCRO also has offices in Bulgaria, Romania and Croatia. The 30-employee company combines U.S. management with local European staff to provide country-specific CRO expertise.

Miami-based **SFBC International**'s subsidiary **Anapharm** has opened a new bioanalytical laboratory at the company's facility in Toronto. The 10,000 square-foot laboratory is solely devoted to the high-pressure liquid chromatography-tandem mass spectrometry, or LC-MS-MS, technology platform. SFBC invested $4 million in the facility. This new laboratory is an extension of SFBC Anapharm's Quebec City bioanalytical laboratory. SFBC currently also has bioanalytical laboratories in Philadelphia; Princeton, N.J. and Barcelona, Spain.

Maryland-based **Medifacts International,** a global contract research organization (CRO) has received $16 million in equity financing from **Ampersand Ventures** and **SV Life Sciences (SVLS).** It is the first institutional funding for Medifacts, a 320-employee company founded in 1985. Medifacts focuses on cardiovascular, renal, pulmonary, stroke and metabolic clinical development programs, providing clinical trial management services such as cardiac safety services. In 2002, the company began a push to become a global CRO by opening offices in several countries. Medifacts International also has offices in Canada, Germany and China.

Parexel International is looking for stronger revenue growth in the next six months after a sluggish couple of quarters when its project cancellation rate rose to 13.4% of its backlog. Normally, Parexel's cancellation rate is 8% to 10%. Company officials told analysts that the higher than normal cancellation rate was fueled by losing a large phase III project. Backlog at Dec. 31, 2004 was $721 million, a 16% increase compared with its backlog reported a year earlier. For the six-month period from July to December 2004, the company reported net new business of $291.2 million. Parexel's sluggish performance in the past two quarters is similar to what other contract research organizations (CROs) have experienced. Its core clinical research services were flat at $94.9 million for the quarter ended Dec. 31, 2004, compared with the year ago quarter. A bright spot for Parexel has been its technology subsidiary, Perceptive Informatics, which was up 22% to $10.7 million for the quarter

March

Geny Research Center, a contract research organization (CRO) founded in 1999, with headquarters in Newton, Mass., and offices in Moscow and St. Petersburg, has opened a phase I unit close to Moscow. It is one of the first phase I units in Russia to be licensed by the Ministry of Health to perform clinical research activities.

Market leading contract research organization **Quintiles,** which was taken private in 2003, reported strong fourth quarter net revenue gains. The stronger overall performance of Quintiles, which must report quarterly financials since its move to become private was financed by public debt, has raised the question of whether the CRO leader will test the public markets once again. Several industry observers believe Quintiles will file for a public offering in the near future.

ClinPro launched a new medical imaging service for scanning and archiving medical images, including X-rays, CT and MRI images. The new medical imaging service is an addition to ClinPro's existing scan center technology. ClinPro's medical imaging system has been implemented and validated over the last several months to support clinical studies of two intervertebral disk devices under development by a large medical device company.

Kendle was selected as the *PharmaTimes*' Clinical Research Team of the Year for 2004. *PharmaTimes* is a global multimedia organization targeted to executives in the biopharmaceutical and healthcare industries. Members of the winning team were from Kendle's office in Crowthorne, England. Kendle becomes the first CRO to win the Clinical Research Team of the Year award.

April

Scirex, a CRO that focuses on analgesia, neurology and psychiatry clinical research, has joined the **DataLabs** CRO Partners Program. Scirex will add the DataLabsXC suite of software to the company's electronic data capture (EDC). "This partnership allows Scirex to build on our strong experience with multiple EDC systems as well as expand on our own internal EDC offerings and industry relationships," said Peter Black, corporate vice president for Strategic Initiatives at Scirex. While not an exclusive arrangement with DataLabs, sponsors working with Scirex will have access to this option for EDC in their clinical trials.

Irvine, Calif.-based **Paragon Biomedical,** a contract research organization (CRO) has entered into a definitive agreement to acquire **InDatum Ltd.,** a United Kingdom-based CRO with 20 employees specializing in data management, biostatistics and related services. Paragon officials said the acquisition of InDatum is part of Paragon's push for geographic service expansion. The InDatum acquisition will give Paragon's customers wider access to clinical trials expertise in Western and Eastern Europe, and India. Headquartered in High Wycombe, U.K., InDatum also has a rapidly growing presence in the southwest coast of Kerala, India.

Toronto, Canada-based **Ventana Clinical Research,** a contract research organization (CRO) specializing in early-phase and central nervous system (CNS) drug development, has opened a new phase I clinical facility that quadruples its capacity from

its previous unit. The phase I market remains a hot area of expansion for CROs and site management organizations (SMOs). Ventana's inpatient unit for phases I and II trials is designed for a variety of clinical studies, including first in human, single and multiple ascending dose, alcohol and drug interaction and neurocognitive assessments. The company, founded in 1997, also specializes in conducting ongoing abuse liability studies. In addition to the inpatient unit, Ventana has an outpatient clinic for later phase studies in a number of therapeutic areas.

Parexel hurriedly announced bad financial news—a $10 million shortfall in its third quarter revenue—on April 18 and its stock plunged nearly 20%. The analysts' conference came three days before the contract research organization was set to announce its full results for the quarter. The company said revenue fell short of management's expectations in the quarter, mainly due to underperformance in its Consulting and Marketing Services unit, but also caused by project delays, timing of contract signatures at a key pharmaceutical client, and staffing shortfalls.

PPD reported first quarter net revenue jumped 25% to $244.1 million. First quarter net revenue included a $10 million milestone payment to PPD related to the filing of the new drug application (NDA) for dapoxetine. First quarter 2005 income from operations was $47.9 million, compared with income from operations of $38.5 million for the same period in 2004. First quarter 2005 income from operations included a $5.1 million pre-tax gain on the exchange of assets associated with PPD's acquisition of **SurroMed**'s biomarker business. First quarter 2005 earnings per diluted share were $0.62, compared with $0.44 for the first quarter 2004. Development segment net revenue, which does not include reimbursed out-of-pocket expenses, for the first quarter of 2005 was $212.9 million, an increase of 21.9% compared with the same period in 2004.

May

AaiPharma and its domestic subsidiaries have filed for relief under chapter 11 of the U.S.

Bankruptcy Code in the U.S. Bankruptcy Court for the District of Delaware. The filing will allow AaiPharma to continue business operations during restructuring proceedings. AaiPharma also announced that it negotiated definitive agreements to receive $210 million in debtor-in-possession financing. The financing, subject to approval by the bankruptcy court, will be used to replace the company's existing $180 million senior credit facility and supplement the Company's cash flow during the reorganization process with a $30 million revolving credit facility.

June

Three companies, including **Quintiles**, have launched a joint venture to commercialize pharmaceutical products in the hot Asia-Pacific region, a market of more than $20 billion that is expected to double within 10 years. The other two partners in the joint venture, which will have an investment fund of $112 million, include Asia Pacific pharmaceutical services group, **Interpharma Asia Pacific**, parent of drug distributor **Zuellig Pharma**; and a Singapore-based investment company **Temasek Holdings Limited**. Each partner is expected to make an equal investment in the joint venture and own one-third of the company. The joint venture will draw on each partner's market knowledge and experience and in the Asia Pacific region to help drug companies focus their resources on R&D and provide outsourcing for product registration and sales and marketing of their mature brand portfolios. **PharmaLink**, the specialist Asia Pacific pharmaceutical marketing services division of Interpharma, will be transferred to the new joint venture and will help negotiate the acquisition of products and their subsequent marketing in the Asia Pacific healthcare market. Zuellig Pharma will provide distribution and logistics expertise while Quintiles will contribute regional commercialization expertise and experience in pharmaceutical outsourcing partnerships.

PRA International has started off an expected set of strategic acquisitions by acquiring two regulatory and product development consultancies: **Regulatory/Clinical Consultants, Inc. (RxCCI)** and **GMG BioBusiness Ltd. (GMG)**. PRA declined to give financial details of the acquisitions. A spokeswoman for the 2,500 employee contract research organization (CRO) said the company wouldn't release the number of employees at each consultancy. An April 2004 *CWWeekly* story estimated RxCCI's staff at 75 full-time employees. The company said both organizations will be integrated into PRA's strategic product development service offering within its global regulatory affairs group or other service groups where appropriate. PRA could be starting on a bit of an acquisition spree. The company still has money from its initial public offering in November for deals. PRA had about $69 million in cash at the end of the quarter.

MDS Pharma Services has opened new facilities in Sydney, Australia, and Petaling Jaya, Malaysia. Located in Pyrmont, Sydney, the new Australian facility offers access to clinical research sites, academic institutions, investigator networks and a significant patient population. The staff at this site provides project management, clinical monitoring and regulatory submission services throughout Australia and New Zealand. The new MDS Pharma Services Malaysian facility in Petaling Jaya, near Kuala Lumpur, was selected because of its location near leading teaching hospitals and national clinical research sites, and access to investigators and patient groups. This site also provides supply project management, clinical monitoring and regulatory submissions services. In addition to the two new global clinical development facilities, MDS Pharma Services' presence in the Asia-Pacific region also includes central lab and global clinical development services in China and Singapore, centralized ECG services based in Singapore serving Asia and Australia, field-based capabilities in Thailand and pharmacology services in Taiwan. The company established partnerships for phase II–IV services in Australia, India, Japan, South Korea and New Zealand.

Parexel will record a charge of $30 million to $35 million as part of a restructuring plan that includes office closures and 150 job cuts or relocations. In addition, the company said Carl Spalding, its chief operating officer, will retire by the end of the month. These moves continue to fuel speculation by industry observers that Parexel is getting ready for a merger or sale.

Pharm-Olam International (POI) has established an office in Boston, Mass. Mark Anderson, business development manager, will direct business development activities in Boston. Anderson has been with POI for nearly three years and in the clinical research industry for more than eight years. He previously held the position of business development manager, Europe and worked in POI's Ascot, England office.

Parexel has aligned its services to make it easier for clients to access the expertise that the company provides. This alignment reinforces the company's new positioning statement: "Expertise that makes the Difference." Parexel recently aligned its clinical research services with technology subsidiary Perceptive Informatics to help clients leverage advanced technologies to improve the speed and efficiency of their drug development programs. In addition, the company aligned Parexel consulting with its medical marketing services to help clients combine and incorporate strategic marketing as well as scientific and regulatory considerations into their drug development planning.

Remedium, a CRO founded in 1996 with headquarters in Espoo, Finland, and offices in Scandinavia and Central Eastern Europe, has entered collaborative agreements with two phase I units in Turkey. Remedium has 120 employees and 70 active projects. Though privately owned phase I units are not allowed to be established in Turkey yet, Remedium was able to form a collaborative agreement with Erciye University for use of its phase I unit in Kayseri and one with Ege University for a unit in Izmir. Both facilities have been inspected and licensed by the Turkish Ministry of Health. The phase I unit in Kayseri was established in 1999 and has 52 beds. It is fully staffed with four physicians, six nurses, four health technicians, two lab technicians and three administrative staff. The clinic manager is a professor of pharmacology and acts as principal

investigator for every clinical trial conducted there. Several trials can be run simultaneously there. The phase I unit in Izmir was established in 1996 and has 16 beds. It has two physicians, two nurses, one pharmacist and one administrative staff, all full-time. The clinical director is a pharmacologist and often acts as principal investigator.

LifeTree eClinical, a member of the FFF Enterprises family of companies and a provider of clinical electronic data capture (EDC) and analysis systems, has entered into a partnership with **Novotech**, a CRO based in Australia. Novotech will partner with LifeTree through its ClinPartners program to provide a suite of clinical services interfaced with the LifeTree eClinical applications. By combining their capabilities, LifeTree and Novotech offer clinical trial sponsors services packages including clinical trial management and monitoring; electronic data capture, analysis

July

Clinigene International, a wholly owned subsidiary of India's biotech company, **Biocon Limited**, and **Scirex**, a wholly owned subsidiary of advertising firm **Omnicom Group**, have signed a letter of intent to collaborate on global clinical trials. The agreement was signed at Scirex's headquarters in Horsham, Pa. during a recent visit by Dr. Kiran Mazumdar-Shaw, chairman and managing director of Biocon and Dr. Arvind Atignal, chief operating officer of Clinigene. The new relationship provides Scirex's clients access to expertise in clinical investigation in India and provides Clinigene the opportunity to expand its markets and participate in global clinical trial programs.

PPD has signed an agreement to exclusively license Duke University the development rights to PPD's patented portfolio of geranylgeranyl transferase (GGTase) inhibitor compounds. Inhibitors of GGTase are potential drug candidates for anticancer treatments. Under the terms of the agreement, researchers at Duke may spend up to three years advancing the development of these GGTase inhibitors in an effort to identify lead candidates for further preclinical and clinical development for the treatment of cancer. Duke will fund this research and development effort. In the event that Duke advances a GGTase inhibitor, PPD will share equally with Duke in future payments by third parties. An initial set of GGTase inhibitors was originally identified at Duke University Medical Center by Patrick J. Casey, Ph.D., James B. Duke professor of pharmacology and cancer biology and director, Center for Chemical Biology. PPD exclusively licensed the technology from Duke in 1998. Since that time, PPD developed a new collection of GGTase inhibitors using its combinatorial chemistry expertise.

Octagon Research Solutions has opened the company's European headquarters in Amersham, United Kingdom. The new office location is 30 miles northwest of London and will be the hub for the company's European business development, customer strategy and relationship management activities.

August

Bridgetech Holdings International, a publicly held company that offers healthcare products and services in the U.S. and Asian markets, has partnered with the Chinese University of Hong Kong (CUHK) to conduct clinical trials in Hong Kong and China. Bridgetech formed a contract research organization (CRO) with Amcare Labs International, an affiliate of **Johns Hopkins Medicine International** in June. Shortly afterward the CRO formed a strategic partnership with the **Mary Crowley Medical Research Center (MCMRC)** for the purpose of performing clinical trials in China on investigational cancer treatments. MCMRC is located within Baylor University Medical Center in Dallas and conducts early phase studies in vaccine, gene and cellular oncology therapies. Under that agreement, the Bridgetech CRO is the exclusive provider of clinical research services to MCMRC in China.

Parexel, which has been struggling financially, acquired **QdotPharma**, a phase I and IIa clinical pharmacology business located in George, South Africa. Parexel already has a strong presence in South Africa in phase I. QdotPharma, established in 1996, operates 32 beds and has therapeutic expertise in drugs to treat central nervous system, psychiatric, cardiovascular and metabolic conditions. Parexel, based in Waltham, Mass., acquired the business and related facilities for approximately $6 million in cash and potential earn-out payments. Still struggling with restructuring charges, Parexel swung to a big loss of $51.5 million for its fourth quarter ended June 30. The company reported an operating loss of $23.7 million, compared with operating income of $8.4 million in the comparable quarter of the prior year and a net loss for the quarter of $51.5 million, or $1.98 per diluted share, compared with net income of $6.5 million, or $0.24 per diluted share, for the prior year quarter. Parexel took $29.8 million in restructuring and special charges during the quarter for costs related to the abandonment of certain property leases, and employee separation benefits.

September

Toronto-based **MDS**, a life sciences company whose core is a Canadian diagnostics laboratory business, has launched a strategic plan to focus resources and management on opportunities within the global life sciences markets, which includes its contract research organization, MDS Pharma Services. The parent company, MDS, will also focus on molecular imaging and radio-therapeutics through its MDS Nordion and analytical instruments at MDS Sciex. The organic growth rate of these markets is expected to increase from 3%-5% to 7%-10% annually, according to the company. Other assets that don't contribute to the company's areas of focus are being evaluated, according to MDS. In addition, through a realignment of its operations and cost structures, the company is focused on near-term improvement in financial performance.

Startup **Aptuit**, which has already announced its planned acquisition of **Quintiles'** early development and packaging business, agreed to acquire **Almedica** for an undisclosed amount of cash. Aptuit plans to merge Almedica with those Quintiles' units. The combination would create a leader in clinical trial material supplies. Almedica already provides clinical trial materials to more than 150 customers globally and has facilities in Allendale, N.J., and Deeside, United Kingdom. Following the closing of both acquisitions, Greenwich, Conn.-based Aptuit will employ nearly 2,000 employees in seven operating facilities, with units that generated total revenues of nearly $225 million. The Quintiles acquisition includes preclinical services, pharmaceutical sciences, in addition to clinical trials supplies. Quintiles' units employ 1,400 people, mostly in Kansas City. The combined units will offer significant clinical supply and packaging capacity, and will provide an integrated global network for drug development, formulation, packaging, distribution and tracking, as well as an information technology platform providing customers with web-enabled inventory management. Aptuit customers will have access to centrally managed resources from five global packaging and logistics facilities, with more than 30 primary and over 50 secondary packaging suites, complemented by 27 clinical supply distribution depots reaching more than 70 countries around the globe. Almedica also offers formulation development capabilities in the U.S. and the U.K.

Philadelphia-based **Archbrook Capital Management, LLC,** an investment firm, has purchased a controlling interest in clinical trials industry financial management firm **Clinical Financial Services (CFS)** through its subsidiary, **Golden Eagle Partners.** Financial details of the transaction were not released by the privately held companies.

Basking Ridge, N.J.-based **i3** has introduced new business unit i3 Drug Safety, which brings together the i3 organization's epidemiology and drug safety resources into one unit to enhance the delivery of safety services to the industry. i3 Aperio, the drug experience registry launched in April to help researchers identify potential safety signals in new drugs faster, also will be part of i3 Drug Safety, under the direction of Arnold Chan, M.D., ScD. Led by Terri Madison, Ph.D, MPH, an epidemiologist from sister business i3 Statprobe, i3 Drug Safety includes a staff of drug safety coordinators—nurses, medical doctors and doctors of phar-

macy—as well as pharmacoepidemiologists. Alec Walker, M.D., Dr.PH, will continue as senior vice president of epidemiology. These experts will support a full range of safety services, including clinical trials, safety surveillance studies and pharmacovigilance activities.

October

In something of a reversal of a recent trend where global contract research organizations (CROs) have been opening offices in India or buying local CROs, an Indian CRO company has bought a CRO in the United States. **Jubilant Organosys Ltd.** has acquired 150-employee **Target Research Associates,** a New Jersey-based, CRO for $33.5 million in cash from **McCann-Erikson Worldwide,** a large advertising firm that purchased the CRO in 2002. At the time of the 2002 deal, McCann hoped its pharmaceutical marketing and CRO services would complement each other. According to Jubilant, it is the first acquisition of a U.S. CRO by an Indian company. The 2,500-employee company plans a major initiative supporting Jubilant's plan to expand its CRO services globally. Jubilant has an Indian subsidiary, Jubilant Clinsys Ltd., which conducts bioavailability studies at its 54-bed facility and bioanalytical laboratory. The company also provides clinical phase I through IV services.

ICON reported first quarter net revenues increased 10% to $85.9 million, thanks to strong performance in Europe and the rest of the world. Revenue from U.S. clinical operations rose just 4%, compared with an 18% jump in revenues outside of the U.S. Excluding the impact of acquisitions, revenue growth was 9% compared with the same quarter last year.

Greenwich, Conn.-based **Aptuit** has come a long way in a short period of time. The company unveiled its new senior management team as it completed its purchase of Quintiles' early development and packaging business units. Startup Aptuit also closed on its acquisition of Almedica International. With the closing of both acquisitions, Aptuit now employs nearly 2,000 staff in seven operating facilities, with units that generated total revenues of nearly $225 million. The Quintiles acquisition includes preclinical services, pharmaceutical sciences, in addition to clinical trials supplies. Quintiles' units employ 1,400 people, mostly in Kansas City. Almedica already provides clinical trial materials to more than 150 customers globally and has facilities in Allendale, N.J., and Deeside, United Kingdom.

Covance reported it has won a lawsuit against People for the Ethical Treatment of Animals (PETA). PETA agreed to a ban on conducting any infiltration of the company for five years. In May, PETA filed a complaint with the U.S. Department of Agriculture against Covance, claiming the company violated the federal Animal Welfare Act in a Virginia laboratory. The animal-rights organization had secretly videotaped a number of alleged animal-welfare violations in an 11-month period. Covance sued the organization for fraud and violation of employee contract.

The Clinical Services division of preclinical company **Charles River Laboratories International** has signed an electronic data capture (EDC) partnership with **DataLabs**, an EDC vendor. Charles River, based in Wilmington, Mass., already has a suite of integrated clinical technologies for managing global clinical trials, including customized interactive voice response (IVR) and web applications, clinical trial management systems (CTMS), drug safety and pharmacovigilance systems.

November

Columbus, Ohio-based non-profit **Battelle**, possibly best known for managing five national laboratories, such as Oak Ridge in Tennessee and Brookhaven in New York, has made its first foray into clinical contract research by acquiring Newton, Mass.-based CareStat, a 100-employee contract research organization (CRO). Battelle has a long history of conducting contract research in a range of industries. Among its innovations are development of the office copier machine for Xerox, pioneering work on compact disc technology, medical technology advancements and fiber optic technologies. CareStat has become a wholly owned subsidiary of Battelle and will be renamed Battelle CRO. CareStat employees will remain in Newton. Terms of the agreement were not disclosed. Battelle, which is expected to generate annual revenue of $3.5 billion, has 19,000 employees. When its government laboratory management business is excluded, the rest of the company has about 5,000 employees and $900 million in revenue. Battelle's Health and Life Sciences Division currently generates annual revenue of about $150 million and hopes to almost double that over the next five years.

Springfield, Missouri-based **Bio-Kinetic Clinical Applications**, a provider of phase I services to the pharmaceutical and biotechnology industry, is planning to build a new 108-bed facility on its corporate campus. The additional beds would brings Bio-Kinetic's total capacity to 240 phase I beds. The new facility is set to open during the second half of 2006. The company now has 40 employees.

Wilmington, Mass.-based **Charles River Laboratories**, whose main focus is preclinical services, continues to look hard at its clinical services business that it acquired as part of its **Inveresk** acquisition in July 2004. Despite a dip in clinical revenue from the previous quarter by $1.1 million, the company saw margin improvements. For the third quarter of 2005, net sales for the clinical services segment were $32.4 million. Operating income was $3.1 million and the operating margin was 9.5%. Excluding amortization of $3 million related to the Inveresk acquisition, operating income was $6 million and the operating margin was 18.7%. The company expects margins to improve in 2006. For the first nine months of 2005, clinical net sales were $97.7 million and the gross margin was 33.5%. Operating income was $5.9 million and the operating margin was 6%. European phase I growth in Edinburgh, Scotland was reported as "exceptional."

December

Quintiles, which already has a strong Asian clinical trials market presence, has opened an office in Hanoi, Vietnam. Quintiles already has clinical development offices in seven other East Asian countries including China, Malaysia, the Philippines, Singapore, South Korea, Taiwan and Thailand. Singapore has been seen as a hub for clinical trial activity in Asia, and China is becoming a place where top pharmaceutical companies, such as AstraZeneca, are establishing clinical research units. The Vietnam Ministry of Health recently issued a revised set of guidelines for the conduct of clinical trials, thereby setting a consistent regulatory framework for clinical trials. Quintiles plans to work closely with the Vietnam Ministry of Health to increase the number of sites trained in Good Clinical Practice (GCP). Quintiles emphasizes local language skills, clinical knowledge and regulatory expertise, so Vietnamese clinical research monitors will be employed by Quintiles in Vietnam.

PPD issued financial guidance for 2006. Net revenue for 2006, excluding reimbursed out-of-pockets, is expected to be in the range of $1.125 to $1.140 billion, an increase of 18% compared with a revised forecast for 2005 net revenue of $955 to $960 million. Earnings per diluted share before non-cash stock option expense for the full year 2006 are expected to be in the range of $2.67 to $2.75.

Quintiles Medical Communications has formed two additional businesses and a separate continuing medical education (CME) accrediting division. Soniq and Cospective join established brands QED Communications and Medical Action Communications (MAC) under the Quintiles Medical Communications umbrella. Scepter becomes the company's CME accrediting arm. The new structure reflects the growing pharmaceutical industry trend toward complete separation of support for accredited CME programs and non-accredited programs deemed promotional by the U.S. Food and Drug Administration (FDA), a move prompted by stricter guidelines issued by the Accreditation Council for CME (AACME) and increased federal scrutiny. Cospective and QED Communications provide CME services, while Soniq and MAC develop non-accredited educational programs for clinicians. The ACCME

accrediting function, under QED since 1998, now resides with Scepter.

Patient Recruitment

January

First Genetic Trust (**FGT**) and the **Vanderbilt University Medical Center** (**VUMC**) said that FGT will provide its web-based entrust study management system to expand VUMC's studies of the genetics of drug-induced prolonged QT, a side-effect for many different classes of drugs. Patients who exhibit prolonged QT may develop heart arrhythmias that can lead to sudden death in some cases. The enTRUST system's "distance enrollment" feature will enable VUMC researchers to expand the study and speed recruitment of participants by providing an electronic basis for enrolling and consenting patients who are referred through VUMC by other clinicians and clinical sites globally.

October

Praxis, a company specializing in centralized patient recruitment for clinical research studies, recently provided services to a major biotech company for a phase II medical research study taking place in approximately 55 sites across the U.S. The study investigated a possible treatment for rheumatoid arthritis in nearly 200 subjects. The study met enrollment two months earlier than projected.

Regulatory

March

Germany has had some rocky times trying to work out the last details of full implementation of Directive 2001/20/EC, but it has now addressed the major issues and is looking for a smoother ride during 2005. During a recent conference held by the **Association for Applied Human Pharmacology** (**AGAH**), the issues surrounding study approval and ethics approval were addressed. The Directive was implemented in Germany by the 12th

Amendment of the Medicinal Drugs Law, which became effective in August 2004, but since that time the details of implementation were still being ironed out.

July

The future is now as a new era of transparency in clinical research dawns, according to panelists at a session at the **Drug Information Association (DIA)** annual meeting in Washington, D.C. "The debate over whether we should have clinical trials registries is now moot," Arthur Caplan, Ph.D., professor of bioethics at the University of Pennsylvania, told the audience at the well-attended session last week. The only question left is how the registries are going to be set up and who is going to run them, Kaplan noted. "It is time in this new era to move to a new ethic," Kaplan said. Kaplan began his presentation by reviewing what he called the "demonization" of the pharmaceutical industry, detailing how recent "scandals"—such as Merck's withdrawal of painkiller Vioxx, Pfizer's withdrawal of Celebrex and the NIH's consulting fees controversy, among others—had hurt the industry's image. The industry's stature has fallen lower than tobacco companies due in part because of a "ludicrous" campaign against Canadian drug importation, "ridiculous" ad campaigns for erectile dysfunction drugs and skyrocketing prices, he added. But Kaplan laid out a plan that would allow pharma to regain its good name with better public relations campaigns and, more importantly, recommit to science. He noted that there are many researchers in the industry who are working hard to help people and cure diseases

August

Pharmaceutical industry, academic and government researchers are calling for new and increased collaborations among pharmaceutical companies, academic researchers and regulatory agencies to strengthen the drug development process, according to a new report released by the **U.S. Food and Drug Administration.** The joint report, "Drug Development Science Obstacles and Opportunities for Collaborations," points out that despite signif-

icant growth in public and private sector funding for scientific research in recent decades, the number of new medical products, especially innovative drugs, submitted to the FDA has declined steadily since 1996. The report came out of a January conference, sponsored by the FDA and the Association of American Medical Colleges (AAMC). It is part of the FDA's Critical Path Initiative.

October

National Institutes of Health (NIH) Director Elias Zerhouni, M.D., launched a new program designed to spur the transformation of clinical and translational research in the United States. The Institutional Clinical and Translational Science Awards (CTSAs) program, unveiled in *The New England Journal of Medicine* (NEJM), is designed to energize the discipline of clinical and translational science at academic health centers around the country. The grants will encourage institutions to propose new approaches to clinical and translational research, including new organizational models and training programs at graduate and post-graduate levels. In addition, they will foster original research in developing clinical research methodologies such as clinical research informatics, laboratory methods, other technology resources and community-based research capabilities. NIH plans to award four to seven CTSAs in fiscal year 2006 for a total of $30 million, with an additional $11.5 million allocated to support 50 planning grants for those institutions that are not ready to make a full application. NIH expects to increase the number of awards annually so that by 2012, 60 CTSAs will receive a total of approximately $500 million per year.

Health information company **Ingenix**, a subsidiary of managed care company United Health Group, has been selected by the U. S. Food and Drug Administration (FDA) to help improve the effectiveness and speed of safety evaluations for pharmaceutical agents. The Ingenix program is built around a team of leading epidemiologists, analytic tools and a large patient database. Ingenix will work with the FDA to monitor the safety of new drugs as well as conduct ad hoc safety studies on established pharmaceutical agents. i3 Aperio, the drug experience registry Ingenix launched in April, helps researchers identify potential safety signals in new drugs faster.

ClinPhone, a clinical technology company, has established a new office in the Southeastern United States in response to growing demand for the company's services in the region. The company said its growth has been driven by the addition of several new biopharmaceutical customers in the Southeast, as well as increased business from current clients.

Sites

January

Long Beach, Calif.-based **West Coast Clinical Trials**, a privately owned clinical research facility, is expanding its clinical facilities on Redondo Avenuc in Long Beach. The new phase I unit is part of a 25,000-square-foot expansion adjacent to its outpatient clinical trials unit. A 40-bed overnight facility, the phase I unit offers private sleeping quarters and examination rooms as well as an entertainment area for study participants. The new facility has state-of-the-art equipment such as atomic clocks, multiple spirometry units, ECG machines, treadmills, freezers, refrigerated centrifuges, stadiometers and a sleep lab.

February

Maryland-based **Accelovance**, a privately funded company founded in 2004, has completed an asset purchase of **nTouch Research**, a Raleigh, N.C.-based site management organization (SMO) with 18 sites (SMO). The deal is the largest in the SMO niche since market leader **Radiant Research** bought rival Protocare in March 2003. Financial details of the deal were not disclosed. The deal is significant because nTouch is the second largest owned-site model SMO behind Radiant Research, which has about 50 sites. Accelovance, based in Rockville, intends to keep nTouch's SMO network intact along with keeping its 30 employees, including its president Lee Palles. The company's name will become Accelovance. The sale to Accelovance

keeps the competitive landscape for SMOs in place. Other major players are Comprehensive Neuoroscience, Americas-Doctor, Research Solutions and Pioneer Behavioral Health. Center-Watch estimated that the market for SMOs reached $282 million in 2004. nTouch's annual revenucs are about $10 million

March

Odyssey Research was recently invited by the **Chinese State Food and Drug Administration (SFDA)** to be what it believes is the first trial management organization (TMO) to participate in a government-sponsored clinical research training program in Beijing to improve the standard of clinical research for physicians and drug approval processes. The Chinese SFDA is working with Odyssey Research to prepare Chinese investigators and the sites for the challenges and demands of establishing large scale, multi-center, global clinical trials in China.

April

Global Spectrum Clinical Research, a joint venture of Eastside Comprehensive Medical Center in New York City and Spectrum Healthcare in Mumbai, India, have entered into an agreement with Clinical Research Centers International (CRCI) to open a dedicated, clinical research site in Mumbai, India. The resulting organization brings together clinical research veterans Ram Shrivastava, M.D., Walter Brown, M.D. and Viral Shah, M.D. Shrivastava founded Eastside Comprehensive Medical Center about 30 years ago as a dedicated site in New York City. Brown also has a long history in clinical research. He founded a site, Clinical Programs in Rhode Island, 20 years ago. From that site, the company grew to more than 20 sites nationwide, and was sold under the name Clinical Studies. In 2000, Brown co-founded CRCI with Max Moss to facilitate implementation of clinical trials in ascending markets.

Healthcare Discoveries, which specializes in phase I and IIa in-patient clinical research, has added a 54-bed dedicated facility within ByWater Hospital in New Orleans. In March, Pasadena, Calif.-based Catalyst Pharma Group acquired Healthcare Discoveries, a 110-bed phase I unit in San Antonio, Texas, for an undisclosed sum. Its new facility in New Orleans will also be named Healthcare Discoveries. Catalyst Pharmaceutical Research is a contract research organization (CRO) that provides clinical development, regulatory and licensing representative services worldwide. The New Orleans unit has 16 employees and four contract physicians. The company said the phase I unit in New Orleans, La., draws from a southern Louisiana-Mississippi area that encompasses nearly two million people.

May

Austin, Texas-based **Benchmark Research**, a site management organization (SMO) with three sites in Texas and one in San Francisco, has opened a fifth site in New Orleans. The New Orleans site has three employees now, but president and CEO Mark Lacy plans to double its staff by the end of the year. The five-site company, founded in 1997, has 37 employees, including 26 that handle site - specific operations and 11 in the corporate office. Its two other sites in Texas, in addition to its headquarters in Austin, are located in San Angelo and Fort Worth. Benchmark also operates its own call center in Texas, but has no plans to seek call center business beyond its own studies. In 2003, the company grew revenues 25% to $2.5 million.

Maryland-based **Accelovance**, a SMO with a wholly foreign-owned enterprise in China, has opened an office in Beijing. The Beijing office will serve as the base of operations for several clinical sites scheduled to be functioning within nine months. The company said sites in China will provide Accelovance's clients with a strategic alternative to their clinical trial needs and will add to its existing 12-site network in the United States. Accelovance made a big move into the site business in February when it bought nTouch Research, a Raleigh, N.C.-based SMO, for an undisclosed amount. The deal was the largest in the SMO niche since market leader Radiant Research bought rival Protocare in March 2003.

Accelovance is the second largest owned-site model SMO behind Radiant Research, which has 45 sites.

Radiant Research, the market leading site management organization (SMO), continued its push into the hot phase I market by opening a large freestanding phase I unit in Dallas. In August 2004, Radiant Research raised $26 million to move quickly into the phase I market in a big way. In addition to opening the new freestanding phase I facility in Dallas, Radiant is using the money to expand six existing early-phase units by adding 24-to-36-bed phase I and IIa capabilities at four of its phase II–IV clinical research sites. By the end of 2005, Radiant expects to have 10 early-phase units with about 500 beds, each having access to special patient populations and the therapeutic expertise of experienced clinical investigators. Radiant already owns more than 45 phase II–IV investigative sites.

Duke Medical Strategies has formed a new business unit known as **COResearch**. Formerly known as the Duke ECG Core Lab, this new unit provides digital core laboratory measures of cardiac safety and efficacy for new molecular entities and devices in phase I through phase IV clinical trials. COResearch has a specific focus on thorough QT studies. Capabilities incorporate a range of cardiac safety and efficacy core laboratory services, including resting and continuous ECG; echocardiography; ischemia and arrhythmia monitoring; trial design; data interpretation and analysis; global study management; and consultation on regulatory strategy.

June

California-based **United States Clinical Research Centers (USCRC)** has opened two phase I units located in Costa Mesa and Cerritos with a total of more than 200 beds in recent months. USCRC is the latest research group to enter the growing phase I market. The phase I market grew 16% to $4.1 billion in 2004. Both USCRC phase I units have more than 100 beds with on-site dietary services. The Costa Mesa site maintains a medical-surgical unit; operating suites; 24-hour, CLIA-certified clinical lab; diagnostics and secured units.

Sydney Bonnick, M.D. and **Mike Maricic, M.D.,** osteoporosis researchers, have joined **OsNET's** network. OsNET is a clinical research alliance of 24 independent investigative sites Sites, that work together to meet enrollment goals. The network's sites are therapeutically focused in all osteoporosis, arthritis, obesity, COPD, and women's health trials.

July

Neeman Medical International, which already has a network of 40 affiliated investigative sites in India, has embarked on a major expansion by signing clinical research agreements with four private hospitals and a medical college. The institutions include P.D. Hinduja National Hospital in Mumbai, Sri Ramachandra Medical College in Chennai, Deenanath Mangeshkar Hospital in Pune, and Mediciti Hospitals and Indo-American Hospital both in Hyderabad. India has become a hotbed of clinical research in recent years with sponsors ramping up research and CROs flocking to the country.

September

CFS provides financial management services to academic medical centers, investigative sites, site management organizations and sponsors in the clinical trials industry. CFS and Archbrook estimate that the market for CFS' financial management services in the clinical research market exceeds $100 million. The current CFS executive committee will remain, with Archbrook Management adding an additional member to the committee. CFS's management team, including Jim Wynn, will remain the same.

October

Clinical Research Centers International (CRCI) is expanding to Latin America, one of the hottest markets for clinical trials. CRCI has opened dedicated clinical trial sites in Mexico and Guatemala. CRCI already operates sites in Romania, South

Africa and, most recently, India. To further establish itself in the region, CRCI is opening an office in Panama this winter. In the coming year, the company plans to open phase I units in Central America, as well as begin working with sites in other Latin American nations. Joseph Uribe, M.D., will direct operations in Mexico and Luis Lombardi, M.D., will do the same in Guatemala.

Seattle-based **LabConnect,** a central laboratory services company, has signed a definitive agreement with Van Nuys, Calif.-based Consolidated Laboratory Services (CLS) to jointly provide esoteric laboratory testing services to the biopharmaceutical industry. As part of the deal, CLS will make an undisclosed equity investment in LabConnect. LabConnect officials believe the exclusive agreement will add significant capabilities to its central laboratory testing at its Johnson City, Tenn., location. Launched in 1995, CLS is a specialty provider of analytic and diagnostic research services for preclinical and clinical studies. It is known for vaccine and HIV/AIDS testing, having a complete menu of assays for all FDA-approved HIV antiretroviral drugs. CLS will integrate its laboratory information system and conduct its preclinical and clinical trial work exclusively under the LabConnect-CLS joint agreement. Through the joint agreement, clinical trial sponsors now have access to esoteric and safety laboratory testing services and long-term storage of biomaterial samples.

December

Synexus, a site management organization (SMO) based in Chorley, Lancashire, United Kingdom has opened an office in Mumbai, India, in a joint venture with Indian Clinical Research Institute (ICRI), a clinical research institute. They plan to open seven sites in India. Synexus, which has 100 employees, owns 12 sites in the United Kingdom and is currently managing 20 active clinical trials. The company plans to open three or four sites in India in the next 18 months. Synexus is also looking to expand into central Europe and is negotiating joint ventures with several investigative sites in that region. They are talking with a UK-based company that operates patient management centers in Russia and Ukraine and with the owners of a patient management site in Poland. Launched in 1998, Synexus has been focusing its sites on patient recruitment for disease prevention studies such as cardiac outcome studies.

The **Mary Crowley Medical Research Center** (**MCMRC**) has signed a research partnership with Ithaca, N.Y.-based biosimulation company Gene Network Services (GNS), to analyze genetic material from cancer patients to improve treatment and clinical trials efficiency. The MCMRC, based in Dallas, Texas, is a nationally known cancer research center with eight affiliate sites across the country, including centers in Spokane, Wash.; Orlando Fla.; and Albany, N.Y. The partnership will enhance the MCMRC's ability to deliver more focused treatments and mine valuable research data to aid patients with advanced cancers. The new tools will also allow the center to attract sponsor grants looking to use the pharmacogenomic data in developing investigative drugs.

West Coast Clinical Trials is expanding once again with another phase I unit and a new corporate headquarters in Costa Mesa, Calif. About 60% of the company's revenues are generated by phase I trials. A year ago, West Coast Clinical Trials expanded its clinical facilities on Redondo Avenue in Long Beach. The new phase I unit is a 25,000-square-foot facility adjacent to its outpatient clinical trials unit. The 40-bed overnight facility offers private sleeping quarters and examination rooms as well as an entertainment area for study participants. The new facility features multiple spirometry units, ECG machines, treadmills, freezers, refrigerated centrifuges, stadiometers and a sleep lab. West Coast was doing phase I research at a local hospital before opening its dedicated facility.

Technology

January

eResearchTechnology, an e-research technology and services provider, has entered into an agreement to provide PRACS Institute, a phase I-

focused CRO, with integrated technology and services that include enterprise EDC, clinical data management, and a web portal for client access to real-time data. Financial terms of the agreement were not disclosed.

Datatrak International, an application service provider (ASP) in the electronic data capture (EDC) niche, and SAS, a business intelligence software company, have signed a joint offering to provide analysis-ready data from information collected in clinical trials. This deal will link Datatrak's clinical trial data software with SAS' clinical trials data integration and analysis solution.

February

Waltham, Mass.-based **Phase Forward**, the market leading electronic data capture (EDC) company, reported strong fourth quarter results, while two other private EDC companies Medidata Solutions and etrials also reported stellar fourth quarter results. The first EDC company to enter the public markets in July 2004, Phase Forward reported fourth quarter revenues jumped 24% to $20.1 million, from $16.2 million for the fourth quarter of 2003. Income from operations was $1.4 million compared with a $4.1 million loss from operations for the prior year's comparable quarter. Net income for the fourth quarter of 2004 was $734,000, or $0.02 per share, compared with a net loss of $5.8 million, or a loss of $1.66 per share, for the prior year quarter. Phase Forward officials were cautious on growth for 2005 as sales cycles lengthen with the pharmaceutical industry under pressure.

April

New York-based **Medidata Solutions**, a provider of electronic clinical data management for clinical trials, signed a major electronic data capture (EDC) licensing deal with Bayer HealthCare AG. Bayer Healthcare is standardizing its method of capturing clinical trial data on Medidata's RAVE solution. The deal with a major pharmaceutical company signals Medidata as a significant challenger to Phase Forward. The deal is also noteworthy because the Medidata software will replace an in-house system that was developed by Sylva Collins, who has created a similar in-house EDC system for Novartis. Industry observers say Novartis is considering proposals to replace its EDC system. Bayer HealthCare expects that 100% of its internally managed clinical trials will implement EDC. Bayer HealthCare has committed to conduct at least 150 clinical studies on Medidata RAVE in the next three years. The first trials using Medidata's software will start in June.

Waltham, Mass.-based **Phase Forward**, the market-leading electronic data capture (EDC) company that provides data management for clinical trials and drug safety, signed two licensing deals last week, including a major deal with the Dana-Farber Cancer Institute (DFCI) in Boston and another with biopharmaceutical company, ZymoGenetics. In a multi-year agreement, Dana-Farber/Harvard Cancer Center licensed Phase Forward's InForm EDC software. The DFCI is standardizing on Phase Forward's software for all of Dana-Farber/Harvard Cancer Center's investigator-initiated clinical studies across its clinical research platform for its member institutions and 20 network affiliates that conduct clinical research in oncology.

In a collaborative effort designed to increase the speed and efficiency of late-phase clinical research, **etrials Worldwide** and **Quintiles** have entered into an arrangement to license etrials' eClinical Suite of software and to collaborate to develop technology specifically for use in peri-approval studies. As part of the deal, etrials will augment its existing eClinical Suite by developing a new phase IV product to take advantage of the data collected in late-stage and post-approval trials. The new products will combine Quintiles' expertise in the post-approval market, including certain technology transferred to etrials. The three-year licensing agreement provides Quintiles' clients with etrials' suite of eClinical tools for use in late-phase studies, including EDC; IVR; and reporting/analytic tools. The contract also provides etrials with backlog and ongoing work relating to 10 late-phase clinical trials already in progress that will be supported by etrials.

May

Phase Forward reported that **GenVec**, has selected Phase Forward's electronic data capture (EDC) solution to manage a randomized, controlled phase II clinical trial of its investigational oncology drug, TNFerade. The trial will assess the clinical benefit of using TNFerade in combination with standard care treatment in patients with locally advanced pancreatic cancer. GenVec will use Phase Forward's hosting service to obtain direct, real-time access to clinical data.

The parade of CROs signing licensing deals with EDC companies continues with new signings from **etrials Worldwide**, **Omnicomm** and **DataLabs**. etrials Worldwide announced that Omnicare Clinical Research, a subsidiary of geriatric services provider, has signed a multi-year, subscription licensing agreement that will enable its clients to use etrials' eClinical platform for collecting, monitoring and analyzing clinical trial data. Meanwhile, DataLabs announced that Axio Research, a CRO based in Seattle, joined the DataLabs CRO Partners Program. And Apex International, a CRO focused on Asia, selected Omnicomm's Trialmaster as its in-house EDC system. Omnicomm will provide a private-label version of its software to Apex.

June

DataLabs, a developer of Internet-based applications for clinical development, has signed a technology development and preferred provider agreement with United BioSource Corporation (UBC), which provides science- and evidence-based services and information to the biopharmaceutical industry. UBC and DataLabs are working together to deliver electronic data capture (EDC) solutions specific for late stage clinical trials. It is the eighth deal that Datalabs has signed with CROs since starting a partnership program a year ago. Other CROs have also been partnering with EDC vendors.

In response to widespread demand throughout the province of Quebec, the **Ministère de la Santé et des Services sociaux/Ministry of Health and Social Services (MSSS)** now offers online training in both

French and English for research ethics board (REB) members and support staff. The online training program went live last month at http://ethique. msss.gouv.qc.ca/didacticiel. At a workshop in 2002 to which all REB members within MSSS' jurisdiction, which includes all hospitals and medical schools as well as some community health centers in Quebec, were invited, many expressed the need for training and education for both REB members and support staff. After conducting a follow-up survey, MSSS sent out a request-for-proposal (RFP) to create the training program.

Cary, N.C.-based **SAS**, a business intelligence software company, signed up Daiichi, a global pharmaceutical firm, as its first client for SAS's Drug Development software as the centerpiece of a suite of hosted solutions. The announcement is a win for Cleveland-based electronic data capture (EDC) company Datatrak, which provides its EDC software to SAS. In January, Datatrak signed a deal that linked its clinical trial data software with SAS' clinical trials data integration and analysis solution. The joint offering is called Datatrak Aware— powered by SAS. The offering gives life sciences companies updated information on their drugs in clinical trials in an analysis-ready format every 24 hours over the Internet.

July

DataLabs, a developer of Internet-based applications for clinical development, has signed up PRA International, a global CRO, to an enterprise-wide agreement to standardize its method of capturing clinical data using DataLabs's electronic clinical data management eCDM solution in all of its clinical trials. The DataLabs-PRA enterprise deal will produce the industry's largest eCDM-CRO technology transfer, according to DataLabs.

August

Waltham, Mass.-based **Phase Forward**, an electronic data capture (EDC) market leader that has been making a push into drug safety, took its effort to the next level last week when it entered into a definitive agreement to acquire Wellesley, Mass.-based

Lincoln Technologies, a provider of clinical trial safety products, in an all-cash transaction valued at $11 million. The deal includes an additional $6 million based on achievement of certain financial targets in 2005 and 2006. Lincoln Technologies generated approximately $4.5 million of revenue and an operating profit in the prior four quarters. The 30-employee company increased its revenue 50% in the past 12 months.

Nextrials, a clinical research software and services company, has established a partnership with **Galt Associates** to offer customers expedited automatic coding of real-time data being exchanged during clinical trials. Through integration with Galt's dsNavigator, Nextrials' Prism software offers researchers an electronic data capture and safety alert system that also auto-codes drug and event terms using MedDRA™ (Medical Dictionary for Regulatory Activities) and WHO Drug (World Health Organization)

As a spate of electronic data capture (EDC) vendors continues to tout their ties to contract research organizations (CROs) and plans to integrate their technology application offerings, database software giant **Oracle** is defending its position in the market niche. Oracle announced that more than 240 major life sciences companies, CROs and academic research organizations use Oracle clinical applications to expedite multinational regulatory approval processes and reduce cycle times in critical clinical trial processes. Overall, 29 of the 30 largest pharmaceutical companies run Oracle applications. Among the CROs that use Oracle Clinical are **Omnicare**, **INC Research**, and **PPD**.

New York-based **Medidata Solutions**, an electronic data capture (EDC) vendor, reported its 18th consecutive quarter of growth, as its second quarter revenue jumped 150%. The private company declined to release actual revenue figures. In its second quarter, Medidata Solutions closed 19 new deals, including biopharmaceutical companies in the U.S., Europe and Asia. Bayer Yahukin in Japan was one of its new clients. Medidata also signed its largest contract to date, but did not provide further details of the deal.

Phase Forward continued to lead the electronic data capture (EDC) sector, reporting solid growth for its second quarter. Revenues for the second quarter increased 17% to $20.7 million, compared with $17.7 million for the same quarter of 2004, and the company swung to a profit. Income from operations was $2 million in the second quarter compared with $946,000 for the prior year's comparable quarter. Net income applicable to common stockholders for the second quarter of 2005 was $1.8 million, or $0.05 per share, on a diluted basis, compared with a net loss of $6.2 million, or a loss of $1.70 per share, for the second quarter of the previous year.

September

Cleveland-based **Datatrak International**, an electronic data capture (EDC) application service provider, has added five new customers within the past month including an American pharmaceutical company, a European medical device firm and three clients delivered through its contract research partner, Cross S.A., based in Switzerland. A number of other EDC vendors and CROs have partnered in recent months. These new contracts include a total of five new clinical trials: four phase I and a phase II study. Datatrak's alliance with Cross was established in May 2004. Cross has undergone a technology transfer and is able to offer its own EDC-based products and services through its relationship with Datatrak.

November

Waltham, Mass.-based **Phase Forward**, a provider of data management for clinical trials and drug safety, reported third quarter revenue increased 17% to $22.2 million, buoyed by its drug safety niche acquisition, **Lincoln Technologies** in August. A privately held competitor, **Medidata Solutions**, also reported strong financial results. Phase Forward's third quarter income from operations grew 44% to $2.4 million. Net income applicable to common stockholders for the third quarter of 2005 was $2.2 million, or $0.06 per diluted share, compared to a GAAP net loss applicable to common stockholders of $95,000, or $0.00 per share,

for the third quarter of the previous year. Results for the third quarter of 2005 Lincoln Technologies. For this period beginning Aug. 25, Lincoln's revenues were $444,000 and operating income was $30,000.

DataLabs, a developer of web-based software applications electronic data capture, has acquired **Broadpeak LLC**, an eClinical collaboration software company that provides applications to the biopharmaceutical and CRO industries to improve the workflow and communication processes in managing clinical trials. Broadpeak was launched in January 2004 and has six employees. Competitors would be document management companies such as Documentum and collaboration software companies like eRooms and Groove. The Broadpeak software facilitates internal and external collaboration for study activities, including recruiting qualified investigators, initiating each site, communicating with investigative sites and providing a central portal from which to manage the progress of each clinical trial.

Medidata Solutions, an electronic data capture (EDC) company appointed Graham Bunn as vice president of strategic alliances for EMEA. Prior to joining Medidata, Bunn served as global vice president of e-clinical business development at Quintiles. After spe

## CHAPTER ONE

Industry Sales

27 ☐ IN FOCUS

Singapore: Hub for Clinical Trials in Asia

The clinical trials market in Singapore has doubled in size since the country adopted ICH-GCP in 1998. Bolstered by well-developed technology and hospital infrastructures, strict adherence to international standards, considerable investment by multinational pharmaceutical, biotech companies and CROs, and a well-educated English-speaking population, Singapore has become an attractive place to conduct clinical trials.

Due to a relatively small population of just under 4.5 million, 1 million of whom are foreigners, Singapore's clinical research market can only grow so large. But, Singapore's geographic location gives it access to the fast growing Asian markets. In addition, the country's pro-business policies have helped make Singapore an important hub for companies' pan-Asian strategy for clinical trials.

33 ☐ ANALYSIS & INSIGHT

Singapore: Hub for Clinical Trials in Asia

By Sara Gambrill
Published August 2005

How does a country with an area of just under 700 square kilometers and a population of just under 4.5 million become one of the most important business hubs for clinical trials in Asia? A little geographic luck and a lot of determination.

Since the Singapore government began the biomedical sciences initiative five years ago, $S3 billion [U.S.$1.78 billion] has been committed to this sector. Funding for biomedical research in the public sector and academia was increased as well as the training of Ph.D.'s in order to attract international pharmaceutical and biotech companies to set up drug discovery operations in Singapore. This, in turn, drew companies to Singapore interested in undertaking clinical trials there as well as in the Asian countries surrounding it. Singapore is in the heart of Asia—roughly equidistant by plane from Sydney, Australia, northern China, eastern Japan and western India. An enviable location, as Asia is the fastest growing clinical research market in the world.

"Having the supportive climate, the scientific climate, the business climate and the regulatory climate really helps companies feel very comfortable about doing trials in Singapore and, equally important, about using Singapore as a base to coordinate their trials in the region. Singapore— along with Hong Kong—is one of the predominant regional hubs in Asia. Because of that, Singapore has close to 7,000 multinational companies, about half of which have regional responsibilities," said Dr. Swan Gin Beh, director, Bio- medical Sciences, Singapore Economic Development Board.

"For several years now, the Singapore government has been investing in life sciences to be the next pillar of the economy here. This has facilitated expansion of both public and private R&D. At present there is emphasis on attracting skills and building infrastructure to allow translation of basic science concepts into the clinical arena. Doctors are being encouraged to get training and experience in clinical research," said Dr. Stephen Wise, director of Lilly NUS [National University of Singapore] Centre for Clinical Pharmacology, which was established in 1997.

Dr. Edmund Leong, director of strategic development for Asia, PPD, which has been in Singapore since 2002, said, "Singapore, in many ways because of our size, started establishing itself as world-class in terms of whatever activities we take part in. The establishment of medical centers and hospitals of world-renowned standards is something that the government always had in their plans to make Singapore the focal point for medical services in southeast Asia and even throughout Asia. The government has injected a lot of interest in terms of skill-intensive and technology-intensive activities. We are a small country with a limited population size. The only way for us to thrive and make ourselves heard in the international arena is to have that edge in terms of outputs that are skill- and technology-driven."

The Singapore Advantage: Timelines and Training

At the same time that the biomedical sciences initiative was being spearheaded by the Singapore government, the Ministry of Health organized all the public hospitals and specialized health institutes in Singapore into two clusters. The re-organization of public hospitals has translated into much faster timelines for clinical trials.

"The timelines for starting a clinical trial in Singapore are amongst the shortest in the world," said Dr. Anand Tharmaratnam, CEO of Quintiles Southeast Asia. Quintiles was the first contract research organization to set up an office in Singapore in 1995. "In Singapore, there are two hospital groups that basically own the seven public hospitals in Singapore, and each of them has an IRB. You just have to go to two IRBs. As soon as you get approval from one IRB, you can make a submission to the health authority of Singapore and that's done online and takes one month. So it's a two-month process. It's a clear process. It's highly conducive to companies getting started with clinical trials."

Each public hospital cluster is under the auspices of one of the two major hospitals in Singapore. Nearly half of all clinical trials conducted in Singapore are conducted in these two public hospital clusters. The eastern cluster, which is under Singapore General Hospital, is called SingHealth and comprises three hospitals, five national specialist centers and a network of primary healthcare clinics. The western cluster is under National University Hospital and comprises four hospitals, one national center, nine polyclinics, three specialty institutes and five business divisions.

Each cluster has a single institutional review board (IRB), which is called the Domain Specific Review Board, making the review process accessible, efficient and relatively quick with a four week–turnaround. Regulatory review cannot be done in parallel and also takes a month. Each cluster also has a centralized clinical trials office that can offer efficiencies to sponsor companies, from finding and training investigators and facilitating the approval process to support services for the conduct of clinical trials. These offices act as a liaison between industry and the institutions in the respective clusters.

In addition, investigator training is strongly emphasized by the Singapore government. The CITI Program in the Protection of Human Research Subjects is the minimum training requirement for clinical research investigators conducting research in the public sector. Potential investigators must complete seven modules: History & Ethics Principle, Overview of Domain Specific Review Board (DSRB) Review Process, Overview of the Regulatory Framework and Guidelines in Singapore, Informed Consent, Social and Behavioral Research for Biomedical Research, Research with Protected Population—Vulnerable Subjects: A definition, and Record Based Research. In addition, principal investigators must select five elective modules out of 21 available based on their relevance to their research and areas of specialty.

Dr. Dan Weng, president of ICON Clinical Research—Rest of World, added, "The majority of physicians have been trained in the U.S. and Europe. The technology for treatment is very similar to Western technology. Hospital infrastructure is like a Western hospital also. Physicians have all had GCP [Good Clinical Practice] training. The Singapore regulatory process is very transparent and it's very short as well. They really adapted the U.S. and European system." ICON established an office in Singapore in 1999.

Just over half of all clinical trials are conducted in private hospitals in Singapore through the Parkway Hospital Group. Gleneagles CRC, a site management organization-contract research organization (SMO-CRO), was initially established in 1999 to harmonize all clinical trials within its Parkway Hospital Group, comprising three private hospitals in Singapore, and seven others throughout Asia, in Malaysia, Indonesia, India and Brunei. It is a subsidiary of Gleneagles Hospital, which in turn is a subsidiary of Parkway Hospital Singapore Pte. The parent company, Parkway Holdings has been in Singapore for about 40 years and in the healthcare business for the last 18 and also has a chain of general practitioner clinics with 200 physicians. "Getting the various hospital departments to work together is very easy for us. Thus, managing clinical trials within our system is efficient because we already have our own healthcare system," said Dr. Kok Wei Yap, president and CEO, GleneaglesCRC.

Size a Limiting Factor

Singapore offers an environment where the regulatory process is transparent and there is good intellectual property rights protection, GCP training opportunities abound and the costs of conducting a clinical trial are lower relative to the U.S. and Europe, though not to some other Asian countries—notably China and India. Singapore also offers a multiracial population mix of Chinese, Malay and Indian as well as a disease demographic that sustains strong interest in the therapeutic areas of oncology and Hepatitis B, with interest also in cardiovascular, tuberculosis, diabetes as well as dengue fever and malaria. But, the size of Singapore's population will always be a limiting factor.

"One of the key challenges that you will always face in Singapore is the limited patient population that you can tap into within Singapore itself. When it comes to large phase III trials, Singapore certainly can provide some patients but clearly will not wind up being the country that recruits the greatest number of patients globally," said Leong.

Growth

Despite its small size, Singapore has fostered rapid growth and there remain pockets of opportunity for more. The number of clinical trial certificates (CTCs) issued has doubled since 1998 when the country adopted ICH-GCP. Although the outbreak of Severe Acute Respiratory Syndrome [SARS] in March 2003 caused a drop in the number of CTCs issued that year, the number rebounded, increasing 25% the very next year and surpassing 2002 levels, according to the Health Sciences Authority (HSA).

Every CRO there has experienced a great deal of growth in the number of its active projects

across Asia since establishing a regional office in Singapore and satellite offices for CRAs in surrounding countries to monitor clinical trials there. Quintiles is celebrating its 10th anniversary in Singapore. Quintiles started off as a clinical business and an Innovex commercialization business, but is now completely focused on clinical, including its clinical management and central lab business. Quintiles had one active study in 1995 and now has 75. Gleneagles-CRC, the only home-grown SMO-CRO in Singapore, was established in 1999 and had a single study in 2000 and has 65 active trials today. ICON Clinical Research has had an office in Singapore since 1999 and started with one large global trial but has 20 active trials now. MDS Pharma Services has had an office in Singapore since 2001, from which time it has grown 300% and expects to experience 30%-50% growth per year. PPD has been in Singapore since 2002 when it acquired ProPharma Limited, which was established in 1998 and already had a presence in Asia beyond Singapore. PPD's staff and presence in Asia has doubled in the past year.

Phase I Opportunities

The kind of growth that Singapore has experienced in its own clinical research market until now cannot go on indefinitely. However, phase I still offers growth opportunities.

Both Eli Lilly and Pfizer have dedicated phase I clinical pharmacology centers in Singapore, where the majority of phase I clinical trials are conducted, according to HSA. In addition, Changi Hospital, part of the eastern cluster of public hospitals in Singapore has a phase I unit.

The Lilly-NUS Centre for Clinical Pharmacology is part of the Exploratory Medicine component of Lilly Research Laboratories. The unit has 60 staff including: four physician investigators; a large nursing/technician staff; about seven Ph.D. scientists in statistics/pharmacokinetics and related disciplines; and IT, quality and administrative personnel. Lilly conducts about 15 studies in-house per year and collaborates externally both within and outside Singapore, e.g., Australia, China, Japan.

"Our studies are generally small and intensive phase I, with an increasing proportion of biomarker studies as well as pharmacokinetic studies to define biopharmaceutical characteristics of new medicines for registration. We also have academic projects and collaborate with local university and university hospital investigators, as well as delivering some teaching and training locally," said Wise.

While phase I growth has been steady in the region, with phase I CTC applications making up around 15% of all CTCs, it is widely believed that the phase I market could grow rapidly in the years to come. "We are not looking at huge patient populations. We are looking at technologically demanding trials where we are talking about phase I or II activities, even preclinical work. As far as we are concerned, we're looking at phase I, II. I think Singapore would want to attract more and more players to run such trials in Singapore," PPD's Leong said.

Possibly having a large role to play in the future of phase I studies in the country is the Biopolis. This seven-building complex is the cornerstone of the much broader vision to build up the biomedical sciences industry in Singapore and was developed for S$500 million [U.S.$296 million] and opened in 2003. Two buildings are dedicated to biomedical companies from the private sector. The other five house the biomedical research institutes of the Agency of Science, Technology and Research (A*STAR)—the BioInformatics Institutes, the Bioprocessing Technology Institute, the Genome Institute of Singapore, the Institute of Molecular and Cell Biology and the Institute of Bioengineering & Nanotechnology. Demand for research laboratories has been so strong that development of phase II of the project began last month, ahead of schedule. Phase I of the project, with 2 million square feet of space, is more than 90% occupied. Phase II will start with two new buildings providing an additional 400,000 square feet of space to house the R&D operations of pharmaceutical and biotech companies.

"I would say that the Biopolis has played a role to the extent that it's attracted our competitors and our clients to come here. It's become a focal point for companies coming to Singapore. I cannot say we've seen any tangible benefits in the last 10 years from it yet. All the benefits have been intangible in terms of the business environment for ourselves. I can see that changing significantly in the next five years as the companies that are set up in Biopolis have got compounds that are a couple of years away from entering human clinical trials. Once that happens, then companies are going to find companies like ourselves at their doorstep to offer them that service," said Quintiles' Tharmaratnam.

He added, "As things move along in Singapore, there certainly is room for a fully independent phase I unit here in Singapore. The phase II, phase III business is established and the gap in that pipeline is phase I. That would be a potential growth opportunity in Singapore."

Important Regional Hub

Multinational CROs have set up their offices in Southeast Asia so that the clinical trial management and administrative functions in addition to a group of clinical research associates are located in Singapore. CRO offices in the surrounding Southeast Asian countries have only monitors. Incentives for CROs to choose Singapore as their regional hub include the business dynamic there and the geographic location, which gives it access to a regional population of 500 million, many of whom are treatment-naïve. The main business that CROs conduct in Singapore are clinical trial management and central laboratory services.

In addition to this, the Singapore government offers tax incentives that CROs can take advantage of. "What we help support is if a CRO, for instance, locates its business operations for the region in Singapore. Pioneer status confers a preferential corporate tax rate and that would make sense if you were a profit center, which means only CROs really will be looking for that. I think the drivers for clinical trials in Singapore and Singapore as a base to coordinate clinical trials in Asia is really the business dynamic and less to do with incentives," said Beh.

Raymond Yeung, director, Asia Pacific, MDS Pharma Services, added, "From a central laboratories perspective, an important advantage is the good logistics of the infrastructure, the many flights in and out per day. I have no problem getting samples from Japan, India, Australia coming into Singapore. We are able to get the samples within 24 hours most of the time."

From the clinical trial management side, while English is the language of business and education as well as a national language of Singapore, that is not always the case in surrounding countries. Official documents to be submitted to ethics committees and informed consent documents must be translated both forward and back to ensure they are correct. The adoption of GCP is uneven, depending on the government's backing of it.

"If you look at Southeast Asian countries, they would certainly fall into two tiers. The first tier, which is the fully developed infrastructure in terms of regulatory, hospital infrastructure and language would be Singapore and Malaysia and, to a certain extent, Thailand. But the next tier would really be Thailand, Phillipines and the other countries in Southeast Asia. If you look beyond Southeast Asia, Taiwan and Korea would fall into the first tier as well," said Tharmaratnam.

"[Some of the investigators from South-east Asia] have learned GCP. They have run through that information, but we haven't seen the government pushing it yet. I think more and more countries are moving into it. The general consensus is that patients are more compliant in Asia, but you have to go through cultural differences, the language differences and the translations because there are many languages used in Asia," said Yeung.

Beh added, "By and large, there is a growing awareness and familiarity with GCP and ICH standards. Singapore's regulatory agency is an active member of fostering harmonization of these standards and these processes in Southeast Asia."

But the spread of the adoption of ICH-GCP guidelines will most likely start with international sponsors' insistence on it.

"I think a big part of Singapore's attractiveness to the clinical research industry is the growing comfort and growing interest of industry to do more trials in Asia as a whole because of the availability of treatment-naïve patients in China and India. Generally speaking it is fair to say that the

cost of clinical trials in Asia is cheaper and Asia itself as a market is becoming more important for them, so conducting clinical trials is one way to better understand your patient population. Asia plays a big role in why Singapore is an attractive place for the industry to locate their business activities," said Beh.

The vast populations of Asia will allow growth to be sustained in the region for quite some time and underscore Singapore's importance as a regional hub. New opportunities for growth come in the form of Japan's beginning to accept non-Japanese data. One reason why may be the relatively long time it takes to conduct a clinical trial in Japan, especially early phase trials. Weng, who also works out of ICON's office in Japan, said, "The Japanese government has begun accepting non-Japan data from Asian countries. [ICON] has successfully done one trial and the data has been accepted by the Japan regulatory agency—not on the core data but on the supporting data. The Japanese government has shown an interest in and that they're willing to take non-Japan data as core data but so far there has not been a single case. It seems like they are willing to do it right now so that's a very good sign. That will be moving a lot of Asia, Singapore and Hong Kong as well, to do early phase trials for the Japanese regulatory agency."

Future Outlook

Although the clinical trial markets in both India and China are growing very rapidly and will increase competition in the region, Singapore's pivotal role as a hub will most likely be secure for the foreseeable future. Both India and China have work to do to achieve the comfort level that Singapore offers in terms of quality data. India and China are huge in terms of area and treatment-naïve populations, and both have had important regulations go into effect in order to make the clinical trials process more transparent and streamlined and to protect intellectual property. How well these regulations are enforced bears watching. India and China could easily take the lion's share of clinical research business in Asia in a decade.

"India and China are the fastest growth countries. But they are facing more challenges than Singapore. In Singapore, it's very easy whereas in India and China it takes longer and there are more problems and challenges as well. People are more willing to accept data from Singapore. Legally it's very transparent. People know how to follow the rules. China and India have more issues in that area," said Weng.

Despite its praiseworthy regulatory reputation, Singapore, too, is working on making its regulatory process more streamlined. Next year, the HSA will be implementing a 30-day regulatory notification system. Under this new framework, applications could be submitted in parallel to both IRBs and HSA. The study can be initiated after a 30-day default timeline if HSA does not raise any objection or query, and the ethics approval has been obtained. No approval letters or CTCs will be issued by HSA.

Quintiles' Tharmaratnam added, "As more companies move clinical development to India and China, they would use countries like Singapore and other countries in Southeast Asia as part of their pan-Asian strategy because it would lend them that extra credibility when they went to the FDA and they had data from Taiwan, Korea, Singapore as well as China, as opposed to China-only data."

It could be tempting to become China-centric in future due to the fact that China does not allow whole blood samples to leave the country, so companies conducting clinical trials in China must have a lab there or have an alliance with a lab there. India does not have such a restriction. MDS has a fully owned lab in Beijing. "Our Beijing lab is the only one so far that is CAP [College of American Pathologies]-accredited. Because of that, the laboratory data of our Beijing lab is widely accepted and FDA will have no issue at all. Basically our operation in China is independent and our operation in Singapore is a complement, so both the Beijing and Singapore offices from MDS provide a pan-Asia service, which is unique to MDS. Regarding India, it's different because we do not have that limitation. But the market is growing rapidly, so I would not be too surprised if there were a need to set up a central lab in India."

But becoming "India-centric" or "China-centric" might not be desirable. "As the volume of trials increases in China and India five or 10 years from now, where it makes sense for them to also have hubs in China or a center in India, that could well happen, but that would be a function of demand. I think today if companies had to pick one location, it would be Singapore for the sheer reason that if you set something up in China, you tend to become China-centric and India quickly becomes forgotten. Likewise in India because these countries are huge countries. So I think sometimes, to maintain that 'helicopter view,' that big picture perspective, companies tend to prefer locating their regional headquarters in a more neutral location like Singapore," said Beh.

Most realize that Singapore cannot look to India and China to learn how to compete for clinical trials sponsored by Western companies. Embracing international, U.S. and European standards and guidelines are what led to Singapore's exponential growth. It is clear that Singapore will continue to look to the West in the future.

As PPD's Leong summed up, "The Singapore government is always looking outwards in terms of the U.S. and the European Union to get ideas in terms of how best to move forward. We believe that it's true innovation and efficiency that will strengthen our position in Southeast Asia and Asia as a whole."

Ethical Pharmaceutical Sales

Total PhRMA-Member-Company Sales, 2000-2005

$US in Billions

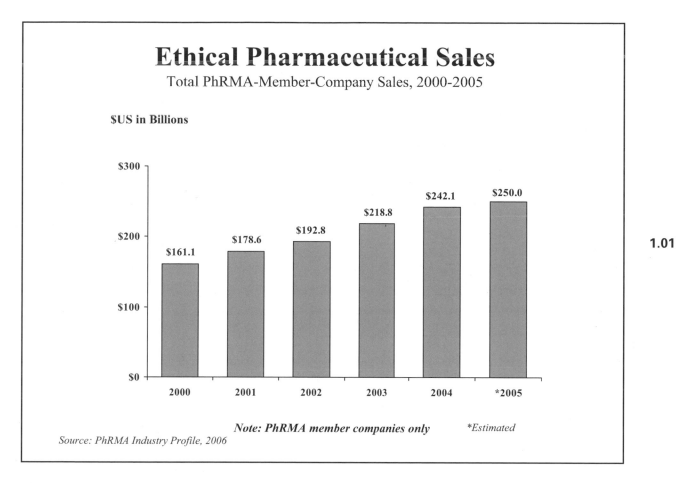

Note: PhRMA member companies only   *Estimated*

Source: PhRMA Industry Profile, 2006

1.01

Major World Markets

Population Size and Sales Growth

Country	Population 2005	Pharmaceutical Sales 2004	Sales Growth (2003 – 2004)
Japan	127 million	$58 billion	2%
Latin America	551 million	$19 billion	13%
North America	328 million	$248 billion	8%
Europe	796 million	$153 billion	6%

1.02

Source: Thomson CenterWatch Analysis, 2004; CIA World Factbook, 2004; IMS World Review, 2005

1.03

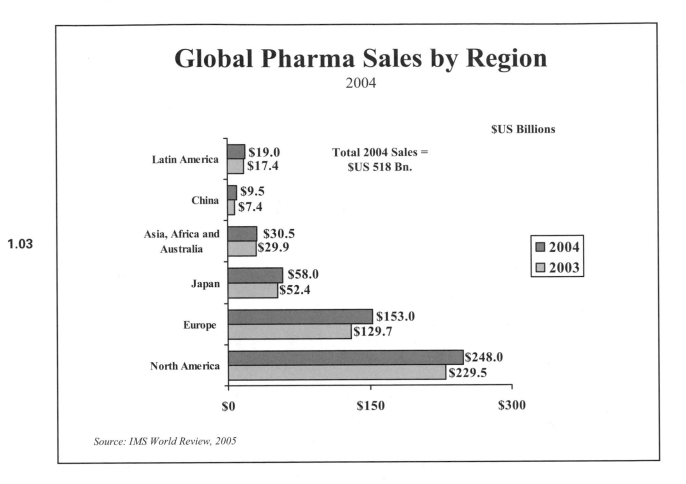

Global Pharma Sales by Region
2004

$US Billions

Total 2004 Sales = $US 518 Bn.

Region	2004	2003
Latin America	$19.0	$17.4
China	$9.5	$7.4
Asia, Africa and Australia	$30.5	$29.9
Japan	$58.0	$52.4
Europe	$153.0	$129.7
North America	$248.0	$229.5

Source: IMS World Review, 2005

1.04

Pharmaceutical Sales by Region
Share of Worldwide Market

% Market Share

	2000	2001	2002	2003	2004
Latin America	6%	5%	4%	4%	4%
Asia/Africa/Australia	6%	8%	8%	8%	8%
Japan	16%	13%	12%	11%	11%
Europe	24%	24%	25%	28%	28%
North America	48%	50%	51%	49%	48%

Source: IMS World Review, 2005

Ethical Pharmaceutical Sales

Growth Rate, 1996-2004

Note: PhRMA member companies only

Estimated

Source: PhRMA Industry Profile, 2005

1.05

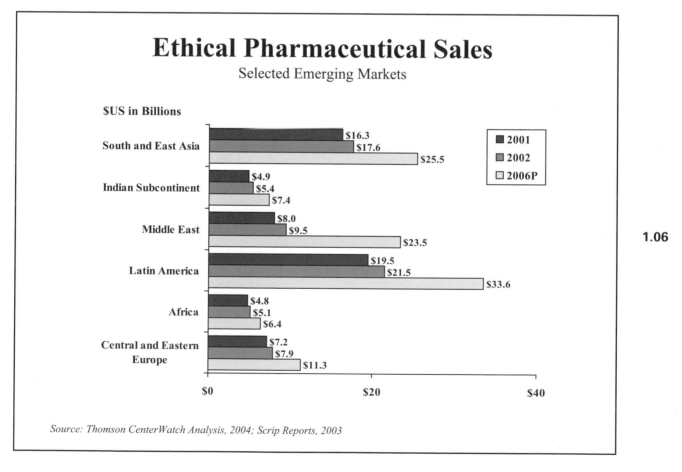

Ethical Pharmaceutical Sales

Selected Emerging Markets

$US in Billions

Source: Thomson CenterWatch Analysis, 2004; Scrip Reports, 2003

1.06

Global Pharma Sales Growth by Region

Regions	2004 Sales		% Growth	
	($ US Billions)	% share	2003	CAGR 1999-2003
North America	$248	47.8%	7.8%	13.7%
Europe (EU)	$144	27.8%	5.7%	8.8%
Eastern and Central Europe	$9	1.8%	12.4%	10.9%
Japan	$58	11.1%	1.5%	3.3%
Asia/Africa/Australia	$40	7.7%	13.0%	10.3%
Latin America	$19	3.8%	13.4%	1.5%
Worldwide	$518	100%	9.0%	10.0%

Source: IMS Health, Intelligence 360, 2005

1.07

Top Pharmaceutical Market Growth Rates

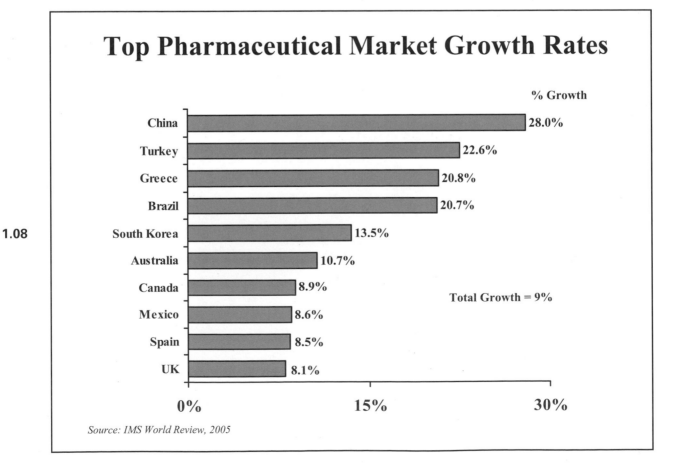

% Growth

China	28.0%
Turkey	22.6%
Greece	20.8%
Brazil	20.7%
South Korea	13.5%
Australia	10.7%
Canada	8.9%
Mexico	8.6%
Spain	8.5%
UK	8.1%

Total Growth = 9%

Source: IMS World Review, 2005

1.08

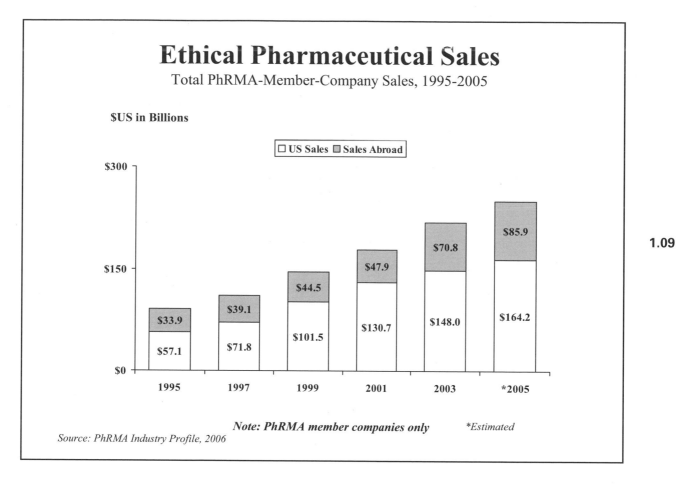

Ethical Pharmaceutical Sales
Total PhRMA-Member-Company Sales, 1995-2005

$US in Billions

1.09

Note: PhRMA member companies only   *Estimated

Source: PhRMA Industry Profile, 2006

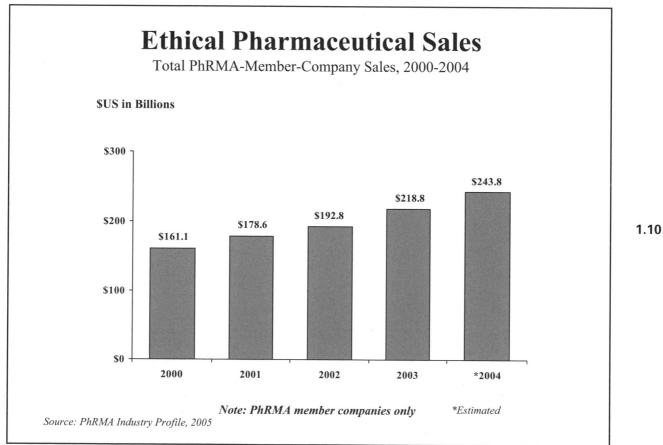

Ethical Pharmaceutical Sales
Total PhRMA-Member-Company Sales, 2000-2004

$US in Billions

1.10

Note: PhRMA member companies only   *Estimated

Source: PhRMA Industry Profile, 2005

Major European Pharmaceutical Sales

$US in Billions

Country	2004 Sales	2004 Growth	Est. 2005 Growth
Germany	$29.4	1.6%	4-5%
France	$28.5	7.2%	5-6%
UK	$20.0	8.1%	7-8%
Italy	$18.9	3.2%	4-5%
Spain	$13.9	8.5%	8-9%
Netherlands	$4.8	<-1%>	0- <-1%>
Belgium	$4.4	7.5%	7-8%
Poland	$3.7	1.5%	5-6%
Greece	$3.3	20.8%	19-20%
Switzerland	$3.3	4.9%	6-7%

Source: IMS Health, Intelligence 360, 2005

1.11

Central and Eastern Europe
Pharmaceutical Sales, 2001-2006

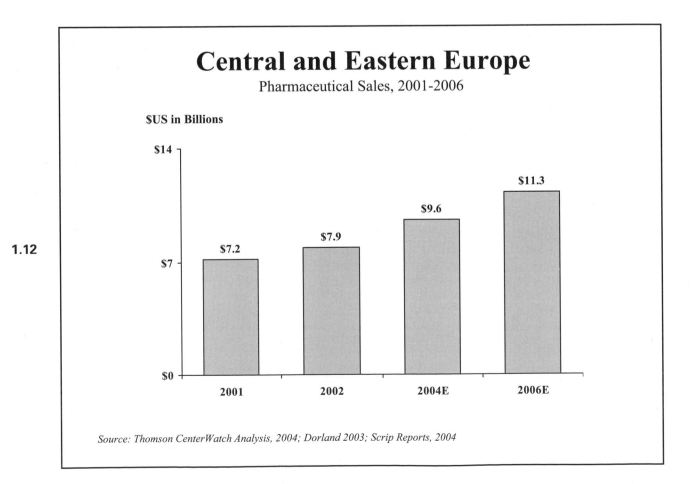

$US in Billions

Source: Thomson CenterWatch Analysis, 2004; Dorland 2003; Scrip Reports, 2004

1.12

Central & Eastern Europe Sales
Pharmaceutical Market Share of Select Countries

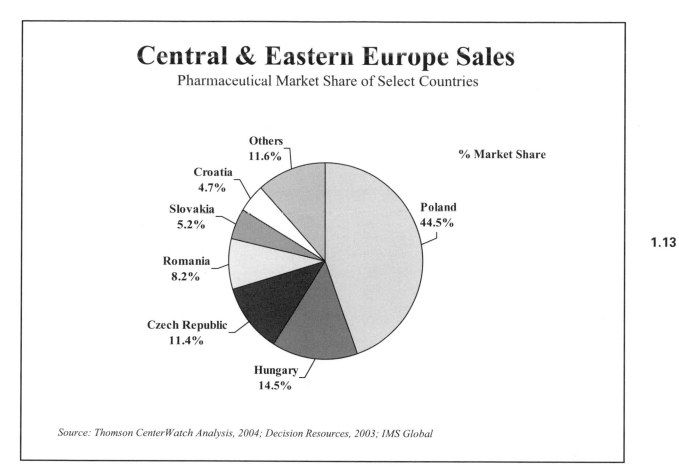

Source: *Thomson CenterWatch Analysis, 2004; Decision Resources, 2003; IMS Global*

1.13

Canadian Healthcare Market

	Value	Year	World Ranking
Population (millions)	31.6	2003	32
GDP per capita (US$)	27,199	2003	18
Health expenditure per capita (US$)	2,740	2003	10
Health expenditure as % of GDP	9.9	2003	8
Hospital beds per 1,000 population	3.2	2000	52
Physicians per 1,000 population	1.9	2001	43
Pharmaceutical market (US$ millions)	15,179	2004	8
Pharmaceutical market per capita (US$)	476	2004	10
Market growth (%)	8.4	2004	~

1.14

Source: *Espicom Business Intelligence, 2004*

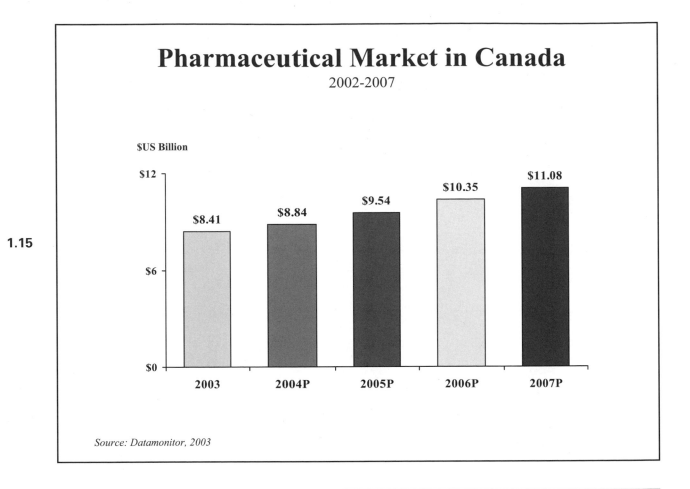

Pharmaceutical Market in Canada
2002-2007

$US Billion

1.15

Source: Datamonitor, 2003

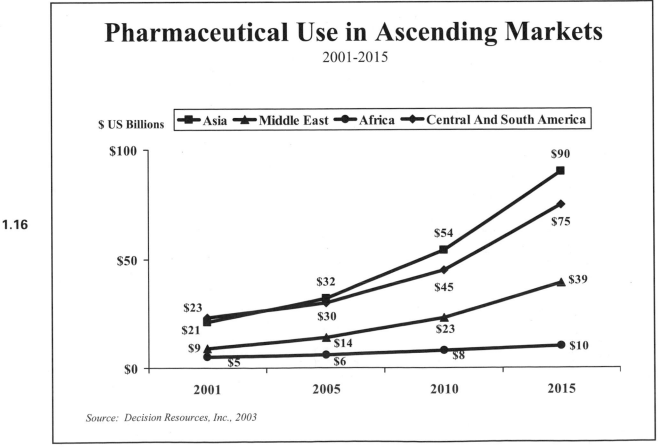

Pharmaceutical Use in Ascending Markets
2001-2015

$ US Billions — Asia — Middle East — Africa — Central And South America

1.16

Source: Decision Resources, Inc., 2003

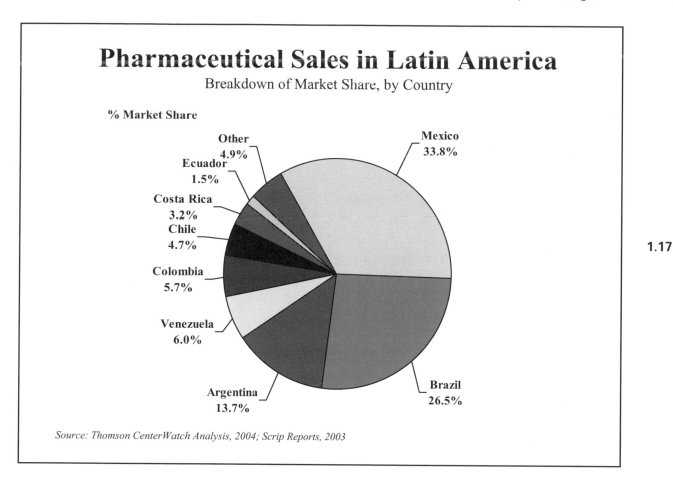

Pharmaceutical Sales in Latin America
Breakdown of Market Share, by Country

% Market Share

- Mexico 33.8%
- Brazil 26.5%
- Argentina 13.7%
- Venezuela 6.0%
- Colombia 5.7%
- Chile 4.7%
- Costa Rica 3.2%
- Ecuador 1.5%
- Other 4.9%

Source: Thomson CenterWatch Analysis, 2004; Scrip Reports, 2003

1.17

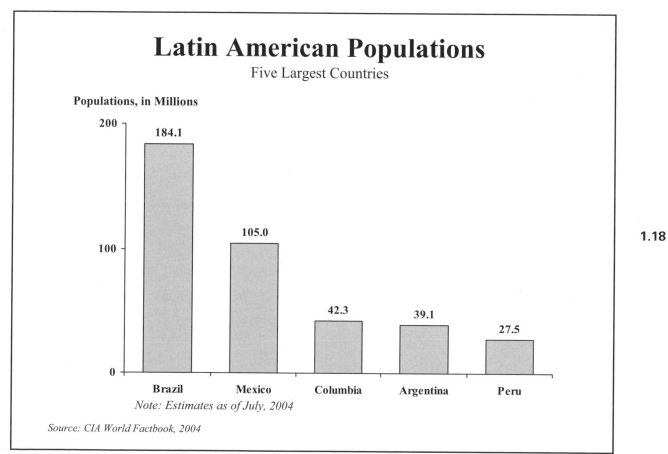

Latin American Populations
Five Largest Countries

Populations, in Millions

Country	Population
Brazil	184.1
Mexico	105.0
Columbia	42.3
Argentina	39.1
Peru	27.5

Note: Estimates as of July, 2004

Source: CIA World Factbook, 2004

1.18

1.19

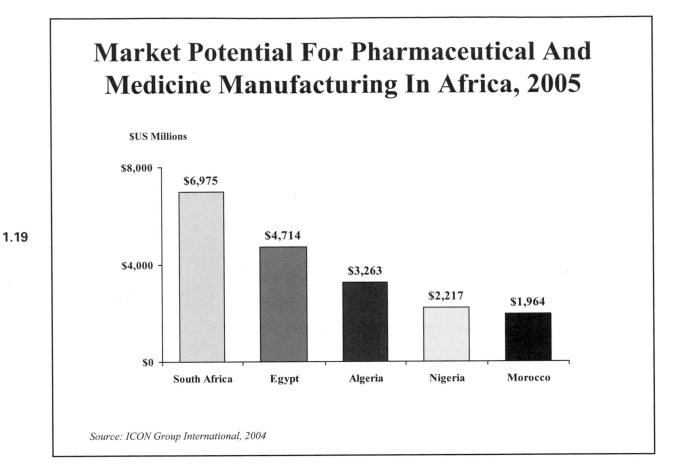

Market Potential For Pharmaceutical And Medicine Manufacturing In Africa, 2005

$US Millions

Source: ICON Group International, 2004

1.20

South African Healthcare Market

	Value	Year	Source
Population (millions)	45.6	2004	*Statistics South Africa*
GDP per capita (US$)	2,780	2003	*BBC*
Health expenditure per capita (Rand) Public	969	2003	*Statistics South Africa*
Health expenditure per capita (Rand) Private	5,724	2003	*Statistics South Africa*
Health expenditure as % of GDP	8.5%	2002	*Espicom Business Intelligence, 2003*
Hospital beds per 1,000 population	3.1	2003	*Espicom Business Intelligence, 2003*
Physicians per 1,000 population	.7	1998	*Espicom Business Intelligence, 2003*
Pharmaceutical market (US$ millions)	1,500	2002	*Espicom Business Intelligence, 2003*
Pharmaceutical market per capita (US$)	$35	2002	*Espicom Business Intelligence, 2003*
Market growth (%)	12%	2002	*Espicom Business Intelligence, 2003*

Source: Espicom Business Intelligence, 2004

Large Market Potential in Asia

	Population	Population Growth (2005 est.)	GDP (PPP)	Per Capita Income (PPP)
Philippines	87,857,473	1.84%	$430.6 billion	$5,000
Indonesia	241,973,879	1.45%	$827.4 billion	$3,500
Malaysia	23,953,136	1.80%	$229.3 billion	$9,700
Singapore	4,425,720	1.56%	$120.9 billion	$27,800
South Korea	48,422,644	0.38%	$925.1 billion	$19,200
Thailand	65,444,371	0.87%	$524.8 billion	$8,100
Taiwan	22,894,384	0.63%	$576.2 billion	$25,300
India	1,080,264,388	1.40%	$3.319 trillion	$3,100

1.21

Source: 2005 CIA Factbook

Major Asia/Pacific Pharmaceutical Sales

$US in Billions

Country	2004 Sales	2004 Growth
Japan	$58.0	1.6%
China	$9.5	7.2%
Australia	$5.8	8.1%
South Korea	$5.7	3.2%
India	$4.6	8.5%
Taiwan	$2.8	<-1%>
Indonesia	$1.9	7.5%
Philippines	$1.3	1.5%
Thailand	$1.1	20.8%
Hong Kong	$0.4	4.9%

1.22

Source: IMS, 2005

1.23

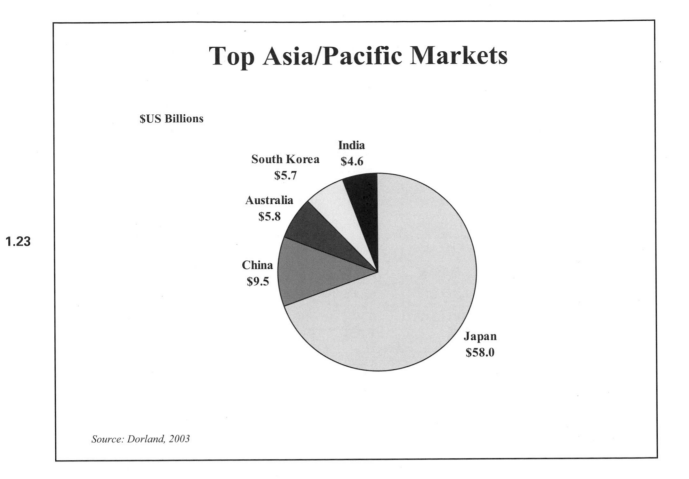

Top Asia/Pacific Markets

$US Billions

South Korea $5.7
India $4.6
Australia $5.8
China $9.5
Japan $58.0

Source: Dorland, 2003

1.24

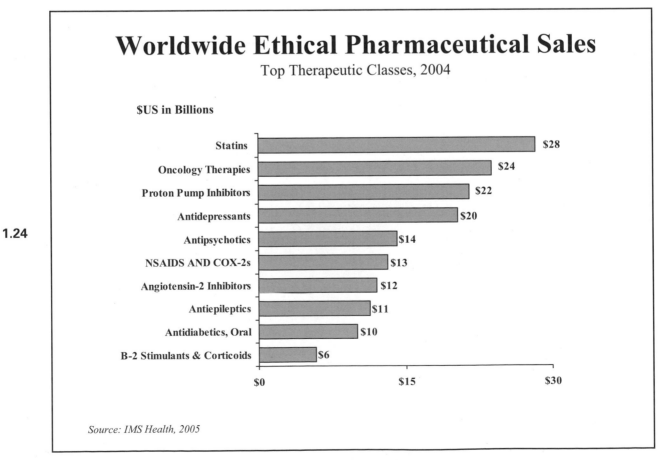

Worldwide Ethical Pharmaceutical Sales
Top Therapeutic Classes, 2004

$US in Billions

Statins	$28
Oncology Therapies	$24
Proton Pump Inhibitors	$22
Antidepressants	$20
Antipsychotics	$14
NSAIDS AND COX-2s	$13
Angiotensin-2 Inhibitors	$12
Antiepileptics	$11
Antidiabetics, Oral	$10
B-2 Stimulants & Corticoids	$6

$0 $15 $30

Source: IMS Health, 2005

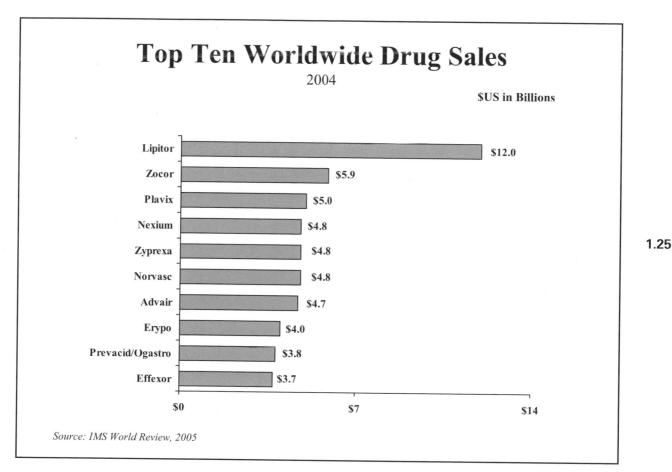

Top Ten Worldwide Drug Sales
2004

$US in Billions

Drug	Sales
Lipitor	$12.0
Zocor	$5.9
Plavix	$5.0
Nexium	$4.8
Zyprexa	$4.8
Norvasc	$4.8
Advair	$4.7
Erypo	$4.0
Prevacid/Ogastro	$3.8
Effexor	$3.7

$0 $7 $14

Source: IMS World Review, 2005

1.25

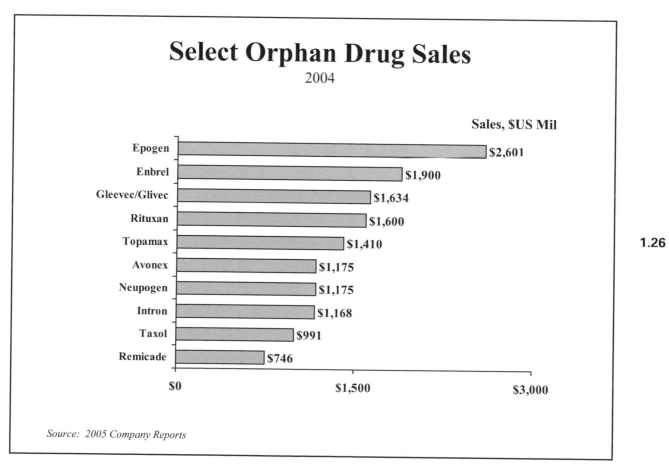

Select Orphan Drug Sales
2004

Sales, $US Mil

Drug	Sales
Epogen	$2,601
Enbrel	$1,900
Gleevec/Glivec	$1,634
Rituxan	$1,600
Topamax	$1,410
Avonex	$1,175
Neupogen	$1,175
Intron	$1,168
Taxol	$991
Remicade	$746

$0 $1,500 $3,000

Source: 2005 Company Reports

1.26

1.27

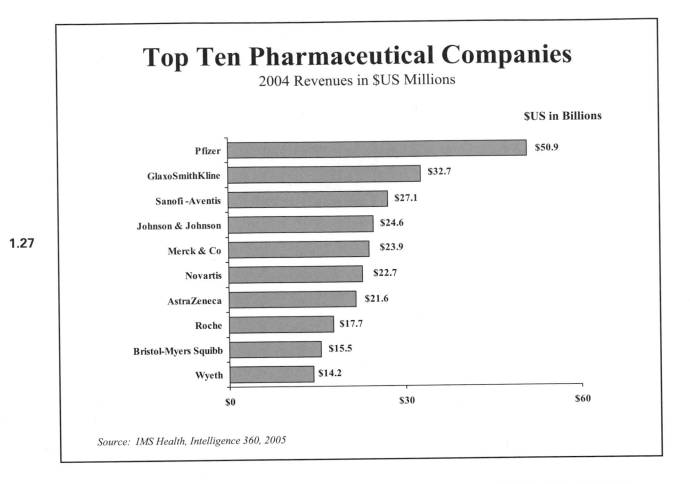

Top Ten Pharmaceutical Companies
2004 Revenues in $US Millions

$US in Billions

Company	Revenue
Pfizer	$50.9
GlaxoSmithKline	$32.7
Sanofi-Aventis	$27.1
Johnson & Johnson	$24.6
Merck & Co	$23.9
Novartis	$22.7
AstraZeneca	$21.6
Roche	$17.7
Bristol-Myers Squibb	$15.5
Wyeth	$14.2

Source: IMS Health, Intelligence 360, 2005

1.28

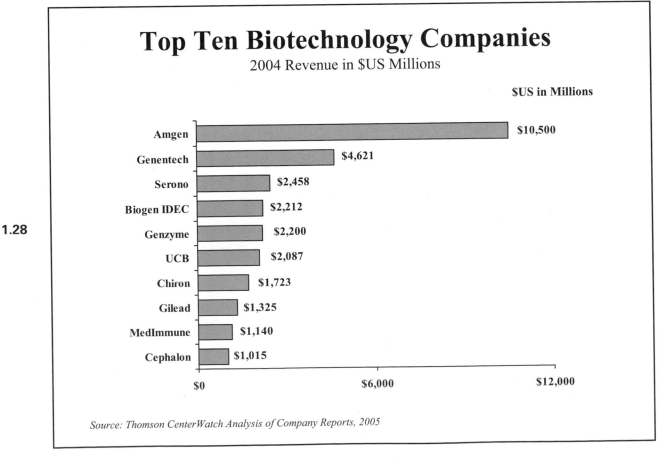

Top Ten Biotechnology Companies
2004 Revenue in $US Millions

$US in Millions

Company	Revenue
Amgen	$10,500
Genentech	$4,621
Serono	$2,458
Biogen IDEC	$2,212
Genzyme	$2,200
UCB	$2,087
Chiron	$1,723
Gilead	$1,325
MedImmune	$1,140
Cephalon	$1,015

Source: Thomson CenterWatch Analysis of Company Reports, 2005

Worldwide Medical Device Market
Projected Sales, through 2009

$US in Billions

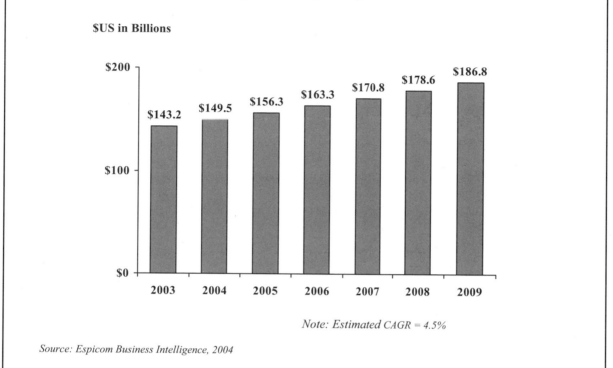

$200

$143.2 $149.5 $156.3 $163.3 $170.8 $178.6 $186.8

$100

$0

2003   2004   2005   2006   2007   2008   2009

Note: Estimated CAGR = 4.5%

Source: Espicom Business Intelligence, 2004

1.29

U.S. Medical Device Market
Projected Sales 2004-2009

$US in Billions

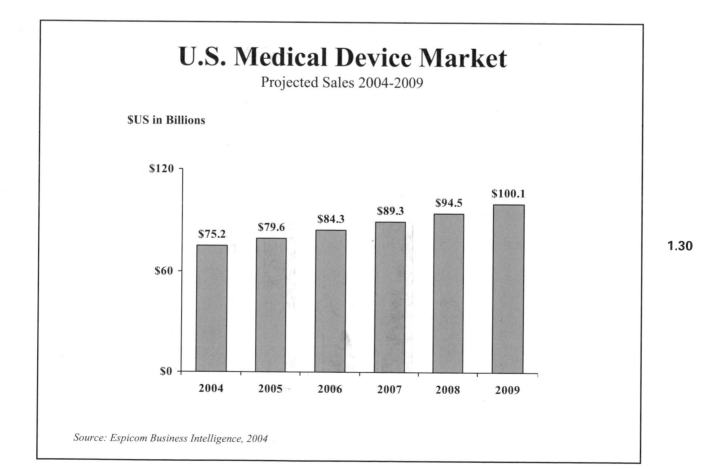

$120

$75.2 $79.6 $84.3 $89.3 $94.5 $100.1

$60

$0

2004   2005   2006   2007   2008   2009

Source: Espicom Business Intelligence, 2004

1.30

1.31

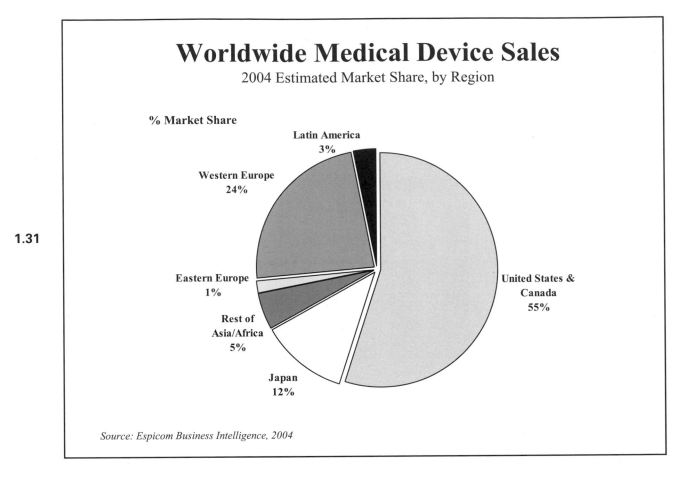

Worldwide Medical Device Sales
2004 Estimated Market Share, by Region

% Market Share

- Latin America 3%
- Western Europe 24%
- Eastern Europe 1%
- Rest of Asia/Africa 5%
- Japan 12%
- United States & Canada 55%

Source: Espicom Business Intelligence, 2004

1.32

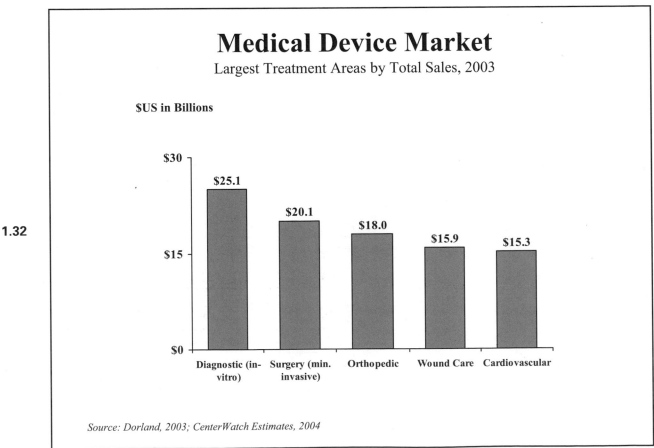

Medical Device Market
Largest Treatment Areas by Total Sales, 2003

$US in Billions

Diagnostic (in-vitro)	$25.1
Surgery (min. invasive)	$20.1
Orthopedic	$18.0
Wound Care	$15.9
Cardiovascular	$15.3

Source: Dorland, 2003; CenterWatch Estimates, 2004

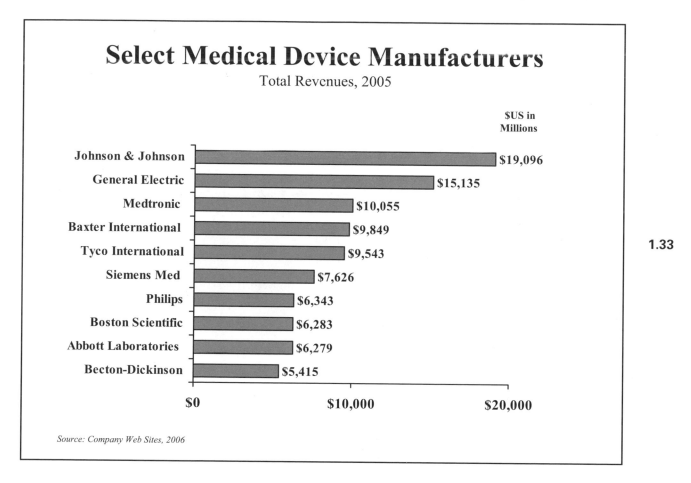

Select Medical Device Manufacturers
Total Revenues, 2005

$US in Millions

Johnson & Johnson	$19,096
General Electric	$15,135
Medtronic	$10,055
Baxter International	$9,849
Tyco International	$9,543
Siemens Med	$7,626
Philips	$6,343
Boston Scientific	$6,283
Abbott Laboratories	$6,279
Becton-Dickinson	$5,415

Source: Company Web Sites, 2006

1.33

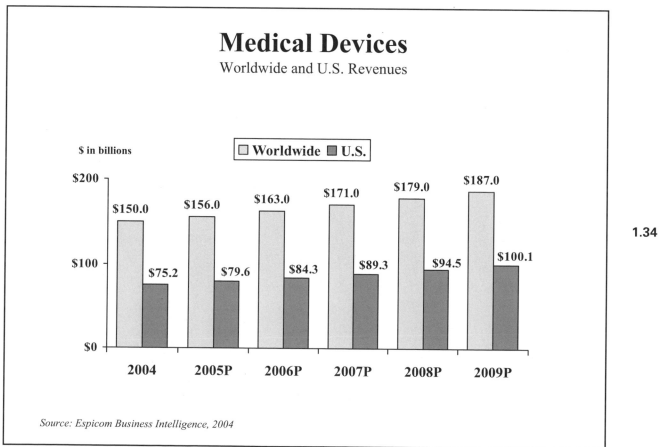

Medical Devices
Worldwide and U.S. Revenues

$ in billions

☐ Worldwide ■ U.S.

	2004	2005P	2006P	2007P	2008P	2009P
Worldwide	$150.0	$156.0	$163.0	$171.0	$179.0	$187.0
U.S.	$75.2	$79.6	$84.3	$89.3	$94.5	$100.1

Source: Espicom Business Intelligence, 2004

1.34

Generic Pharmaceutical Market
Total Worldwide Sales, 1998-2003

$US in Billions

Source: Thomson CenterWatch Analysis, 2004; Datamonitor, 2003

1.35

Generic Pharmaceutical Market
Total U.S. Sales, 2000-2007

$US in Billions

Source: Thomson CenterWatch Analysis, 2004; Dorland , 2003

1.36

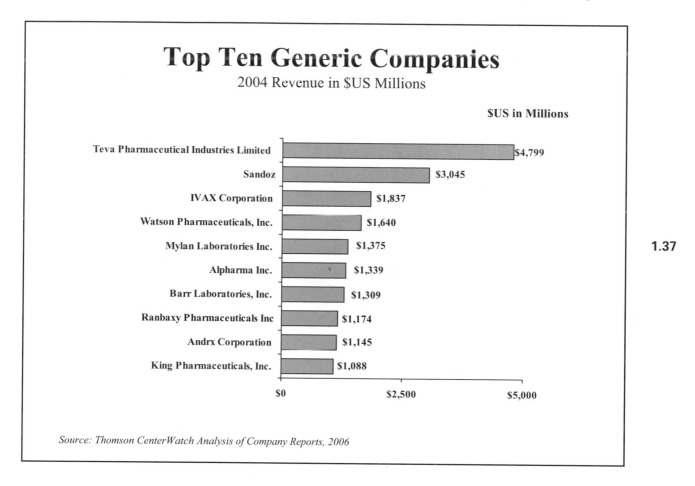

Top Ten Generic Companies
2004 Revenue in $US Millions

$US in Millions

Company	Revenue
Teva Pharmaceutical Industries Limited	$4,799
Sandoz	$3,045
IVAX Corporation	$1,837
Watson Pharmaceuticals, Inc.	$1,640
Mylan Laboratories Inc.	$1,375
Alpharma Inc.	$1,339
Barr Laboratories, Inc.	$1,309
Ranbaxy Pharmaceuticals Inc	$1,174
Andrx Corporation	$1,145
King Pharmaceuticals, Inc.	$1,088

$0 $2,500 $5,000

Source: Thomson CenterWatch Analysis of Company Reports, 2006

1.37

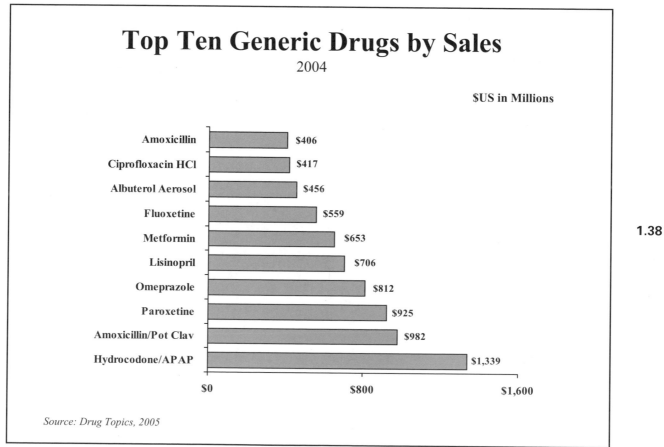

Top Ten Generic Drugs by Sales
2004

$US in Millions

Drug	Sales
Amoxicillin	$406
Ciprofloxacin HCl	$417
Albuterol Aerosol	$456
Fluoxetine	$559
Metformin	$653
Lisinopril	$706
Omeprazole	$812
Paroxetine	$925
Amoxicillin/Pot Clav	$982
Hydrocodone/APAP	$1,339

$0 $800 $1,600

1.38

Source: Drug Topics, 2005

1.39

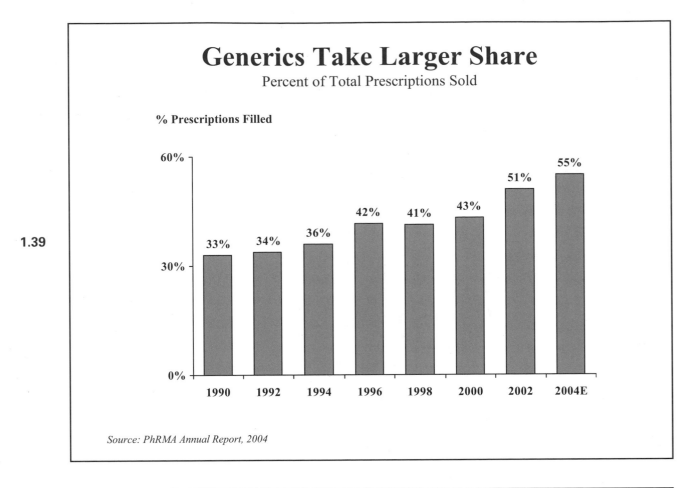

Generics Take Larger Share
Percent of Total Prescriptions Sold

% Prescriptions Filled

Source: PhRMA Annual Report, 2004

1.40

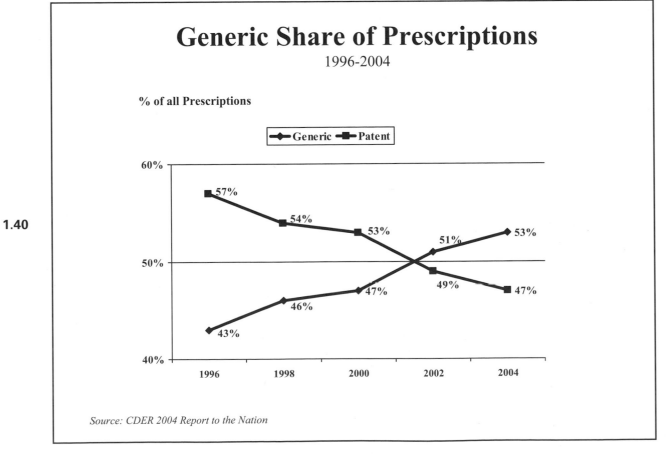

Generic Share of Prescriptions
1996-2004

% of all Prescriptions

Source: CDER 2004 Report to the Nation

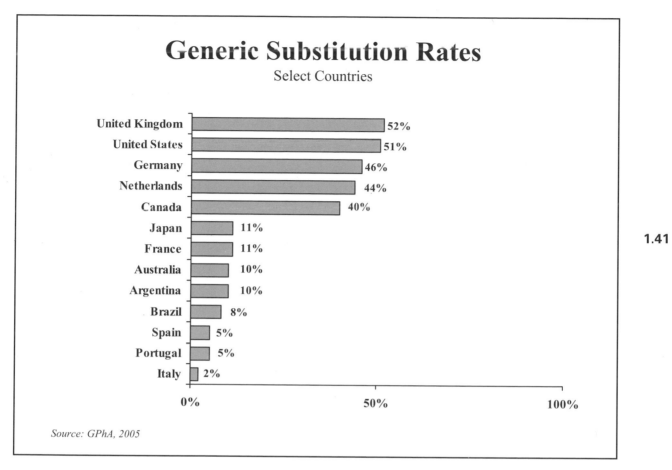

Generic Substitution Rates
Select Countries

Country	Rate
United Kingdom	52%
United States	51%
Germany	46%
Netherlands	44%
Canada	40%
Japan	11%
France	11%
Australia	10%
Argentina	10%
Brazil	8%
Spain	5%
Portugal	5%
Italy	2%

Source: GPhA, 2005

1.41

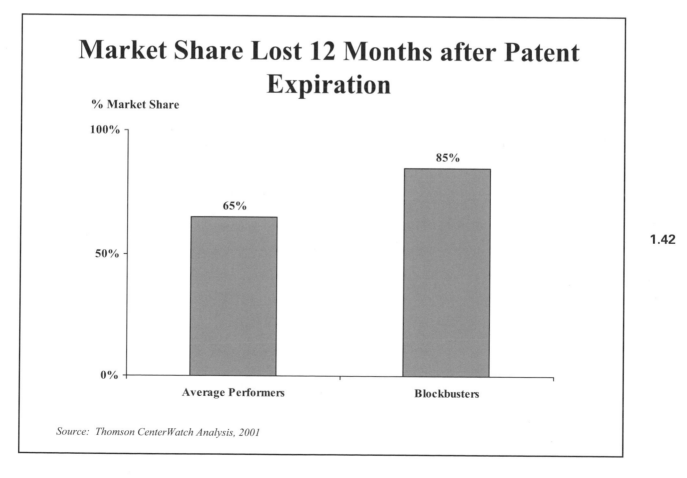

Market Share Lost 12 Months after Patent Expiration

% Market Share

Average Performers	65%
Blockbusters	85%

Source: Thomson CenterWatch Analysis, 2001

1.42

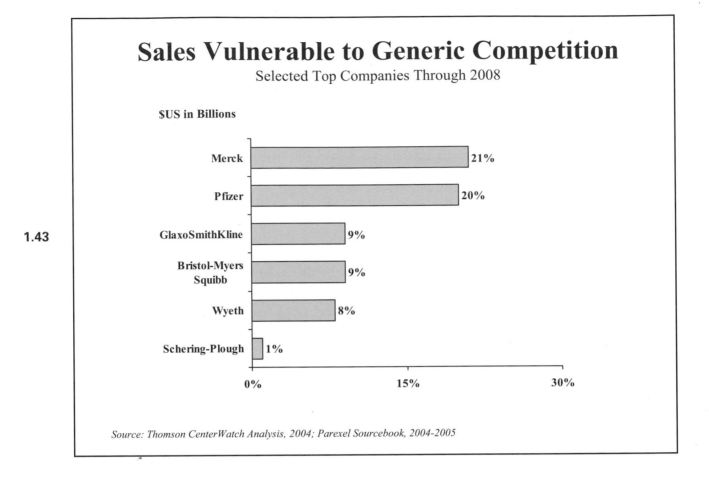

Sales Vulnerable to Generic Competition
Selected Top Companies Through 2008

$US in Billions

1.43

Merck — 21%
Pfizer — 20%
GlaxoSmithKline — 9%
Bristol-Myers Squibb — 9%
Wyeth — 8%
Schering-Plough — 1%

(0% — 15% — 30%)

Source: Thomson CenterWatch Analysis, 2004; Parexel Sourcebook, 2004-2005

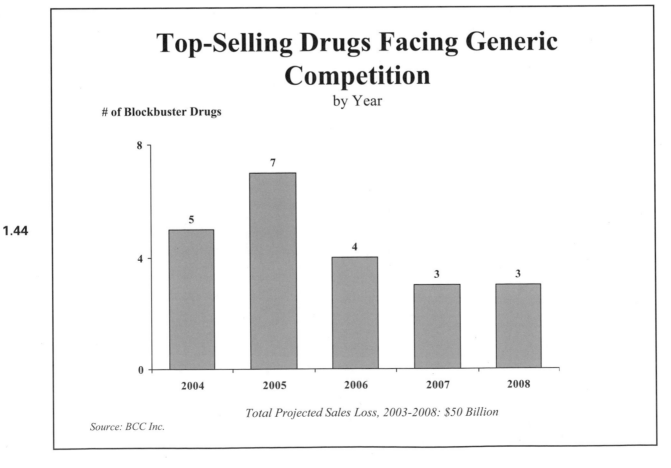

Top-Selling Drugs Facing Generic Competition
by Year

# of Blockbuster Drugs

1.44

2004 — 5
2005 — 7
2006 — 4
2007 — 3
2008 — 3

Total Projected Sales Loss, 2003-2008: $50 Billion

Source: BCC Inc.

R&D Expenditure

Clinical Trial Transparency Efforts Multiply

By Karyn Korieth
Published November 2005

Pharmaceutical companies, under growing pressure to provide more information about clinical research on new drugs and to restore public trust in the industry, have taken significant steps towards clinical trials transparency. This year alone, companies will have spent an estimated $89 million, up from $60 million spent in the last half of 2003 and all of 2004 combined, to publicize active and completed trials on publicly accessible web sites.

As part of industry-wide efforts to expand access to clinical trial data, during the past year major drug companies have published results of hundreds of hypothesis-testing studies completed on some 200 marketed drugs through a centralized web site created by the industry trade group Pharmaceutical Research Manufacturers of America, known as PhRMA. In addition, several major pharmaceutical companies, including Eli Lilly, GlaxoSmithKline, AstraZeneca and Roche, have invested considerable resources to establish trial registries on their company web sites. And while pharmaceutical companies are legally required to register trials for products treating serious or life-threatening diseases on a National Institutes of Health web site, in the last year they have begun to voluntarily post clinical trials for other types of studies on the government-sponsored site, as well as listing an increasing number of active studies on company web pages or on commercial registries.

In fact, a Thomson CenterWatch analysis found that the number of studies listed on public online registries grew by 51% from July 2004 to July 2005; during the past five years, the average number of active listings has grown from 12,300 to 32,000 per month. "I think that we are moving in a direction of greater levels of transparency, which I think will be very good for patients and the public," said Alan Breier, M.D., vice president and chief medical officer at Eli Lilly and Company.

Industry-wide efforts to improve access to clinical trials information are on the rise, yet significant problems remain. While the top 15 biopharmaceutical companies have begun aggressive transparency initiatives, the remaining companies in the top 50 have lagged in their disclosure efforts. Those 35 companies represent more than 40% of the pipeline. Existing initiatives for clinical trials transparency are fragmented, with no agreement on common standards or the scope of disclosed information. Reporting of clinical trials results remains voluntary. And public criticism of the pharmaceutical industry's efforts to publicize its clinical research ranges from charges of hiding data to publishing information not useful to patients; even those in the industry admit the vast number of study summaries available on the Internet can be overwhelming for those who don't understand the clinical trials process. "A lot of what is up online so far isn't really useful to anybody. Right now, just registering a trial and disguising a lot of the key facts isn't helpful to anybody," said Arthur Caplan, Ph.D., director of the Center for Bioethics at the University of Pennsylvania in Philadelphia. "But the move toward registries is underway. That will continue and we will see more efforts to make the information useable and meaningful."

Irrespective of the criticism, the amount of activity involving clinical trials transparency in the past 18 months, especially in an industry notoriously slow to change, is unprecedented. Major pharmaceutical companies say they are committed to clinical trial transparency initiatives and want both patients and physicians to not only use the registries and results databases, but also give these new resources a fair chance to work. "We need to be open enough to play fair game. But also, from the people watching this, they need to realize that a lot of effort is being done by the industry," said Beat E. Widler, Ph.D., global head of clinical quality at Roche. "If there is something not perfect, then we should have a fair debate. But the wish is really that people use this resource before they make new claims for disclosure of information or make an argument for adding additional hurdles."

Michael Berelowitz, M.D., senior vice president, worldwide medical and outcomes research at Pfizer, added, "We hope that it is a useful source of information for patients and investigators and we hope they actually go to it and use it. We also hope that the people who are most interested in determining that we maintain transparency will actually agree that we are conforming and give credit where credit is due. An enormous number of people put an enormous amount of effort into this and I think they deserve credit for doing the work."

Demand for Transparency Grows

By law, drug companies are required to post information about drug effectiveness trials for serious or life-threatening diseases on clinicaltrials.gov, a registry launched by the National Institutes of Health five years ago. Overall industry compliance, however, had been poor with less than 50% of serious or life-threatening clinical trials posted during the first three-and-a-half years of the site's existence.

For years, academics and physicians have pushed for more clinical trial disclosures from pharmaceutical companies. The issue gained

momentum in 2004 when New York Attorney General Eliot Spitzer sued GlaxoSmithKline for allegedly hiding results from trials showing that its antidepressant Paxil might increase suicidal thoughts in children and adolescents.

GlaxoSmithKline, which settled the suit for $2.5 million without admitting wrongdoing, in September, 2004, launched the first public clinical trial register to post results and protocol information from GSK-sponsored trials of marketed medicines on its company web site. Other companies, including Roche, Eli Lilly and AstraZeneca, soon followed suit with their own online registries. Then the Pharmaceutical Research and Manufacturers of America, an industry lobbying group known as PhRMA, announced plans in September, 2004, to create a central site for companies to voluntarily post results for drugs that have received marketing approval.

Earlier this year, the introduction of federal legislation called the Fair Access to Clinical Trials Act, or the FACT Act, which would require the reporting of all clinical trial results and expand the current mandate for trial registration, helped to focus the industry's attention on the issue of clinical trials transparency. But what had the biggest impact on getting companies to take the issue seriously was the International Committee of Medical Journal Editors (ICMJE) announcement in September, 2004, that it would consider an article about a research project for publication only if it was posted to a central registry before September 13, 2005. ICMJE defined "research project" as "Any research project that prospectively assigns human subjects to intervention and comparison groups to study the cause-and-effect relationship between a medical intervention and a health outcome." In conjunction with the publication of the ICMJE statement, clinicaltrials.gov expanded its scope and modified data fields to accommodate the ICMJE's registration requirements.

On the whole, the pharmaceutical industry has signed on to the idea of

voluntarily registering clinical trials on publicly accessible sites. In January, the International Federation of Pharmaceutical Manufacturers and Associations (IFPMA) and three trade associations, including PhRMA, issued a Joint Position on the Disclosure of Clinical Trial Information, which recommended that pharmaceutical companies voluntarily submit information about all non-exploratory industry-sponsored trials to publicly accessible registries such as clinicaltrials.gov. The statement also suggests that members submit summary results of industry-sponsored trials, regardless of outcome, for drugs that have received marketing approval.

Transparency Increases

The ICMJE policy has driven growth in terms of the number of ongoing trials registered during the past year. Overall, companies have made significant progress with registering their data in a relatively short time period. A CenterWatch analysis found that 100% of the top 15 biopharmaceutical companies are posting their active clinical trials online in some capacity. Specifically, 93% of the companies registered their studies on clinicaltrials.gov, while 60% of the drug companies posted their information on commercial registries such as centerwatch.com and 33% post on their own web sites. In the past 18 months alone, the top 15 biopharmaceutical companies have posted more than 1,300 trials.

At the same time, however, efforts to post trial results lag behind the progress made in registering active clinical trials. CenterWatch analysis found that currently about 87% of the top 15 companies are posting trial results online; most companies are posting results to the new PhRMA site (clinicalstudyresults.org).

Industry Response Divided

In this new drive toward transparency, within the industry companies are divided about how much information to reveal, both about new studies and completed studies for drugs already being sold.

The World Health Organization's technical advisory group developed registration standards, which have been adopted by clinicaltrials.gov and other registries, requiring sponsors to complete 20 data fields when registering a clinical trial. Five of

the data elements, however, have been hotly debated in the industry. Some companies hold that the level of detail required in those five fields, including the official scientific title of the study, interventions, target sample size and primary and secondary outcome measures, could tip off competitors about the types of drugs they are developing. Major pharmaceutical companies, including GSK, Eli Lilly and Pfizer, have decided not to submit data in all 20 fields when posting certain clinical trials in order to protect intellectual property. Some drug companies have argued that it's not necessary to disclose this data until the drug is available for prescribing. "At the initiation of a trial, the purpose of registering the trial is to acknowledge that it exists. The detailed methodology really serves no clinical purpose. It doesn't help prescribers to prescribe the drug. It doesn't help patients understand what drug they are taking. That comes in the second piece, when you put the results out," said Eli Lilly's Breier.

Meanwhile, other biopharmaceutical companies, including Wyeth and Amgen, have decided to complete all 20 data fields when registering clinical trial protocols. "We are going for transparency and we feel that this is the appropriate thing to do," said Maryann Foote, Ph.D., director, global regulatory writing, for Amgen. "We feel transparency is really the issue here and people need to know."

Drug companies also have chosen different paths to disclose information concerning both active trials and results. Many major biopharmaceutical companies register clinical trials on clinicaltrials.gov and results on clinicalstudyresults.org, which is the PhRMA web site. In addition, some pharmaceutical companies have developed their own online registries and databases; some of these company web sites post only active trials, others only publish clinical trial results of marketed drugs, and still others include data from both ongoing trials and results.

Companies also have made different decisions about which study results to post online. GSK has committed to posting on its web site the trial results of all GSK-marketed medicines they have sponsored since the company's formation; if the product has been marketed in at least one country,

GSK will post results of all studies, from every phase, in every country. The more widespread approach adopted by pharmaceutical companies has been to post clinical study results from phase II to IV trials.

Companies that register clinical trial protocols on clinicaltrials.gov and results for marketed products on PhRMA's web site face a dilemma about how to disclose study results from failed drugs. At Amgen, for example, the policy on the public disclosure of clinical trials and clinical trials results calls for posting information about investigational drug candidates that will no longer be developed, including new uses that will not be pursued for marketed purposes, within two years of ending the product development. The policy calls for disclosing any medically or scientifically important information from all Amgen-sponsored phase II or III studies of safety or efficacy that enroll patients. Since the PhRMA site and the clinicaltrials.gov site both lack the ability to post this information, Amgen is working to redesign its own web site in order to include information about trials that have ended. "We're trying to find a place to get the information out about trials for drugs that we've stopped that would not have a package insert," Foote said. "That is one limitation of the PhRMA web page now—drugs posted need to have a package insert, which makes it more difficult to get out information about drugs that will no longer be developed."

Eli Lilly, on the other hand, has developed a web site that lists both clinical trial registry and results. The Lilly site includes more than 100 clinical trial result summaries across 16 different products dating back 10 years. In addition, the web site includes information on more than 170 initiated and ongoing Lilly-sponsored phase II to IV clinical trials. Lilly decided to post both registry and results on one site, in part, to avoid the appearance of incomplete disclosure; companies cannot easily hide the results of trials that have been disclosed in advance. "It helps build trust because there is knowledge of what trials are occurring globally. And at some point those trials will end and the second part of clinical registry is appending the results of those trials to the web. Then you have the complete set. You have the initiation of the trial, then

when the trial is completed, you have the results available," said Breier.

Other companies also have plans in the works to develop their own web sites that publicize both active trials and results. Bristol-Myers Squibb, for example, is developing its own web site to supplement clinicaltrials.gov and clinicalstudyresults.org for the centralized reporting of registration and results, and Wyeth plans to include all study postings and trial results on a re-designed web site in the second quarter of next year.

Roche, which has headquarters in Basel, Switzerland, chose a different approach to disclosing trial registry and results data when it decided to publish its clinical trials data through an independent host. In April, Roche announced an agreement with Thomson CenterWatch to list its clinical trial protocol registry and results on CenterWatch's web site and on a new Roche clinical trial web site. Ultimately, Roche's database will include protocol information and results from all phase II to IV clinical trials completed after October 1, 2004; in addition, all results from phase II to IV clinical trials for medicines first marketed after October 1, 2002, will be included retrospectively. As of September, Roche has posted data from 195 studies representing more than 30 medicines; 170 postings were to register clinical trials and the other 25 postings were trial results. The data will be posted to be consistent with the information disclosure principles published earlier this year by the European Federation of Pharmaceutical Industry Associations (EFPIA). "Any trial that is on the registry will eventually appear on the results section. Whether a trial has positive or negative results, the results will be visible. For projects that have failed, we will publish a short summary of results," Widler said.

When deciding how to disclose clinical trials information, Roche wanted both registry and results on the same site to make finding information easier for users. The company also wanted a global clinical trials registry and results database that was not associated with either a single country or a trade association. At the same time, senior management decided to place the registry and results database outside of Roche in order to keep the process at arms length. "Once the data is transferred from Roche to CenterWatch, we can no longer change it, access it or modify it in any way unless we make a modification package that then gets uploaded. The quality control and the hosting of the data does not come under the direct control of Roche," said Widler.

Other companies, including Pfizer, have decided against developing their own web site to publish clinical research data. Instead, Pfizer has posted enrollment information for 265 ongoing studies on the clinicaltrials.gov site and results from 314 studies involving 35 marketed medicines on the PhRMA web site; information contained in the PhRMA database includes summary results of late-stage efficacy and safety studies completed after October 2002. "We wanted people to have the widest possible access and the easiest possible access to this so we went with web sites that were accommodating more than a single pharmaceutical company," said Pfizer's Berelowitz. "The results are posted on the PhRMA web site, and the studies are posted on the NIH web site. These are public access locations. Multiple pharmaceutical companies will eventually put their material on these sites. We decided to go in that direction rather than the different path chosen by other companies."

Resources Applied

Major biopharmaceutical companies have committed significant personnel, time and money to the issue of clinical trials transparency since 2003. Thomson CenterWatch estimates that the top 15 biopharmaceutical companies will have spent an estimated total of $146 million by the end of this year in various efforts to disclose clinical trials information, including registering their listings in public databases and creating their own registries; this amount does not include initiatives to recruit patients. Roche, for example, has spent more than 1 million Swiss francs, or US$775,000, this year alone to ramp up its clinical trials registry and results database. "It's not a cheap exercise," said Widler.

CenterWatch analysis, based on PhRMA and company reports, estimates industry spending on

registry initiatives, including development, posting and maintenance, will continue to rise for the next four years. Industry spending on registry initiatives is expected to reach $89 million next year and continue to increase through 2009 to $107 million. These growth projections are based on expected increases in labor and technology costs, annual contract increases, staff training costs, lack of efficiencies and the amount of past trial data companies will need to post. In future years, total spending will level off as companies develop better internal workflow of these functions and sponsors finish posting retrospective trial data. "Over time, it will not be the work bite that it has been. It will become more streamlined and a matter of practice," said Eli Lilly's Breier.

At a time when big pharma is under pressure to keep down headcount, on average, major biopharmaceutical companies have dedicated anywhere from 25 to 40 full-time equivalents (FTEs), depending on the retrospective work required, to clinical transparency efforts. In order to produce and maintain registries, personnel are needed in areas such as project management, web development, data entry, medical writing, regulatory and legal. Once the backlog of trial data has been processed and systems established, large pharmaceutical companies will require somewhere between five and 10 FTEs to maintain the registries depending on the volume of research.

GlaxoSmithKline has dedicated about 40 FTEs to work on summaries and databases for its clinical trial results register. For the initial year to year-and-a-half following the launch of its database, the company has retrospectively generated summaries for studies that have been completed since the merger of the company in 2000. In some cases, the company will post results of studies completed before 2000 if they are likely to inform medical judgment. Since the introduction of the clinical trial register last September, GSK has posted the results of more than 1,100 trials representing more than 30 medicines; once retrospective work has been finished, the company expects to have posted between 1,800 and 2,000 clinical trial results on its register. "We've had a bit of a retrospective exercise to conduct in addition to the prospective exercise of imbedding all of this activity moving forward into our normal practices," said Craig A. Metz, Ph.D., vice president of CEDD Regulatory Affairs at GlaxoSmithKline.

When GSK moves into its registry maintenance phase next year, the company will need somewhere between six to 10 FTEs per year to cover the entire spectrum of activities, from registering the study protocols on clinicaltrials.gov to providing the results both on GSK's Clinical Trial Register and on the PhRMA site.

Pfizer, which has posted information on more than 500 company-sponsored clinical trials, also has dedicated significant resources to its effort. "It was a huge effort on the part of many, many, many of our product teams," said Berelowitz. "Results of our clinical trials were posted for 35 medications. Each medication involves a team of people who are normally working on that medication; that team put aside time, resource and effort to obtain all of the information that was needed, get it into the format that was required and get it up on the web site. We haven't really broken out those particular headcount or dollars because it's essentially a part of business and it's going to be a part of ongoing business in the future."

Establishing registries at pharmaceutical companies is more than a matter of posting information on a web site. Roche contracted with an external consulting company to help with project managing for its effort. "The actual posting of the trial is the very least of the concerns. The alignment of all of the internal processes around this new process needs a lot of time and effort," said Widler. "Because we are in the regulated environment, we have to regulate the SOPs [standard operating procedures] and we have to change certain workflows. It's a major undertaking."

Implementing Amgen's policy to list clinical trials and disclose trial results involved a company-wide training program. "We take this quite seriously. Just about everybody in clinical development has been required to take training on this to know the right thing to do. There is a core group of people whose main job is to make sure that things get up on the web site. Other people have it as part of their job description to track the publications, track when the trials close, or track the clinical study reports," said Foote.

At Eli Lilly, 300 employees worldwide have been trained to contribute to the company's web site, which posts both active trials and results. In addition to a core group of employees dedicated to the registry, the company relies on its medical writers, medical directors and physicians all over the world to comply with its requirements. "Our requirements for the clinical trials registry, our SOPs, are mandatory at Lilly. We have educated everyone. Then it requires people who work on molecules at different phases, literally all over the world, to gather the information and make it available. It's a substantial number of personnel hours," said Breier.

Wyeth Research, which registers its ongoing global trials on clinicaltrials.gov and posts results on the PhRMA website, hired four to five full-time employees in an effort to post all recruiting trials by the ICMJE's September 13, 2005, deadline; the team posted 130 trials to the registry and successfully met the deadline. Wyeth has committed to posting all phase II to IV trials, along with phase I trials in patients. A team in the Clinical Recruitment Services group, which has responsibility for the clinical trials posting process at Wyeth, is now ensuring that trials are updated and that new trials are posted before the first patient is enrolled as required by the ICMJE policy. "The process required significant effort and time from our clinical organization—people like clinical scientists, medical monitors and trial managers," said Mark Ridge, associate director of clinical recruitment services at Wyeth Research. "We've also had a good relationship with our legal group, who reviews and approves all postings prior to going up on public web sites and we've had direction and feedback from our therapeutic area directors."

Moving forward, Wyeth plans to have at least two full-time employees in the United States focused on this effort, along with another one or two resources outside of the U.S. The amount of resources needed to maintain the process, however, remains a challenge at Wyeth and other companies. "This didn't exist before and it doesn't necessarily fit on as a piece of someone's existing job," said Ridge. "It takes a lot of time and effort to make sure that on a regular basis trials are updated. The effort and time it takes to get through the details is a challenge."

Challenges for the Future

As biopharmaceutical companies move forward with providing clinical trials information to the public through registries and results databases, the industry faces a multitude of challenges: how to collect information internally and how to get it into the right format for posting; meeting staffing requirements for processing, posting and maintaining this information; guarding against competitors using detailed clinical trial information to make adjustments to their own strategies; and deciding which results, positive or negative, are statistically significant enough to report.

Another critical challenge involves explaining to the public what all the clinical trial information available on web sites truly means. "There is an overwhelming number of studies out there. It's very difficult for someone who may not understand clinical trials to go to these web sites and find something that makes sense for them. The menu is too big now and I think it actually loses some of the value," said Wyeth's Ridge. "I think one of the challenges is providing clarity around what we are talking about."

At the same time, as the issues of transparency and increasing the public trust in the conduct of clinical research have grown in importance, so has the number of web sites disclosing clinical trials and clinical trial results. The state of Maine, for example, recently passed a law requiring drug manufacturers who do business in the state to disclose clinical trial data, including adverse impacts, on a publicly accessible web site approved by the Maine Department of Health and Human Services. At least nine states this year introduced legislation that would require public registry and disclosure of clinical drug trials. Multiple web sites, with differing data requirements, present a problem for biopharmaceutical companies. "If every state and every country comes online with a different web site, how do you do quality control on that? It would be a problem for pharmaceutical companies to make sure all the data are always

correct," said Amgen's Foote. "It also has the potential to inadvertently not help patients. It might confuse patients if the data are in different formats."

Many biopharmaceutical companies have been working with the World Health Organization's Institute of Medicine and with academic and industry organizations as they develop standards for registration and posting of results. In addition, the International Federation of Pharmaceutical Manufacturers & Associations in September launched a worldwide clinical trials portal, which is an Internet search engine that allows access to online clinical trials information, including both listings of ongoing trials and results of clinical trials. The portal can access online sources of clinical trial information posted by individual pharmaceutical company sites, sites run by third parties working on behalf of these companies, and pharmaceutical industry association resources such as the PhRMA site and clinicaltrials.gov.

At the same time, for true transparency, the industry needs more commitment not only from small to medium sized biopharmaceutical companies, which often lack internal resources needed for these types of initiatives, but also from academic sites doing clinical research. "The question is how do we ensure that all sponsors of clinical research embrace this initiative?" asks GSK's Metz. "That's something we have to look at moving forward."

2.01

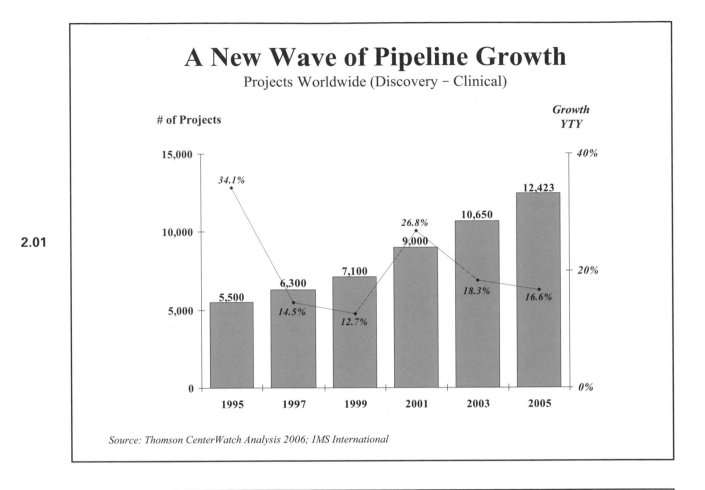

A New Wave of Pipeline Growth
Projects Worldwide (Discovery – Clinical)

of Projects

Growth YTY

34.1%

26.8%

18.3%
16.6%

14.5%
12.7%

5,500   6,300   7,100   9,000   10,650   12,423

1995   1997   1999   2001   2003   2005

Source: Thomson CenterWatch Analysis 2006; IMS International

2.02

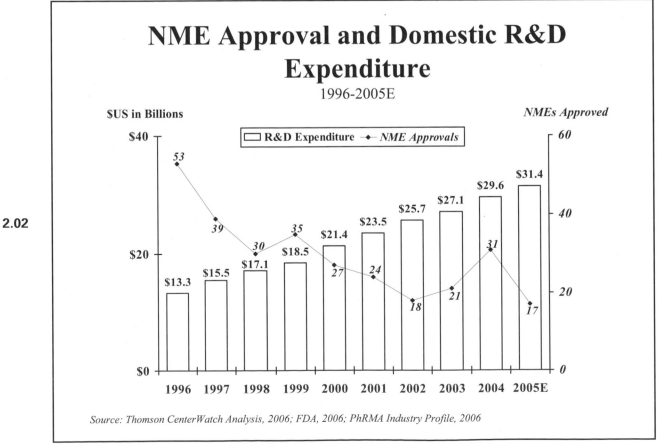

NME Approval and Domestic R&D Expenditure
1996-2005E

$US in Billions

NMEs Approved

☐ R&D Expenditure   ◆ NME Approvals

53
39
30   35
27   24
18   21
31
17

$13.3 $15.5 $17.1 $18.5 $21.4 $23.5 $25.7 $27.1 $29.6 $31.4

1996   1997   1998   1999   2000   2001   2002   2003   2004   2005E

Source: Thomson CenterWatch Analysis, 2006; FDA, 2006; PhRMA Industry Profile, 2006

Projected R&D Spending
Pharmaceutical and Biotech Companies, 2005-2009

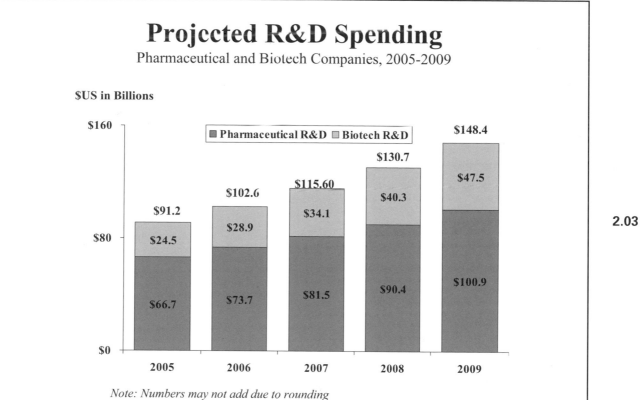

$US in Billions

Legend: ■ Pharmaceutical R&D ■ Biotech R&D

Year	Pharmaceutical R&D	Biotech R&D	Total
2005	$66.7	$24.5	$91.2
2006	$73.7	$28.9	$102.6
2007	$81.5	$34.1	$115.60
2008	$90.4	$40.3	$130.7
2009	$100.9	$47.5	$148.4

Note: Numbers may not add due to rounding

Source: Goldman Sachs, 2005

2.03

R&D Spending Growth Rates
PhRMA Member Companies, 1980-2004

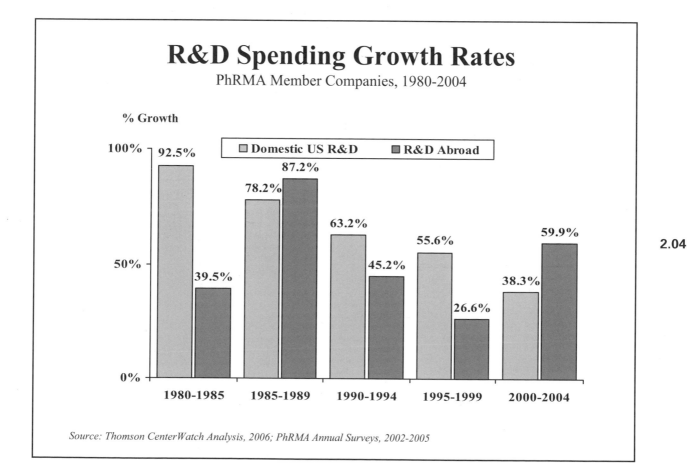

% Growth

Legend: ■ Domestic US R&D ■ R&D Abroad

Period	Domestic US R&D	R&D Abroad
1980-1985	92.5%	39.5%
1985-1989	78.2%	87.2%
1990-1994	63.2%	45.2%
1995-1999	55.6%	26.6%
2000-2004	38.3%	59.9%

Source: Thomson CenterWatch Analysis, 2006; PhRMA Annual Surveys, 2002-2005

2.04

2.05

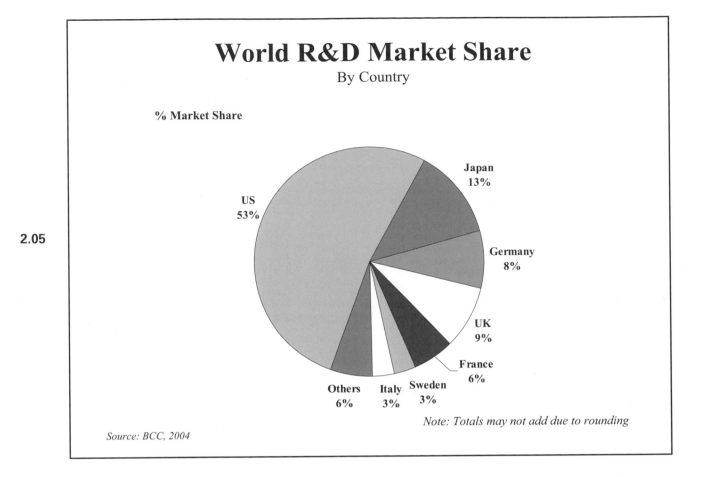

World R&D Market Share
By Country

% Market Share

Japan 13%

US 53%

Germany 8%

UK 9%

France 6%

Others 6%

Italy 3%

Sweden 3%

Note: Totals may not add due to rounding

Source: BCC, 2004

2.06

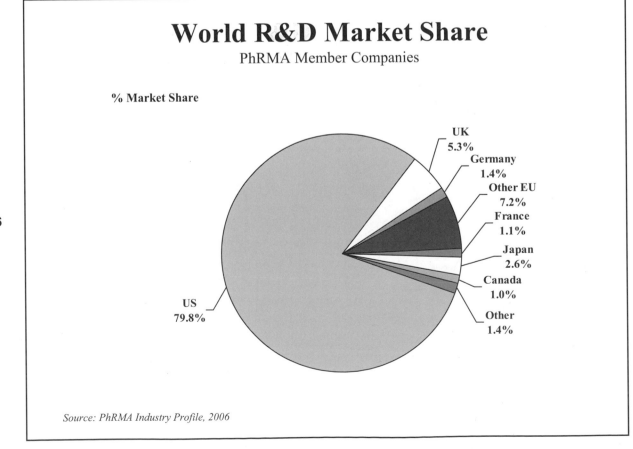

World R&D Market Share
PhRMA Member Companies

% Market Share

UK 5.3%

Germany 1.4%

Other EU 7.2%

France 1.1%

Japan 2.6%

Canada 1.0%

Other 1.4%

US 79.8%

Source: PhRMA Industry Profile, 2006

Domestic R&D Spending
PhRMA Member Companies, 1996-2005

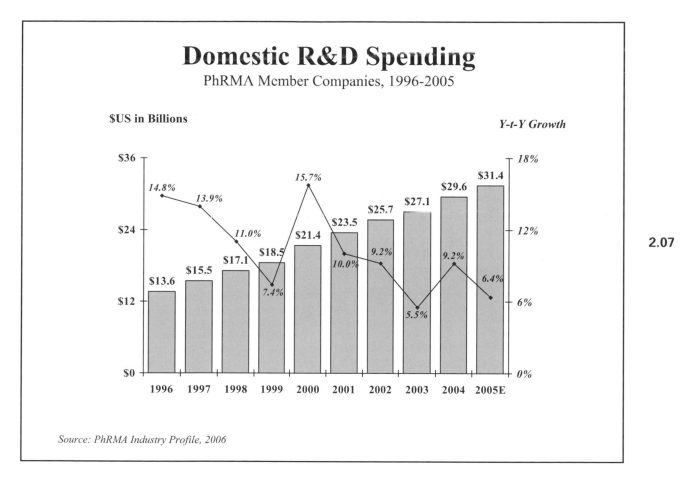

2.07

Source: PhRMA Industry Profile, 2006

R&D Spending Abroad
PhRMA Member Companies, 1996-2006

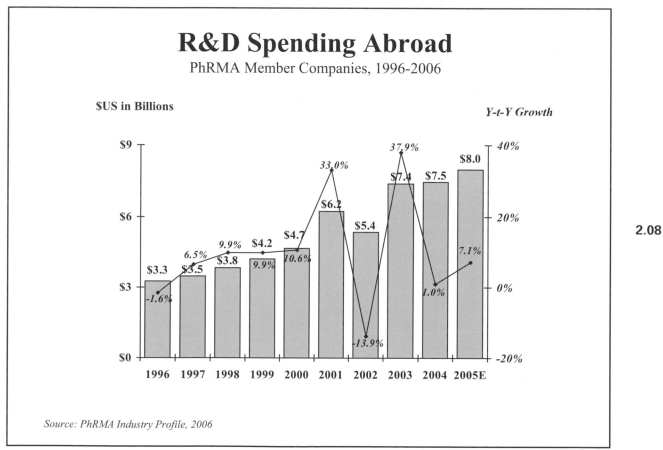

2.08

Source: PhRMA Industry Profile, 2006

2.09

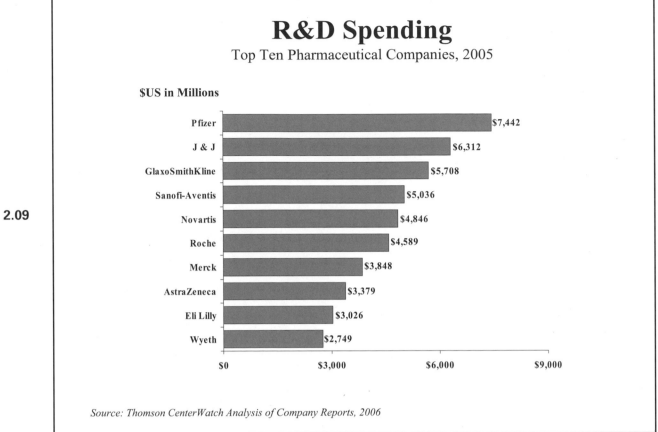

R&D Spending
Top Ten Pharmaceutical Companies, 2005

$US in Millions

Company	Spending
Pfizer	$7,442
J & J	$6,312
GlaxoSmithKline	$5,708
Sanofi-Aventis	$5,036
Novartis	$4,846
Roche	$4,589
Merck	$3,848
AstraZeneca	$3,379
Eli Lilly	$3,026
Wyeth	$2,749

Source: Thomson CenterWatch Analysis of Company Reports, 2006

2.10

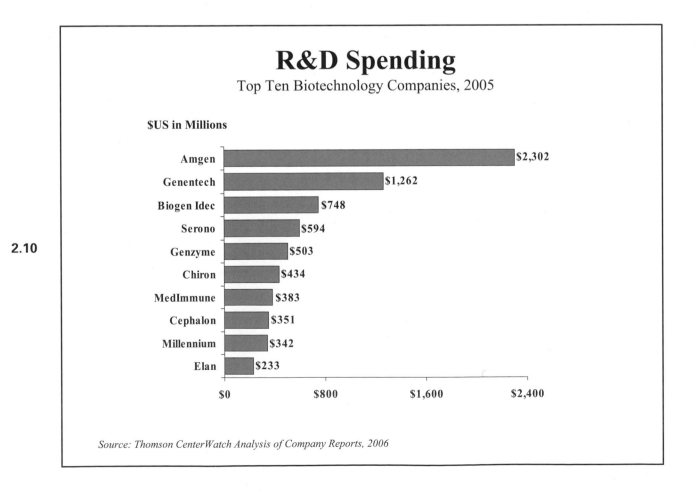

R&D Spending
Top Ten Biotechnology Companies, 2005

$US in Millions

Company	Spending
Amgen	$2,302
Genentech	$1,262
Biogen Idec	$748
Serono	$594
Genzyme	$503
Chiron	$434
MedImmune	$383
Cephalon	$351
Millennium	$342
Elan	$233

Source: Thomson CenterWatch Analysis of Company Reports, 2006

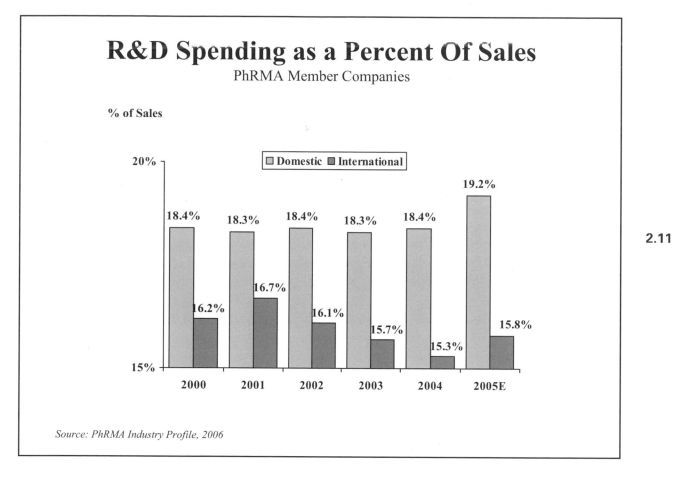

R&D Spending as a Percent Of Sales
PhRMA Member Companies

2.11

Source: PhRMA Industry Profile, 2006

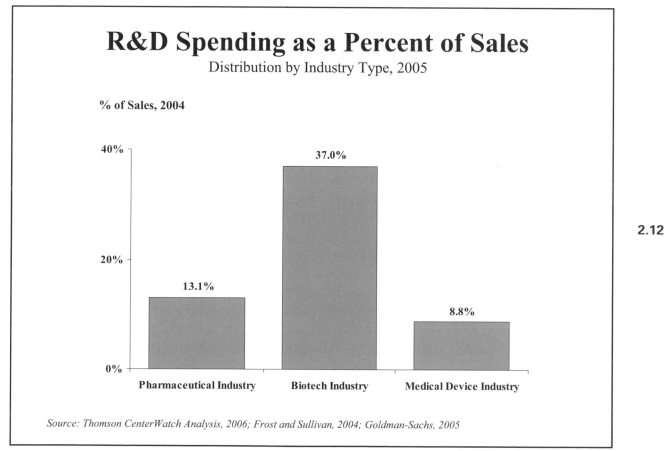

R&D Spending as a Percent of Sales
Distribution by Industry Type, 2005

2.12

Source: Thomson CenterWatch Analysis, 2006; Frost and Sullivan, 2004; Goldman-Sachs, 2005

2.13

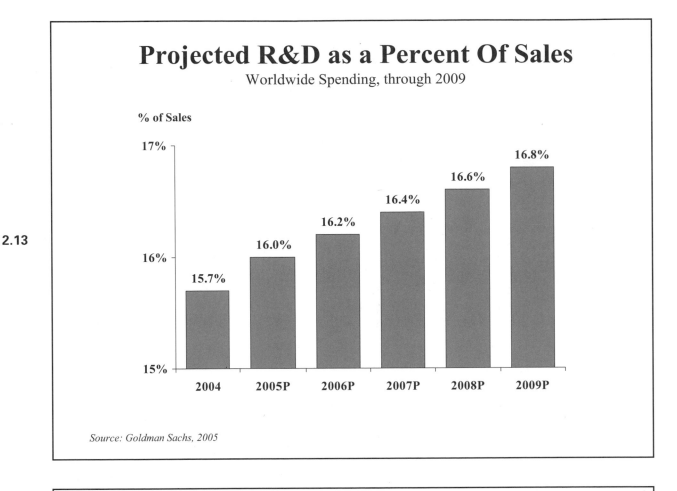

Projected R&D as a Percent Of Sales
Worldwide Spending, through 2009

% of Sales

Source: Goldman Sachs, 2005

2.14

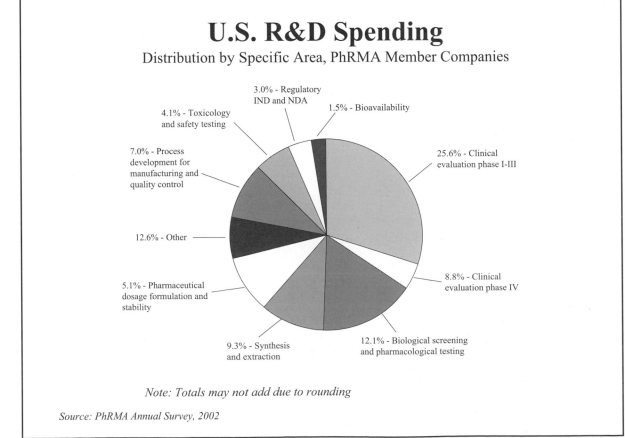

U.S. R&D Spending
Distribution by Specific Area, PhRMA Member Companies

3.0% - Regulatory IND and NDA

1.5% - Bioavailability

4.1% - Toxicology and safety testing

7.0% - Process development for manufacturing and quality control

25.6% - Clinical evaluation phase I-III

12.6% - Other

5.1% - Pharmaceutical dosage formulation and stability

8.8% - Clinical evaluation phase IV

9.3% - Synthesis and extraction

12.1% - Biological screening and pharmacological testing

Note: Totals may not add due to rounding

Source: PhRMA Annual Survey, 2002

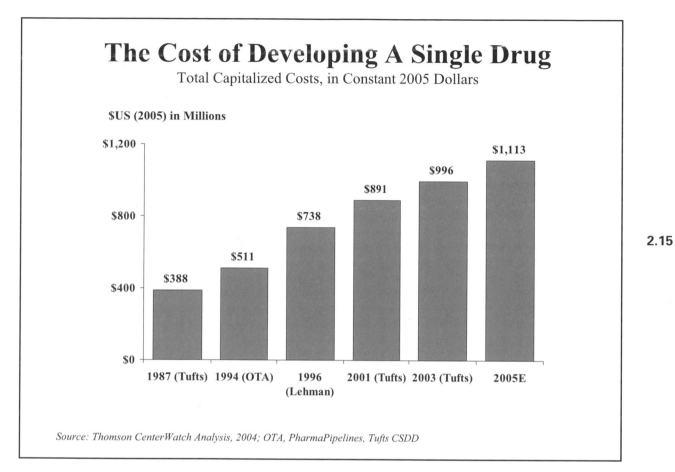

The Cost of Developing A Single Drug
Total Capitalized Costs, in Constant 2005 Dollars

2.15

Source: Thomson CenterWatch Analysis, 2004; OTA, PharmaPipelines, Tufts CSDD

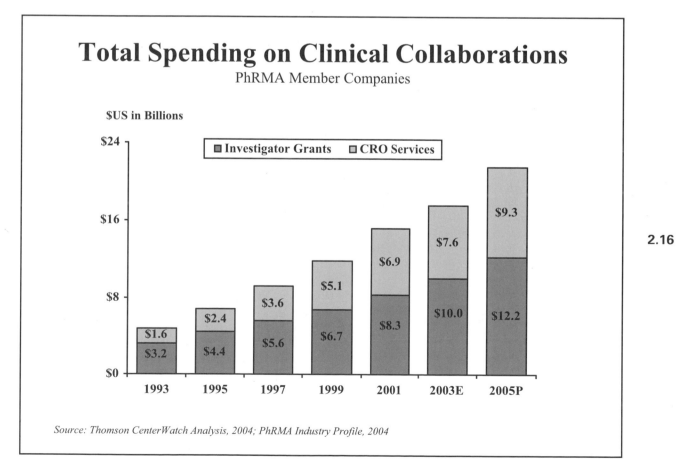

Total Spending on Clinical Collaborations
PhRMA Member Companies

2.16

Source: Thomson CenterWatch Analysis, 2004; PhRMA Industry Profile, 2004

2.17

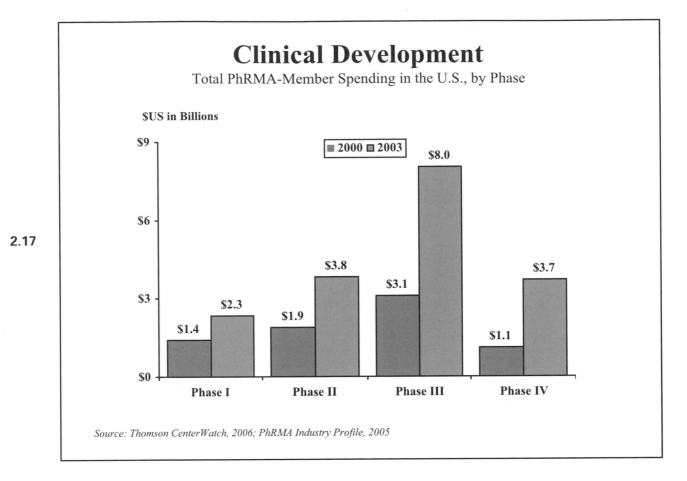

Clinical Development
Total PhRMA-Member Spending in the U.S., by Phase

$US in Billions

Legend: ■ 2000 ■ 2003

- Phase I: $1.4, $2.3
- Phase II: $1.9, $3.8
- Phase III: $3.1, $8.0
- Phase IV: $1.1, $3.7

Source: Thomson CenterWatch, 2006; PhRMA Industry Profile, 2005

2.18

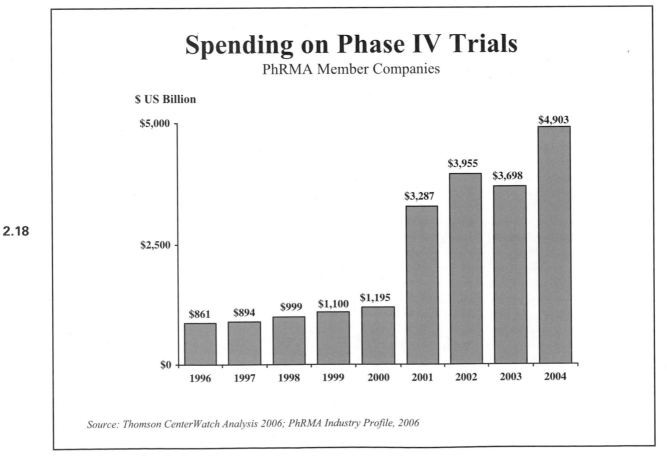

Spending on Phase IV Trials
PhRMA Member Companies

$ US Billion

- 1996: $861
- 1997: $894
- 1998: $999
- 1999: $1,100
- 2000: $1,195
- 2001: $3,287
- 2002: $3,955
- 2003: $3,698
- 2004: $4,903

Source: Thomson CenterWatch Analysis 2006; PhRMA Industry Profile, 2006

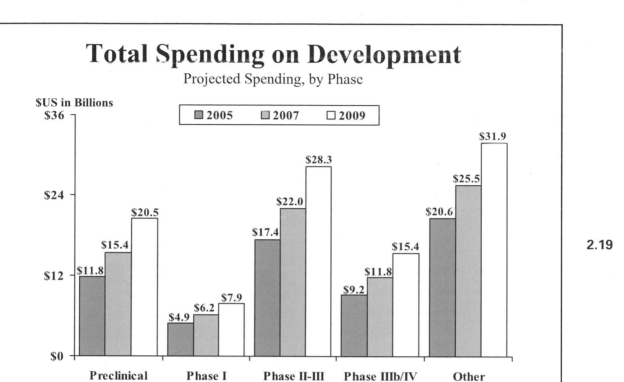

Total Spending on Development
Projected Spending, by Phase

$US in Billions

Legend: ■ 2005 ■ 2007 □ 2009

	Preclinical	Phase I	Phase II-III	Phase IIIb/IV	Other
2005	$11.8	$4.9	$17.4	$9.2	$20.6
2007	$15.4	$6.2	$22.0	$11.8	$25.5
2009	$20.5	$7.9	$28.3	$15.4	$31.9

| 15.80% CAGR | 14.53% CAGR | 12.85% CAGR | 15.76% CAGR | 14.85% CAGR |

Source: Thomson CenterWatch Analysis, 2006; Goldman Sachs, 2005

2.19

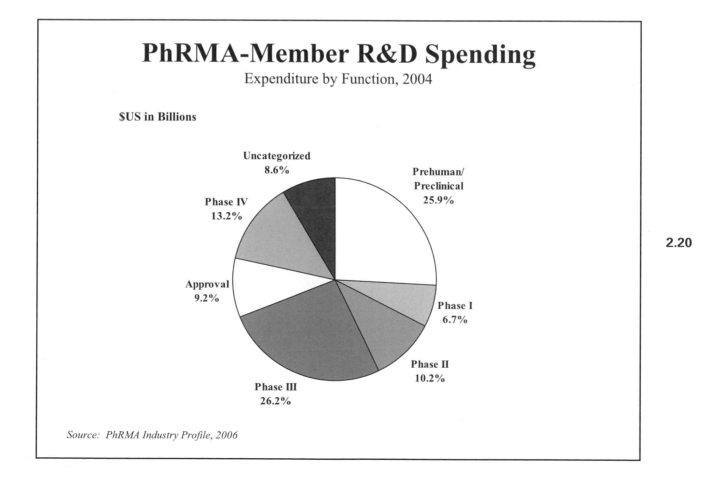

PhRMA-Member R&D Spending
Expenditure by Function, 2004

$US in Billions

- Uncategorized 8.6%
- Prehuman/Preclinical 25.9%
- Phase IV 13.2%
- Phase I 6.7%
- Approval 9.2%
- Phase II 10.2%
- Phase III 26.2%

Source: PhRMA Industry Profile, 2006

2.20

2.21

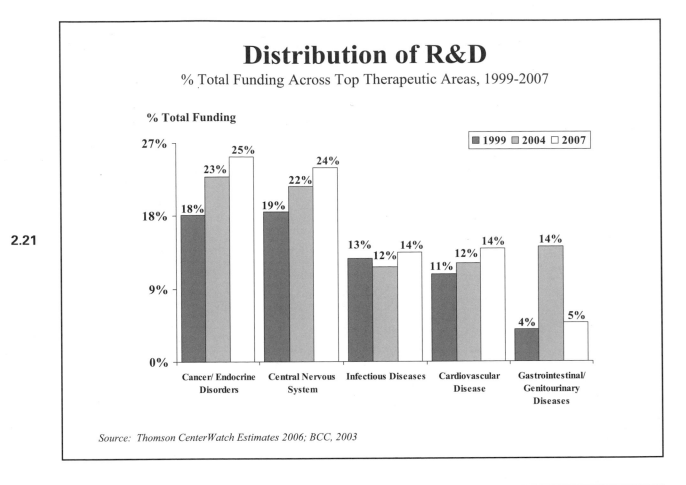

2.22

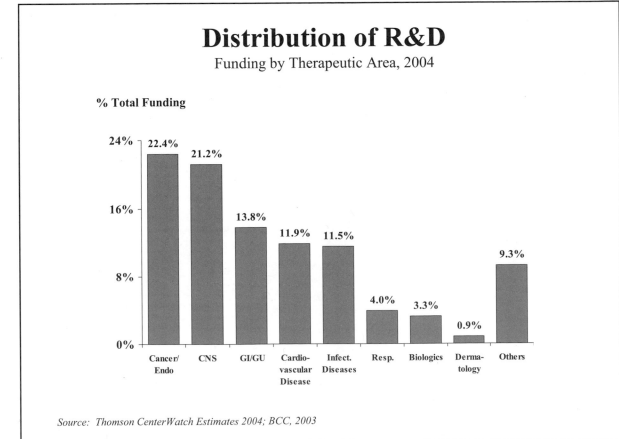

Pharmaceutical R&D

Funding by Therapeutic Area, 1999- 2007

Disease	1999	2002	2004	2007	AAGR% 2002-2007
Cancer / Endocrine Disorders	$3,872	$9,250	$10,157	$14,740	9.8%
Central Nervous System	$3,955	$8,760	$9,618	$13,958	9.8%
Infectious Diseases	$2,717	$4,715	$5,224	$7,856	10.8%
Cardiovascular Disease	$2,305	$4,875	$5,397	$8,122	10.7%
Gastrointestinal / Genitourinary Diseases	$847	$7,680	$6,275	$2,800	-18.3%
Respiratory Diseases	$697	$1,625	$1,799	$2,707	10.7%
Biologicals	$665	$1,320	$1,481	$2,343	12.2%
Dermatology	$182	$360	$407	$690	13.0%
Diagnostics	$108	$375	$394	$147	5.0%
Nutrients	N/A	$115	$121	$147	5.0%
Others	$6,015	$3,470	$3,699	$4,772	6.6%

2.23

Source: Thomson CenterWatch Analysis, 2006; BCC, 2003

Sources of Trial Funding

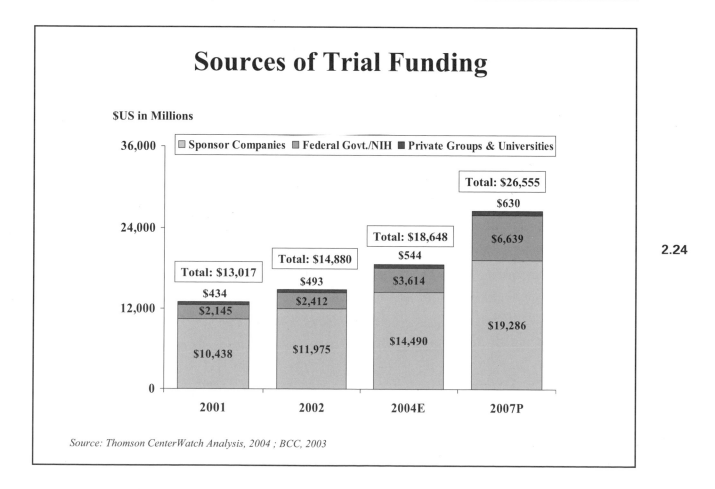

2.24

Source: Thomson CenterWatch Analysis, 2004 ; BCC, 2003

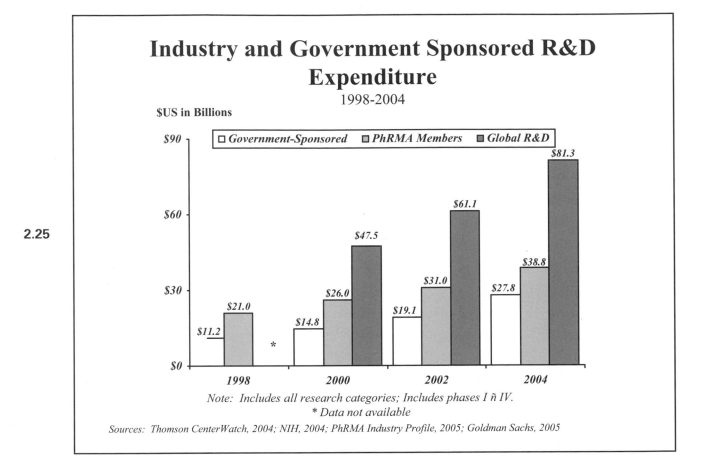

Industry and Government Sponsored R&D Expenditure
1998-2004

$US in Billions

Legend: □ *Government-Sponsored* ▨ *PhRMA Members* ▓ *Global R&D*

- 1998: Government-Sponsored $11.2; PhRMA Members $21.0; Global R&D *
- 2000: Government-Sponsored $14.8; PhRMA Members $26.0; Global R&D $47.5
- 2002: Government-Sponsored $19.1; PhRMA Members $31.0; Global R&D $61.1
- 2004: Government-Sponsored $27.8; PhRMA Members $38.8; Global R&D $81.3

Note: Includes all research categories; Includes phases I ñ IV.
* Data not available

Sources: Thomson CenterWatch, 2004; NIH, 2004; PhRMA Industry Profile, 2005; Goldman Sachs, 2005

2.25

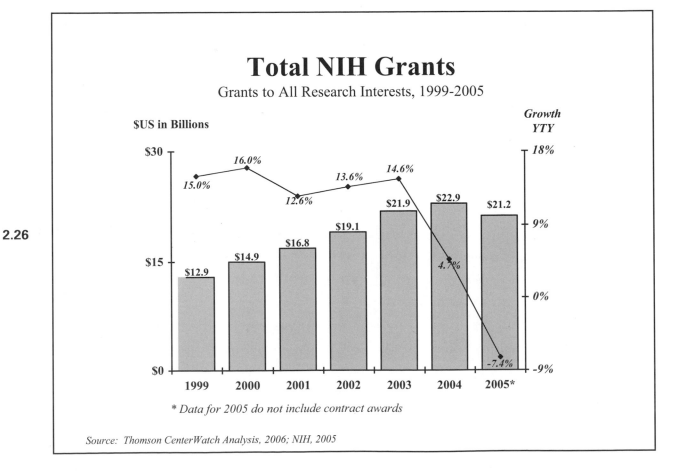

Total NIH Grants
Grants to All Research Interests, 1999-2005

$US in Billions | *Growth YTY*

- 1999: $12.9 — 15.0%
- 2000: $14.9 — 16.0%
- 2001: $16.8 — 12.6%
- 2002: $19.1 — 13.6%
- 2003: $21.9 — 14.6%
- 2004: $22.9 — 4.7%
- 2005*: $21.2 — -7.4%

* Data for 2005 do not include contract awards

Source: Thomson CenterWatch Analysis, 2006; NIH, 2005

2.26

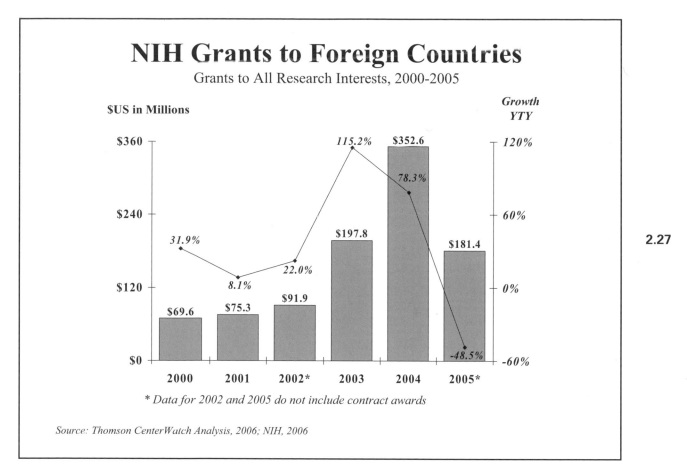

NIH Grants to Foreign Countries
Grants to All Research Interests, 2000-2005

$US in Millions

Growth YTY

31.9%   8.1%   22.0%   115.2%   78.3%   -48.5%

$69.6 $75.3 $91.9 $197.8 $352.6 $181.4

2000   2001   2002*   2003   2004   2005*

* Data for 2002 and 2005 do not include contract awards

Source: Thomson CenterWatch Analysis, 2006; NIH, 2006

2.27

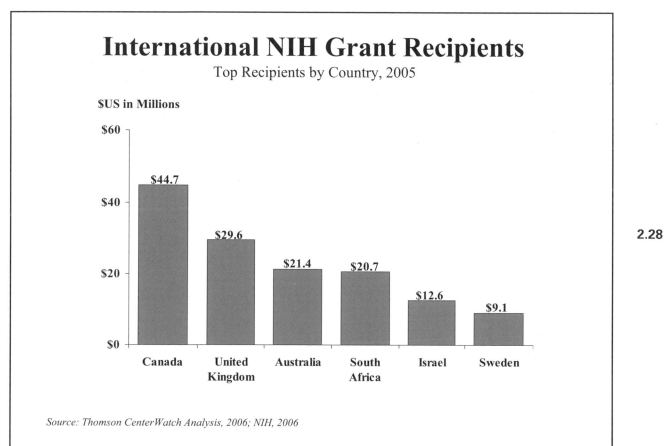

International NIH Grant Recipients
Top Recipients by Country, 2005

$US in Millions

$44.7 $29.6 $21.4 $20.7 $12.6 $9.1

Canada   United Kingdom   Australia   South Africa   Israel   Sweden

Source: Thomson CenterWatch Analysis, 2006; NIH, 2006

2.28

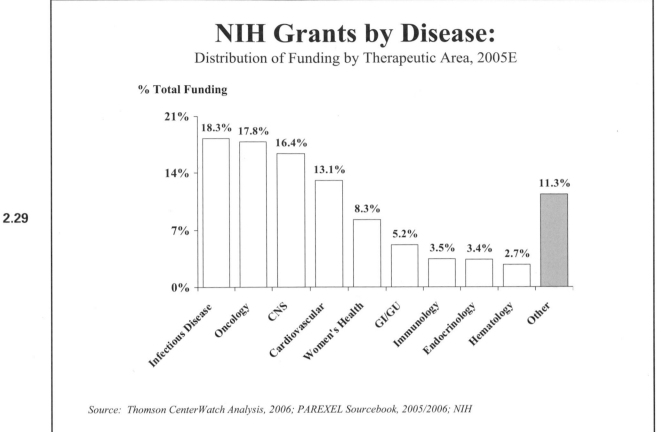

NIH Grants by Disease:
Distribution of Funding by Therapeutic Area, 2005E

2.29

Source: Thomson CenterWatch Analysis, 2006; PAREXEL Sourcebook, 2005/2006; NIH

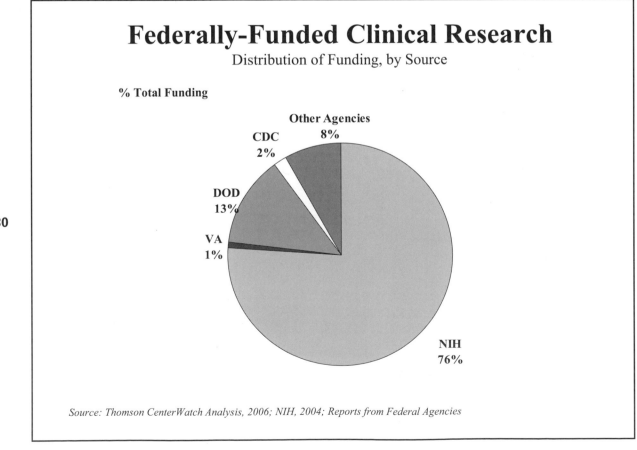

Federally-Funded Clinical Research
Distribution of Funding, by Source

2.30

Source: Thomson CenterWatch Analysis, 2006; NIH, 2004; Reports from Federal Agencies

NIH Budget, FY 2004

Distribution of Total NIH Budget, by Destination

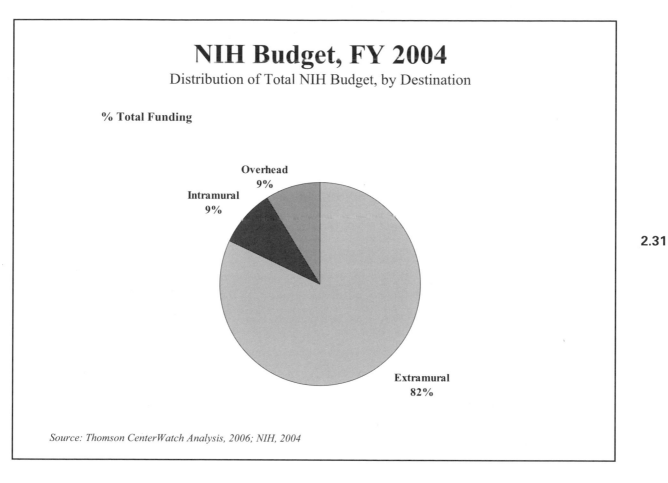

% Total Funding

Overhead 9%

Intramural 9%

Extramural 82%

Source: Thomson CenterWatch Analysis, 2006; NIH, 2004

2.31

New NIH Grants

Type I Research Project Grants, 1996-2004

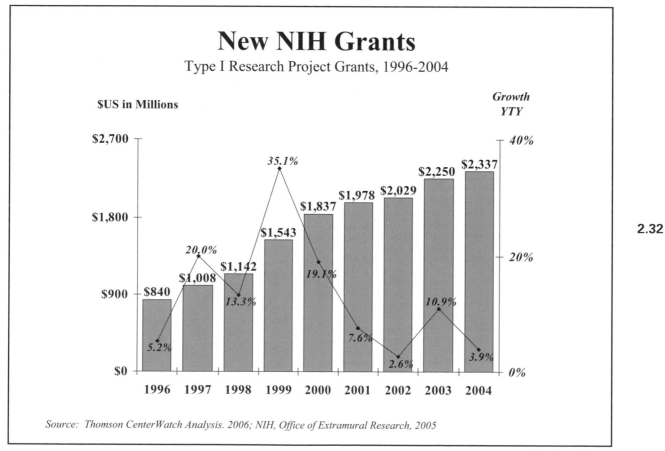

$US in Millions

Growth YTY

Source: Thomson CenterWatch Analysis. 2006; NIH, Office of Extramural Research, 2005

2.32

2.33

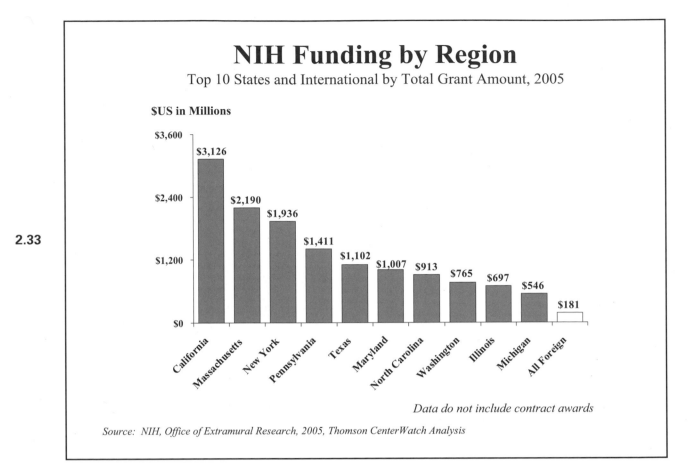

NIH Funding by Region
Top 10 States and International by Total Grant Amount, 2005

$US in Millions

Data do not include contract awards

Source: NIH, Office of Extramural Research, 2005, Thomson CenterWatch Analysis

2.34

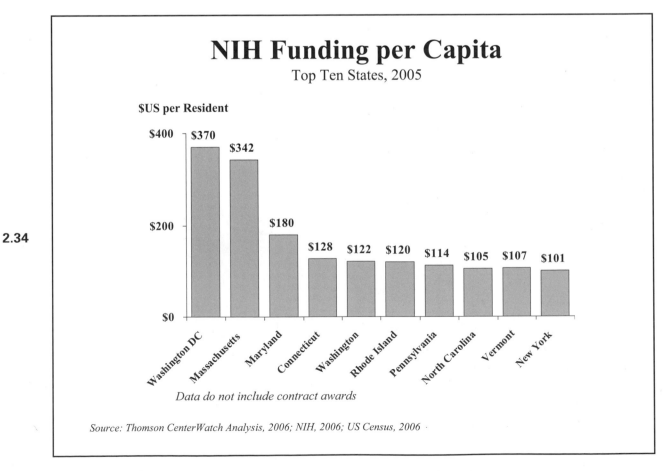

NIH Funding per Capita
Top Ten States, 2005

$US per Resident

Data do not include contract awards

Source: Thomson CenterWatch Analysis, 2006; NIH, 2006; US Census, 2006

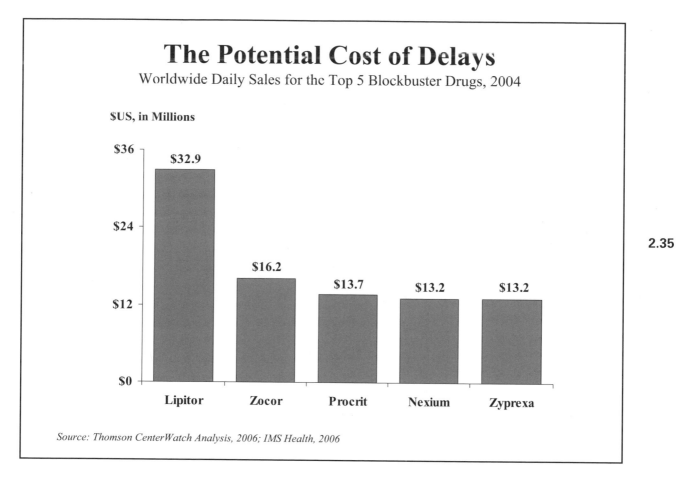

The Potential Cost of Delays

Worldwide Daily Sales for the Top 5 Blockbuster Drugs, 2004

$US, in Millions

Lipitor	$32.9
Zocor	$16.2
Procrit	$13.7
Nexium	$13.2
Zyprexa	$13.2

Source: Thomson CenterWatch Analysis, 2006; IMS Health, 2006

2.35

Clinical Development

Zeroing in on Microdosing

Industry observers expect the number of microdose studies, also called human phase 0 trials, to increase in the United States once the U.S. Food and Drug Administration issues a draft guidance next month that will ease preclinical safety data requirements for microdose studies, making it easier to conduct them as exploratory studies rather than traditional phase I programs.

During the past year, acceptance of microdose studies has grown more quickly in Europe. The growth of phase 0 could cut into the rapid rise of phase I trials, which sponsors have also used to kill drug candidates earlier.

Zeroing in on Microdosing

By Karyn Korieth
Published February 2005

Microdose studies, during which trace doses of new drugs are tested in humans to evaluate pharmacokinetics and drug metabolism before entering phase I trials, are being touted as a new way to speed up early drug discovery efforts, identify failures sooner and cut study costs. These early human microdose studies aim to weed out drug candidates with inappropriate metabolism, such as too short a half-life or poor bioavailability, before significant amounts are spent advancing the drugs into clinical trials.

While some pharmaceutical companies in the United States have done pre-phase I exploratory studies in humans for years, during the past 18 months the industry has seen acceptance of microdose studies grow more quickly in Europe, where a recent guidance defines abbreviated animal toxicology requirements to allow microdose studies of drugs in humans.

However, many expect the number of microdose studies, also called human phase 0, to increase in the United States once the U.S. Food and Drug Administration (FDA) issues a draft guidance in March that will ease preclinical safety data requirements for microdose studies, making it easier to conduct them as exploratory studies rather than traditional phase I programs.

Since the FDA began developing its guidelines for early human microdose studies, interest in the concept has heightened. Microdosing has become a hot topic at industry conferences; analysts at Frost & Sullivan included the concept of micro-

dosing in a recent report discussing technologies that can accelerate early phase drug discovery efforts. And the top 20 pharmaceutical companies are exploring the possibility of using first-in-human microdosing studies in order to select drug candidates that offer a greater likelihood of success in later-phase clinical trials; while today sponsors use data from microdose studies mainly for in-house decision making rather than regulatory submission, a few major pharmaceutical companies have had microdose studies approved by the FDA through the traditional IND process.

At the same time, CROs have stepped up efforts in the United States to offer services for microdose studies and accelerator mass spectrometry (AMS), the technology most often used to analyze trace drug doses in the human body. Accium BioSciences, a Seattle-based contract clinical and analytical facility that specializes in phase 0/I technology and clinical trials, will open a dedicated clinical trials facility in April designed for the low-radiation dose delivery and sample collection required for AMS microdose studies. Vitalea Sciences Inc., a niche-CRO based in Davis, Calif., recently opened a commercial AMS facility in Woodland, Calif. Meanwhile, two U.K. companies that have completed many successful microdosing studies in Europe, Xceleron and Pharmaceutical Profiles, have established bases in the United States and plan to grow these activities substantially.

Microdose studies allow for more efficient, faster drug development by providing early information about pharmacokinetics (PK) and a drug's absorption, distribution, metabolism and excretion (ADME) characteristics in humans before investment is made in the resources needed for traditional phase I clinical development. The data help sponsors not only identify drug candidates that are likely to succeed in later-phase clinical trials, but also to kill no-go drug candidates earlier, which saves time, money and resources during preclinical and clinical development.

While some believe microdosing has the potential to transform the drug development process, others are more cautious about embracing this new concept. Microdose testing can have negative effects on the scheduling of drug development since scale-up of chemical synthesis must be put on hold for six months or more pending results of the microdose study, and many remain unconvinced about the value of data from these studies, which only test PK and not safety and efficacy. Others, meanwhile, are waiting for data to answer the fundamental question about whether a correlation exists between the PK of microdoses and the PK of therapeutic doses.

New FDA Guidance

Momentum for microdose studies has built in Europe during the past 18 months since the European Medicines Agency (EMEA) issued guidance on the nonclinical safety package to support human microdosing studies. At Xceleron, for example, which pioneered AMS microdosing studies in Europe, researchers have studied 10 molecules during the past 12 months. Three years ago, just one molecule was studied during the year. And some European drug sponsors have begun to incorporate microdosing techniques into their early studies; Tripep, for example, a Swedish biotech research company, recently used microdosing for the development of alphaHGA, an HIV-inhibiting drug.

The FDA expects that the number of microdosing studies and exploratory IND studies will grow in the United States as well once the preclinical safety testing guidelines for microdosing studies are issued. "Sponsors start off with hundreds or thousands of chemical structures. Using a series of

assays, for both efficacy and safety, they wean them down to a single drug, which they then synthesize—often in kilogram quantities—and take into the clinic. In some instances, you find out very quickly once you introduce it into humans that it doesn't have the characteristics of a successful drug," said David Jacobson-Kram, the FDA's associate director for pharmacology and toxicology, Office of New Drugs, Center for Drug Evaluation and Research. "This guidance will give sponsors the opportunity to not have to choose a single molecular entity—they will be able to choose between a number of molecular entitites based on human data. Our hope is that we can really facilitate the drug development process."

The FDA will release its document, called "Guidance for Industry Investigators and Reviewers: Exploratory IND Studies," as a draft before the end of March. The draft guidance will be open for comment for 90 days; the FDA then will respond to the comments, make appropriate changes and publish the document as a final guidance.

The guidance addresses requirements for many types of exploratory IND studies; microdose studies are a subset of studies included in the guidance. "The whole notion behind this guidance is it enables sponsors to do clinical trials for different reasons. In some cases it would be to do imaging studies, in some cases they may have a handful of potential lead compounds that they want to choose between based on human data. This guidance provides a vehicle for doing those studies. It also provides the preclinical safety testing requirements for the various kinds of exploratory INDs," said Jacobson-Kram.

With the new guidance, microdose studies will require fewer tests than conventional phase I trials. "The premise is that the amount of preclinical safety testing that a sponsor has to do will be gauged to what they want to do clinically," Jacobson-Kram said. "Microdose studies are an extreme case here. Typically these are going to be single dose studies in very small numbers of people with doses that are sub-pharmacologic. Because of the very limited nature of those clinical trials, the amount of preclinical safety data that we would ask is really quite minimal and much less than a sponsor would be expected to submit for a traditional IND."

The guidance has been prioritized as supporting the FDA's Critical Path initiative, which includes developing tools that could allow sponsors to identify unsuccessful drug candidates earlier in the development process. "We see this guidance as an important tool for sponsors to make very early decisions in drug development," said Jacobson-Kram. "We see it as an important piece in the Critical Path in enabling sponsors to make good decisions and not waste time and resources on drugs that will ultimately fail."

Until the FDA issues its guidance, which could allow sponsor companies to expedite the microdose process, sponsor companies that submit microdosing INDs usually must meet requirements for traditional phase I studies, including IRB approval and two-species toxicology studies. "We're in kind of a gray area since the guidance hasn't been issued," said Jacobson-Kram. "In some instances, what sponsors might find until this guidance is available is that some divisions would adhere to traditional requirements, which this guidance suggests is probably overkill for these kinds of studies. This guidance would hone down that battery of tests to a much more minimal level."

Industry leaders remain cautious about endorsing the FDA's guidance until they can review the document, including preclinical work requirements and submission standards, yet most welcome efforts to address regulatory obstacles to microdosing studies. "One of our significant limitations under 21 CRF 361.1 is that we are restricted to radioactive drugs that have been previously evaluated in humans," said Dennis Swanson, director of the University of Pittsburgh Research Conduct and Compliance Office. "First-in-humans, under a microdosing concept, certainly would allow us to do more types of studies and significantly expand our research efforts under the current regulations. That would be a big benefit."

The new guidance could address these restrictions on studying radioactive drugs first-in-humans since the exploratory IND process allows FDA staff to evaluate each study on a case-by-case basis.

Microdosing Benefits

During the past two decades, advances in genomics and proteomics, along with high-throughput screening and combinatorial chemistry, have resulted in thousands of new drug leads, yet drug developers often struggle to identify the molecules that can become useful drugs. In fact, while the amount pharmaceutical companies spend on research and development has increased to an estimated $59.2 billion last year, according to a Goldman Sachs report, only 23 new molecular entities were registered by the FDA in 2004. "There are a lot of new technologies that have focused primarily on the discovery portion of drug development," said Michael Chansler, vice president of business development at Accium BioSciences. "The problem is that we're still doing clinical trials the same way we've always done clinical trials. We're following the same regimen. There haven't been any new technologies adapted. Microdosing is a new technology that changes the way people are thinking. The goal is to bring some new technologies to the second half of the discovery chain; microdosing is one of those technologies."

Ian Wilding, executive chairman of Pharmaceutical Profiles, a Nottingham, U.K.-based CRO that specializes in early clinical development capabilities, added, "With so many drug candidates exiting discovery and entering development, the task of choosing and then advancing the right molecules into the clinic has become more and more difficult. In the future, for pharmaceutical companies to be successful, it will be necessary for them to determine, at a very early stage, which of their drug candidates is the most likely to pass the necessary safety and efficacy hurdles to become approved medications. Chemists and development scientists need to be confident that only the compounds with the best chance of success are taken forward, a task that is becoming increasingly difficult as the biopharmaceutical properties of molecules gain in complexity. Human microdosing studies can provide this key decision-making information."

At present, up to 40% of compounds entering clinical development fail because of inappropriate drug metabolism and pharmacokinetics, despite extensive preclinical screening of drug candidates with a broad range of in silico, in vitro, ex vivo and animal models. Animal models, in particular, can be problematic in predicting PK for humans since different types of animals, such as rats, dogs and monkeys, can metabolize the same drug in different ways. "Each animal species could handle the drug differently—sometimes we get contradictory results. The so-called allometric scaling from animals to humans is very difficult even if these results are not confounding or contradictory," said Nenad Sarapa, M.D., director of clinical pharmacology at Pfizer Global Research & Development. "Sometimes the whole process doesn't work very well because of the nature of the breakdown of the compound in animals versus humans. That is why, at some point very early on, microdosing in humans can reveal information which wouldn't have been apparent from any preclinical species."

Human microdosing studies involve the administration of microgram quantities of drug candidates in a very small number of healthy volunteers in order to gain pharmacokinetic and pharmacodynamic information. Because of the low doses of drugs used in microdose studies, usually 100 micrograms or less, ultrasensitive methods are needed for PK measurement; most microdosing studies rely on AMS, an isotopic measurement tool, although positron emission tomography (PET) also has the sensitivity to measure compounds administered in the low microgram range. PET provides real-time data on drug disposition, whereas AMS is used to analyze drug and metabolite concentrations in body fluids withdrawn after dosing. Both methods require radioactive labeling of the drug being studied.

While microdosing studies can't provide safety or efficacy data, since the drug doses used are sub-pharmacological, they do provide PK and ADME information, which can allow sponsors to select drugs with appropriate PK parameters for further development. "The main purpose of microdosing is really de-selecting of the compound," said Pfizer's Sarapa. "People usually speak of speeding up drug development or making it more innovative, but taking off the table a compound that would eventually prove to be unsuccessful based on properties that can be gleaned out of microdosing much earlier than would have been the case in classical, conventional data is an important benefit. It can be translated to de-selecting the compound; if you have two or three compounds which are different between themselves, doing microdosing with all three of them early will enable you to park one, kill another and possibly develop the third."

Sponsor companies often use microdose testing on a compound that has shown issues in preclinical development. But Sarapa believes the most efficient, productive use of microdosing is testing similar compounds that are difficult to distinguish. "Pre-phase I studies are best used in cases in which several drug candidates target a novel therapeutic principle from which one wants to select one for further development," Sarapa said.

Microdose studies also hold potential use in other phases of drug development. "One could consider microdosing in pediatric studies, where you are administering sub-pharmacological doses so you are not putting babies at risk in any way. It could be used in patient studies as well, where you want to study the metabolism of your drug in patients, but not put the patient at any risk," said R. Colin Garner, CEO of Xceleron, a York, U.K.-based company that is the world leader in biomedical applications of AMS. "Microdosing probably will broaden in terms of groups that are studied using the approach."

Significant Cost Savings

Drug sponsors are interested in microdosing studies because of their potential to reduce development costs. Microdosing doesn't provide shortcuts to drug development, but rather can help improve the attrition rate of compounds in later-phase clinical trials by allowing sponsors to choose the best candidates for further development. "Microdosing appears to be a promising new, safe and rapid methodology to derive human PK data as an aid in candidate selection prior to committing large resources to a full-scale phase I study," said Carl Peck, M.D., founder and director of the Center for Drug Development Science at Georgetown

University Medical Center, Washington and former director of the FDA's CDER.

"The main reason companies are looking at microdosing is to help decrease failure rates in later clinical development," Accium's Chansler added. "If you could save just one year, you could save a lot of money in the development process. Hopefully, these types of technologies will be able to decrease the overall cost of drugs in the market."

At Xceleron, Garner estimates microdose studies cost one-tenth of a conventional phase I study, not only in the amount spent on toxicology studies, but also in costs to synthesize chemical compounds since microdose studies use very low amounts of the pharmaceutical ingredient or bulk drug. "The low amount of bulk drug clearly translates to a low cost. It also means low usage of experimental animals, and low environmental and human exposure risk. But most importantly for drug companies is the aspect of low costs," said Pfizer's Sarapa. "If we can kill the compound at an early stage based on human microdosing, before the very costly business of pharmaceutical scale-up has been initiated, it translates into savings anywhere between $500,000 and $2.5 million, depending on how expensive the compound is to make. There are very direct, very real savings.

"Otherwise, if you continue the development of this compound," Sarapa added, "you would have to scale up the manufacturing to a point where you would be utilizing raw materials and chemical plants and numerous outsourced partners. Equally important, you would start utilizing this newly synthesized compound for new tests that eventually prove to have poor PK properties in humans. If you do microdosing and realize those poor properties sooner, then all of that subsequent cost and subsequent studies will be unnecessary and you can save both in human resource and the cost."

Microdosing studies also can be completed more quickly than traditional phase I studies. For example, Xceleron recently worked with a company that carried out three human microdose studies on a compound within a 12-month period. "They did the studies in sequence, rather than in parallel," Garner said. "They got the microdose data, decided that the molecule could be improved in

some way, improved it, repeated the process, got some more microdose data and then improved the molecule a little more. They ultimately got a molecule which they think has the optimum pharmacokinetic characteristics. If you were to do classical phase I studies for three molecules, they would take two to three years."

In another example, a recent microdosing study Pharmaceutical Profiles carried out for the Swedish biotech research company Tripep took less than six months from inception to completion. The study examined the PK of an HIV-inhibiting molecule in healthy subjects. The microdosing study, according to Anders Vahlne, Tripep's acting CEO and head of research, gave the company early human PK data on the performance of their candidate drug more quickly than would have been possible using conventional development strategies.

However, microdose testing has drawbacks. In and of itself, microdosing won't speed up drug development. "While you prepare radio-label compounds and while you evaluate microdosing, everything else to do with this compound must be stopped," said Sarapa. "Drug companies do what's called advanced scheduling or scale up of chemical synthesis—while I'm doing a set of preclinical experiments, I'm already scaling up synthesis of the chemical compound for human studies. Synthesis, to be made more efficient, must account for larger quantities than those that are required for microdosing. But if I want to do microdosing, I do not want to scale up chemical synthesis of the compound for later phases because I don't know what the microdosing study will reveal. Therefore, there will be a period between three and six months that my chemical synthesis will be stalled and that is not really favorable for most compounds."

Adoption Slow in the U.S.

In the United States, microdosing techniques have not been widely adopted by pharmaceutical researchers. Some estimates show that microdosing studies are done before formal phase I studies less than 5% of the time.

Chansler said there are three main reasons that microdosing techniques and AMS technology have lagged in the United States. First, companies have little or no access to specialized AMS equipment since currently there are about 50 AMS centers in the world and only two analyze biological samples. The United States also lacks dedicated clinical trials facilities designed for the low 14C dose delivery and sample collection required for AMS microdosing studies. The third obstacle has been an FDA regulation that states no radioactive drugs may be studied first in humans because investigators must first provide pharmacological dose calculations based on published literature or other human data.

Yet for many in the industry, the main obstacle to wider acceptance of microdosing remains the fundamental question about whether a correlation exists between metabolism at a microdose and at a pharmacological dose. At Xceleron, which has been the principal advocate in driving the microdosing debate since its inception in 1997, Garner said data from AMS microdosing studies has begun to establish a link between microdose and full dose. "Certainly the pharmacokinetic data that you obtain from these microdose studies on whole does seem to reflect that which you would obtain at pharmacological doses," said Garner.

An ongoing clinical program, called Consortium for Resourcing and Evaluating AMS Microdosing (CREAM) has begun to build a database to compare PK parameters at micro and pharmaceutical doses; data collected by the consortium may help validate the microdosing concept. Sponsor companies in the consortium, which include Eli Lilly and Company from the United States along with three European pharmaceutical companies, F. Hoffmann-La Roche, Servier Laboratories and Schering AG, recently participated in a trial conducted by Xceleron to compare the metabolism of five drugs at pharmacological doses and microdoses. Results of the study will be announced at a drug symposium on microdosing to be held at the American Society for Clinical Pharmacology and Therapeutics' annual meeting in March. After the meeting, study results also will be written as a peer-reviewed scientific paper.

In the study, which was completed last year, five 14C-labelled drugs were examined in a crossover study design in which human volunteers received both a microdose and a pharmacological dose of the respective drug. The drugs were all fully commercialized, but had complex metabolism properties in which animal models or in vitro studies failed to predict human PK; the drugs had specific issues associated with their development, such as a long half-life. The CREAM trial was designed to determine whether AMS microdosing could have predicted the problems. "The idea behind the consortium was to take a number of drugs with known metabolism at pharmacological doses and compare metabolism at microdoses with the metabolism at the high dose," Garner said. "The results are still bound by confidentiality agreements. But the bottom line is that the CREAM trial seems to support the microdose concept."

But even positive results from the CREAM trial may not convince some skeptics about the value of microdosing. P. David Mozley, M.D., senior medical director, Department of Imaging at Merck, formerly a medical fellow at Eli Lilly, believes the field should introduce some "harsh reality testing" into the microdosing conversation. Mozley said that any microdosing paradigm, including both PET techniques and AMS, will fail to produce data of value unless issues of cost-effectiveness and the variability in approaches can be addressed.

"The effectiveness of weaving molecular imaging into new drug development seems to be directly related to how well the study conditions reflect the actual circumstances in which the therapeutic drug candidate will be administered. The validity of some results can appear to be questionable when some conditions, such as the dose administered, vary too much, said Mozley." Although Mozley's comments mainly reflect concerns with the microdosing paradigm that uses PET techniques, which involves an imaging modality, he believes AMS models also will fail to produce data of value unless these issues he raised are addressed.

The FDA's Jacobson-Kram added, "If you talk to the pharmaceutical industry in the United States, they are not that excited about microdose studies. It seems to be more of a European kind of initiative; my sense is that there is more enthusiasm across the pond for these kinds of studies than there is in this country," he said. "You basically only can get PK information from these studies. Sponsors feel that to really understand and be able to make decisions about a compound, you need pharmacologic data. There is not unanimity about how valuable the data from these studies are."

Moving Forward With Caution

Will human phase 0 studies ever become a routine part of late-stage drug discovery? "That's the question which is hotly debated," said Garner. "My view is that it should become routine. I would envisage, ultimately, that microdosing would become the first-in-human study. We take the view that getting early information about human metabolism must be good for developing drugs. We also think there is an ethical aspect to this—is it ethical to expose humans to higher doses, then subsequently kill a compound for metabolism reasons when the same information could have been found out with a safe microdose?" he asks.

Yet others hold a more modest view. Pfizer's Sarapa believes microdosing can be a valuable tool in making development decisions based on ADME/PK data, yet he cautions it can't be used in every drug development program. Sarapa said, "I hope to see microdosing being used more, but in a meaningful way. It's not a panacea. One needs to be very selective in using it because it has some negative repercussions on scheduling of drug development."

"It also has some very clear advantages," Sarapa concluded. "If it is used meaningfully in appropriately chosen cases, I see great potential that it contributes to resolving issues in picking out compounds that will reach human testing with a greater likelihood of success. A greater likelihood of success in phase I will translate directly into greater speed and greater ability of these compounds to help patients that need them."

3.01

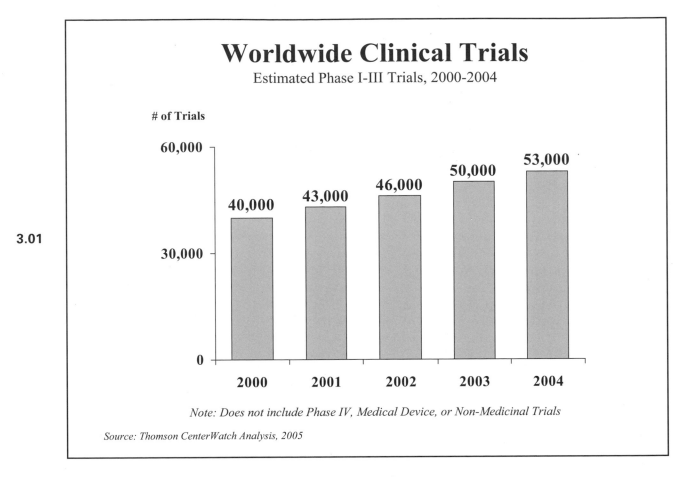

Worldwide Clinical Trials
Estimated Phase I-III Trials, 2000-2004

of Trials

60,000

53,000

50,000

46,000

43,000

40,000

30,000

0

| 2000 | 2001 | 2002 | 2003 | 2004 |

Note: Does not include Phase IV, Medical Device, or Non-Medicinal Trials

Source: Thomson CenterWatch Analysis, 2005

3.02

The Clinical Development Cycle

STUDY PHASE	Number of Patients	Duration	Primary Purpose
Phase I	20 – 100 healthy, normal patients	Up to one year	Safety
Phase II	Up to several hundred patients	One to two years	Safety Efficacy
Phase III	Several hundred to several thousand patients	Two to four years	Efficacy Cost benefits
Phase IV (Post-Marketing)	Several hundred to several thousand patients	Two to ten years	Cost benefits Outcomes

Source: FDA

Distribution of Clinical Development
Active Projects by Phase, as of October 2005

% of Projects

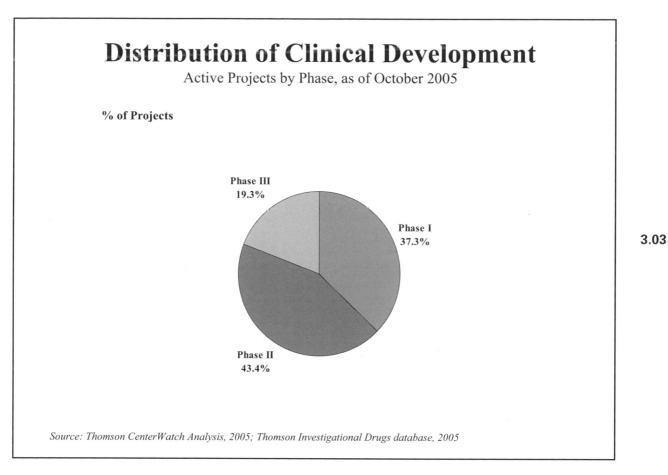

Phase III
19.3%

Phase I
37.3%

Phase II
43.4%

3.03

Source: Thomson CenterWatch Analysis, 2005; Thomson Investigational Drugs database, 2005

Clinical Trials Per NDA
Mean Number of Trials in Drugs Reaching Approval, by Phase

Number of Trials

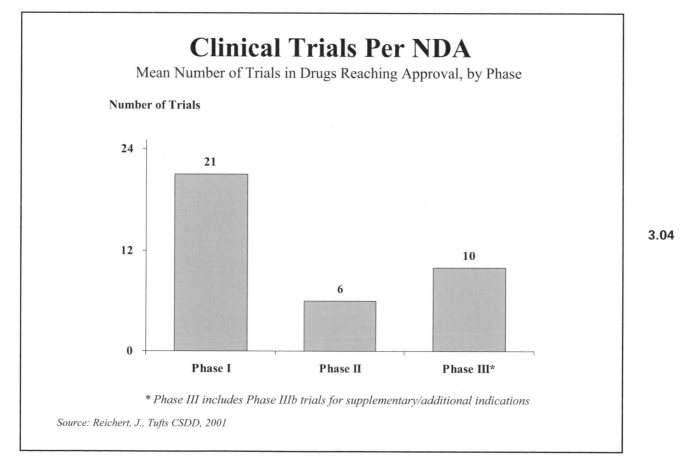

3.04

* Phase III includes Phase IIIb trials for supplementary/additional indications

Source: Reichert, J., Tufts CSDD, 2001

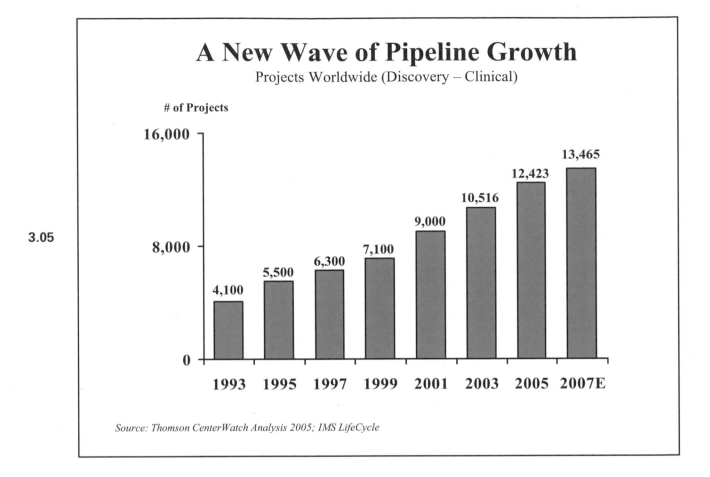

A New Wave of Pipeline Growth

Projects Worldwide (Discovery – Clinical)

3.05

Source: Thomson CenterWatch Analysis 2005; IMS LifeCycle

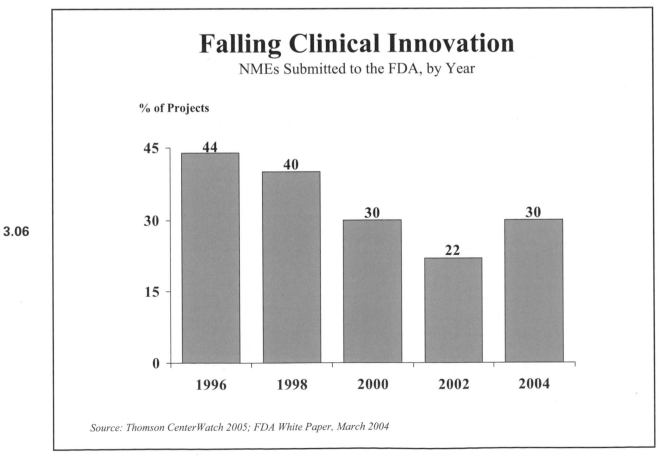

Falling Clinical Innovation

NMEs Submitted to the FDA, by Year

3.06

Source: Thomson CenterWatch 2005; FDA White Paper, March 2004

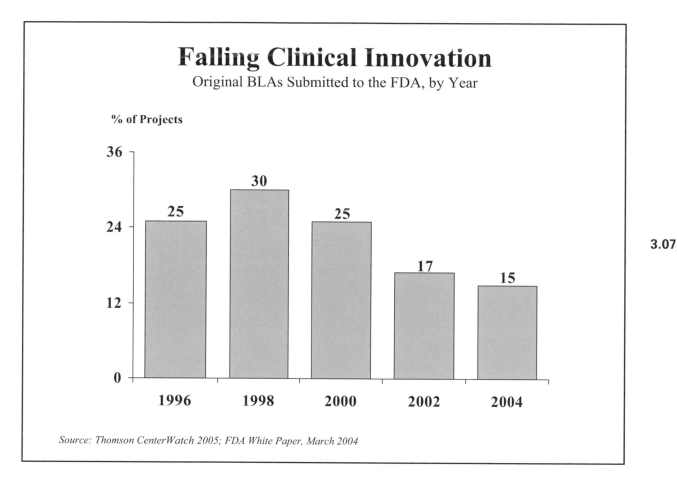

Falling Clinical Innovation
Original BLAs Submitted to the FDA, by Year

% of Projects

3.07

Source: Thomson CenterWatch 2005; FDA White Paper, March 2004

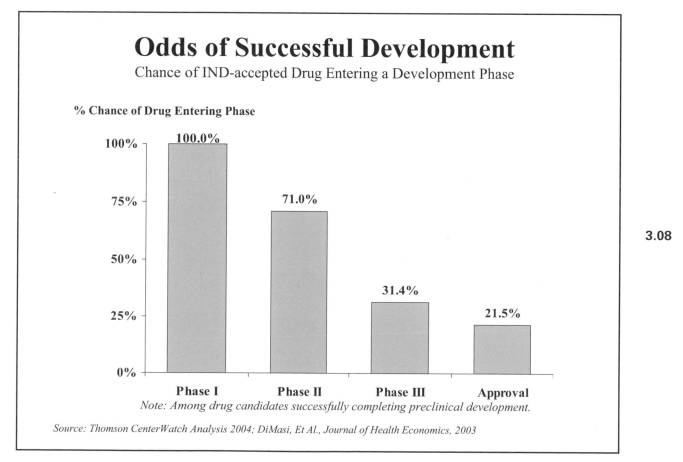

Odds of Successful Development
Chance of IND-accepted Drug Entering a Development Phase

% Chance of Drug Entering Phase

3.08

Note: Among drug candidates successfully completing preclinical development.

Source: Thomson CenterWatch Analysis 2004; DiMasi, Et Al., Journal of Health Economics, 2003

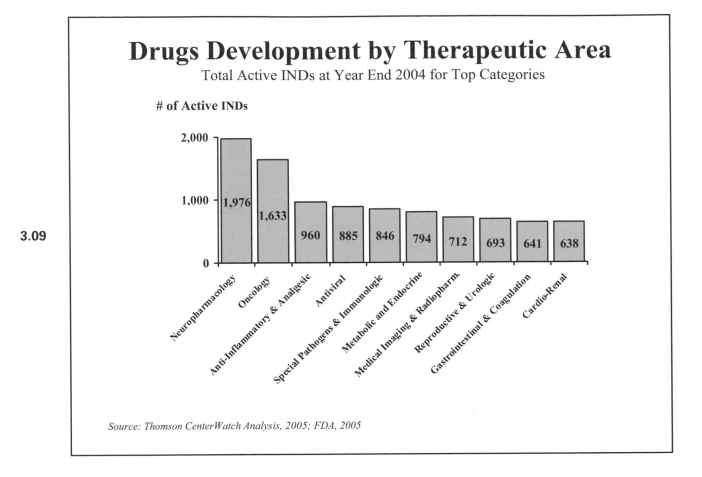

Drugs Development by Therapeutic Area
Total Active INDs at Year End 2004 for Top Categories

3.09

Source: Thomson CenterWatch Analysis, 2005; FDA, 2005

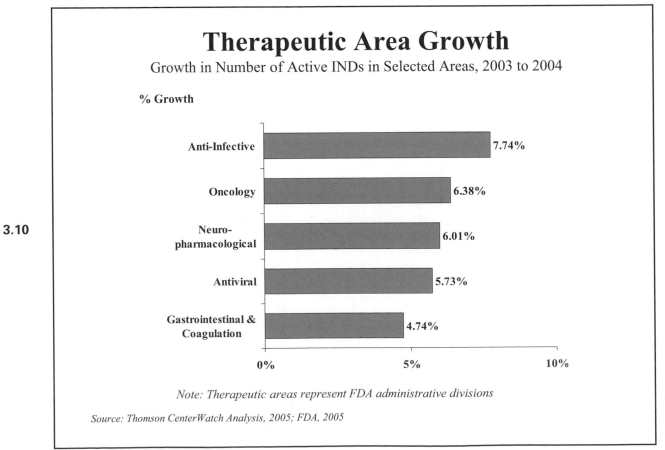

Therapeutic Area Growth
Growth in Number of Active INDs in Selected Areas, 2003 to 2004

3.10

Note: Therapeutic areas represent FDA administrative divisions

Source: Thomson CenterWatch Analysis, 2005; FDA, 2005

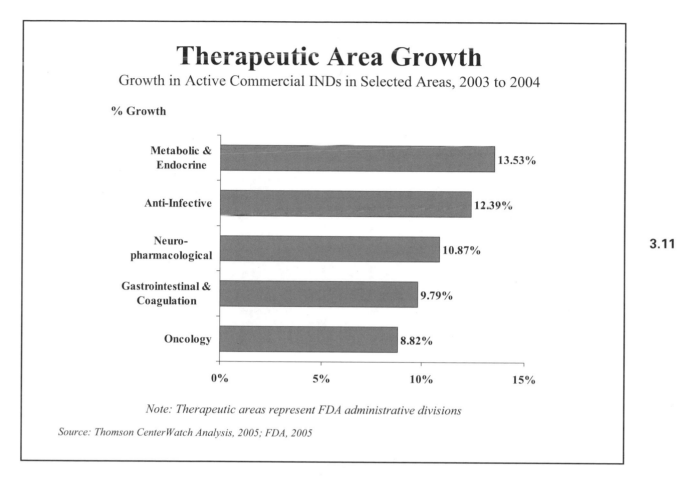

Therapeutic Area Growth

Growth in Active Commercial INDs in Selected Areas, 2003 to 2004

% Growth

Metabolic & Endocrine — 13.53%
Anti-Infective — 12.39%
Neuro-pharmacological — 10.87%
Gastrointestinal & Coagulation — 9.79%
Oncology — 8.82%

3.11

Note: Therapeutic areas represent FDA administrative divisions

Source: Thomson CenterWatch Analysis, 2005; FDA, 2005

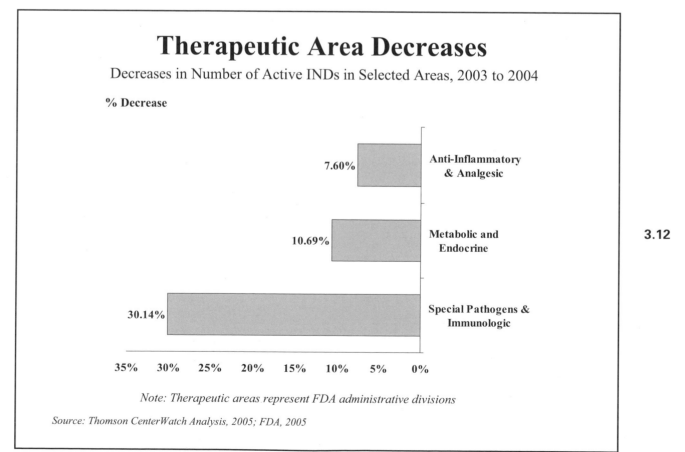

Therapeutic Area Decreases

Decreases in Number of Active INDs in Selected Areas, 2003 to 2004

% Decrease

Anti-Inflammatory & Analgesic — 7.60%
Metabolic and Endocrine — 10.69%
Special Pathogens & Immunologic — 30.14%

3.12

Note: Therapeutic areas represent FDA administrative divisions

Source: Thomson CenterWatch Analysis, 2005; FDA, 2005

3.13

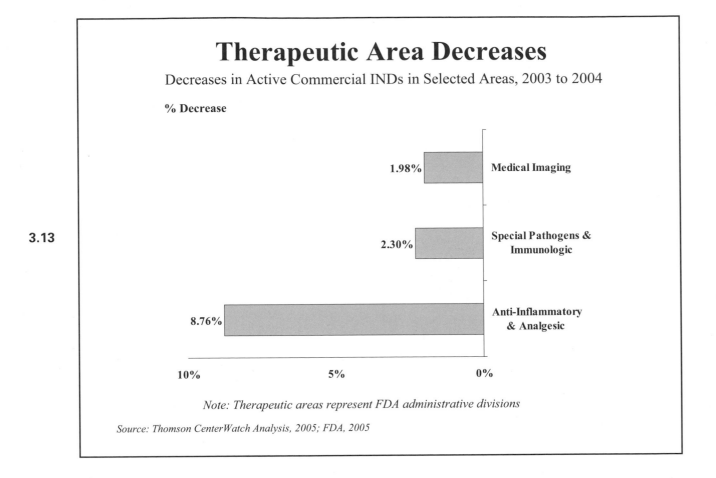

Therapeutic Area Decreases

Decreases in Active Commercial INDs in Selected Areas, 2003 to 2004

% Decrease

1.98%	Medical Imaging
2.30%	Special Pathogens & Immunologic
8.76%	Anti-Inflammatory & Analgesic

10%   5%   0%

Note: Therapeutic areas represent FDA administrative divisions

Source: Thomson CenterWatch Analysis, 2005; FDA, 2005

3.14

Annual Change in R&D Pipeline

Change in Number of Active INDs by Top Therapeutic Areas

	2000-2001 Growth Rate	2001-2002 Growth Rate	2002-2003 Growth Rate	2003-2004 Growth Rate
Cardio-Renal	-17.0%	7.4%	7.3%	3.7%
Neuropharmacological	-0.6%	4.8%	10.4%	6.0%
Oncology	-11.0%	39.1%	-12.9%	6.4%
Gastrointestinal & Coagulation	17.4%	7.4%	2.9%	4.7%
Medical Imaging	-12.1%	2.0%	2.7%	2.9%
Metabolic & Endocrine	-17.6%	-23.6%	1.6%	-10.7%
Anti-Infective	-40.7%	-0.6%	0.6%	7.7%
Antiviral	1.0%	4.9%	2.6%	5.7%
Anti-Inflammatory, Analgesic & Ophthalmologic	5.3%	3.6%	-2.2%	-7.6%
Reproductive & Urologic	7.4%	11.8%	2.6%	0.1%
Special Pathogen & Immunologic	-17.4%	4.2%	-7.6%	-30.1%

Source: Thomson CenterWatch Analysis, 2005; FDA, 2005

Annual Change in Commercial Pipeline

Change in Active Commercial INDs by Top Therapeutic Areas

	2000-2001 Growth Rate	2001-2002 Growth Rate	2002-2003 Growth Rate	2003-2004 Growth Rate
Cardio-Renal	2.3%	12.3%	-12.6%	3.7%
Neuropharmacological	3.3%	10.3%	-1.6%	10.9%
Oncology	3.5%	6.9%	-1.8%	8.8%
Gastrointestinal & Coagulation	8.4%	8.2%	4.9%	9.8%
Medical Imaging	7.0%	-0.9%	-4.7%	-2.0%
Metabolic & Endocrine	11.5%	6.3%	-6.2%	13.5%
Anti-Infective	2.3%	5.3%	-18.1%	12.4%
Antiviral	16.4%	0.0%	-5.8%	8.2%
Anti-Inflammatory, Analgesic & Ophthalmologic	6.7%	1.5%	-7.4%	-8.8%
Reproductive & Urologic	7.0%	12.1%	-8.0%	4.8%
Special Pathogen & Immunologic	10.6%	5.9%	-12.6%	-2.3%

3.15

Source: Thomson CenterWatch Analysis, 2005; FDA, 2005

Commercial Pipeline Focus

Number of Active INDs at Year's-End 2004

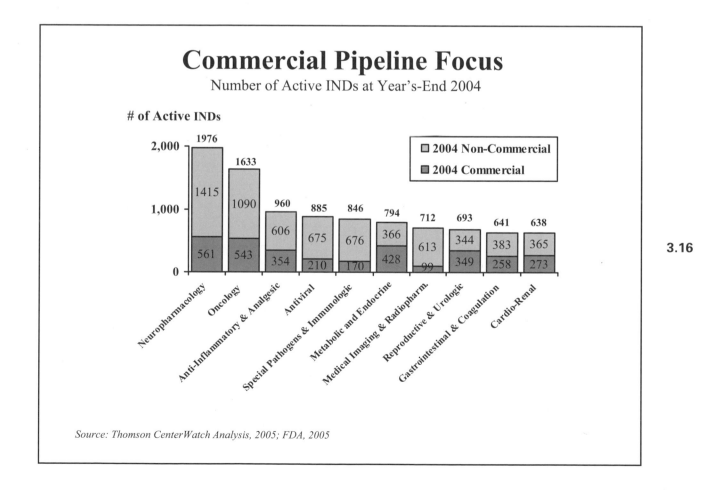

3.16

Source: Thomson CenterWatch Analysis, 2005; FDA, 2005

3.17

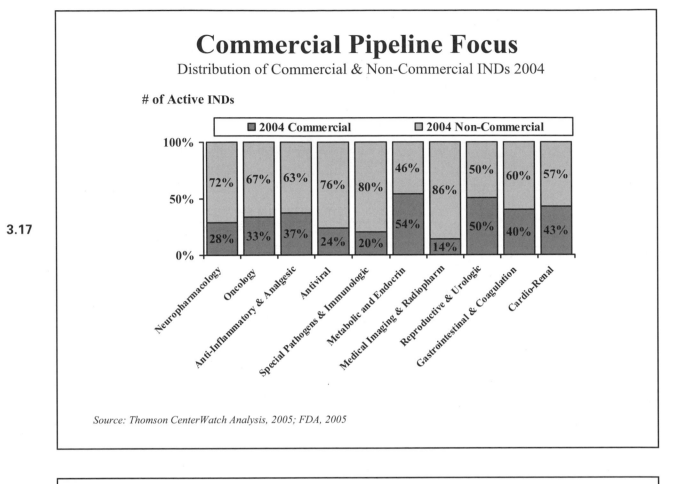

Commercial Pipeline Focus
Distribution of Commercial & Non-Commercial INDs 2004

Source: Thomson CenterWatch Analysis, 2005; FDA, 2005

3.18

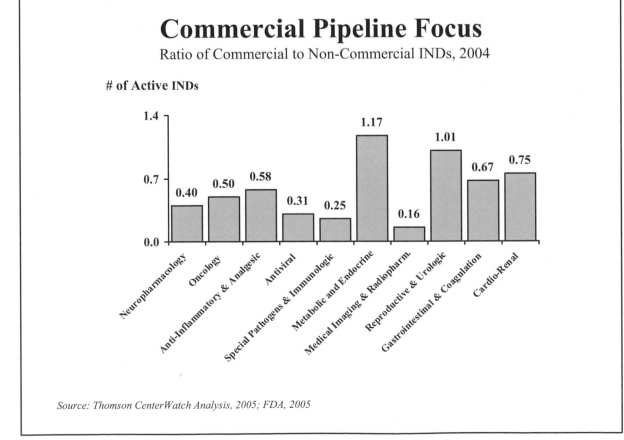

Commercial Pipeline Focus
Ratio of Commercial to Non-Commercial INDs, 2004

Source: Thomson CenterWatch Analysis, 2005; FDA, 2005

Drugs in Pediatric Trials

Distribution of Projects, by Phase

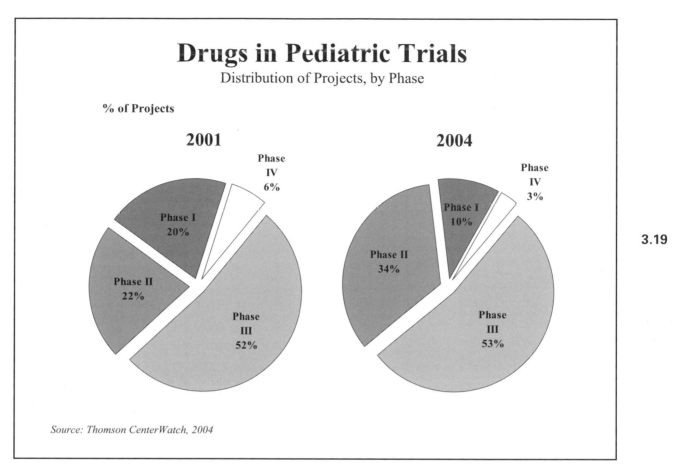

% of Projects

2001

2004

Source: Thomson CenterWatch, 2004

3.19

Pediatric Drugs in Clinical Trials

Total Active Development Projects, PhRMA Member Companies

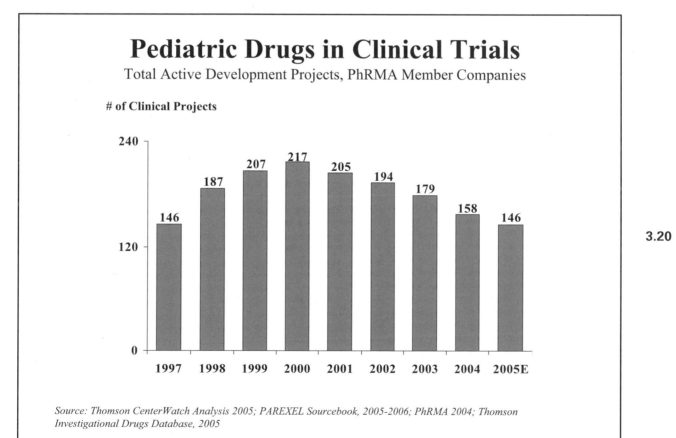

# of Clinical Projects

Source: Thomson CenterWatch Analysis 2005; PAREXEL Sourcebook, 2005-2006; PhRMA 2004; Thomson
Investigational Drugs Database, 2005

3.20

3.21

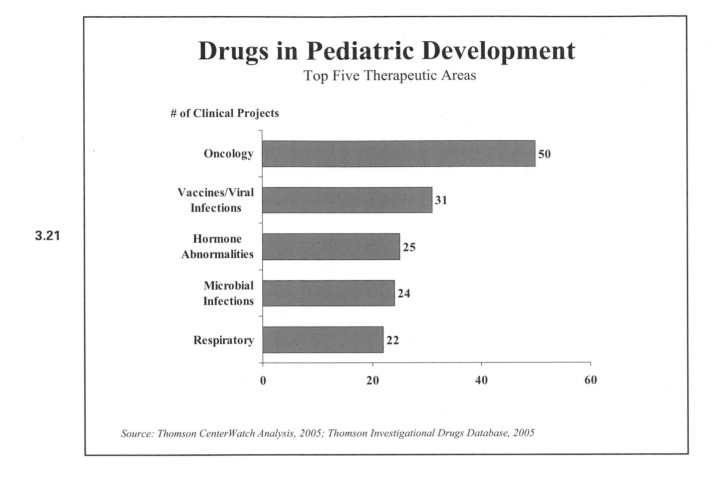

Drugs in Pediatric Development
Top Five Therapeutic Areas

# of Clinical Projects

Therapeutic Area	#
Oncology	50
Vaccines/Viral Infections	31
Hormone Abnormalities	25
Microbial Infections	24
Respiratory	22

Source: Thomson CenterWatch Analysis, 2005; Thomson Investigational Drugs Database, 2005

3.22

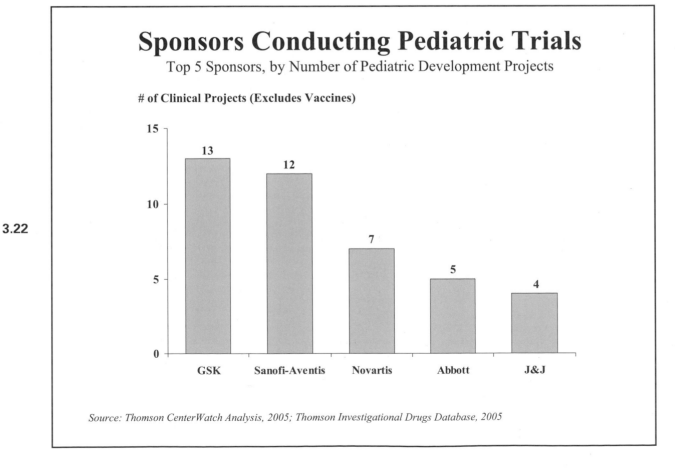

Sponsors Conducting Pediatric Trials
Top 5 Sponsors, by Number of Pediatric Development Projects

# of Clinical Projects (Excludes Vaccines)

Sponsor	#
GSK	13
Sanofi-Aventis	12
Novartis	7
Abbott	5
J&J	4

Source: Thomson CenterWatch Analysis, 2005; Thomson Investigational Drugs Database, 2005

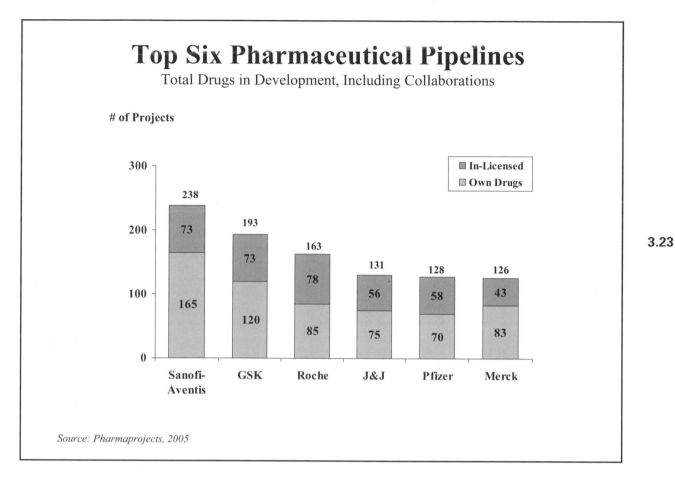

Top Six Pharmaceutical Pipelines
Total Drugs in Development, Including Collaborations

# of Projects

Legend:
- In-Licensed
- Own Drugs

Company	In-Licensed	Own Drugs	Total
Sanofi-Aventis	73	165	238
GSK	73	120	193
Roche	78	85	163
J&J	56	75	131
Pfizer	58	70	128
Merck	43	83	126

Source: Pharmaprojects, 2005

3.23

R&D Pipelines of Top Companies
Number of Total Drugs in Development, 15 Largest Pipelines

Company	2001	2003	2005	2001-2005 Change
Abbott	108	98	79	-27%
AstraZeneca	98	98	108	10%
Bristol-Myers Squibb	61	82	87	43%
Eli Lilly	78	65	83	6%
Genzyme	58	58	60	3%
GlaxoSmithKline	170	193	193	14%
Johnson & Johnson	96	111	131	36%
Merck	76	82	126	66%
Novartis	96	83	123	28%
Pfizer	270	107	128	-53%
Roche	97	138	163	68%
Sanofi-Aventis*	274	202	238	-13%
Schering AG	86	84	67	-22%
Schering-Plough	59	59	54	-8%
Wyeth	88	95	101	15%

Note: Pipelines for companies completing mergers during sample time are combined values

Source: Pharmaprojects, 2001-2005; R&D Directions, 2005; Decision Resources, 2000,2003; Datamonitor, 2001, 2002; Investigational Drug Database, 2005

3.24

R&D Pipelines of Top Companies

Number of Own-Drugs in Development, 15 Largest Pipelines

3.25

Company	2001	2003	2005	2001-2005 Change
Abbott*	52	48	41	-21%
AstraZeneca	57	63	83	46%
Bristol-Myers Squibb	28	47	40	43%
Eli Lilly	44	30	47	7%
Genzyme	44	46	41	-7%
GlaxoSmithKline*	85	110	120	41%
Johnson & Johnson	36	48	75	108%
Merck	48	54	83	73%
Novartis	57	51	72	26%
Pfizer*	152	57	70	-54%
Roche	53	73	85	60%
Sanofi-Aventis*	160	125	165	3%
Schering AG	51	53	37	-27%
Schering-Plough	22	32	29	32%
Wyeth	42	61	69	64%

Note: Pipelines for companies completing mergers during sample time are combined values

Source: Pharmaprojects, 2001-2005; R&D Directions, 2005; Decision Resources, 2000,2003; Datamonitor, 2001, 2002; Investigational Drug Database, 2005

A Shift Towards In-House Development

Mean Distribution of Own-Drugs and Licensed Drugs in Pipelines

3.26

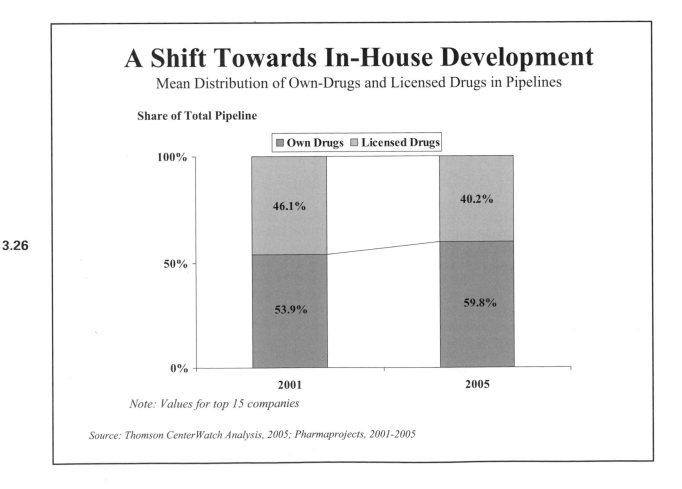

Share of Total Pipeline

☐ Own Drugs ☐ Licensed Drugs

- 2001: 46.1% / 53.9%
- 2005: 40.2% / 59.8%

Note: Values for top 15 companies

Source: Thomson CenterWatch Analysis, 2005; Pharmaprojects, 2001-2005

The Pharmaceutical Development Cycle
Total Cycle Time: 20 Years

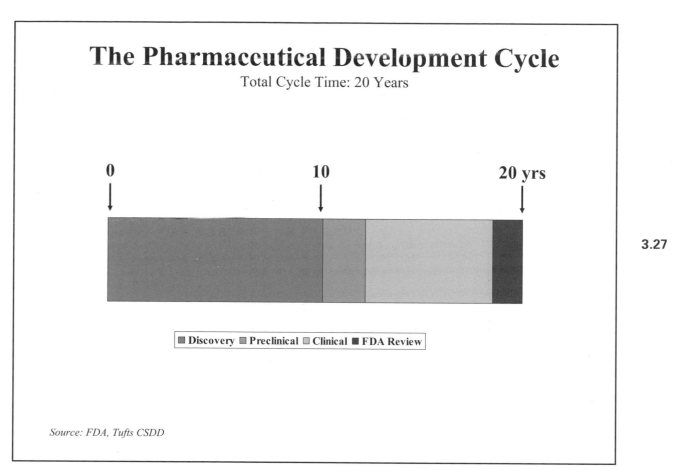

Source: FDA, Tufts CSDD

3.27

Mean Development Cycle Time
New Biopharmaceuticals

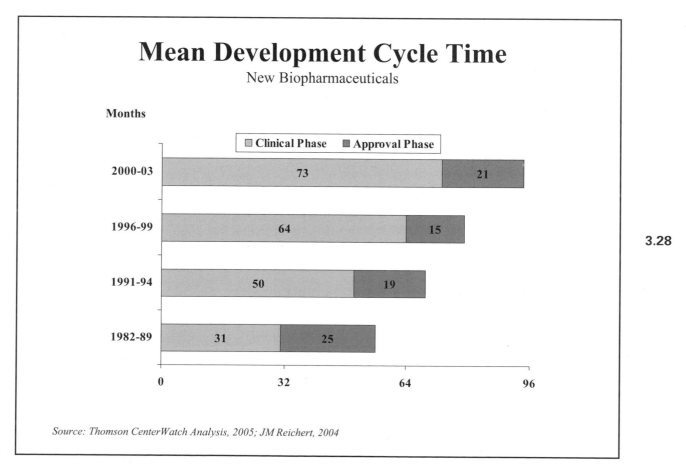

Source: Thomson CenterWatch Analysis, 2005; JM Reichert, 2004

3.28

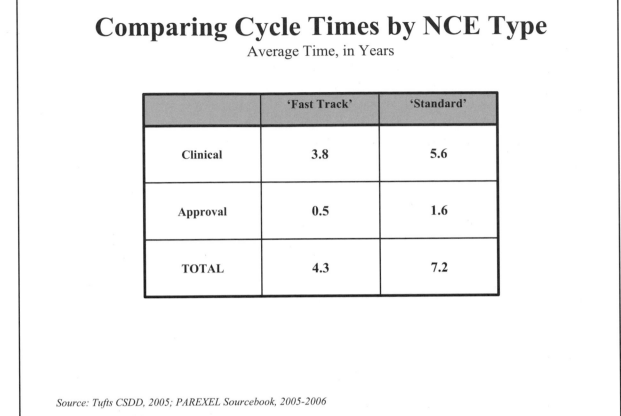

Comparing Cycle Times by NCE Type
Average Time, in Years

	'Fast Track'	'Standard'
Clinical	3.8	5.6
Approval	0.5	1.6
TOTAL	4.3	7.2

Source: Tufts CSDD, 2005; PAREXEL Sourcebook, 2005-2006

3.29

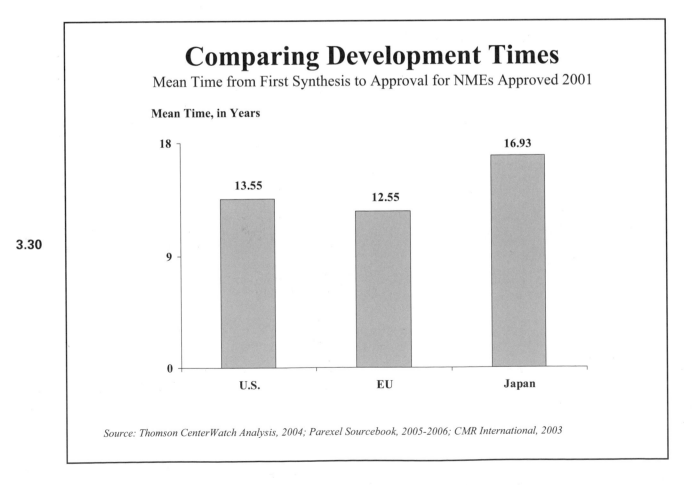

Comparing Development Times
Mean Time from First Synthesis to Approval for NMEs Approved 2001

Mean Time, in Years

	U.S.	EU	Japan
	13.55	12.55	16.93

Source: Thomson CenterWatch Analysis, 2004; Parexel Sourcebook, 2005-2006; CMR International, 2003

3.30

Japanese Approvals Accelerating
Time from NDA to Approval by Year of Submission, 1993-2003E

Mean Time, in Months

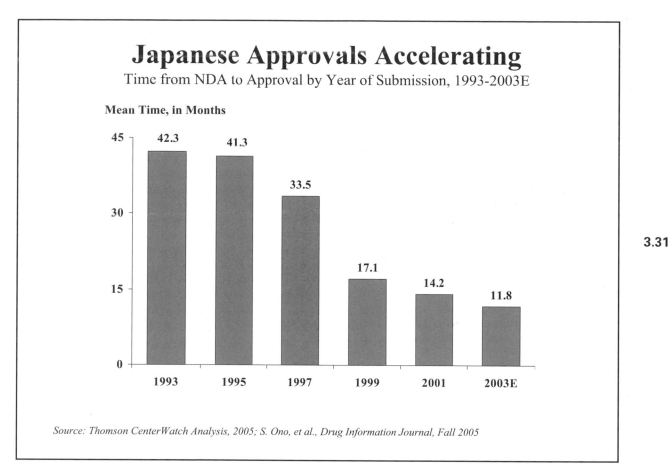

Source: Thomson CenterWatch Analysis, 2005; S. Ono, et al., Drug Information Journal, Fall 2005

3.31

Canadian Drug Approval Times
NDS to Approval for Standard and Priority Reviews, 1998-2004

Mean Time, in Days

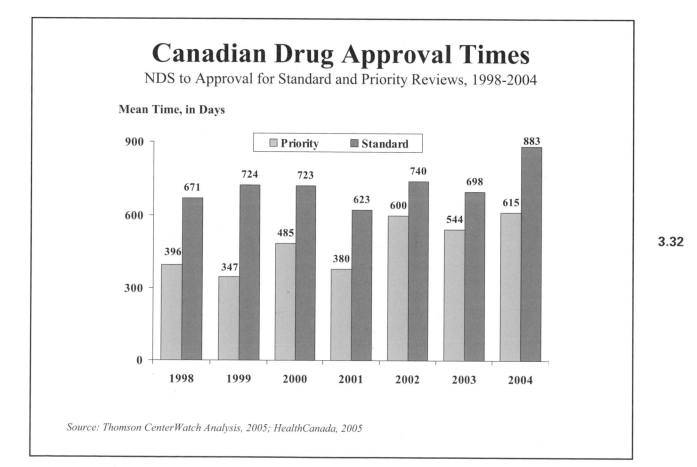

Source: Thomson CenterWatch Analysis, 2005; HealthCanada, 2005

3.32

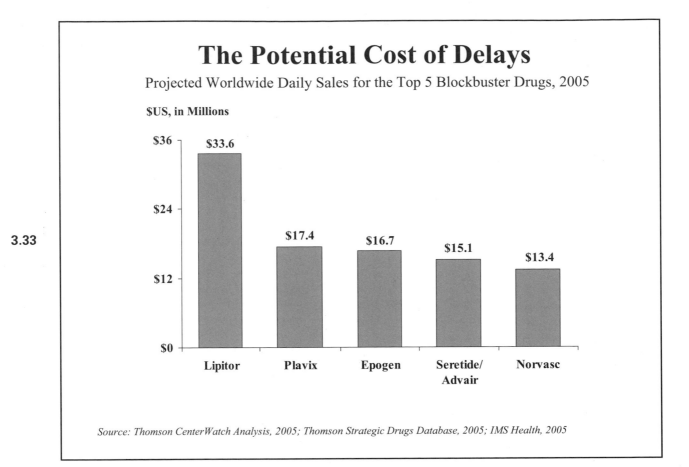

The Potential Cost of Delays

Projected Worldwide Daily Sales for the Top 5 Blockbuster Drugs, 2005

$US, in Millions

Source: Thomson CenterWatch Analysis, 2005; Thomson Strategic Drugs Database, 2005; IMS Health, 2005

3.33

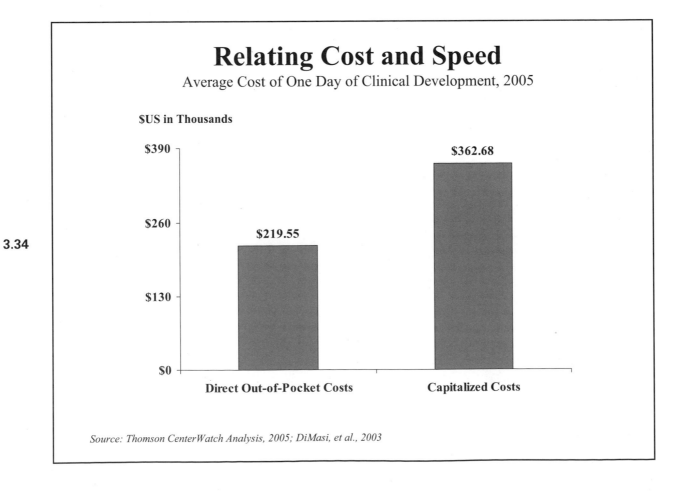

Relating Cost and Speed

Average Cost of One Day of Clinical Development, 2005

$US in Thousands

Source: Thomson CenterWatch Analysis, 2005; DiMasi, et al., 2003

3.34

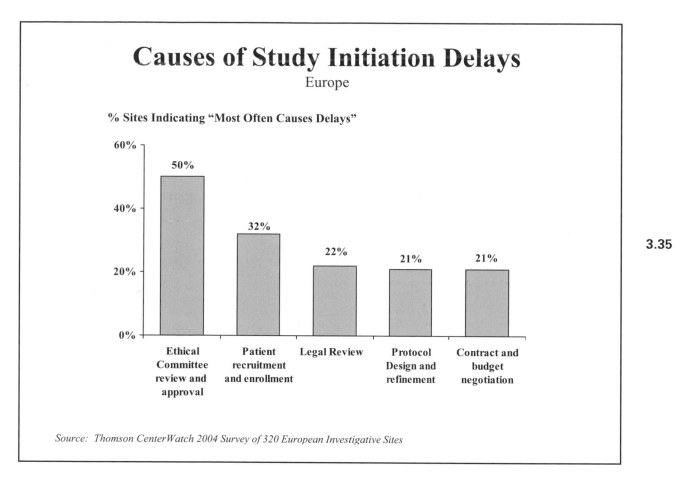

Causes of Study Initiation Delays
Europe

% Sites Indicating "Most Often Causes Delays"

Source: Thomson CenterWatch 2004 Survey of 320 European Investigative Sites

3.35

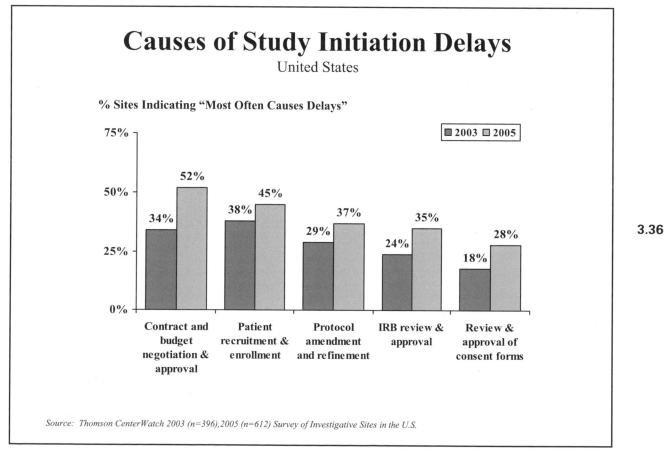

Causes of Study Initiation Delays
United States

% Sites Indicating "Most Often Causes Delays"

Source: Thomson CenterWatch 2003 (n=396),2005 (n=612) Survey of Investigative Sites in the U.S.

3.36

3.37

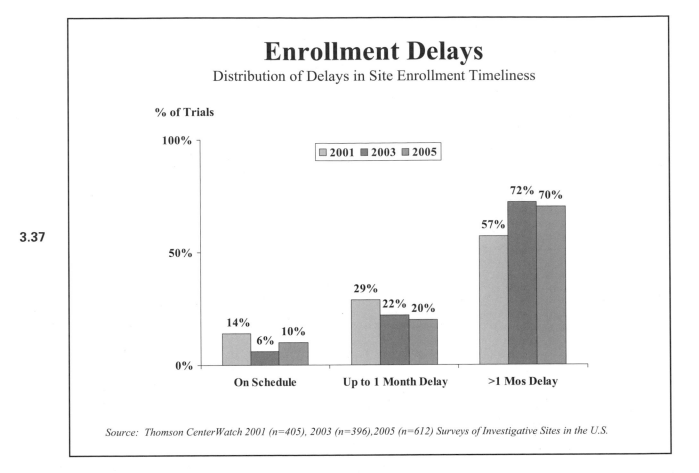

Enrollment Delays
Distribution of Delays in Site Enrollment Timeliness

% of Trials

Legend: 2001 2003 2005

On Schedule: 14%, 6%, 10%
Up to 1 Month Delay: 29%, 22%, 20%
>1 Mos Delay: 57%, 72%, 70%

Source: Thomson CenterWatch 2001 (n=405), 2003 (n=396),2005 (n=612) Surveys of Investigative Sites in the U.S.

3.38

Sponsor Development Time Goals

Development Activity	Current Average Time (months)	Emerging Standards (months)	Time Reduction (months)
Protocol Development	7.5	3	4.5
Investigator Recruitment	6	3.5	2.5
Trial Initiation	6	.5	5.5
Patient Recruitment	15	9	6
Clinical Trial Supplies	4	2	2
Last Patient to Data Lock	10	.5	9.5
Data Analysis	11	1.5	9.5
NDA Dossier Preparation	9	2	7

Source: Thomson CenterWatch Analyses, PriceWaterhouseCoopers, 2000

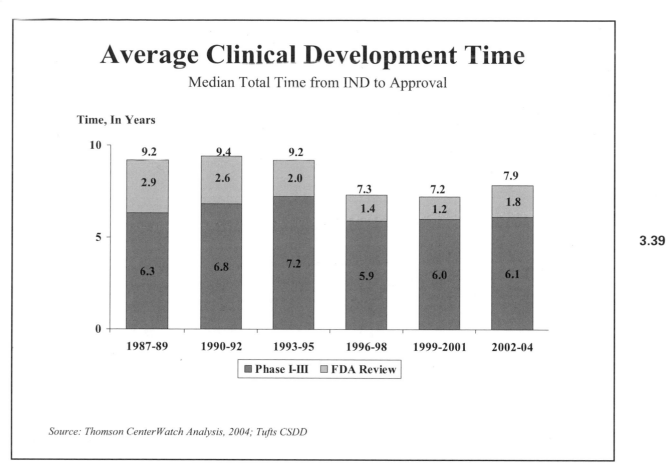

Average Clinical Development Time
Median Total Time from IND to Approval

Time, In Years

Source: Thomson CenterWatch Analysis, 2004; Tufts CSDD

3.39

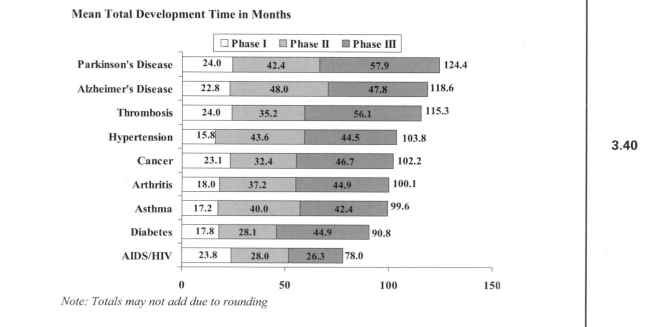

Average Clinical Development Time
Mean Total Time by Therapeutic Area and Phase

Mean Total Development Time in Months

Note: Totals may not add due to rounding

Source: Thomson CenterWatch Analysis, 2005; RA Abrantes-Metz, et al., FTC Bureau of Economics., 2004

3.40

3.41

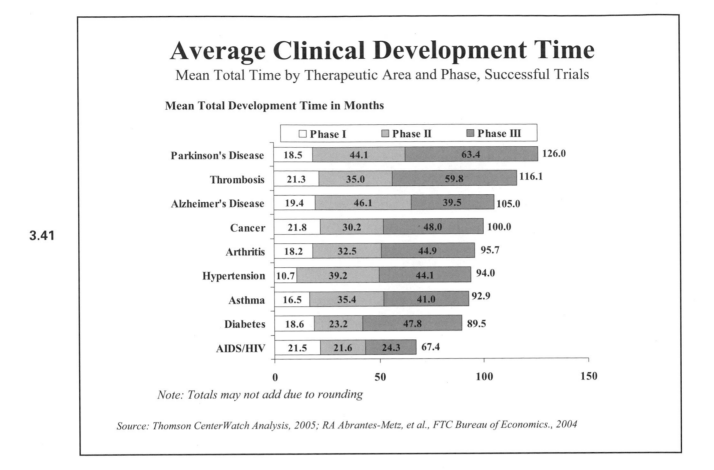

Average Clinical Development Time
Mean Total Time by Therapeutic Area and Phase, Successful Trials

Mean Total Development Time in Months

	Phase I	Phase II	Phase III

Parkinson's Disease	18.5	44.1	63.4	126.0
Thrombosis	21.3	35.0	59.8	116.1
Alzheimer's Disease	19.4	46.1	39.5	105.0
Cancer	21.8	30.2	48.0	100.0
Arthritis	18.2	32.5	44.9	95.7
Hypertension	10.7	39.2	44.1	94.0
Asthma	16.5	35.4	41.0	92.9
Diabetes	18.6	23.2	47.8	89.5
AIDS/HIV	21.5	21.6	24.3	67.4

Note: Totals may not add due to rounding

Source: Thomson CenterWatch Analysis, 2005; RA Abrantes-Metz, et al., FTC Bureau of Economics., 2004

3.42

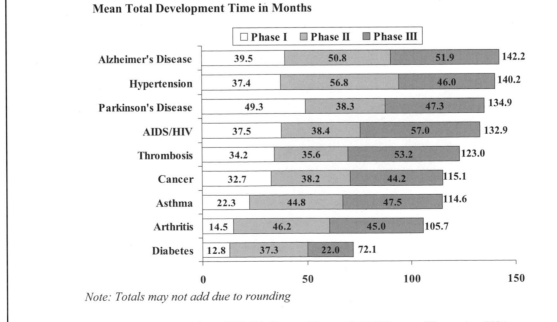

Average Clinical Development Time
Mean Total Time by Therapeutic Area and Phase, Unsuccessful Trials

Mean Total Development Time in Months

	Phase I	Phase II	Phase III

Alzheimer's Disease	39.5	50.8	51.9	142.2
Hypertension	37.4	56.8	46.0	140.2
Parkinson's Disease	49.3	38.3	47.3	134.9
AIDS/HIV	37.5	38.4	57.0	132.9
Thrombosis	34.2	35.6	53.2	123.0
Cancer	32.7	38.2	44.2	115.1
Asthma	22.3	44.8	47.5	114.6
Arthritis	14.5	46.2	45.0	105.7
Diabetes	12.8	37.3	22.0	72.1

Note: Totals may not add due to rounding

Source: Thomson CenterWatch Analysis, 2005; RA Abrantes-Metz, et al., FTC Bureau of Economics., 2004

Average Clinical Development Time
Mean Total Time by Company Size and Phase, All TAs

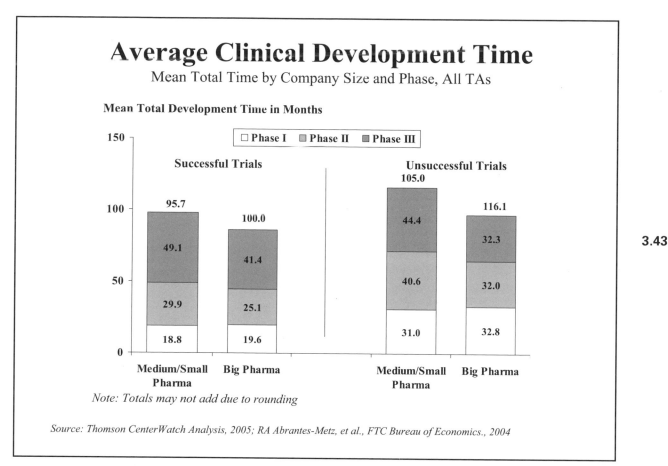

Mean Total Development Time in Months

Note: Totals may not add due to rounding

Source: Thomson CenterWatch Analysis, 2005; RA Abrantes-Metz, et al., FTC Bureau of Economics., 2004

3.43

The Speed of Major Pharma Companies
Median Clinical Development Speed, 1996-2001

Note: Time from IND submission to FDA approval, all drugs across all therapeutic areas

Source: Thomson CenterWatch Analysis of NMEis Approved 1998 - 2001

3.44

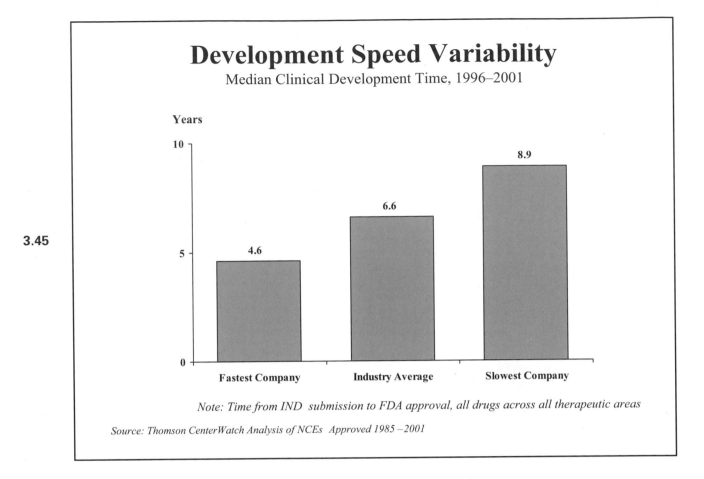

Development Speed Variability
Median Clinical Development Time, 1996–2001

3.45

Note: Time from IND submission to FDA approval, all drugs across all therapeutic areas

Source: Thomson CenterWatch Analysis of NCEs Approved 1985–2001

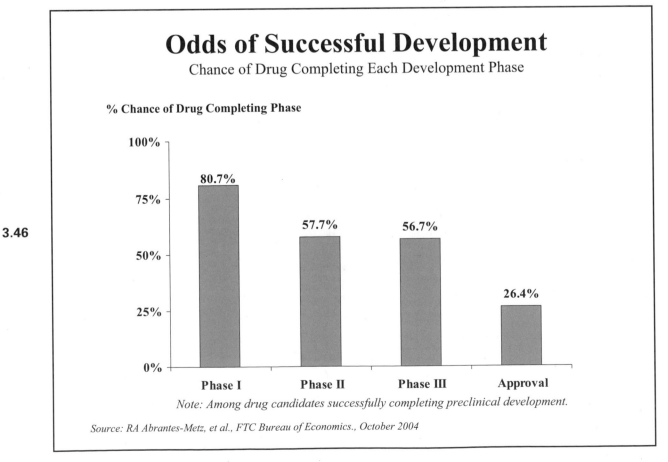

Odds of Successful Development
Chance of Drug Completing Each Development Phase

3.46

Note: Among drug candidates successfully completing preclinical development.

Source: RA Abrantes-Metz, et al., FTC Bureau of Economics., October 2004

Time to Completing Phase for Successful and Failed Trials

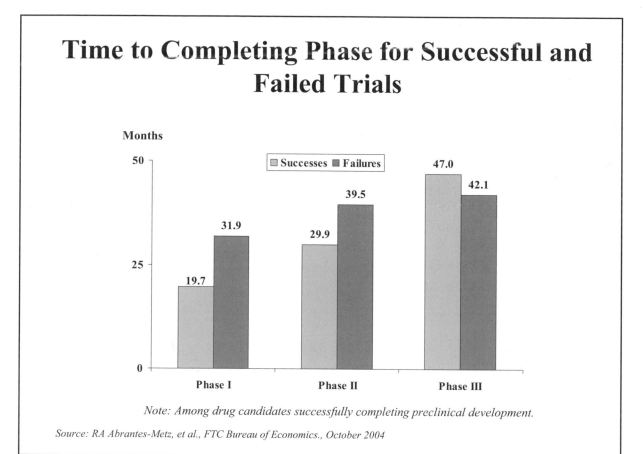

Note: Among drug candidates successfully completing preclinical development.

Source: RA Abrantes-Metz, et al., FTC Bureau of Economics., October 2004

3.47

Weeding Out Failures Earlier

Increases in Phase I Spending Improve Phase III Success

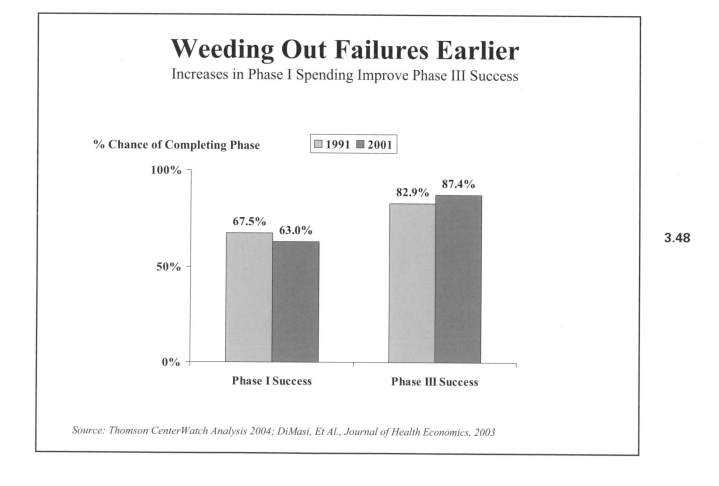

Source: Thomson CenterWatch Analysis 2004; DiMasi, Et Al., Journal of Health Economics, 2003

3.48

3.49

Scope of Clinical Projects
Mean Number of Subjects and Sites per Trial

	Phase I	Phase I/II	Phase II	Phase II/III	Phase III
Mean Subjects per Trial	32.6	52.1	151.4	372.3	868.6
Mean Sites per Trial	2.0	6.0	16.2	23.4	69.0

Note: Average across all therapeutic areas and countries.

Source: Thomson CenterWatch Analysis of 912 Trials, 2005

3.50

Differences in Phase I trials
Index of Number of Subjects in Phase I Trials for Selected TAs

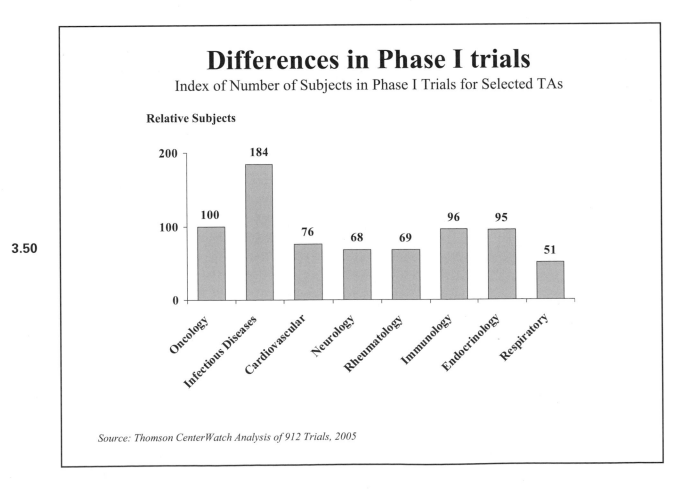

Source: Thomson CenterWatch Analysis of 912 Trials, 2005

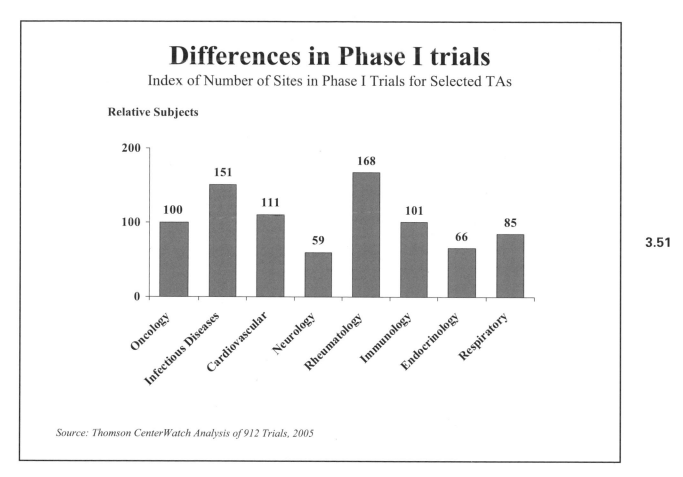

3.51

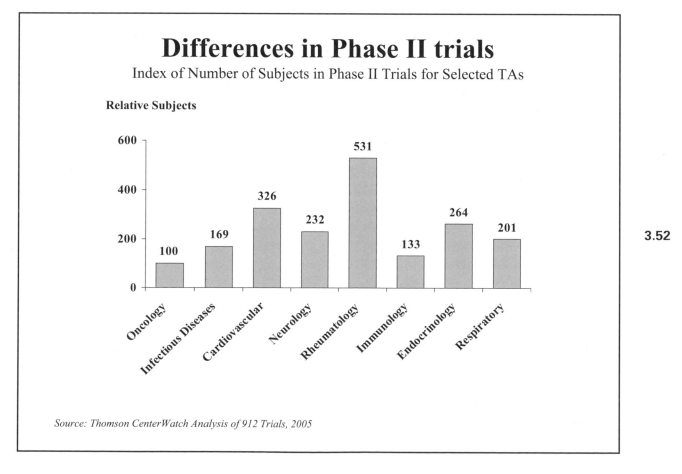

3.52

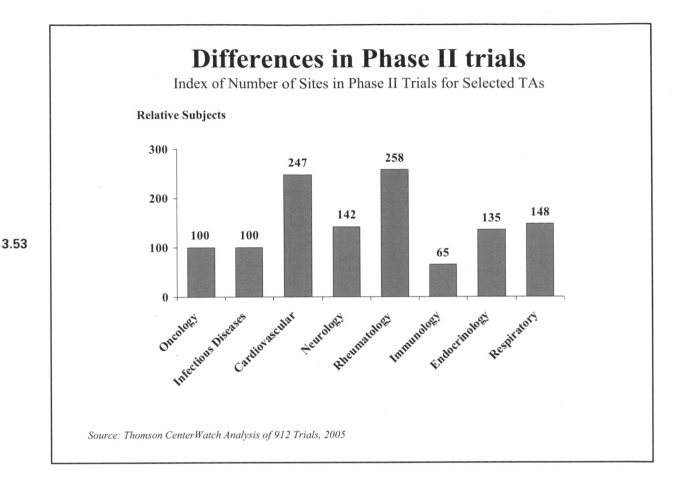

Differences in Phase II trials

Index of Number of Sites in Phase II Trials for Selected TAs

Relative Subjects

3.53

Source: Thomson CenterWatch Analysis of 912 Trials, 2005

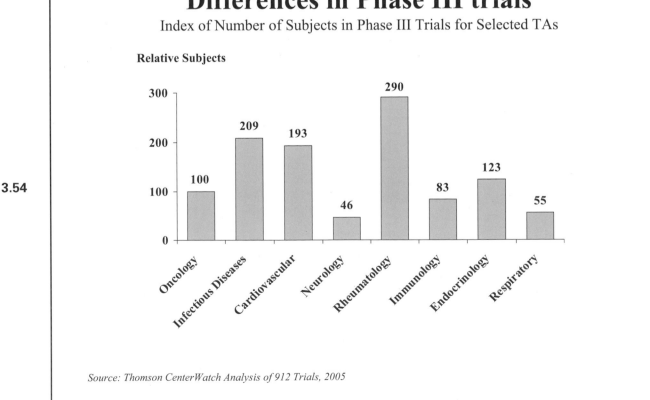

Differences in Phase III trials

Index of Number of Subjects in Phase III Trials for Selected TAs

Relative Subjects

3.54

Source: Thomson CenterWatch Analysis of 912 Trials, 2005

Differences in Phase III trials
Index of Number of Sites in Phase III Trials for Selected TAs

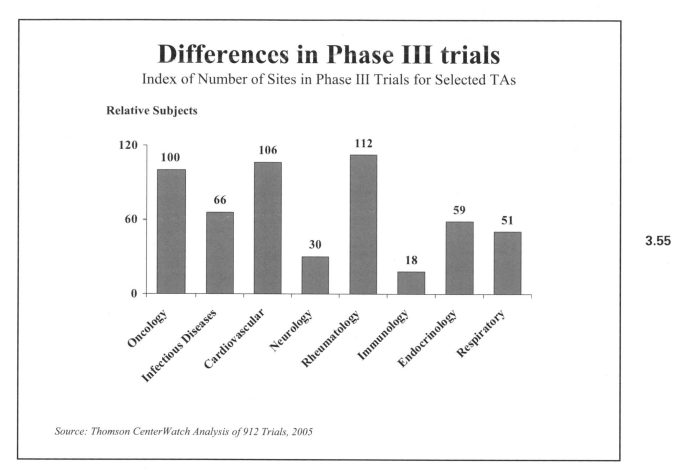

Relative Subjects

Oncology: 100
Infectious Diseases: 66
Cardiovascular: 106
Neurology: 30
Rheumatology: 112
Immunology: 18
Endocrinology: 59
Respiratory: 51

Source: Thomson CenterWatch Analysis of 912 Trials, 2005

3.55

Rising Project Complexity
Mean Number of Procedures per Patient

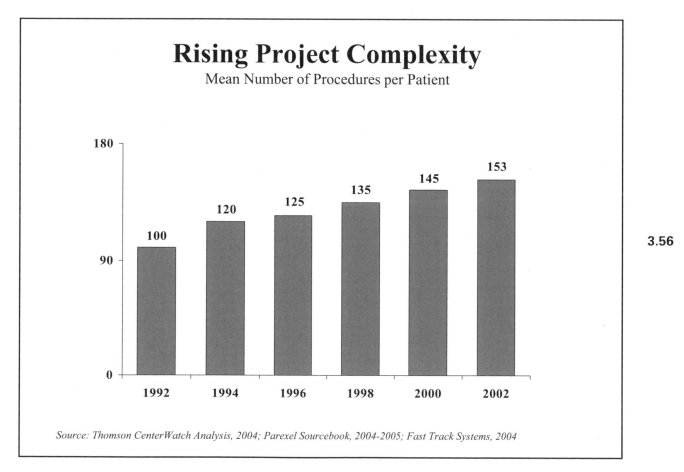

1992: 100
1994: 120
1996: 125
1998: 135
2000: 145
2002: 153

Source: Thomson CenterWatch Analysis, 2004; Parexel Sourcebook, 2004-2005; Fast Track Systems, 2004

3.56

3.57

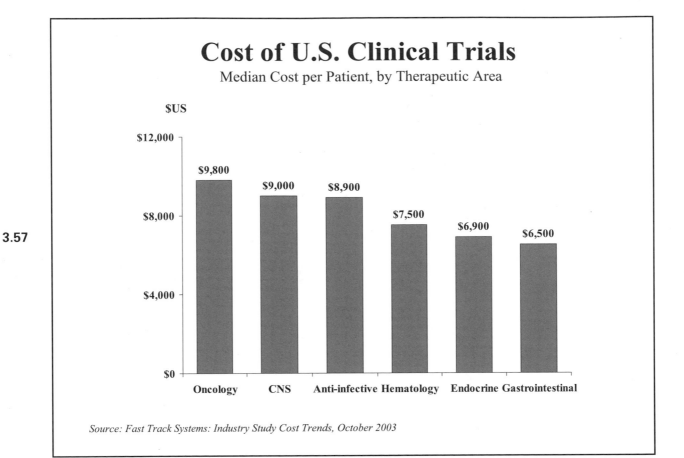

3.58

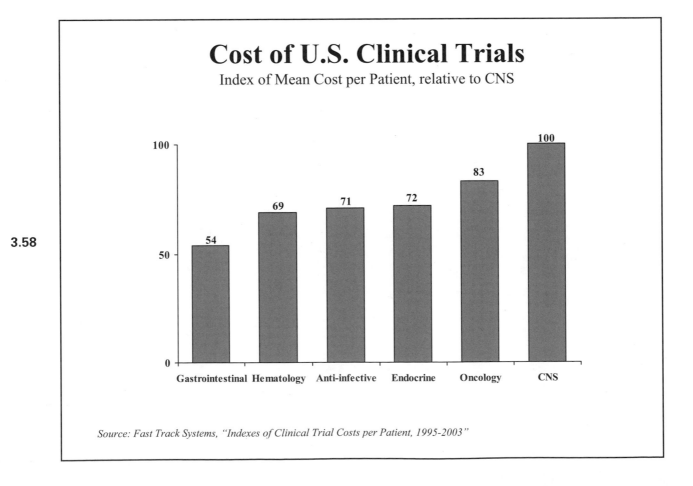

Eye Ons and Pipelines

Bacterial Infections

By Laurie Barclay, M.D.
Published July 2005

Bacterial infections are caused by growth within body tissues of harmful bacteria that normally do not reside in the body in large numbers. Release of toxins from the invading bacteria damages tissues, causing symptoms of inflammation, swelling, pain, heat, redness and loss of function. Depending on the organ system involved, there may be pneumonia, gastrointestinal symptoms, urinary tract symptoms or meningitis. Invasion of the bloodstream by large numbers of virulent bacteria causes sepsis, with fever, chills, circulatory collapse and ultimately death.

Worldwide, bacterial infections are the leading cause of death, and they are a significant cause of morbidity and healthcare expenditures. According to the England Department of Health, more than half of consultations for bacterial intestinal infections required emergency hospital admissions during 2002–2003, with a mean length of stay of 16.8 days. About 2 million hospitalized U.S. patients acquire serious or fatal bacterial infections each year.

Risk factors for bacterial infections include immunocompromised state from cancer, AIDS or other chronic diseases, burns, severe trauma, low white blood cell counts, drug or alcohol use, malnutrition and vitamin deficiency. Spread of bacterial infection occurs by inhalation of airborne bacteria, oral ingestion from dirty hands or contaminated food or water, direct contact with an infected lesion or contaminated blood, or by insect bite.

The body's protective mechanisms against bacterial infection include antibacterial chemicals naturally present in body tissues, such as lysozymes in tears, gastric acid in the stomach, pancreatic enzymes in the bowel, and fatty acids in the skin. If bacteria penetrate these defenses, a nonspecific immune response involving inflammation occurs first, followed by a specific immune response involving the activation of T- and B-lymphocytes. T-cells activate cytotoxic cells, which engulf and destroy the invading bacteria, and B-cells generate antibodies, or immunoglobulins, directed against specific bacteria.

One of the most revolutionary and miraculous medical discoveries of all time was the advent of modern antibiotics. Penicillin, the natural product of the soil mold Penicillium, was first discovered in 1896 by Ernest Duchesne, a French medical student, and then rediscovered in 1928 by Scottish physician Alexander Fleming. During World War II, this one drug single-handedly eradicated the greatest source of wartime deaths, namely wound infections.

But merely four years later, the specter of penicillin-resistance appeared, spurring the search for new antibiotics and even new classes of antibiotics. Even today, despite the plethora of approved antibiotics, bacterial resistance is a significant and increasing threat. In 1998, strains of *Staphylococcus aureus*, a significant cause of sometimes fatal hospital-associated infections were detected that were resistant to vancomycin, the most potent antibiotic then available.

Natural selection pressure fosters the growth of resistant organisms through genetic adaptation. Other factors encouraging microbial resistance include increased transmission of infections, higher numbers of immunocompromised patients, use of antibiotics in livestock, and widespread prescription of potent, broad spectrum antibiotics, often taken in incomplete courses and for unclear indications.

In the U.S., antibiotic prescriptions for sinusitis and for middle ear infections doubled between 1985 and 1992, according to a 1995 report in the *Journal of the American Medical Association*. The National Center for Health Statistics reported that from 1980 to 1992, there has been a tendency for doctors to prescribe more expensive, broader spectrum antibiotics.

To counteract the problem of microbial resistance to existing agents, possible solutions include development of new antibiotics, vaccines to prevent bacterial infection and immunotherapeutic agents to stimulate the body's own defenses to bacterial attack. CenterWatch has identified a pipeline of 35 such agents in various phases of development.

Depomed has submitted a New Drug Application (NDA) for Ciprofloxacin GR, a gastric retention dosage form of ciprofloxacin used to treat urinary tract infections. In a phase III trial involving 580 patients, a three-day course of this once daily formulation was as effective as twice daily CIPRO, but with fewer episodes of nausea, diarrhea and other gastrointestinal adverse effects. Hopefully, this extended release formulation will also improve patient convenience and compliance.

Vicuron Pharmaceuticals has also submitted an NDA for dalbavancin, a second-generation glycopeptide agent. Members of this antibiotic class, such as vancomycin and teicoplanin, have proven effective against serious and difficult-to-treat hospital infections. In preclinical studies, dalbavancin was the most potent antibiotic in its class against the most resistant Staph infections, including methicillin-resistant *Staphylococcus aureus* (MRSA) and methicillin-resistant *Staphylococcus epidermidis* (MRSE). Pivotal phase III trials enrolling more than 1,500 patients and evaluating once weekly dalbavancin in skin and soft tissue infections (SSTIs) caused by Gram-positive bacteria met primary and secondary endpoints. Dalbavancin is the first once weekly injectable antibiotic, which may reduce the need for continued intravenous lines in some patients.

Cipro (ciprofloxacin) is an approved fluoroquinolone antibiotic, now in phase IIIb testing by Bayer for pediatric indications. It is rapidly absorbed after oral administration and easily penetrates extravascular tissues and other body compartments. This synthetic bactericidal antibiotic inhibits nuclear DNA synthesis by targeting the enzyme DNA gyrase (topoisomerase II).

Another orally administered fluoroquinolone is Factive (gemifloxacin mesylate). In Europe, Oscient Pharmaceuticals is in phase III development of this broad spectrum antibiotic.

Cubist Pharmaceuticals is in phase IIIb development of the antibiotic lipopeptide Cubicin (daptomycin) for urinary tract infections. Cubicin is the first cyclic lipopeptide, with a distinct mechanism of action. It binds to the bacterial cell membrane, causing rapid depolarization of membrane potential, which inhibits protein, DNA and RNA synthesis, resulting in bacterial cell death.

At doses up to 6 mg/kg administered once daily for seven days, Cubicin pharmacokinetics are nearly linear and time-independent, with steady-state concentrations achieved by the third daily dose. In a concentration-independent manner, Cubicin reversibly binds to human plasma proteins, primarily to serum albumin. The primary route of elimination is renal excretion, so dosage adjustment is needed in patients with severe renal insufficiency.

Iclaprim (AR-100) is a diaminopyrimidine dihydrofolate reductase inhibitor, in phase III testing by Arpida for the treatment of severe bacterial infections requiring hospitalization. Iclaprim is a broad spectrum antibiotic highly active against MRSA and other bacterial pathogens. Arpida is developing iclaprim both as intravenous and oral formulations.

In a phase II trial, iclaprim injected twice daily was effective and well tolerated in hospitalized patients with infected burns, ulcers, surgical abscesses and cellulitis. As part of a global phase III program, U.S. trials are planned for injectable iclaprim in the treatment of complicated skin infections, including infected burns, ulcers and surgical wounds. Oral iclaprim is currently being tested in phase I clinical trials.

Another broad spectrum antibiotic for the treatment of serious bacterial infections in hospitalized patients is doripenem (S-4661), in phase III testing by Peninsula Pharmaceuticals. This synthetic, parenteral agent belongs to the class of carbapenem antibiotics, which have potent activity, broad antibacterial spectrum and stability against most ß-lactamases.

In preclinical testing, the overall antimicrobial potency of doripenem is comparable to that of other new and established carbapenem drugs, with enhanced activity against *S. aureus* and *Pseudomonas aeruginosa*, as well as coverage of penicillin-resistant Streptococcus pneumoniae (PRSP). Its spectrum of bactericidal activity in animal models includes aerobic and anaerobic gram-positive and gram-negative microorganisms. Like other ß-lactams, doripenem targets penicillin-binding proteins (PBPs) to inhibit biosynthesis of the bacterial cell wall. Phase III trials of doripenem for injection are underway in complicated urinary tract infections (including pyelonephritis), complicated intra-abdominal infections, and hospital-acquired pneumonia (including ventilator-associated pneumonia).

Another ultra-broad spectrum injectable carbapenem antibiotic is Merrem/Meronem (meropenem), in phase IIIb development by Astra-Zeneca. This agent targets a wide variety of serious infections such as meningitis and pneumonia.

Ceftobiprole (BAL5788) is the first of a new generation of cephalosporins with good activity against MRSA, now entering phase III development by Basilea Pharmaceutica for the treatment of complicated SSTIs. Preclinical studies suggest a high degree of resistance to bacterial ß-lactamases and potent inhibition of important penicillin-binding proteins, resulting in good bactericidal activity against resistant gram-positive pathogens. In addition to MRSA, these include methicillin-resistant S. epidermidis and penicillin-resistant *S. pneumoniae*.

In March 2003, the U.S. Food and Drug Administration granted ceftobiprole Fast-Track designation for treatment of complicated SSTIs caused by MRSA, with an additional designation in June 2004 for treatment of ventilator-associated or other hospital-acquired pneumonia caused by MRSA.

Telavancin (TD-6424) is a multivalent lipoglycopeptide antibiotic, in phase III testing by Theravance for serious infections due to *S. aureus*

and other Gram-positive bacteria. This rapidly bactericidal, injectable antibiotic has multiple mechanisms of action, inhibiting formation of the bacterial cell wall and disrupting bacterial cell membrane integrity. Synergy between these mechanisms of action may improve bactericidal activity while lowering the risks of inducing resistance to telavancin or cross-resistance with other antibiotics.

InterMune is in phase III testing of oritavancin, a semi-synthetic glycopeptide antibiotic for the treatment of a broad range of gram-positive bacterial skin infections, including those resistant to most other glycopeptides. Unlike other glycopeptides, oritavancin is bactericidal rather than bacteriostatic. Oritavancin met the primary efficacy endpoint in two phase III trials for complicated SSTIs.

Another glycopeptide antibiotic is ramoplanin (glycolipodepsipeptide), in phase III development by Oscient Pharmaceuticals for the treatment of *Clostridium difficile*-associated diarrhea. This agent binds to lipid II intermediate, thereby inhibiting further steps of cell wall biosynthesis.

A distinct approach to treatment of diarrhea associated with *C. difficile* is tolevamer (GT-160246), in phase III testing by Genzyme. This non-antibiotic polymer therapy binds to *C. difficile* toxins A and B implicated in causing diarrhea.

Toyama Chemical/Schering Plough is in phase III development of Garenoxacin (T-3811; des-F(6)-quinolone), a novel quinolone synthetic antibacterial agent.

Yet another approach to bacterial infection is prevention rather than cure. Sanofi pasteur is in phase III development of Pentacel, a childhood vaccine designed to protect against diphtheria, tetanus, polio, Haemophilus influenzae type B and pertussis. Unlike the old vaccine, the new Pentacel vaccine has an improved pertussis component with fewer adverse effects but with the same or better protection from whooping cough. Common adverse effects of Pentacel are fever, irritability and local vaccination site reactions. Convulsions, shock or allergic reaction are very rare and typically transient.

Another vaccine is StaphVAX, in phase III testing by Nabi Biopharmaceuticals. This polysaccharide conjugate vaccine targets *S. aureus* types 5 and 8, which account for approximately 85% of *S. aureus* infections. StaphVAX is designed for patients at high risk of *S. aureus* infections who are able to produce their own antibodies in response to a vaccine. At approximately 200 sites across the U.S., a phase III, double-blind, placebo-controlled, randomized trial is ongoing in approximately 3,600 patients on hemodialysis for end-stage renal disease.

Other vaccines in the pipeline in phase II development include Holavax-typhoid, a live attenuated oral typhoid vaccine by Acambis; Antex Biologics' Activax, a multi-component vaccine to prevent diarrheal diseases caused by Shigella, Campylobacter and E. coli bacteria; CholeraGarde (Peru-15), a single dose, recombinant cholera vaccine by Avant Immunotherapeutics; rPA102, an alum-adjuvanted single-component anthrax vaccine based on recombinant protective antigen (rPA) by VaxGen; and ID Biomedical's product StreptAvax, a multivalent recombinant vaccine developed to cover 26 serotypes of group A streptococcus (GAS). The GAS infections include strep throat, impetigo, toxic shock syndrome, flesh-eating bacteria, boils and skin abscesses (pyoderma), scarlet fever and pneumonia.

An alternate pathway for prevention of Staph as well as Candida bacterial infections is antibody-based immunotherapy such as Veronate (INH-A21), in phase III testing by Inhibitex. This polyclonal immune globulin product contains concentrated amounts of antibodies targeting specific Microbial Surface Components Recognizing Adhesive Matrix Molecules (MSCRAMM) proteins found on the surface of staphylococci. The intended indication is for prevention of hospital-associated infections in very low birth weight (VLBW) infants.

Inhibitex is also in phase II development of Aurexis (tefibazumab), a humanized monoclonal antibody recognizing an MSCRAMM protein found on most strains of *S. aureus*. Aurexis is currently being tested as first-line therapy, in combination with standard antibiotics, for the treatment of serious *S. aureus* bloodstream infections in hospitalized patients.

Demegen has received Orphan Drug Designation for P113D, an antibacterial peptide derived from histatins found in human saliva, for treatment of infections associated with cystic fibrosis. P113D has shown activity against resistant bacterial isolates from patients with cystic fibrosis, and the peptide appears to be stable and to maintain its activity in sputum.

As pathogenic bacteria become increasingly resistant, treatment of infections may require a multipronged approach: use of antibiotics designed to overcome resistance, vaccination of high-risk patients, and immunotherapy alone or in combination with conventional antibiotics. However, clinicians must continue to regulate prescribing patterns to avoid overuse or misuse of antibiotics that can foster selection of resistant microbes.

Drug	Company	Additional Information
IND Filed		
Anthim (ETI-204)	Elusys (973) 808-0222 www.elusys.com	bispecific monoclonal antibody, targets the primary toxins produced by Bacillus anthracis
Phase I		
ABthrax (PA mAb)	Human Genome Sciences (301) 309-8504 www.hgsi.com	human monoclonal antibody to Bacillus anthracis protective antigen
PGCvax	ID Biomedical (604) 431-9314 www.idbiomedical.com	chimeric pneumococcal protein vaccine a fusion of the surface proteins BVH3 and BVH11
Parenteral Cephalosporin	Johnson & Johnson (732) 524-0400 www.jnj.com	cell wall synthesis inhibitor

Drug	Company	Additional Information
ETEC vaccine, oral	Microscience +44 (118) 944 3300 www.microscience.com	a vaccine expressing a gene from the ETEC bacterium
MP-601,205,	Mpex Pharmaceuticals (619) 594-3567 www.mpexbio.com	bacterial efflux pump inhibitor MP-601205
TAK-599 (PPI-0903)	Peninsula Pharmaceuticals (510) 747-3900 www.peninsulapharm.com	N-phosphono prodrug of the cephalosporin derivative T-91825

Phase II

CdVax (*C. difficile* vaccine)	Acambis (617) 761-4200 www.acambis.com	contains chemically inactivated A and B toxins to stimulate high-level antitoxin antibodies
Holavax-typhoid	Acambis (617) 761-4200 www.acambis.com	live attenuated oral typhoid vaccine
ACTIVAX	Antex Biologics (301) 590-0129 www.antexbiologics.com	multi-component vaccine to prevent diarrheal diseases caused by *Shigella, Campylobacter* and *E. coli* bacteria
CholeraGarde (Peru-15)	Avant Immunotherapeutics (781) 433-0771 www.avantimmune.com	single dose, recombinant cholera vaccine
BAL5788	Basilea Pharmaceutica +41 (61) 606 11 11 www.basileapharma.com	broad-spectrum cephalosporin antibiotic for the treatment of complicated skin and soft tissue infections
P113D	Demegen (412) 621-9625 www.demegen.com	antibacterial derived from histatins, found in human saliva
StreptAvax	ID Biomedical (604) 431-9314 www.idbiomedical.com	multivalent recombinant vaccine developed to cover 26 serotypes of group A *streptococcus*
Aurexis (tefibazumab)	Inhibitex (678) 746-1100 www.inhibitex.com	humanized monoclonal antibody that recognizes an MSCRAMM protein found on most strains of *S. aureus*
rPA102, anthrax	VaxGen (650) 624-1000 www.vaxgen.com	alum-adjuvanted single-component vaccine based on vaccine recombinant protective antigen (rPA)

Phase III

iclaprim (AR-100)	Arpida +41 (61) 417 96 60 www.arpida.com	diaminopyrimidine dihydrofolate reductase inhibitor
desquinolone (garenoxacin)	Schering-Plough (908) 298-4000 www.schering-plough.com	oral formulation of the des-F(6)-quinolone garenoxacin
tolevamer (GT-160246)	Genzyme (617) 252-7500 www.genzyme.com	non-antibiotic polymer therapy that binds to toxins that cause *Clostridium difficile*-associated diarrhea
Factive (gemifloxacin mesylate)	Oscient Pharmaceuticals www.oscient.com	broad spectrum fluoroquinolone, phase III in Europe

Drug	Company	Additional Information
oritavancin	InterMune (415) 466-2200 www.intermune.com	glycopeptide antibiotic being developed for the treatment of gram-positive bacterial skin infections
MBI 226	Migenix (604) 221-9666 www.mbiotech.com	from the company's Bactolysins category, antibiotic peptides for drug-resistant pathogens
ramoplanin	Oscient Pharmaceuticals (781) 398-2300 www.oscient.com	glycolipodepsipeptide, binds to lipid II intermediate with resulting inhibition of further steps of cell wall biosynthesis
doripenem (S-4661)	Peninsula Pharmaceuticals (510) 747-3900 www.peninsulapharm.com	synthetic, parenteral carbapenem antibiotic
Pentacel	Sanofi pasteur (570) 839-4267 www.sanofipasteur.com	a vaccine effective against diphtheria, tetanus, polio, Haemophilus influenzae type B and pertussis
telavancin (TD-6424)	Theravance (877) 275-8479 www.theravance.com	multivalent lipoglycopeptide antibiotic
Garenoxacin (T-3811)	Toyama Chemical/ Schering Plough +81-3-5381-3889 www.toyama-chemical.co.jp	des-F(6)-quinolone
StaphVAX	Nabi Biopharmaceuticals (561) 989-5800 www.nabi.com	polysaccharide conjugate vaccine
Veronate (INH-A21)	Inhibitex (678) 746-1100 www.inhibitex.com	antibody-based immunotherapy for prevention of Staph and Candida infections
Phase IIIb		
Merrem, Meronem (meropenem)	AstraZeneca (781) 839-4000 www.astrazeneca.com	carbapenem antibiotic in injectable formulation for bacterial pneumonia
Cipro (ciprofloxacin)	Bayer (412) 777-2000 www.bayer.com	fluoroquinolone antibiotic, for pediatric
Cubicin (daptomycin)	Cubist Pharmaceuticals (781) 860-8660 www.cubist.com	antibiotic lipopeptide, for urinary tract infections
NDA Submitted		
Ciprofloxacin GR	Depomed (650) 462-5900 www.depomedinc.com	gastric retention dosage form of ciprofloxacin
dalbavancin	Vicuron Pharmaceuticals (610) 205-2300 www.vicuron.com	second-generation glycopeptide agent
Tygacil (tigecycline, GAR-936)	Wyeth (484) 865-5000 www.wyeth.com	glycylcycline derivative of minocycline

Breast Cancer

By Laurie Barclay, M.D.
Published October 2005

Second only to skin cancer, breast cancer is the most common type of cancer in American women, and incidence has increased from one in 20 in 1960 to one in seven in 2005. Estimates of new cases of invasive breast cancer range from 180,000 to more than 210,000 each year, causing approximately 40,000 deaths.

Mortality is higher in African American than in white women.

Although breast cancer is rare in men, annual incidence is more than 1,000 men in the U.S., and the disease tends to be more aggressive and lethal in men than in women.

Risk factors for breast cancer include female sex, advancing age, heredity, early puberty, late childbearing, obesity, heavy alcohol use and smoking. Genetic screening is possible for BRCA1, BRCA2, and other genes increasing susceptibility, but 85% of women who develop breast cancer have no known family history.

Symptoms may include a new breast lump, localized breast swelling, skin irritation or dimpling over the lump, nipple pain or inversion, redness or scaliness of the nipple or breast skin, nipple discharge, and axillary lymph node swelling. Many asymptomatic breast cancers are detected by screening mammography. In addition to mammography, diagnostic procedures may include breast MRI or ultrasound, with definitive diagnosis made at biopsy, lumpectomy or mastectomy.

Treatment options include surgery, radiotherapy, traditional chemotherapy and hormonal therapy such as tamoxifen for hormone-receptor-positive tumors. Tamoxifen can reduce the risk of recurrence after surgery for ductal carcinoma in situ (DCIS) and early-stage invasive disease; it can arrest progression of metastatic disease; and it can reduce the risk of new breast cancer. Herceptin (trastuzumab) is an anti-HER2 protein antibody effective against HER2-positive breast cancer, and it is FDA-approved for metastatic disease.

CenterWatch has identified a pipeline of 27 drugs in various phases of development for breast cancer. Most target the immune system with vaccines or monoclonal antibodies, whereas others affect angiogenesis, hormone receptors or other processes vital to tumor growth.

Theratope (STn-KLH), in phase III testing by Biomira, is a synthetic Sialyl-Tn (STn) antigen vaccine designed to stimulate an immune response to the tumor-associated STn marker. In a large pivotal phase III trial of Theratope in 1,030 women with metastatic breast cancer, two predetermined statistical endpoints of time to disease progression and overall survival were not met, but women on hormonal treatment following chemotherapy had a favorable trend toward improved survival. Theratope appeared to elicit no safety concerns and was well tolerated by patients, with the most common side effects being flu-like symptoms and local injection site reactions.

Eli Lilly is in phase III testing of arzoxifene (LY353381) as a potential chemoprevention agent. This benzothiophene second-generation selective estrogen-receptor modulator (SERM) has strong antiestrogen activity in the breast but not in the uterus.

In a phase Ia trial, 50 women with newly diagnosed DCIS or T1/T2 invasive cancer were randomized to 0, 10, 20 or 50 mg of arzoxifene daily in the interval between biopsy and repeat surgery. In a phase Ib trial, 76 postmenopausal women were randomized to 20 mg of arzoxifene or placebo. Both trials showed increases in serum sex hormone binding globulin, decreases in insulin-like growth factor (IGF)-I and the IGF-I:IGF binding protein-3 ratio, and a nonsignificant decrease in estrogen receptor expression for arzoxifene versus placebo. Because of the favorable adverse effect profile and the observed changes in biomarkers, the investigators suggest that arzoxifene should be studied further as a preventive agent for breast cancer.

Another SERM is raloxifene, in phase III testing by Eli Lilly. Based on a prospective study in more than 5,000 women, long-term use of this drug appears to lower the risk of breast cancer. Compared with women given placebo, those given raloxifene for eight years had a 59% lower risk of developing invasive breast cancer. This lower risk was only for estrogen-receptor-positive breast cancers, and did not extend to estrogen-receptor-negative breast cancer or to DCIS. During the eight-year study, raloxifene was not associated with increased uterine bleeding or uterine cancer, but rate of thrombosis was twice as high as in the placebo group.

Genentech is in phase III development of Avastin (bevacizumab, R-435), a recombinant humanized antibody to vascular endothelial growth factor (VEGF). Inhibition of VEGF reduces angiogenesis, choking off blood vessels supplying the tumor. Although the FDA has already approved Avastin in combination with intravenous 5-fluorouracil-based chemotherapy for first-line treatment of metastatic colorectal cancer, Genentech is now preparing to file a supplemental Biologics License Application for the use of Avastin as treatment of first-line metastatic breast cancer.

Another angiogenesis inhibitor is Panzem (2-methoxyestradiol), in phase I development by EntreMed. This multifaceted compound also disrupts microtubule formation needed for cell division, downregulates the survival protein hypoxia inducible factor one-alpha (HIF-1a,a), and induces apoptosis, or cell death.

Lapatinib (GW 572016), in phase III testing by GlaxoSmithKline, is a dual tyrosine kinase inhibitor (TKI) directed against epidermal growth factor receptor (EGFR) and ErbB-2 (Her2/neu). Tyrosine kinases, which function as vital regulators of cellular signal transduction, and therefore of cell proliferation, metabolism, survival and apoptosis, may be activated in various cancer cells to promote tumor growth and progression. Lapatinib appears to prevent progression in some patients with metastatic, treatment-refractory breast cancer. By targeting both the EGFR and Her2/neu receptor, dual TKIs such as lapatinib may reduce drug resistance resulting from treatment with trastuzumab or other single receptor inhibitors.

In a phase II trial of women with breast cancer that progressed on trastuzumab-containing regimens, 46% of the 41 patients studied had either a partial response or stable disease at eight weeks, and 24% were still progression-free at 16 weeks. Once daily oral lapatinib was generally well tolerated, with the most common side effects being rash, fatigue and diarrhea.

Neuvenge (APC-8024), a vaccine in phase II testing by Dendreon, is designed to elicit an antibody response against tumor cells over-expressing HER-2/neu. Using an Antigen Delivery Cassette technology, Neuvenge delivers small fragments of the HER-2/neu protein to specialized immune cells known as antigen-presenting cells (APCs). The APCs then activate other immune cells to attack cancer cells containing HER-2/neu.

Another vaccine specific for HER-2/neu is AE37, a li-key/MHC class II epitope hybrid peptide in phase I testing by Generex Biotechnology. AE37 consists of a small piece of the HER-2/neu protein attached to a fragment of the MHC class II-associated invariant chain (li protein), which greatly increases stimulation of T helper cells.

Wyeth is conducting phase III testing of temsirolimus (CCI-779), a derivative of rapamycin with antifungal, immunosuppressant and antitumor activities. In a trial of 109 women with stage IIIb or IV breast cancer refractory to chemotherapy, who were randomized to 75 mg or 250 mg temsirolimus once weekly for six months, 9% had a partial response. Adverse effects included mucositis, low white blood cell levels, high blood sugar, somnolence, thrombocytopenia and depression.

Tesmilifene is an intracellular histamine antagonist, in phase III testing by YM Biosciences. An ongoing multicenter trial in 700 women with metastatic breast cancer is comparing overall survival for the combination of tesmilifene, epirubicin and cyclophosphamide versus that with epirubicin and cyclophosphamide alone. In an earlier trial in 305 patients, overall survival with tesmilifene plus anthracycline was increased by more than 50% compared with anthracycline alone.

ADVENTRX Pharmaceuticals is in phase II development of CoFactor (ANX-510; 5,10-methylenetetrahydrofolate), a novel folate inhibiting thymidylate synthase and modulating 5-fluorouracil (5-FU). This drug stimulates DNA synthesis and 5-FU entry into cancer cells, leading to irreversible inhibition of thymidylate synthase and cancer cell death. In phase I/II Swedish trials, CoFactor was associated with fewer side effects than 5-FU alone or with leucovorin, and with improved survival in breast cancer patients. Among patients with treatment-refractory advanced disease who were switched to CoFactor with 5-FU, 63% showed stabilization or response to therapy.

The antisense drug Oncomyc-NG (AVI-4126), in phase II testing by AVI BioPharma, uses a cellular transcription factor to target c-myc, an oncogene involved in cell proliferation. Preclinical studies have shown favorable preclinical anti-cancer activity with essentially no toxicity, and a phase I/II study is evaluating the ability of Oncomyc-NG's ability to accumulate within tumors.

Cell Therapeutics and Chugai are in phase II development of XYOTAX (paclitaxel poliglumex, CT-2103), an intravenously administered poly-(L-glutamic acid)-conjugate of paclitaxel. Coupling paclitaxel to the biodegradable, water soluble polyglutamate protein polymer allows this chemotherapeutic taxane to be more selectively delivered to tumors, with potentially higher efficacy and lower toxicity.

Telcyta (TLK286), a phase II Telik product, is an alkylating agent prodrug activated by glutathione S-transferase P1-1 (GST P1-1), an enzyme overexpressed in many cancer cells. In preclinical studies, GST P1-1 splits Telcyta into a glutathione analog fragment, and a cytotoxic fragment that reacts with RNA, DNA and proteins, causing cell death. Because the glutathione analog fragment remains bound to GST P1-1, this limits inactivation of other cancer drugs by GST P1-1. Preclinical studies also demonstrate synergy of Telcyta with platinum, taxane and anthracycline chemotherapeutic agents.

The available standard of care for pharmacologic therapy of breast cancer forms a solid basis from which to begin treatment. Investigational drugs enhancing immune system activity or interfering with tumor cell biology may further enhance survival and improve response rates in refractory patients.

Drug	Company	Additional Information
Phase I		
AN-152	AEterna Zentaris (418) 652-8525 www.aeternazentaris.com	a formulation of doxorubicin linked to luteinizing hormone releasing hormone (LHRH), Germany
ONCase (AC-930, methioninase)	Anticancer (858) 654-2555 www.anticancer.com	an enzyme therapeutic
Her-2/neu vaccine	Corixa/GSK (206) 754-5711 www.corixa.com	a peptide vaccine based on the Her-2/neu antigen
AE37	Generex Biotechnology (416) 364-2551 www.generex.com	a Ii-key/MHC class II epitope hybrid peptide immunomodulator vaccine specific for HER-2/neu

Drug	Company	Additional Information
Panzem (2-methoxyestradiol)	EntreMed (240) 864-2600 www.entremed.com	an angiogenesis inhibitor
R-1550 (formerly Therex)	Roche/Antisoma +41-61-688 1111 www.roche.com	a humanized monoclonal antibody based on HMFG1
Phase II		
CoFactor (ANX-510)	ADVENTRX Pharmaceuticals (858) 271-9671 www.adventrx.com	a thymidylate synthase inhibitor and modulator of 5-fluorouracil
batabulin T-67	Amgen (805) 447-1000 www.amgen.com	a pentafluorobenzene sulfonamide tubulin polymerization inhibitor
Oncomyc-NG (AVI-4126)	AVI BioPharma (503) 227-0554 www.avibio.com	antisense drug that specifically targets c-myc
XYOTAX (paclitaxel poliglumex, CT-2103)	Cell Therapeutics/Chugai (206) 282-7100 www.cticseattle.com	an iv poly-(L-glutamic acid)-conjugate of paclitaxel
Seliciclib (R-roscovitine, CYC-202)	Cyclacel Limited +44 1382 206 062 www.cyclacel.com	an inhibitor of CDK2/cyclinE activity that induces apoptosis in cancer cells
Neuvenge (APC-8024)	Dendreon (206) 256-4545 www.dendreon.com	designed to elicit an antibody response to attack tumor cells which over-express HER-2/neu
epothilone	Kosan/Roche (510) 732-8400 www.kosan.com	a microtubule-stabilizing agent obtained from the fermentation of cellulose degrading myxobacteria
Advexin (INGN 201)	Introgen Therapeutics (512) 708-9310 www.introgen.com	an adenoviral p53 tumor suppressor gene therapy product
Targretin (bexarotene)	Ligand Pharmaceuticals (858) 550-7500 www.ligand.com	capsule formulation of the retinoid X receptor (RXR)-selective retinoid bexarotene
GTI-2040	Lorus Therapeutics (416) 798-1200 www.lorusthera.com	targets R2 ribonucleotide reductase mRNA
Irofulven (MGI-114)	MGI Pharma (952) 346-4700 www.mgipharma.com	an acylfulvene derived from mushroom toxins
Lutrin (motexafin lutetium)	Pharmacyclics (408) 774-0330 www.pharmacyclics.com	a photosensitizer that belongs to a class of drugs called texaphyrins
Telcyta (TLK286)	Telik (650) 845-7700 www.telik.com	an alkylating agent prodrug activated by cancer cell enzyme GST P1-1
Tariquidar (XR9576)	QLT/Xenova (604) 707-7000 www.qltinc.com	designed to overcome multi-drug resistance caused by P-glycoprotein

Drug	Company	Additional Information
Phase III		
Theratope (STn-KLH)	Biomira (780) 450-3761 www.biomira.com	a synthetic Sialyl-Tn antigen vaccine
Arzoxifene LY353381	Eli Lilly (317) 276-2000 www.lilly.com	benzothiophene second-generation selective estrogen-receptor modulator (SERM)
raloxifene LY-139481	Eli Lilly (317) 276-2000 www.lilly.com	a selective estrogen receptor modulator
Avastin (bevacizumab, R-435)	Genentech (650) 225-1000 www.gene.com	a humanized antibody to vascular endothelial growth factor (VEGF)
lapatinib (GW 572016)	GlaxoSmithKline (888) 825-5249 www.gsk.com	an ErbB2 and EGFR dual tyrosine kinase inhibitor
Temsirolimus (CCI-779)	Wyeth (484) 865-5000 www.wyeth.com	a derivative of rapamycin, exhibits antifungal, immunosuppressant and antitumor activities
tesmilifene	YM Biosciences (905) 629-9761 www.ymbiosciences.com	an intracellular histamine antagonist

Gastroesophageal Reflux Disease (GERD)

By Laurie Barclay, M.D.
Published April 2005

astroesophageal reflux disease (GERD) refers to heartburn and sometimes other symptoms associated with backflow of gastric acid from the stomach into the esophagus. Approximately 5% to 7% of the total population experiences heartburn, or burning beneath the breastbone, at least once daily, and nearly 20% have this symptom at least weekly. Other symptoms may include acid regurgitation, belching, chronic sore throat or throat irritation, laryngitis, gum inflammation, erosion of tooth enamel, bad breath and hoarseness in the morning.

The mechanism underlying GERD is inappropriate relaxation of the lower esophageal sphincter (LES), a band of muscles at the junction of the stomach and esophagus. Normally the LES and diaphragm prevent reflux of stomach contents into the esophagus. In addition to causing heartburn and other symptoms, acid reflux may damage the esophageal lining, causing esophagitis or erosive GERD.

Chronic erosive GERD may result in stricture (narrowing) of the esophagus or a potentially precancerous condition known as Barrett's esophagus, in which specialized intestinal metaplasia replaces the normal esophageal lining. About 10% of individuals with GERD develop Barrett's esophagus, and approximately 1% of those develop esophageal cancer. Risk factors for Barrett's esophagus include severity and frequency of GERD symptoms, presence of heartburn or reflux for more than five to 10 years, age over 50 years, and

being a white male. Endoscopic screening every two or three years is recommended for patients with Barrett's esophagus.

Diagnosis is usually based on relief of symptoms after a two-week trial of a proton pump inhibitor (PPI) that inhibits gastric acid secretion, because confirmatory pH monitoring in the esophagus is perceived by many as overly invasive.

Treatment goals are symptom relief and maintenance of remission, esophageal healing and prevention or management of Barrett's esophagus or stricture. Although there is no cure for chronic reflux and it does not resolve spontaneously, long-term pharmacological therapy with promotility agents, H2 blockers, or PPIs is usually effective. Lifestyle modifications may be somewhat helpful, and surgery is seldom required. Endoscopic procedures are also available but are less well studied than surgery and pharmacotherapy.

Promotility drugs can help relieve symptoms of non-erosive GERD. However, adverse effects and drug interactions associated with cisapride (Propulsid) led Janssen Pharmaceutica to stop marketing Propulsid in the U.S. as of July 14, 2000.

Currently available H2 blockers, which lower gastric acid secretion, relieve symptoms and permit esophageal healing in approximately half of patients, but lead to sustained remission in only about one-quarter of patients.

Available PPIs reduce gastric acid secretion through their effect on H+, K+-ATPase, and they may be helpful in managing stricture. Compared with H2 blockers, they are more effective, allowing rapid symptom resolution and esophageal healing in 80% to 90% of patients.

Because GERD is a chronic condition often requiring long-term or even lifelong therapy, safety and tolerability of pharmacotherapy are important considerations. Potential areas of improvement in pharmacotherapy include faster onset of complete acid inhibition and improved duration of efficacy.

CenterWatch has identified a pipeline of 12 drugs in various phases of development for GERD, including drugs that limit transient LES relaxation, serotonergic agents acting as prokinetics, potassium-competitive acid blockers, mucosal protectants, histamine H3 agonists and anti-gastrin agents.

Santarus is in phase III development of the PPI SAN-15 (Zegerid, Rapinex) a formulation of omeprazole as 20 mg chewable tablets and oral capsules. In 2004, Santarus received Food and Drug Administration (FDA) approval of Zegerid powder for oral suspension, an immediate-release formulation allowing rapid absorption into the bloodstream and sustained acid control.

Omeprazole is a potent inhibitor of gastric acid secretion, with a good safety profile and the convenience of once-a-day dosing. In powder form, Zegerid reaches peak plasma levels in approximately 30 minutes, maintaining a median 24-hour stomach pH of greater than 4 for 18.6 hours. Zegerid is effective for heartburn and other GERD symptoms, and for short-term treatment (four to eight weeks) of erosive esophagitis diagnosed on endoscopy. It appears to maintain healing of erosive esophagitis, but follow-up in controlled studies is limited to 12 months.

Adverse events of Zegerid may include headache, diarrhea and abdominal pain. In patients receiving long-term omeprazole treatment, stomach biopsies have occasionally revealed atrophic gastritis. Because Zegerid contains 460 mg sodium per dose as sodium bicarbonate, caution is warranted in patients on a sodium-restricted diet, and it is contraindicated in patients with metabolic alkalosis and hypocalcemia.

Prevacid (Takepron, lansoprazole, AG 1749) is another PPI, in phase III development by TAP Pharmaceuticals in Japan for a new indication. Prevacid is indicated for the short-term treatment of heartburn and other GERD symptoms. In ero-sive esophagitis, it is indicated for short-term (up to eight weeks) healing, symptom relief and maintenance. Controlled studies for maintenance have been limited to 12 months; those for healing to eight weeks; and those for risk reduction of recurrence to twelve weeks.

As with omeprazole and other PPIs, symptom relief with Prevacid does not preclude the presence of serious stomach problems. Adverse events include diarrhea in 3.8%, abdominal pain in 2.1%, and nausea in 1.3%.

ARYx Therapeutics is in phase I development of ATI-7505, an analog of cisapride (Propulsid) acting as an acetylcholine release stimulator. This drug is being tested in diabetic gastroparesis as well as GERD. Unlike the originally marketed version of cisapride, this product is said to have prokinetic activity with no metabolic or cardiac liabilities.

Sankyo/Novartis is in phase II testing of S-526 (R-105266, AKU-517), an orally administered, reversible acid-pump antagonist (APA). In comparison with existing antacid therapies, potential advantages of this drug may include more rapid acid reduction and longer duration of action, allowing faster symptom relief and ulcer healing. Soraprazan (B9106-086, BYK-359) is another APA, in phase II development by Altana AG. The first two phase IIa trials offered evidence supporting proof of concept and tolerability.

By selectively targeting the serotonin 5-HT receptor, mosapride citrate (TAK-370), in phase II development by Takeda Chemical Industries, enhances gastrointestinal motility. Mosapride is said to be the world's first selective serotonin 5-HT4 receptor agonist to stimulate gastrointestinal propulsion. In October 1998, Dainippon first launched this drug in Japan to reduce heartburn, nausea, vomiting and other symptoms associated with chronic gastritis. It was then licensed out to Daewoong Pharmaceutical Co., Ltd. of South Korea in April 1999, and was subsequently developed by Takeda.

A different approach to reducing acid secretion is a vaccine directed at the growth hormone gastrin, such as Insegia (G17DT, Gastrimmune), in phase II development by Aphton.

Gastrin is a key hormone in the embryological development of the gastrointestinal system.

Although most gastrin receptors and gastrin itself are inactive in the mature gastrointestinal system, the hormone and its receptors remain active in the stomach. Insegia is an immunogen that enlists the immune system to generate high levels of antibodies to gastrin and the gastrin receptor. Because some cancers also express gastrin receptors, this drug is also being tested in pancreatic cancer and in combination with chemotherapy in gastric cancer.

Other hormonal receptors of potential utility as targets for GERD treatment are cholecystokinin (CCK) receptors. Rottapharm is in phase I testing of itriglumide (CR 2945), a CCK-B (CCK2) antagonist that reduces stomach secretions and is therefore being developed in gastric ulcer disease as well as GERD. Rottapharm has not yet submitted an

IND application for dexloxiglumide (CR 2017), a CCK-A (CCK-1) antagonist acting as a prokinetic and digestive antispasmodic of potential value in GERD, irritable bowel syndrome and chronic constipation.

Thanks to several different pathways regulating LES control and acid secretion, drugs targeting GERD can have several different mechanisms of action. Given the need for chronic and even long-term treatment, prolonged follow-up for safety and tolerability are just as important as demonstrated efficacy in reducing acid reflux and its complications. Other key considerations are rapidity of onset and the ability to maintain remission of symptoms and of esophageal healing for long periods.

Drug	Company	Additional Information
Pre-IND		
dexloxiglumide, (CR 2017)	Rottapharm/ Forest Laboratories +39-039-7390-1 www.rotta.com	CCKA antagonists target receptors in the gastrointestinal system
Phase I		
ATI-7505	ARYx Therapeutics (408) 869-2761 www.aryx.com	an analog of cisapride (Propulsid), an acetylcholine release stimulator
AZD 3355	AstraZeneca (781) 839-4000 www.astrazeneca.com	a GABA B agonist and inhibitor of transient lower sphincter relaxations
itriglumide (CR 2945)	Rottapharm +39-039-7390-1 www.rotta.com	CCK-B (CCK2) antagonist
Phase II		
Soraprazan (B9106-086; BYK-359)	Altana AG +49 (0)7531/ 84-0 www.altana.de	an acid pump antagonist (APA)
Insegia (G17DT, Gastrimmune)	Aphton (305) 374-7338 www.aphton.com	An anti-gastrin vaccine, which neutralizes G17 to treat GERD and gastrointestinal ulcerations.
DWP-301	Daewoong Pharmaceutical 82-2-550-8800 www.daewoong.com	potential antacid (South Korea)
mosapride citrate (TAK-370)	Takeda Chemical Industries (847) 383-3000 www.takedapharm.com	enhances gastrointestinal motility by acting on the serotonin 5-HT receptor selectively
CS-526 (R-105266; AKU-517)	Sankyo/Novartis +81 3-5255-7111 www.sankyo.co.jp	oral acid pump antagonist

Drug	Company	Additional Information
Z-360	Zeria Pharmaceutical (03)3663-2351 www.zeria.co.jp	orally available CCK B receptor (gastrin receptor)
Phase III		
SAN-15 (Rapinex, Zegerid)	Santarus (858) 314-5700 www.santarus.com	20 mg chewable tablets and oral capsules of omeprazole
Prevacid, Takepron (lansoprazole, AG 1749)	TAP Pharmaceuticals (847) 582-2000 www.tap.com	proton pump inhibitor (phase III in Japan for new indication)

Multiple Sclerosis (MS)

By Laurie Barclay, M.D.
Published May 2005

Multiple sclerosis (MS) is a chronic, inflammatory demyelinating disease of the central nervous system. Damage to the myelin sheath, which coats nerve fibers, interferes with their ability to transmit impulses to each other and to other parts of the body, causing problems with muscle control, coordination, walking, vision, balance, sensation, thinking, and bowel and bladder function.

MS is the most common, non-traumatic, neurological disease in young adults, affecting approximately 400,000 Americans and two million people worldwide. Age of onset is typically between 20 and 40 years, and women are more likely to be affected than men. The relapsing-remitting form of MS, characterized by flares interspersed with symptom-free periods for up to 10 years, accounts for about 90% of cases. The remaining 10% are primary progressive, meaning that neurologic impairment and disability continue to worsen. Even in relapsing-remitting MS, however, the exacerbations may not clear completely, and each relapse tends to increase the patient's residual level of disability.

About 70% of people with MS are still able to work five years after the onset of symptoms. Complications may include urinary infections, pneumonia, malnutrition because of swallowing impairment, depression, and dementia in the late stages.

Although the exact cause of MS is unknown, it is thought to be an autoimmune disease, possibly triggered by viral infections, genetic factors, and/or other environmental factors such as climate.

Diagnosis is usually by clinical history of dissemination in time (two or more episodes of neurological symptoms) and in space (involvement of more than one part of the central nervous system). Other tests that may be helpful include magnetic resonance imaging (MRI) showing characteristic white matter lesions, cerebrospinal fluid analysis for protein and anti-myelin antibodies, and visual and other evoked potential testing.

Although there is no cure for MS, disease-modifying drugs affect the course of the disease, helping to reduce relapses. These include steroids such as prednisolone, interferon beta-1a (Avonex or Rebif), interferon beta-1b (Betaferon), and glatiramer acetate (Copaxone). Long-term complications of steroids may include gastrointestinal bleeding, immunosuppression and psychosis. Adverse effects of the interferons may include pain at the injection site, flu-like symptoms, diarrhea and insomnia, whereas glatiramer acetate may cause side effects such as flushing and breathlessness after injection.

Drugs that control symptoms include muscle relaxants for spasms, and specific treatments for incontinence, constipation and sexual dysfunction. Physiotherapy, exercise, and attention to diet and lifestyle also play a role in management.

CenterWatch has identified a pipeline of 17 drugs in various phases of development for MS. These include interferons and other immune system modulators, as well as a few drugs aimed at symptomatic relief.

GW Pharmaceuticals has submitted a new drug application (NDA) in the U.K. and Canada for Sativex (GW-1000, Tetranabinex), but queries from U.K. regulators have repeatedly delayed approval. This whole plant medicinal cannabis extract is administered via oral spray to target MS symptoms such as pain and spasm. The Cannabinoids in Multiple Sclerosis Research (CAMS) group compared cannabinoid treatment over 15 and 52 weeks in patients with MS, and long-term data released in September 2004 suggest that chronic use of cannabinoids is more effective in relieving MS symptoms than short-term use.

Although cannabis is illegal, estimates suggest that about 10% to 30% of MS patients in Europe smoke cannabis to relieve symptoms. Sativex contains tetranabinex (THC) and nabidiolex (cannabidiol; CBD), but to avoid intoxication, it does not contain the active substance found in recreational cannabis. Phase III placebo-controlled trials in about 350 patients with MS suggest that Sativex sublingual spray is safe and effective, with improvement in spasticity compared with placebo ($P < .05$).

In collaboration with Serono, IVAX is in phase III development of Mylinax (cladribine), an orally administered adenosine deaminase inhibitor. This purine nucleoside analogue interferes with activity and proliferation of lymphocytes involved in the immunological basis of MS. A two-year, double-blind, placebo-controlled study enrolling more than 1,200 patients with relapsing forms of MS is now underway. Endpoints in this multicenter, international study will include assessments of relapses, progression of disability, and serial MRI scans. Earlier trials using a parenteral formulation of cladribine suggested clinical benefits and reduction in new MRI lesions.

BioMS Medical is in phase II/III testing of MBP8298, a synthetic Myelin Basic Protein (MBP) peptide that reduces production of MBP-antibody by B lymphocytes. It consists of 17 amino acids linked in a sequence identical to that of a portion of human myelin basic protein (MBP). This sequence is the point of attack in MS patients with HLA haplotypes DR-2 or DR-4, which account for 65% to 75% of all MS patients. When administered in high doses intravenously, MBP8298 appears to induce or restore tolerance to ongoing immune attack at this specific molecular site. A phase II clinical trial showed statistically significant clinical benefit in patients with HLA haplotypes DR-2 or DR-4.

Rituximab, in phase II/III development by Genentech, is a monoclonal antibody that binds to the CD20 antigen on the surface of normal and malignant B lymphocytes. In a recent study in the Archives of Neurology (2005;62:258-264), four patients with primary progressive MS received rituximab and underwent analysis of cerebrospinal fluid (CSF) and peripheral blood. Rituximab temporarily suppressed the activation state of B cells in CSF, but the B cells in CSF were not depleted to the extent that B cells were depleted in peripheral blood. Furthermore, the remaining B cells multiplied after rituximab treatment.

Antisense Therapeutics is in phase IIa testing of ATL1102, a second generation antisense inhibitor targeting production of Very Late Antigen-4 (VLA-4), a receptor on the surface of lymphocytes. VLA4 mediates adhesion of immune cells to blood vessel walls and subsequent migration of lymphocytes into the tissue, which is a pivotal event in inflammatory diseases. In MS, excessive amounts of VLA4 are thought to allow the inappropriate entry of lymphocytes into the central nervous system. In earlier studies, blocking VLA4 has reportedly been associated with a reduction of new MRI lesions in patients with MS.

In August 2003, Antisense Therapeutics began phase I testing of ATL1102 in 54 healthy volunteers. This double-blind, dose-escalation, placebo-controlled, randomized study suggested that 6mg/kg/week of ATL1102 appeared to be well tolerated and would be an appropriate dose for phase II development. Trials were temporarily suspended pending a TYSABRI safety issue. However, in December 2004, Antisense announced their intention to conduct a phase IIa, multicenter, double-blinded trial of ATL1102 in approximately 60 patients with relapsing-remitting MS. These subjects are to be randomized to receive subcutaneous ATL1102 twice weekly at a dose of 400 mg per week, or placebo, over eight weeks, and efficacy is to be evaluated with monthly MRI.

Alferon N, or interferon alfa-n3, is in phase IIa testing by Hemispherx Biopharma. This form of interferon is derived from human leukocytes and contains at least 14 alpha interferon molecules. In a retrospective, uncontrolled study, brain MRI with gadolinium contrast enhancement was performed in 69 patients treated with MS, including 38 who declined treatment with interferon alfa-n3, and 31 who were treated with subcutaneous interferon alfa-n3 for three to six months. MRI revealed gadolinium enhanced lesions in two of 31 patients (6%) treated with interferon alfa-n3, and in 14 of 38 patients (37%) in the untreated group. During a mean follow-up of 11 months, mean Expanded Disability Status Scale (EDSS) score decreased in the interferon alfa-n3 treated group from 4.8 to 3.4, reflecting less disability, but mean score in the untreated group increased from 3.8 to 4.5. However, prospective, controlled trials are needed to obtain regulatory approval.

Acorda Therapeutics has completed phase II testing of Fampridine SR, an oral, sustained-release tablet formulation of 4-aminopyridine (4-AP), which is a potassium channel blocker enhancing conduction in damaged nerves. In the laboratory, Fampridine has improved impulse conduction in demyelinated nerve fibers. In phase II clinical trials in MS, treatment with Fampridine-SR has been associated with faster walking and improved leg strength on standard neurological assessments. Most of the adverse effects, including insomnia, paresthesias (numbness/tingling), dizziness and nausea, were rated as mild to moderate. At higher doses than those used in the most recent trials, a few patients had seizures.

Active Biotech/Teva Pharmaceutical has completed phase II development of the oral immunomodulatory agent laquinimod (SAIK-MS). In a phase II study in MS, 24 weeks of treatment with laquinimod was associated with a statistically significant 28% to 44% reduction in new brain MRI lesions, and a very favorable safety profile. Patients with active disease when beginning treatment had a 52% decrease in new lesions.

ABT-874, a fully human anti-interleukin-12 (IL-12) monoclonal antibody, is a protein mediating inflammatory response and present in MS lesions. Abbott Laboratories has begun a Phase II, randomized trial in North America and Europe to evaluate the efficacy of ABT-874 in reducing MS brain lesions. The 48-week study will consist of a 24-week, placebo-controlled phase followed by a 24-week active open-label extension.

Genzyme is in phase II testing of CAMPATH-1H (alemtuzumab), a lymphocyte-depleting humanized monoclonal antibody targeting CD52, and thereby killing T cells thought to initiate the pathological processes underlying MS. In 27 patients with secondary progressive MS (SPMS), CAMPATH-1H treatment was associated with no new MRI lesions for at least eighteen months. Although 14 of these patients had stable disease during that time, the remaining 13 had continued worsening of MS symptoms despite the absence of new MRI lesions. The latter group had the greatest amount of existing lesions and brain atrophy at baseline, leading the investigators to conclude that CAMPATH-1H therapy is more effective if given early in the course of MS. A new clinical trial in 180 patients with early relapsing-remitting MS will compare low- and high-dose CAMPATH-1H with high-dose Rebif. Preliminary findings are anticipated in 2006.

Surprisingly, CAMPATH-1H appears to be reasonably well tolerated even though it destroys T cells. In studies thus far, there have been few serious infections and no deaths. However, one third of subjects developed Graves disease, an autoimmune form of thyroid disease relatively easily managed with thyroid supplements. Another drawback is that most study subjects reported a transient worsening of symptoms immediately following the first CAMPATH-1H injection.

Also in phase II testing is NeuroVax (IR208), a synthetic T-cell receptor (TCR) peptide vaccine developed by Immune Response Corporation. In a multicenter, three-arm, randomized 24-week trial enrolling 60 subjects, 94% of patients treated with NeuroVax had a statistically significant, peptide-specific immune response compared with those receiving three peptides in saline (7%) or adjuvant alone (0%). NeuroVax was well tolerated with no serious adverse effects.

Pirfenidone, in phase II development by InterMune, is an inhibitor of Tumor Necrosis Factor-alpha (TNF-alpha). In an open-label, two-year study in 20 patients with chronic progressive MS, three patients dropped out early because of gastrointestinal adverse reactions, and another three patients dropped out for personal reasons after one year. However, the remaining 14 patients completed the study and did not report any other drug-related adverse reactions or complications. Most patients had improvement or stabilization at about three months, which was sustained at six, 12 and 24 months, and MRI did not reveal any new lesions.

Zenapax (daclizumab), manufactured by Protein Design Labs, is an intravenously administered immunosuppressive monoclonal antibody targeting the alpha chain of the human interleukin-2 (IL-2) receptor. A phase II trial sponsored by the National Institute of Neurological Disorders and Stroke is currently recruiting patients with relapsing-remitting MS. By blocking the activity of IL-2, Zenapax interferes with the growth of T lymphocytes that damage myelin.

Recent advances in molecular biology and genetics have paid dividends for research in MS therapeutics. By targeting specific pathways thought to be involved in myelin destruction, one or more of these agents may ultimately prove to be a "silver bullet" reducing or preventing relapses while maintaining a reasonably good safety and tolerability profile. For the agents in earlier phases of development, only time will tell to what extent these disease-modifying drugs may accomplish these goals.

Drug	Company	Additional Information
Phase I		
interferon beta (intranasal)	Nastech Pharmaceutical (425) 908-3600 www.nastech.com	intranasal formulation of interferon beta
Phase Ia		
REN-850	Renovis (650) 266-1400 www.renovis.com	oral leukocyte traffic inhibitor and chemokine-receptor-driven cell migration modulator
Phase II		
ABT-874	Abbott Laboratories (847) 937-6100 www.abbott.com	monoclonal interleukin -12 (IL-12) antibody
alemtuzumab (CAMPATH)	Genzyme (210) 949-8230 www.genzyme.com	lymphocyte-depleting humanized monoclonal antibody against CD52
NeuroVax (IR208)	Immune Response Corporation (760) 431-7080 www.imnr.com	synthetic T-cell receptor (TCR) peptide vaccine
pirfenidone	InterMune (415) 466-2200 www.intermune.com	TNF-alpha inhibitor
tiplimotide	Neurocrine Biosciences (858) 658-7600 www.neurocrine.com	vaccine designed from an immunodominant region of the neuroantigen myelin basic protein (MBP)
Zenapax daclizumab	Protein Design Labs (510) 574-1400 www.pdl.com	immunosuppressive monoclonal antibody that targets the alpha chain of the human IL-2 receptor
EMZ-701, interferon enhancing therapy	Transition Therapeutics (416) 260-7770 www.transitiontherapeutics.com	interferon enhancing combination product (Canada)

Drug	Company	Additional Information
Phase II Completed		
Fampridine SR, 4-aminopyridine (4-AP)	Acorda Therapeutics www.acorda.com	4-aminopyridine potassium channel blocker that enhances conduction in damaged nerves
laquinimod, SAIK-MS	Active Biotech/ Teva Pharmaceutical +46 46 19 20 00 www.activebiotech.com	SAIK-MS immunomodulatory, controls and regulates the immune system
Phase IIa		
ATL1102	Antisense Therapeutics + 61 3 9827 8999 www.antisense.com.au	antisense inhibitor of VLA-4 (Very Late Antigen-4), a receptor on the surface of lymphocytes (Trials temporarily suspended pending TYSABRI safety issue)
Alferon N (interferon alfa-n3)	Hemispherx Biopharma (215) 988-0080 www.hemispherx.net	derived from human leukocytes and contains at least 14 alpha interferon molecules
Phase II/III		
MBP8298	BioMS Medical (780) 413-7152 www.biomsmedical.com	synthetic Myelin Basic Protein (MBP) peptide, reduces B cell MBP-antibody production
rituximab	Genentech (650) 225-1000 www.gene.com	binds to the CD20 antigen on the surface of normal and malignant B cells
Phase III		
Mylinax (cladribine)	IVAX/Serono (305) 575-6000 www.ivax.com	adenosine deaminase inhibitor
NDA Submitted		
Sativex (GW-1000, Tetranabinex)	GW Pharmaceuticals 01 980-557 000 www.gwpharm.com	whole plant medicinal cannabis extract containing tetrahydrocannabinol and cannabidiol (UK/Canada)

Obesity

By Laurie Barclay, M.D.
Published November 2005

Obesity affects more than 20% of adults in developed countries, and at least half of adults in developed countries are overweight. However, obesity is no longer exclusively the provenance of the Western world, but rather has become a global problem adversely affecting health worldwide. More than 1 billion people are overweight, defined as a body mass index (BMI; weight in kilograms divided by the square of the height in meters) greater than 25 kg/m2. More than 300 million are clinically obese (BMI >30 kg/m2), according to the World Health Organization.

In some countries, obesity has more than tripled over the past 25 years, resulting from increased intake of food high in calories, sugar and saturated fats, coupled with reduced physical activity. The health burden associated with obesity is significant, because it increases overall morbidity and mortality as well as the risk of cardiovascular disease, type 2 diabetes, hypertension, stroke, osteoarthritis and certain cancers. In developed countries, between 2% and 7% of healthcare dollars are allocated to obesity and related complications.

Attention to diet and lifestyle factors are the first step and may be the mainstay of treatment, but unfortunately, these are often ineffective. The U.S. Food and Drug Administration (FDA) has thus far approved only two prescription drugs (Sibutramine and Orlistat) for long-term obesity treatment. Adverse effect profile and need for daily administration limit the use of these drugs.

Furthermore, their efficacy is modest, with weight loss of 5%-10% from baseline in fewer than 50% of treated patients.

Other anti-obesity drugs initially showing promise, such as Xenical, Meridia and phentermine, have proven to have a poor safety profile exceeding their limited benefits. Although fenfluramine and dexfenfluramine were effective as appetite suppressants, reports of valvular heart disease and pulmonary hypertension led to their withdrawal from the market in 1997.

In selected patients, gastric bypass surgery to remove or bypass part of the stomach may result in 35%-40% loss of body weight, with long-term maintenance of weight loss. However, gastric bypass surgery is a treatment of last resort because of high risks including 0.5%-1% morbidity related to surgical and post-operative complications. It is therefore contraindicated in all but the morbidly obese (BMI > 38 kg/m2).

New, effective treatments well tolerated over the long-term are therefore desperately needed. CenterWatch has identified a pipeline of 17 anti-obesity drugs in various stages of development. Many of these target hormonal or neural systems are involved in appetite and weight control.

Sanofi-Aventis has submitted a new drug application (NDA) for Acomplia (rimonabant), a selective CB1 cannabinoid receptor antagonist. The CB1 receptor is one of two receptors involved in the Endocannabinoid System (EC System) regulating eating behavior and energy expenditure. These receptors are located on the surfaces of fat cells, where they regulate lipid and glucose metabolism, and in hypothalamic cells, where they affect appetite.

In the overweight and obese, increased activity of cannabinoids leads to increased binding to CB1 receptors, thereby increasing appetite. Animal studies have shown that Acomplia blocks this action. In clinical trials with overweight and obese patients, Acomplia reduces cravings and hunger pangs, resulting in weight loss and improvement of cardiovascular and metabolic risk factors.

Regeneron Pharmaceuticals is in phase III development of Axokine (CNTF-AX15), a synthetic analogue of ciliary neurotrophic factor (CNTF) affecting the leptin pathway. Obesity is characterized by leptin resistance and inability to respond normally to signals of satiety. Axokine bypasses this resistance, allowing patients to feel full after eating smaller portions.

In a placebo-controlled trial of 173 obese volunteers given a low-calorie diet for 12 weeks, those receiving placebo injections gained an average of .2 pound, whereas those receiving an optimal dose of Axokine by injection lost an average of nine pounds. Weight loss was maintained for up to one year, but then weight began to increase. Adverse effects associated with Axokine treatment were injection site reactions, nausea and increased cough.

Arena Pharmaceuticals is in phase II testing of APD-356, a novel small molecule 5-HT2C receptor agonist. APD-356 may stimulate the 5-HT2C serotonin receptor more selectively than do fenfluramine and dexfenfluramine, and therefore may be less likely than these drugs to have adverse cardiovascular effects.

Cytos Biotechnology is in phase II development of CYT-009-GhrQb, an immunodrug vaccine carrying the 28 amino acid ghrelin peptide on the surface of the carrier Qb. Ghrelin, which is mostly synthesized in the stomach, regulates appetite. As ghrelin levels increase shortly before and decrease shortly after every meal, this hormone is thought to stimulate appetite by signalling pre-meal hunger and meal initiation. After diet-induced weight loss, ghrelin levels increase in obese subjects, which may explain the rapid rebound in weight when dieting ceases. A vaccine directed against ghrelin may decrease ghrelin levels, thereby reducing appetite and facilitating weight loss.

A different hormonal approach is AOD9604, in phase II development by Metabolic Pharmaceuticals. This compound, which mimics the effect of human growth hormone (hGH) on stimulating fat metabolism, induced weight loss in clinical trials. Tolerability was good, with no adverse effects typical of currently available obesity drugs. In a 12-week trial, AOD9604 administered orally, 1 mg once daily, was associated with average weight loss of 2.8 kg, compared with 0.8 kg for placebo.

Yet another approach is 1426 (HMR-1426), in phase II testing by Sanofi-Aventis. This anti-obesity drug does not affect the central nervous system or energy expenditure, but reduces food consumption by slowing gastric emptying.

7TMPharma is in phase I/II development of TM30338, a selective agonist of two subclasses of neuropeptide Y receptors that suppress appetite. In obese animals, this compound is superior to the natural hormone PYY3-36, which only targets one of the Y receptors, in terms of long-term reduction of food consumption and weight.

Fluasterone (HE-2500) is an immune regulating hormone (IRH) designed to correct Th1/Th2 dysregulation, in phase I testing by Aeson Therapeutics. In animal models of type 2 diabetes, fluasterone has impressive anti-diabetic and triglyceride-lowering activity. A multicenter phase II study is underway in patients with metabolic syndrome.

A phase I pharmacokinetic trial of Alizyme's drug cetilistat, a lipase inhibitor blocking fat digestion, has completed recruitment of 80 obese subjects. This randomized, double-blind, parallel-group design trial will compare four doses of cetilistat in terms of pharmacokinetics, fat excretion, safety and tolerability.

Amgen is in phase I development of AMG-076, a small molecule antagonist of the melanin concentrating hormone (MCH-1) receptor. MCH neurons in the lateral hypothalamus affect feeding, reward and mood regulation. In animals, MCH-1 receptor antagonists reduce food consumption while increasing energy expenditure.

The Karo Bio compound KB2115, a thyroid hormone receptor beta (TR-beta) agonist, is being tested in phase I clinical trials for treatment of obesity and dyslipidemia. Primary endpoints of these trials are safety, tolerability and pharmacokinetics, with secondary outcomes being effects on high blood lipids and other cardiovascular risk factors. In animal models, KB2115 increases energy expenditure, reduces body weight, and dramatically lowers blood lipids and blood glucose.

Manhattan Pharmaceuticals is in phase I testing of oleoyl estrone (OE), a signaling molecule that may act on the hypothalamus to communicate satiety. In animal studies, orally administered OE is associated with significant weight loss and reduced calorie intake without dietary modifications, without adverse effects or rebound weight gain after treatment was stopped. In obese individuals, circulating OE levels are thought to be lower than would be expected for the level of body fat.

A phase Ia trial was a single-dose, dose-escalation trial in six cohorts each containing six patients, randomized in a 2:1 ratio to OE or placebo. A repeat-dose, dose-escalation phase Ib trial is underway in four cohorts of six patients each, randomized 2:1 study drug to placebo.

Peptimmune is in phase I development of GT 389-255, a pancreatic lipase inhibitor conjugated to a fat binding hydrogel polymer. This novel formulation acts within the gastrointestinal tract to inhibit more than 30% of fat absorption. Compared with the currently marketed pancreatic lipase inhibitor Orlistat, GT 389-255 is expected to be well-tolerated and to have fewer adverse effects such as oily incontinence.

Various pharmacological strategies targeting obesity include hormonal manipulation of appetite, modulation of fat absorption metabolism and delaying gastric emptying. Because of the chronic nature of obesity, long-term safety and tolerability are important considerations.

Drug	Company	Additional Information
Phase I		
Fluasterone (HE-2500)	Aeson Therapeutics (520) 748-4462	an Immune Regulating Hormone (IRH) designed to correct Th1/Th2 dysregulation
cetilistat ATL-962	Alizyme +44 (0)1223 896000 www.alizyme.com	a lipase inhibitor that works by blocking the digestion of fat
AMG-076,T71	Amgen www.amgen.com	(805) 447-1000 melanin concentrating hormone (MCH-1) antagonist
AC162352, PYY 3-36	Amylin Pharmaceuticals (858) 552-2200 www.amylin.com	a synthetic analog of the human gut peptide PYY 3-36
KB2115	Karo Bio +46 8 608 6000 www.karobio.se	a thyroid hormone receptor beta (TR-beta) agonist
oleoyl estrone	Manhattan Pharmaceuticals (212) 582-3950 www.manhattanpharma.com	a signaling molecule that may act on the hypothalamus
PYY3-36	Nastech Pharmaceutical/ Merck (425) 908-3600 www.nastech.com	naturally occurring hormone produced by the gut
GT 389-255	Peptimmune (617) 715-8000 www.peptimmune.com	a lipase inhibitor conjugated to a fat binding hydrogel polymer
Phase I/II		
TM30338	7TMPharma +45 3925 7777 www.7tm.com	a selective agonist of two subclasses of neuropeptide Y receptor

Drug	Company	Additional Information
Leptin	Amgen (805) 447-1000 www.amgen.com	recombinant methionyl human leptin

Phase II

Drug	Company	Additional Information
APD-356	Arena Pharmaceuticals (858) 453-7200 www.arenapharm.com	small-molecule 5-HT 2c receptor agonists
CYT-009-GhrQb	Cytos Biotechnology +41 1 733 47 47 www.cytos.com	immunodrug vaccine that carries the ghrelin peptide on the surface of the carrier Qb
AOD9604	Metabolic Pharmaceuticals +61 3 9860 5700 www.metabolic.com.au	mimics the fat metabolic properties of human growth hormone (hGH)
CP-945598	Pfizer (212) 733-2323 www.pfizer.com	a cannabinoid-1 (CB-1) antagonist
1426 (HMR-1426)	Sanofi-aventis (33) 1 53 77 40 00 www.sanofi-aventis.com	anti-obesity agent that does not affect the central nervous system

Phase III

Drug	Company	Additional Information
Axokine (CNTF-AX15)	Regeneron Pharmaceuticals (914) 345-7400 www.regeneron.com	related to ciliary neurotrophic factor (CNTF)

NDA submitted

Drug	Company	Additional Information
Acomplia (rimonabant)	Sanofi-aventis (33) 1 53 77 40 00 www.sanofi-aventis.com	a selective CB1 cannabinoid receptor antagonist

Parkinson's Disease

By Laurie Barclay, M.D.
Published February 2005

Parkinson's disease is a progressive degenerative disorder of brain cells controlling muscle movement, leading to symptoms including tremor, muscle rigidity and problems with gait, balance and coordination. The characteristic hand tremor is known as "pill rolling" because the thumb and forefinger rub back and forth. Tremors may also involve the head, lips or feet, and they tend to disappear during sleep.

Other typical symptoms include slowed movement (bradykinesia), slow and shuffling gait, stooped posture, "freezing" of gait and of other movement (akinesia), "masked" expressionless face, and softer voice volume. Disturbances of autonomic function include slowed digestion, swallowing problems, constipation, increased salivation and decreased sweating.

If dementia develops, it may be heralded by slowed thought processes and difficulty concentrating. Nearly half of patients with Parkinson's disease develop depression, which is thought to result from the neuropathology rather than being situational in response to disability. Sleep disturbances and sexual dysfunction are not unusual.

Onset is typically after age 50, with very low prevalence under age 40 and increasing prevalence over age 70. In the United States, approximately 500,000 people have Parkinson's disease, with about 50,000 new cases reported each year.

In Parkinson's disease, decreased control over movement results from loss of brain cells in the substantia nigra. These neurons normally use the neurotransmitter dopa-mine to communicate with other brain cells in the corpus striatum.

Although the cause of Parkinson's disease is poorly understood, it most likely is a combination of genetic and environmental factors. Some drugs, diseases and toxins are associated with parkinsonism, lending credence to this theory. Other risk factors include male sex, reduced estrogen levels and reduced folate levels.

Involvement of dopaminergic neurons in the substantia nigra suggests the possibility of treatment with levodopa (L-dopa), which has long been the therapeutic standard. However, this drug is limited by adverse effects, by decreased efficacy as the disease worsens and by less predictable response over time. Combining levodopa with carbidopa (Sinemet) allows more levodopa to cross the blood-brain barrier and reduces adverse effects.

Other available drugs include dopamine agonists, which are used both as adjuncts to levodopa therapy and as initial treatment in early Parkinson's disease, especially in younger adults. These include bromocriptine (Parlodel), pergolide (Permax), pramipexole (Mirapex) and ropinirole (Requip). Although the adverse effects of dopamine agonists are similar to those of levodopa, they are less likely to cause involuntary movements and more likely to cause hallucinations or sleepiness.

Selegiline (Atapryl, Carbex, Eldepryl) is a monoamine oxidase B (MAO-B) inhibitor that helps prevent the breakdown of dopamine occurring naturally or formed from levodopa. Catechol-

O-methyltransferase (COMT) inhibitors, including Tolcapone (Tasmar) and entacapone, prolong the effect of levodopa by blocking an enzyme that metabolizes dopamine. Drawbacks of Tasmar include liver toxicity.

Anticholinergic drugs, such as trihexyphenidyl (Artane) and benztropine (Cogentin), are mildly effective in controlling tremors, but their use is seriously limited by adverse effects including dry mouth, nausea, urinary retention, constipation and central nervous system symptoms.

Other pharmacological options include amantadine (Symmetrel, Symadine), an antiviral drug sometimes used in patients with involuntary movements (dyskinesias) induced by levodopa.

Coenzyme Q-10 is a nutritional supplement targeting inefficient mitochondrial metabolism in Parkinson's disease.

Nonpharmacologic treatments include deep brain stimulation (DBS) via implantable electrodes similar to a heart pacemaker. In some patients, improved control with DBS reduces the need for drug therapy. Other surgical treatments include thalamotomy to reduce tremor, and pallidotomy to counteract dyskinesias. Newer approaches include neurotrophins, or molecules that support growth and survival of neurons, and cell transplantation.

In a preclinical model of Parkinson's disease, activation of the Hedgehog signaling pathway, which regulates the normal development of the brain and spinal cord, appears to spare dopaminergic neurons from additional damage and to improve function and movement. Curis, Inc., a therapeutic drug development company, has licensed Hedgehog pathway agonist technologies to Wyeth Pharmaceuticals, in hopes that this may ultimately lead to a novel treatment for Parkinson's disease.

CenterWatch has identified a pipeline of 23 drugs in various stages of development for Parkinson's disease. These include genetic therapies, neuroprotective agents and neurotransmitter analogues or modulators.

For early diagnosis of Parkinson's disease, Boston Life Sciences is in phase III testing of Altropane, a small, 123I-based radioactive molecule that specifically binds to dopamine transporters (DATs) in the brain. If single photon emission computed tomography (SPECT) scannning

reveals low levels of DATs using this agent, the patient may have Parkinson's disease, whereas excessively high levels may indicate attention deficit hyperactivity disorder.

Istradefylline (KW-6002) is an adenosine A2a receptor antagonist, in phase III testing by Kyowa Hakko. In a 12-week, double-blind, randomized, placebo-controlled study, patients with levodopa-treated Parkinson's disease (PD) with both motor fluctuations and peak-dose dyskinesias were randomized to treatment with placebo (n = 29), istradefylline up to 20 mg/day (n = 26), or istradefylline up to 40 mg/day (n = 28).

Home diaries revealed that subjects assigned to istradefylline experienced a mean reduction in the proportion of awake time spent in the "off" state of 7.1 ± 2.0%, compared with an increase of 2.2 ± 2.7% in the placebo group (p = .008). This corresponded to a decrease in "off" time of 1.2 ± 0.3 hours in the istradefylline group and an increase of 0.5 ± 0.5 hour in the placebo group (p = .004). However, "on" time with dyskinesia was significantly increased in the istradefylline group compared with the placebo group, and there were no differences between groups in change in Unified Parkinson's Disease Rating Scale scores or Clinical Global Impression of Change. Istradefylline was generally well tolerated, although nausea was the most common adverse event.

Newron Pharmaceuticals is in phase III development of safinamide (NW-1015), a unique molecule with multiple mechanisms of action and a very high therapeutic index. It inhibits dopamine uptake and is a potent, selective and reversible inhibitor of monoamine oxidase (MAO)-B, without a MAO-A effect. It is also a potent blocker of the sodium (Na+) channel and modulator of the calcium (Ca2+) channel. Through these multiple activities, safinamide can selectively affect those neurons with abnormal firing patterns without affecting normal activity.

In a multinational phase II, controlled trial, safinamide improved motor disability in early Parkinson's disease by about 30% compared with placebo, and it was equally well tolerated. The greatest benefit was in those patients receiving stable treatment with a single dopamine agonist. Advantages of safinamide include excellent bioavailability, linear kinetics and suitability for once-daily administration.

Rotigotine CDS (Neupro; SPM-962), a novel dopamine receptor-agonist and neuroprotective agent formulated as a skin patch for continuous transdermal delivery, is in phase III testing by Schwarz Pharma. Fifteen multinational clinical trials enrolling more than 1,500 patients with Parkinson's disease have demonstrated the efficacy and safety of the patch, which is applied to the skin once a day.

In the U.S. phase III trial with Neupro as adjunctive therapy, patients with advanced Parkinson's disease tolerated the patch well and had a statistically significant and clinically relevant reduction in "off" time, with no increase in dyskinesias. As a nasal spray, rotigotine has entered phase I development for treatment of acute symptoms in patients with Parkinson's disease.

Solvay Pharmaceuticals is in phase III testing of DU127090, a controlled-release formulation of Luvox. This selective serotonin reuptake inhibitor is a partial dopamine D2 receptor agonist. Because a partial agonist suppresses activity when a neurotransmitter system is hyperactive but increases activity when the system is hypoactive, DU 127090 is theoretically poised to address dyskinesias and tremor, as well as bradykinesia and akinesia.

CEP-1347, a selective inhibitor of the stress-activated protein kinase pathway, is in phase II/III testing by Cephalon. The kinases inhibited by CEP-1347 have been shown to play a key role in apoptosis, or programmed cell death, in neurons. A randomized, double-blind, placebo-controlled, phase II/III clinical trial in 800 patients with early-stage Parkinson's disease should help determine if CEP-1347 can slow progression.

Amgen has completed phase II testing of Liatermine, a glial-derived neurotrophic factor (GDNF). After six months of continuous infusion into the putamen region of the brain in patients with advanced Parkinson's disease, GDNF was safe and well-tolerated and had a documented biological effect, but it did not meet the primary endpoint of clinical improvement on the Unified Parkinson's Disease Rating Scale. However, 11 of 34 patients enrolled in the double-blind trial are now receiving GDNF in an open-label extension study.

ACP-103, an orally administered selective inverse agonist at the 5-HT2A receptor, is in phase II development by Acadia Pharmaceu-ticals for treatment-induced psychosis and other drug-related dysfunction. In a phase Ib/IIa clinical trial, ACP-103 was safe and well tolerated with no adverse events reported, no worsening in pre-existing motor deficits, and fewer treatment-induced dyskinesias in a subgroup of patients.

NeuroSearch is in phase II development of the monoamine reuptake inhibitor NS-2330. Preclinical experiments suggest that NS-2330 reverses akinesia in monkeys treated with L-dopa, that it has a relatively long duration of action, and that the quality of movement in Parkinson test animals treated with NS-2330 is at least as good as that seen with L-dopa and other anti-Parkinson drugs. To determine the optimal dosages and clinical effect of NS-2330, three clinical phase II studies are enrolling a total of approximately 930 patients.

Fipamezole (JP-1730), an alpha-2 adrenoceptor antagonist, is in phase II development by Juvantia Pharma. Unlike other drugs targeting the loss of dopaminergic neurons, this drug is designed to counteract the loss of noradrenergic neurons in the locus ceruleus and generalized depletion of noradrenaline in the brain, which may contribute significantly to the non-motor syndromes in Parkinson's disease, and which may also make dopaminergic terminals more susceptible to drug-induced damage. In clinical trials, fipamezole appears to be able to suppress dyskinesia, and in an animal model with MPTP-treated primates, it appears to extend the duration of action of L-dopa. Three clinical phase I studies showed that fipamezole was safe and well tolerated.

A unique therapeutic approach to Parkinson's disease is spheramine, in phase II testing by Titan Pharmaceuticals. This treatment involves dopamine-producing retinal pigment epithelial (RPE) cells grown in tissue culture, uniformly and in large quantities, from normal, fully-differentiated human cells. Providing a bead matrix on which the cells attach allows them to survive when transplanted and eliminates the need for immunosuppression. After positive results in primate studies, six patients with moderately severe to severe Parkinson's disease had an improvement in motor function of 48% over baseline three to four years post treatment with spheramine. A 68-patient, randomized, blinded, controlled phase IIb clinical study is underway.

Guilford Pharmaceuticals is in phase II testing of GPI-1485, a neuroimmunophilin ligand that stimulates growth and regeneration of damaged neurons. In animal models, neuroimmunophilin ligands preferentially target only damaged nerve cells, whereas earlier compounds stimulated regrowth of both normal and damaged nerves. Other benefits include oral route of administration and penetration of the blood-brain barrier without direct injection into the brain. A phase II, two-year, randomized, double-blind, placebo-controlled,

multicenter trial of GPI 1485 in 200 patients with mild to moderate Parkinson's disease should be completed soon.

From the early days of pharmacotherapy in Parkinson's disease, understanding of the relevant neurotransmitter deficits and of selective neuronal loss has always allowed rational development of pharmaceutical agents. Recent advances in drug delivery technology and in clarifying the role of neurotrophic agents should hopefully allow further breakthroughs, not only in treating the paucity of movement characterizing this disease, but also in preventing or reversing the dyskinesias associated with drug therapy.

Drug	Company	Additional Information
Phase I		
PYM-50028	Phytopharm/Yamanouchi 44 (0)1480 437697 www.phytopharm.co.uk	synthetic neuroprotective and neuroregenerative agent
Mito-4509 (ABP-150)	MitoKor (858) 793-7800 www.mitokor.com	non-feminizing estrogen analog
Phase I/II		
AV201	Avigen (510) 748-7150 www.avigen.com	gene therapy using an adeno-associated virus (AAV)
DAR-0100	DarPharma (919) 403-4348 www.darpharma.com	D1 dopamine receptor agonist
Phase II		
ACP-103	Acadia Pharmaceuticals (858) 558-2871 www.acadia-pharm.com	selective inverse agonist at the 5-HT2A receptor
apomorphine	Britannia Pharmaceuticals +44 (17) 37 773741 www.britannia-pharm.co.uk	dopamine agonist in a nasal powder formulation nasal powder
Provigil (modafinil)	Cephalon (610) 344-0200 www.cephalon.com	excessive daytime sleepiness associated with Parkinson's disease
GPI-1485	Guilford Pharmaceuticals (410) 631-6300 www.guilfordpharm.com	a neuroimmunophilin ligands that stimulates nerve growth
talampanel (LY-300164)	IVAX (305) 575-6000 www.ivax.com	oral agent designed to block the AMPA receptor
fipamezole (JP-1730)	Juvantia Pharma +358-2-6517 1500 www.juvantia.com	alpha-2 adrenoceptor antagonist

Drug	Company	Additional Information
NS-2330	NeuroSearch +45-4460 8000 www.neurosearch.dk	monoamine reuptake inhibitor
SR-57667	Sanofi-Aventis (33) 1 5377 4000 www.sanofi-aventis.com	neuroprotective agent in an oral formulation
SLV 308	Solvay (770) 778-9000 www.solvay.com	affects several different types of neuro-transmitters, including noradrenaline, dopamine and 5-HT
Spheramine	Titan Pharmaceuticals (650) 244-4990 www.titanpharm.com	retinal pigment epithelial (RPE) cells
Phase II Completed		
Liatermine	Amgen (805) 447-1000 www.amgen.com	glial derived neurotrophic factor (GDNF)
Phase II/III		
CEP-1347	Cephalon (610) 344-0200 www.cephalon.com	selective inhibitor of the stress-activated protein kinase pathway
Phase III		
Altropane	Boston Life Sciences (617) 425-0200 www.bostonlifesciences.com	radioactive molecule that binds specifically to dopamine transporters (DATs) in the brain
CHF-1512	Chiesi Farmaceutici +39 0521 2791 www.chiesigroup.com	fixed combination of melevodopa and carbidopa (Europe)
ReQuip (ropinirole)	GlaxoSmithKline (888) 825-5249 www.gsk.com	controlled release GEOMATRIX technology
istradefylline,	Kyowa Hakko (212) 319-5353 www.kyowa-usa.com	adenosine A2a receptor antagonist KW-6002
safinamide, NW-1015	Newron Pharmaceuticals +39 02 610 3461 www.newron.com	combines NA+ channel blocking activity, CA2+ channel modulation and MAO-B inhibition
rotigotine CDS (Neupro; SPM-962)	Schwarz Pharma +49 2173 48 1866 www.schwarzpharma.com	neuroprotective agent formulated as a skin patch
DU127090	Solvay Pharmaceuticals (770) 578-9000 www.solvay.com	controlled-release version of Luvox—a selective serotonin reuptake inhibitor

Prostate Cancer

By Laurie Barclay, M.D.
Published March 2005

Prostate cancer is the second most common cancer (after skin cancer) in American men. According to the American Cancer Society, about 232,090 new cases of prostate cancer will be diagnosed in the U.S. during 2005. Although approximately one in every six men will be diagnosed with prostate cancer during his lifetime, only one man in 33 will die from this disease, or about 30,350 deaths in the U.S. during 2005.

More than 99% of prostate cancers are adenocarcinomas originating from the glandular cells secreting seminal fluid. Prostate cancer may develop from prostatic intraepithelial neoplasia (PIN), which may first be evident in men in their 20s, and which may affect almost 50% of men by their fifth decade. High-grade PIN detected on prostate biopsy conveys a 30% to 50% likelihood of cancer also being present.

Growth of most prostate cancers is typically slow, with about 86% of all prostate cancers detected in the local and regional stages, and many are found incidentally at autopsy. Five-year survival is about 99%, 10-year survival 92%, and 15-year survival 61%.

Risk factors for prostate cancer include advancing age, with more than 70% of all prostate cancers diagnosed in men over 65 years of age; African-American race, North American and northwestern European nationality, family history, diet high in red meat or high-fat dairy products, low intake of fruits and vegetables, sedentary lifestyle, obesity and possibly vasectomy in men younger than age 35. Gene mutations predisposing to prostate cancer may include HPC1, HPC2 (ELAC2), HPCX, and CAPB. High levels of androgens or insulin-like growth factor-1 (IGF-1) may increase prostate cancer risk in some men.

Early prostate cancer is usually asymptomatic, and is typically detected by digital rectal examination and prostate-specific antigen (PSA) blood test, with confirmation by biopsy. Advanced prostate cancers may cause urinary frequency, decreased stream, blood in the urine, or impotence, as well as bony metastases.

Treatment options depend on stage. Early cancers may respond to radiation therapy by external beam or brachytherapy, or radical prostatectomy. For more advanced cancers, treatment options also include hormone therapy, cryosurgery and chemotherapy. Recent combination therapies including docetaxel have been promising in boosting survival by several months, as well as improving quality of life. Bisphosphonates appear to reduce pain and slow cancer growth of skeletal metastases.

CenterWatch has identified a pipeline of 52 new agents in various stages of development for prostate cancer, including vaccines, monoclonal antibodies and hormonal therapies.

Abbott Laboratories has submitted a new drug application (NDA) for Xinlay (ABT-627, atrasentan), an oral, once daily, non-hormonal, non-chemotherapy agent. This selective endothelin A receptor antagonist (SERA) inhibits the activity of endothelin protein thought to be involved in stimulating the spread of cancer cells.

Barr Laboratories is in phase III development of CyPat (cyproterone acetate), a steroid inhibiting the action of testosterone needed to sustain most prostate cancers. CyPat's mechanism of action is to bind surface receptors on the prostate cancer cells, preventing the attachment of testosterone. It may be given in combination with injections of other hormonal therapies such as goserelin, buserelin, triptorelin or leuprorelin, which block production of leuteinising hormone that normally stimulates testosterone production.

GVAX prostate cancer vaccine, in phase III development by Cell Genesys, uses modified tumor cells to secrete granulocyte-macrophage colony stimulating factor (GM-CSF), a hormone that stimulates the body's immune response to vaccines. This non patient-specific vaccine is irradiated for safety, and can be used "off-the-shelf" to stimulate a systemic immune response against prostate cancer, destroying prostate cancer cells still present after surgery, hormone treatment, or radiation. In trials to date for advanced-stage, hormone-refractory prostate cancer, GVAX has had a favorable safety profile.

A different type of vaccine is Gonadimmune (GnRH pharmaccine), in phase II testing by Aphton for hormone-failed or hormone-resistant prostate cancer. This anti-gonadotropin releasing hormone (GnRH) immunogen neutralizes the GnRH hormone.

Pentrix is Australian Cancer Technology's version of a novel vaccine for prostate cancer, now in phase II development. This p53-gene-based vaccine induces an antibody cascade, which triggers an immune response against tumor cells with a mutated p53 gene (present in nearly half of all cancer patients).

Another investigational immunotherapy is Provenge (APC8015), in phase III testing by Dendreon. This dendritic, ex vivo cell therapy stimulates the immune system to attack cells expressing prostatic acid phosphatase (PAP), a protein expressed on about 95% of prostate cancer cells. Using Antigen Delivery Cassette technology, Provenge delivers small pieces of the PAP protein to a patient's antigen presenting cells (APCs). In turn, the APCs activate other immune cells to find and destroy PAP-containing prostate cancer cells.

Myriad Genetics is in phase III testing of Flurizan MPC-7869, the R-enantiomer of the non-steroidal anti-inflammatory drug (NSAID) flurbiprofen. Unlike other NSAIDs, Flurizan does not inhibit cyclooxygenase enzymes (COX-1 and COX-2), and it is therefore devoid of severe gastrointestinal adverse effects. It modulates signal transduction and transcription activation pathways involving nuclear factor kappa B (NFkB), which is a principal transcription factor regulating cell growth and death, as well as inflammation. In animal models, Flurizan is safe and effective.

Satraplatin (JM-216) is a third generation oral platinum drug, in phase III development by Spectrum Pharmaceuticals for use in hormone refractory prostate cancer. This chemotherapeutic agent binds to DNA, causing disruption of cell division and ultimately cell death. In preclinical models, anti-tumor activity is comparable to that of cisplatin and carboplatin with less cross-resistance. This compound also appears to enhance the antitumor activity of ionizing radiation.

A novel immunological approach is CG-7870, an oncolytic virus designed to target and selectively destroy cancer cells while sparing normal cells. Cell Genesys is in phase II testing of this virus therapy in early-stage prostate cancer, both by intratumoral and by intravenous routes of administration. Cell Genesys hopes that CG7870 will be a less toxic alternative to radiation seed therapy in newly diagnosed, intermediate to high-risk prostate cancer patients.

Panzem (2-methoxyestradiol), in phase II testing by EntreMed, is a natural metabolite of estrogen with multiple mechanisms of action targeting prostate cancer. In addition to inhibiting angiogenesis, Panzem disrupts microtubule formation, downregulates hypoxia inducible factor one-alpha (HIF-1a), inhibits bone resorbing osteoclasts, and induces apoptosis, or programmed cell death. This compound has activity in cell lines resistant to various chemotherapeutic agents.

Yet another approach to selective targeting of cancer cells is Genasense (oblimersen G-3139), in phase II development by Genta and Sanofi-Aventis. In preclinical studies, this antisense oligonucleotide-targeting Bcl-2 has been shown to directly kill certain types of cancer cells, and Genta is developing this agent to enhance the effectiveness of standard anticancer therapy.

Another antisense compound is GTI-2501, in phase II development by Lorus Therapeutics. This drug, which contains antisense sequences directed against R1 and R2 components or ribonucleotide reductase, is being tested in combination with GTI-2501 and docetaxel in patients with Hormone Refractory Prostate Cancer (HRPC).

Gloucester Pharmaceuticals/NCI is in phase II testing of depsipeptide (FK-228, FR-901228), an inhibitor of histone deacetylase (HDAC) crucial to regulation of gene expression. This compound therefore causes cell cycle arrest, differentiation and apoptotic cell death.

Acapodene (toremifine, GTx-006) is a nonsteroidal selective estrogen receptor modulator (SERM). Based on encouraging results in phase II testing, in late January GTx began a phase III, placebo-controlled trial for the prevention of prostate cancer in high-risk men with high-grade prostatic intraepithelial neoplasia.

MDX-070, in phase II development by Medarex, is a fully human antibody targeting prostate-specific membrane antigen PSMA, a cell surface marker expressed on cancer cells. Based on phase I clinical data showing a favorable safety and tolerability profile. Medarex has started a multi-dose, dose-escalation phase II trial of MDX-070 in men with hormone refractory prostate cancer.

Vitaxin (LM-609), an investigational monoclonal antibody blocking the alpha-v/beta-3 integrin receptor (vitronectin), is in phase II testing by MedImmune. By inhibiting angiogenesis, Vitaxin blocks the growth and spread of solid tumors, at least in animal models. The phase II trial of Vitaxin in combination with chemotherapy is a randomized, open label, two-arm study enrolling approximately 110 patients with androgen-independent prostate cancer and bone metastases.

Based on the drugs reviewed by CenterWatch, common themes unifying the approaches to prostate cancer involve hormonal manipulation or immunological strategies enhancing the body's natural defense against foreign tumor antigens. The slow course, frequent detection in early stages, and identification of an apparent precursor to prostate cancer offer the opportunity for early intervention in this widespread, sometimes fatal, disease.

Drug	Company	Additional Information
Phase I		
CTP-37 (Avicine)	AVI Biopharma (503) 227-0554 www.avibio.com	vaccine elicits a highly specific immune response to human chorionic gonadotropin (hCG) peptide
Gossypol	Bioenvision (212) 750-6700 www.bioenvision.com	cytostatic agent that inhibits retinoic acid metabolizing enzyme
Modrenal (trilostane)	Bioenvision (212) 750-6700 www.bioenvision.com	blocks the action of estrogen through a mechanism involving a protein called AP1
Regressin, Urocidin, MCC	Bioniche Life Sciences (613) 966-8058 www.bioniche.com	MCC is a cell wall complex prepared from the MCC bacterium M. phlei that inhibits cancer cell division, induces apoptosis and stimulates a immune response
ThermoDox	Celsion (410) 290-5390 www.celsion.com	doxorubicin encapsulated in a heat-activated liposome technology
rsPSMA	CYTOGEN and Progenics (609) 750-8200 www.cytogen.com	combines a protein called prostate-specific membrane antigen (PSMA) with an immune stimulant to induce an immune response

Drug	Company	Additional Information
IDD-1	Medarex/Immuno-Designed Molecules (609) 430-2880 www.medarex.com	consists of dendritophages that are loaded *in vitro* with tumor antigens and then reinjected into the subject
INSM-18	Insmed (804) 565-3022 www.insmed.com	insulin-like growth factor-I receptor (IGF-I) and human epidermal growth factor receptor (Her2/neu) inhibitor
Advexin (INGN 201)	Introgen Therapeutics (512) 708-9310 www.introgen.com	p53 gene therapy product, kills cancer cells or stops tumor growth with an adenoviral delivery system
NBI-42902	Neurocrine Biosciences (858) 658-7600 www.neurocrine.com	GnRH antagonist
Phase I/II		
Oncomyc-NG (AVI-4126)	AVI BioPharma (503) 227-0554 www.avibio.com	Neugene antisense drug, that specifically targets and inhibits the c-myc gene
Combretastatin A4	OXiGENE (781) 547-5900 www.oxigene.com	anti-tumor vascular targeting agent prodrug (CA4P)
Phase II		
Gonadimmune (GnRH pharmaccine)	Aphton (305) 374-7338 www.aphton.com	anti-gonadotropin releasing hormone (GnRH) immunogen
Pentrix	Australian Cancer Technology 61 8 9486 4622 www.austcancer.com.au	p53-gene-based vaccine
Hectorol (doxercalciferol)	Bone Care International (608) 662-7800 www.bonecare.com	provides vitamin D-hormone replacement, which reduces elevated parathyroid hormone levels
Actimid (CC-4047)	Celgene (732) 271-1001 www.celgene.com	thalidomide derivatives that inhibits TNF-alpha overproduction
Thalomid (thalidomide)	Celgene (732) 271-1001 www.celgene.com	oral formulation of the immunomodulatory agent thalidomide
CG-7870	Cell Genesys (650) 266-3000 www.cellgenesys.com	oncolytic virus engineered to target and destroy cancer cells
BBR 3576	Cell Therapeutics (206) 282-7100 www.cticseattle.com	aza-anthrapyrazolic intercalating agent
CEP-701, KT-5555	Cephalon (610) 344-0200 www.cephalon.com	active inhibitor of the enzyme tyrosine kinase
ChemGenex (amonafide)	ChemGenex Therapeutics (650) 474-9800 www.chemgenex.com	isoquinoline topoisomerase inhibitor

Drug	Company	Additional Information
Panzem (2-methoxyestradiol)	EntreMed (240) 864-2600 www.entremed.com	natural metabolite of estrogen that works as an angiogenesis inhibitor
Genasense (oblimersen G-3139)	Genta and Sanofi-Aventis (908) 286-9800 www.genta.com	Bcl-2 targeting antisense oligonucleotide
depsipeptide, FK-228, FR-901228	Gloucester Pharmaceuticals/ NCI (617) 621-1561 www.gloucester-pharma.com	histone deacetylase (HDAC) inhibitor
ILX-651	Genzyme (617) 252-7500 www.genzyme.com	analog of the microtubule stabilizer dolastatin
GTI-2501	Lorus Therapeutics (416) 798-1200 www.lorusthera.com	antisense sequences directed against R1 and R2 components or ribonucleotide reductase
MDX-010	Medarex/Bristol-Myers Squibb (609) 430-2880 www.medarex.com	fully human antibody that targets the CTLA-4, molecule on T cells that suppresses the immune response
MDX-070	Medarex (609) 430-2880 www.medarex.com	fully human antibody that targets PSMA, a cell surface marker that is expressed on cancer tissues
Vitaxin (LM-609)	MedImmune (301) 398-0000 www.medimmune.com	blocks the alpha-v/beta-3 integrin receptor (vitronectin)
Irofulven (MGI-114)	MGI Pharma (952) 346-4700 www.mgipharma.com	derived from *illudin S*, a toxin from the Omphalotus illudens mushroom
adecatumumab (MT-201)	Cell Therapeutics/ Micromet/Serono +49 (0) 89 / 895277-0 www.micromet.de	single-chain antibody technology (SCAs) utilizing small antibody fragments
MLN2704 (MLN591, J591)	Millennium Pharmaceuticals (617) 679-7000 www.millennium.com	humanized monoclonal antibody (T-MAV) that targets the prostate- specific membrane antigen molecule
phenoxodiol, NV-06 (intravenous)	Novogen (203) 327-1188 www.novogen.com	cytotoxic investigational anti-cancer drug
OGX-011	OncoGenex/Isis (604) 736-3678 www.oncogenex.ca	inhibitor of clusterin, a protein that makes tumors resistant to conventional treatment
Reolysin, Reosyn	Oncolytics Biotech (403) 670-7377 www.oncolyticsbiotech.com	mammalian reovirus that infects and kills cancer cells with an activated Ras pathway
Onyvax P	Onyvax +44 (0)20 8682 9494 www.onyvax.com	an allogeneic whole-cell vaccine
SR-31747	Sanofi-Aventis +33 1 53 77 40 00 www.sanofi-aventis.com	peripheral sigma opioid agonist with immunosuppressive activity

Drug	Company	Additional Information
Prostvac-VF	Therion Biologics (617) 475-7500 www.therionbio.com	vaccine that targets cells expressing prostate-specific antigen (PSA)
Triapine	Vion Pharmaceuticals (203) 498-4210 www.vionpharm.com	ribonucleotide reductase inhibitor
XLS-001 (amonafide malate)	Xanthus Life Sciences (617) 225-0522 www.xanthus.com	derivative of naphthalic acid
Xcellerated T-Cells	Xcyte Therapies (206) 262-6200 www.xcytetherapies.com	T-cell infusion treatment
Tesmilifene	YM Biosciences (905) 629-9761 www.ymbiosciences.com	intracellular histamine antagonist
Norelin	YM Bioscience (905) 629-9761 www.ymbiosciences.com	immuno-pharmaceutical product based on a proprietary recombinant antigen

Phase III

Drug	Company	Additional Information
CyPat (cyproterone acetate)	Barr Laboratories (845) 362-1100 www.barrlabs.com	steroid that blocks the action of testosterone
GVAX	Cell Genesys (650) 266-3000 www.cellgenesys.com	modified tumor cells that secrete a granulocyte-macrophage colony stimulating factor
Provenge (APC8015)	Dendreon (206) 256-4545 www.dendreon.com	dendritic ex vivo cell therapy
Acapodene (toremifine, GTx-006)	GTx (901) 523-9700 www.gtxinc.com	non-steroidal selective estrogen receptor modulator (SERM)
Flurizan, MPC-7869	Myriad Genetics (801) 584-3600 www.myriad.com	R-enantiomer of flurbiprofen
Aptosyn (exisulind)	OSI Pharmaceuticals (613) 962-2000 www.osip.com	selective apoptotic anti-neoplastic drugs (SAANDs)
Taxoprexin, DHA-paclitaxel	Protarga (610) 592-4000 www.protarga.com	paclitaxel chemically linked to doco-sahexaenoic acid (DHA), an approved natural additive
satraplatin (JM-216)	Spectrum Pharmaceuticals (949) 788-6700 www.spectrumpharm.com	oral platinum drug, binds to DNA causing disruption of cell division, resulting in cell death

NDA Submitted

Drug	Company	Additional Information
Xinlay (ABT-627, atrasentan)	Abbott Laboratories (847) 937-6100 www.abbott.com	selective endothelin A receptor antagonist

Rare Disorders

By Laurie Barclay, M.D.
Published December 2005

The Orphan Drug Act (ODA) allows the U.S. Food and Drug Admini-stration (FDA) to grant special status to a drug designed to treat a rare disease or condition, when requested by a sponsor. The prevalence of the disease or condition in the United States must be less than 200,000 people or, if the drug is a vaccine, diagnostic drug or preventive drug, the number of people to whom the drug will be administered must be fewer than 200,000 per year.

Orphan designation qualifies the sponsor of the product for a tax credit and marketing incentives, such as exemption from a prescription drug user fee and several years of marketing exclusivity when the drug is approved. However, there must be no reasonable expectation that costs of research and development of the drug for the rare disease can be recovered from United States sales.

Since 1983, when the ODA was implemented, more than 200 drugs and biological products for rare diseases have been brought to market, compared with fewer than 10 such products during the decade before 1983.

CenterWatch has identified a pipeline of 12 orphan drugs in various stages of development for rare diseases or conditions. These include some of the lysosomal storage disorders, or genetic inborn errors of metabolism in which undegraded toxic material accumulates within the lysosomes. About 5 million people in the United States have one of these disabling, life-threatening childhood diseases for which there is no cure to date.

Myozyme (alpha-glucosidase) is in phase III development of Genzyme, an enzyme replacement therapy for late stage Pompe's disease. This disabling, often fatal muscle disease is a lysosomal storage disorder resulting from an inherited deficiency of alpha-glucosidase, which causes excessive accumulation of glycogen in the muscles, heart and other organs.

An ongoing trial is evaluating the use of Myozyme in severely affected children with Pompe's disease aged 6 months to 3 years of age. Approximately 100 patients with Pompe's disease are currently receiving Myozyme in clinical trials, through Gen-zyme's expanded access program, or through pre-approval access mechanisms sponsored by several European governments.

Another enzyme replacement therapy for a lysosomal storage disorder is iduronate-2-sulfatase, in phase III testing by Shire Pharmaceuticals for Hunter syndrome, an X chromosome-linked disease. Iduronate-2-sulfatase is required for lysosomal breakdown of heparan sulfate and dermatan sulfate.

Shire Pharmaceuticals is also in phase II development of Gene-Activated Human Glucocerebrosidase (GA-GCB), a recombinant glucocerebrosidase enzyme replacement therapy for the lysosomal storage disorder Gaucher disease. Interim six-month data from a phase I/II study showed that GA-GCB was very well tolerated in patients with Gaucher disease, and that it resulted in improved hemoglobin levels and platelet counts, reduced liver and spleen size, and lowered levels of biomarkers of disease activity (chitotriosidase and CCL-18).

Migalastat (AT-1001; Amigal) is a phase II product of Amicus Therapeutics being tested for Fabry disease, another lysosomal storage disorder resulting from a deficiency in the enzyme alpha-galactosidase A (a-GAL). This enzyme normally breaks down a specialized fat molecule known as globotriaosylceramide (GL-3), but in Fabry disease, a-GAL is misfolded because of a genetic mutation, resulting in GL-3 accumulation in the kidneys, heart, nervous system and skin.

Amigal is an orally administered alpha-galactosidase A modulator belonging to a class of molecules known as pharmacological chaperones. After binding to the misfolded a-GAL enzyme, Amigal facilitates proper folding, processing and moving of the enzyme from the endoplasmic reticulum to the lysosome. Within the lysosome, Amigal is displaced, allowing a-GAL to function normally in breaking down GL-3.

In phase I clinical trials in healthy volunteers, Amigal was safe and well-tolerated, and showed a dose-dependent increase in a-GAL activity. The FDA granted Amicus orphan designation for Amigal for the treatment of Fabry disease in February 2004.

Stem Cells Inc. has submitted an investigational new drug application for HuCNS-SC, a brain stem cell transplant for the lysosomal storage disorder Batten disease. In mouse studies, HuCNS-SC produces the missing enzyme in the brain and can protect specific neurons from death.

Eisai has submitted a new drug application (NDA) for rufinamide (Inovelon), an antiepileptic drug (AED) for children ages four and over with Lennox-Gastaut syndrome (LGS), a severe form of epilepsy beginning in early childhood that is typically refractory to currently approved drugs. This orally administered triazole derivative is a GABA-B antagonist structurally different from currently approved AEDs.

Based on findings from a multicenter, double-blind, placebo-controlled trial showing clinical benefit for seizures associated with LGS, rufinamide was designated by the FDA as an orphan drug for this indication in October 2004. The most frequently reported adverse events are headache, dizziness, fatigue, somnolence and nausea.

Pfizer has submitted an NDA for Sutent (sunitinib malate, SU-11248) for patients with Gleevec-resistant gastrointestinal stromal tumor (GIST), and it is also being tested in patients with refractory metastatic renal cell carcinoma. The FDA has granted Sutent fast-track status because it may be more effective than existing therapy for potentially fatal diseases.

Sutent is an orally administered, multi-targeted inhibitor of vascular endothelial growth factor receptor (VEGFR2), platelet-derived growth factor receptor (PDGFR-beta), KIT and Flt3 tyrosine kinase signaling pathways. Inhibition of these tyrosine kinase pathways may deprive tumors of blood and nutrients needed for growth while directly attacking cancer cells.

The most frequent adverse effects associated with Sutent in clinical trials were fatigue, gastrointestinal symptoms, skin discoloration, dysgeusia, and anorexia. These adverse effects are typically mild to moderate, and reversible with delay or reduction in dosage or when treatment is discontinued.

ICAgen and McNeil Pharmaceuticals are in phase III testing of ICA-17043 for sickle cell anemia. This drug is a novel inhibitor of the Gardos channel, a calcium-activated potassium channel on red blood cell membranes. In a transgenic mouse model, ICA-17043 prevents dehydration of sickled red blood cells from loss of potassium, chloride and water through the Gardos channel.

Savient Pharmaceuticals is in phase II testing of Puricase (PEG-uricase), which has received FDA Orphan Drug designation for gout refractory to available therapy. This drug is a genetically engineered polyethylene glycol (PEG) conjugate of uricase, an enzyme that converts uric acid into a soluble, more easily excreted product. Puricase is being tested for its ability to eliminate excess uric acid in patients with symptomatic gout unresponsive to conventional treatment.

Drug	Company	Additional Information
IND accepted		
HuCNS-SC	Stem Cells Inc (650) 475-3100 www.stemcellsinc.com	Batten disease: brain stem cell transplant
Phase I		
Alphagen	geneRx+/Aradigm (615) 783-2165 www.generxplus.com	Cystic Fibrosis: an alpha-1-antitrypsin (AAT) gene in a plasmid vector
AAV-factor IX gene therapy	University of Pennsylvania (215) 898-5000 www.upenn.edu	Hemophilia A: factor IX gene therapy
Phase II		
migalastat (AT-1001; Amigal)	Amicus Therapeutics (609) 662-2000 www.amicustherapeutics.com	Fabry disease: orally available alpha-galactosidase A modulator
CFx (CFTR-001)	Copernicus Therapeutics (216) 231-0227 www.cgsys.com	Cystic Fibrosis: a gene therapy containing the gene for CF transmembrane conductance regulator
Puricase (PEG-uricase)	Savient Pharmaceuticals (732) 418-9300 www.savientpharma.com	Gout: glycol (PEG) conjugates of uricase
Gene-Activated Human Glucocerebrosidase (GA-GCB)	Shire Pharmaceuticals +44 1256 894 000 www.shire.com	Gaucher disease: a recombinant glucocere-brosidase enzyme replacement therapy
Phase III		
ICA-17043	ICAgen/McNeil Pharmaceuticals (919) 941-5206 www.icagen.com	Sickle Cell Anemia: inhibitor of the Gardos channel, a potassium channel on red blood cell membranes
Myozyme (alpha-glucosidase)	Genzyme (617) 252-7500 www.genzyme.com	Late stage Pompe's disease: an enzyme replacement therapy
iduronate-2-sulfatase	Shire Pharmaceuticals +44 1256 894 000 www.shire.com	Hunter's disease: enzyme replacement therapy idursulfase (12S)
NDA submitted		
rufinamide (Inovelon)	Eisai 81-3-3817-3700 www.eisai.co.jp	Lennox-Gastaut syndrome: an oral GABA B antagonist
Sutent (sunitinib malate, SU-11248)	SUGEN (Pfizer) (212) 733-2323 www.pfizer.com	Gastrointestinal stromal tumor: inhibitor of VEGFR2, PDGFR-beta, KIT and Flt3 tyrosine kinase signaling pathways

Schizophrenia

By Laurie Barclay, M.D.
Published June 2005

Schizophrenia is a chronically disabling psychiatric disease characterized by disturbances in thinking, emotional response and behavior. Negative symptoms typically include lack of emotional range, disturbed relationships with others and cognitive disturbances, whereas positive symptoms include hallucinations and delusions. Typically, patients require lifelong medical treatment and suffer from chronically impaired social and vocational adjustment.

Lifetime incidence of schizophrenia is 1%, prevalence in the developed world is 8 million, and U.S. prevalence is between 2 and 3 million, according to the National Institute of Mental Health.

The mainstay of therapy is currently first-generation (typical), or second-generation (atypical) antipsychotic agents. First-generation antipsychotics, which were introduced in the late 1950s, block dopamine receptors. Although they are effective against the positive symptoms of schizophrenia, they have a wide range of adverse effects.

Most disabling are the motor disturbances, including tardive dyskinesia (uncontrollable smacking movements of the lips and tongue) and extrapyramidal rigidity (stiffness, tremor and other Parkinsonian symptoms). Furthermore, the typical antipsychotic agents are ineffective for the negative symptoms of schizophrenia, and their use has therefore decreased in the U.S. and Europe.

Atypical antipsychotic drugs target both dopamine and 5-HT2A receptors. Although they have fewer motor adverse effects than do the typical antipsychotics, they are only partially effective in addressing the negative symptoms. Among the atypical antipsychotics, clozapine may partially relieve cognitive symptoms, whereas typical antipsychotics often worsen cognitive function.

Adverse events associated with atypical antipsychotics include severe obesity, type 2 diabetes, and cardiovascular effects. Depending on the specific drug, adverse effects may also include agranulocytosis, a life-threatening loss of white blood cells; movement disorders; and lens changes in the eye that may eventually cause cataracts.

Both typical and atypical antipsychotic agents may give rise to hyperprolactinemia, often associated with increased risk of osteoporosis, and decreased libido and enlarged breasts in men. Both classes may also cause akathisia, a highly unpleasant sensation of inner restlessness and a relentless urge to move, which often contributes to non-compliance. Some evidence suggests that increasing relative activity at 5-HT2A receptors while decreasing relative activity at dopamine D2 receptors may reduce the risk of akathisia.

Because of these often disabling and sometimes serious side effects, compliance with available antipsychotic agents is typically poor. In fact, some experts estimate that nearly half of patients with schizophrenia are not receiving medical treatment because of poor tolerability.

CenterWatch has identified 14 drugs in various phases of development for schizophrenia, most of which act at one or more neurotransmitter receptors. Agonists mimic the action of the naturally found neurotransmitter, whereas antagonists counteract it.

Solvay Pharmaceuticals is in phase III testing of bifeprunox (DU127090), a mixed dopamine D2 partial agonist and 5-HT 1a partial agonist. This full spectrum, atypical antipsychotic targets both the positive and negative symptoms of schizophrenia.

Also in phase III development is Zomaril (iloperidone), Vanda Pharmaceu-ticals' novel antipsychotic agent for the treatment of schizophrenia and related psychoses. Zomaril is one of a new class of drugs known as serotonin/dopamine receptor antagonists (SDAs), which inhibit serotonin and dopamine activity by binding to these receptors in the brain. Specifically, it is a mixed 5-HT 2a /dopamine D2 antagonist.

Seven phase III clinical trials of Zomaril to date have included more than 3,700 patients at approximately 300 sites in 27 countries. At doses ranging from 4 to 24 mg per day, Zomaril was safe and effective, except for QTc interval prolongation with 24 mg daily. This change in QTc interval was similar to that of ziprasidone, a currently approved active comparator in the study. Nonetheless, this adverse effect may potentially limit use of Zomaril as first-line therapy.

ACP-103, a potent and selective 5-HT2A inverse agonist, is in phase II testing by ACADIA Pharmaceuticals as adjunctive therapy. The hope is that adding ACP-103 to currently available antipsychotic agents may achieve the best combination of dopamine receptor blockade and 5-HT2A inverse agonism. In theory, this should reduce adverse effects while expanding the range of efficacy.

Results from a double-blind, placebo-controlled clinical study were announced in September 2004. Of 18 healthy Swedish volunteers, 11 developed measurable akathisia after receiving a single 7.5 mg dose of haloperidol. Prolactin secretion also increased about threefold. After a single treatment with ACP-103, four of the subjects had complete disappearance of haloperidol-induced akathisia, and most subjects had reduced akathisia symptoms.

ACP-103 treatment was also associated with a highly statistically significant (33%; P < .001) reduction in haloperidol-induced increases in pro-

lactin secretion. Coadmini-stration of haloperidol and ACP-103 did not affect their pharmacokinetics, suggesting a lack of drug-drug interactions between these two agents.

In a drug receptor occupancy study using PET (positron emission tomography) scanning conducted at the Karolinska Institute, ACP-103 administered at single, low acute doses targeted 5-HT2A receptors without affecting motor control in healthy volunteers. In 2003, ACADIA completed two phase I clinical trials evaluating safety, tolerability and blood drug levels of ACP-103. Tolerability was good in all trials thus far, with no serious adverse effects.

ACADIA plans to conduct multiple phase II clinical trials of ACP-103 as adjunctive therapy in schizophrenia, testing its ability to ameliorate motor disturbances and improve efficacy of currently available antipsychotic drugs. One trial will study the effect of ACP-103 on haloperidol-induced adverse effects in patients with schizophrenia, and another trial will determine the effect of six weeks of adjunctive ACP-103 treatment in combination with low doses of haloperidol or risperidone.

Blonanserin (AD-5423) is a D2/5-HT2 antagonist in phase II testing by Dainippon Pharmaceutical. This novel antipsychotic agent differs in chemical structure from currently available antipsychotic agents. Because it has dopamine 2 and 5-HT2 receptor antagonistic properties, it is expected to be effective for both positive and negative symptoms.

Compared with other agents with a similar mechanism of action, blonanserin appears to be associated with fewer adverse drug reactions, including extrapyramidal symptoms, hypotension and weight gain. Another 5-HT2a/dopamine D2 antagonist is ocaperidone (ND-1087), in phase II testing by Neuro3d.

Abbott Laboratories is in phase II development of ABT-089 (2-methyl-3-(2-(S)-pyrrolidinyl-methoxy) pyridine dihydrochloride), a selective neuronal cholinergic channel modulator. Like nicotine, ABT-089 binds to nicotinic acetylcholine receptors, but with reduced adverse effects and improved oral bioavailability.

In surgically brain-injured rats, ABT-089 given short-term was associated with marginal improvement in performance on a water maze test of spatial discrimination. However, there was greater improvement, with 45% error reduction on the last training day, when ABT-089 was given continuously by subcutaneous osmotic pumps at a minimum effective dose of 1.3 µmol/kg/day. In monkeys, short-term administration of ABT-089 modestly improved a delayed memory task in young adult monkeys, with greater improvements in aged monkeys.

Another nicotinic agonist is MEM 3454, in phase I testing by Memory Pharma. In several preclinical models, this novel nicotinic alpha-7 receptor partial agonist showed robust activity and beneficial pharmacokinetics. The alpha-7 receptor, located primarily in the brain, appears to play important roles in nerve cell function, protection and plasticity.

Ampalex, an ampakine (AMPA) receptor enhancer, is in phase II development by Cortex Pharmaceuticals as a potential treatment for schizophrenia. Results in phase I trials were encouraging, with improvements in memory in healthy young and elderly, and in measures of attention, memory and cognition in schizophrenic patients. Another AMPA-receptor modulator is ORG-24448 (CX-619), in phase II testing by Organon.

DarPharma is in phase II testing of DAR-0100, a D1 dopamine receptor agonist targeting deficits in working memory and cognition associated with schizophrenia. An ongoing trial at the Medical University of South Carolina has enrolled patients with schizophrenia that is stabilized on available medications. Using functional magnetic resonance imaging (fMRI), the investigators will evaluate the effect of DAR-0100 on brain activation.

GlaxoSmithKline is in phase II testing of talnetant (SB 223412), a tachykinin (neurokinin 3; NK3) receptor antagonist. Because neurokinin receptors are involved in movement, this drug may in theory relieve some of the movement-related adverse effects associated with other antipsychotics.

In early trials, a small subset of patients on a high dose of talnetant had a positive response with good tolerability and minimal adverse effects such as weight gain. Talnetant may also help improve cognitive deficits associated with schizophrenia. Another NK3 antagonist is osanetant (SR 142801), in phase II development by Sanofi-Aventis.

On March 29 of this year, Saegis Pharmaceuticals, Inc., announced the completion of a phase I clinical study of SGS518, a 5HT-6 antagonist targeting cognitive impairment associated with schizophrenia (CIAS). Two cohorts of healthy volunteers were enrolled in a placebo-controlled, blinded study to evaluate safety, tolerability and pharmacokinetics. This was followed by a multi-dose study.

The therapeutic challenge in schizophrenia appears to be not only efficacy in reducing both positive and negative symptoms, but tolerability, which thus far has greatly limited compliance. Novel agents in development may achieve these goals by targeting a range of different neurotransmitter receptors, with the added benefit of relieving memory impairment associated with schizophrenia.

Drug	Company	Additional Information
Phase I		
LU-31130	H. Lundbeck A/S +45 36 30 13 11 www.lundbeck.com	acts at the dopamine D4 receptors in the cortex
MEM 3454	Memory Pharma (201) 802-7100 www.memorypharma.com	nicotinic alpha-7 partial agonists
SGS-518	Saegis Pharmaceuticals (650) 560-0210 www.saegispharma.com	5HT 6 antagonist

Drug	Company	Additional Information
Phase II		
ABT-089	Abbott Laboratories (847) 937-6100 www.abbott.com	selective neuronal cholinergic channel modulator
ACP-103	ACADIA Pharmaceuticals (858) 558-2871 www.acadia-pharm.com	5-HT2a inverse agonist
Ampalex (CX-516, SPD 420)	Cortex Pharmaceuticals (949) 727-3157 www.cortexpharm.com	ampakine (AMPA) receptor enhancer
DAR-0100	DarPharma (919) 403-4348 www.darpharma.com	D1 dopamine receptor agonist
blonanserin (AD-5423)	Dainippon Pharmaceutical 81-6-6337-5875 www.dainippon-pharm.co.jp	D2/5-HT2 antagonist
talnetant (SB 223412)	GlaxoSmithKline (888) 825-5249 www.gsk.com	tachykinin (NK3) receptor antagonist
ocaperidone (ND-1087)	Neuro3d +33 (0) 389 36 91 70 www.neuro3d.fr	5-HT2a/dopamine D2 antagonist
ORG-24448, CX-619	Organon (973) 325-4500 www.organon.com	modulate ampakine (AMPA) receptor
osanetant (SR 142801)	Sanofi-Aventis (33) 1 53 77 4000 www.sanofi-aventis.com	neurokinin-3 receptor antagonist.
Phase III		
bifeprunox, DU127090	Solvay Pharmaceuticals/ H. Lundbeck (770) 578-9000 www.solvay.com	mixed dopamine D2 partial agonist/5-HT 1a partial agonist
Zomaril (iloperidone)	Vanda Pharmaceuticals (650) 244-4990 www.titanpharm.com	mixed 5-HT 2a/dopamine D2 antagonist

Sexually Transmitted Diseases

By Laurie Barclay, M.D.
Published August 2005

According to latest estimates from Thomson, 1.4 million U.S. adults have sexually transmitted diseases (STDs). Prevalence is highest in young adults 25 to 34 years of age, and falls dramatically with increasing age thereafter. Although prevalence in men is nearly double that in women aged 18 to 24 years, gender prevalence is equal at ages 55 to 64, and becomes greater in females over 65 years of age.

In the U.S. as well as globally, human immunodeficiency virus (HIV) infection leading to acquired immune deficiency syndrome (AIDS) poses the most significant threat to public health of all the STDs. Although the estimated total number of deaths globally from AIDS at the end of 2003 was 3 million, HIV is no longer considered a terminal illness. In that year, estimated prevalence of HIV/AIDS worldwide was 38 million.

However, other STDs, especially herpes virus, are also important causes of morbidity. The STD with highest incidence in the U.S. is chlamydia, with an estimated 4 million new cases each year. In 75% of women and 50% of men, chlamydia is asymptomatic, but if left untreated, it may cause infertility in women. Annual incidence of gonorrhea in the U.S. is about 1 million, with possible complications of arthritis, tubal pregnancy and sterility if untreated.

Currently, standard HIV treatment is a cocktail containing drugs from each of the three drug classes targeting viral replication: nucleoside reverse transcriptase inhibitors (NRTIs), non-nucleoside reverse transcriptase inhibitors (NNRTIs) and protease inhibitors (PIs). Because of problems with these regimens including drug resistance, latent viral reservoirs, and drug-induced toxic effects, new classes of anti-HIV drugs with different mechanisms of action are clearly needed.

About three-quarters of HIV-infected patients carry a strain of virus resistant to one or more classes of antiretroviral agents. Adverse effects from currently available AIDS drugs include blood and liver abnormalities, rashes, diarrhea, diabetes, abnormal fat deposits and drug interactions.

CenterWatch has identified a pipeline of 40 drugs in various phases of development for STDs, mostly directed against the HIV virus, as well as some targeting herpes. Although some inhibit viral replication, some are preventive agents, vaccines or immune system stimulants.

Glyminox, in phase III development by Biosyn, is a broad-spectrum microbicide with activity against enveloped viruses. Therefore, it may have potential for STD prevention. In vaginal gel form, it is being tested as a topical contraceptive that may also prevent the transmission of HIV and other STDs, such as chlamydia and gonorrhea.

A similar prophylactic approach is Ushercell, a high molecular weight cellulose sulfate compound in phase III testing by Polydex Pharmaceuticals. This contraceptive antimicrobial gel is designed to protect against HIV, gonorrhea, chlamydia trachomatis and herpes simplex virus (HSV) 1 and 2. In three phase I trials, Ushercell was shown to be safe and effective.

An alternate strategy for prevention of HIV and other STDs is PRO-2000, in phase III testing by Indevus. This drug targets the CD4 molecule, thereby preventing the gp120 molecule of HIV from binding to and infecting cells. In pilot studies of continuous intravenous infusions of PRO-2000, some reversible changes in liver enzymes and platelet levels were noted. The drug is now being tested at various doses as a single daily injection, and like Glyminox, it is also being tested as a topical vaginal or anal microbicide.

While existing AIDS therapies attempt to reduce viral load, a different and complementary approach may be to stimulate the immune system to help fight off the attack. Dimethaid Research is in phase III testing of WF10, an intravenous formulation of tetra-chlorodecaoxide directed against HIV infection. This drug targets the macrophage, attempting to correct the immune deficiency underlying AIDS.

In recent trials of WF10, patients with late-stage AIDS have experienced significant improvements in clinical outcome, including fewer opportunistic infections and hospitalizations, and increased survival. Reported adverse effects have been negligible to date. Analysis of findings from 240 late-stage AIDS patients enrolled in a phase III, multicenter, double-blind, placebo-controlled study in the U.S. and Canada is ongoing.

For HIV infection, Hemispherx/Interferon Sciences is in phase III development of an oral interferon alfa-n3 formulation derived from human leukocytes and containing at least 14 alpha interferon molecules. As a class, interferons orchestrate the immune system's attack on viruses and other foreign substances, slowing or blocking their growth or function.

Side effects of interferons are predominantly flu-like symptoms occurring in nearly 50% of patients.

Remune (HIV-1 immunogen) is in phase III testing by Immune Response Corporation. This inactivated virus-based immune therapy is designed to restore HIV-specific immune responses lost early in the course of HIV infection, and to stimulate the immune system to launch an attack against HIV. In earlier clinical studies, Remune boosted HIV-specific immune responses and appeared to slow the progression of HIV infection when used alone or combined with antiretroviral

therapy. Remune may also stimulate production of cytokines and chemokines that naturally protect immune system components from HIV infection.

In 18 separate clinical trials in North America, Europe and Southeast Asia enrolling more than 2,000 patients, injection of Remune in the deltoid muscle once every three months was well tolerated. The most common adverse effect was transient injection-site reactions, including pain, tenderness and swelling. Findings from these studies suggest that Remune may have the potential to delay the start of antiretroviral drug therapy in drug-naïve patients, to induce an HIV-specific T-cell response, to induce HIV immunity broader than that achieved with vaccines based on subunits of the virus, to induce chemokines interfering with viral attachment and infection and to induce cytokines stimulating helper CD4 T-cells and CD8 "killer" T-cells.

A more traditional approach to HIV infection is capravirine, a non-nucleotide reverse transcriptase inhibitor (NNRTI) tested by Pfizer. This drug prevents HIV from entering the nucleus of healthy T-cells, thereby blocking viral replication and decreasing viral load. In June 2005, Pfizer halted development of capravirine when early phase II studies did not show any statistically significant advantages in patients refractory to other NNRTIs.

However, capravirine combined with two nucleotide reverse transcriptase inhibitors (NRTIs) may be effective against HIV in individuals naïve to NNRTI therapy. Whether or not capravirine will be effective against strains of HIV resistant to currently available NNRTIs is still unknown. HIV must acquire two or three key mutations to develop resistance to capravirine. Adverse effects may include cardiac problems (shown in dogs, but not reported in humans to date), nausea and a metallic taste.

A vaccine designed to protect against genital herpes is Simplirix, in phase III testing by GlaxoSmithKline. This consists of the gD2 subunit of herpes virus together with SBAS4, an adjuvant containing Corixa's MPL adjuvant to elicit T-cell responses. Drawbacks are that efficacy appears to be limited primarily to women who are seronegative for both HSVs 1 and 2.

The findings of two large, double-blind, placebo-controlled, multicenter trials suggest that widespread use of Simplirix could reduce the prevalence of genital herpes by 43% in women and by 32% in men. In a study of 847 participants seronegative for both HSV-1 and HSV-2, Simplirix was ineffective in men, but in women it was 73% effective in preventing laboratory-confirmed genital herpes. This difference may result from gender-specific infection routes: mucous membranes in women, and small skin abrasions on the penis in men.

In a second study of 2,491 individuals, efficacy of Simplirix was 74% in women who were seronegative for both HSV-1 and HSV-2, but the vaccine was ineffective in women who were HSV-1 positive/HSV-2 negative. Adverse effects were mild and transient, and primarily included local reactions at the vaccination site.

AuRx is in phase II development of another antiherpes vaccine, an attenuated recombinant vaccine designed to prevent HSV-2 infections. Through its effect on cell-mediated immunity, the AuRx therapy decreases the proportion of virus-specific T cells while increasing the proportion of protective T cells (helper type 1) and cytotoxic, CD8+ killer T cells that destroy virus-infected cells. Although genetic sequences of HSV-l and HSV-2 are similar, suggesting that this vaccine may also prevent HSV-1 recurrences, large, long-duration clinical trials are needed to test this hypothesis.

Cervarix (MEDI-517) is being promoted by GlaxoSmithKline as the first vaccine with potential for 100% efficacy against HPV16 and HPV18, the two types of human papillomavirus (HPV) with the highest risk for causing cervical cancer. This combination vaccine consists of self-assembling, virus-like particles (VLPs). In phase II studies, Cervarix was 100% effective in preventing persistent HPV16 and HPV18, suggesting that it could potentially prevent more than 70% of cervical cancers. Phase III trials enrolling 25,000 women are underway in the U.K., with filing expected in 2008 for the U.K.

A similar vaccine, being developed by Novavax and the National Cancer Institute, is a recombinant HPV16 VLP vaccine designed to prevent HPV infection. Based on a study of HPV infection in HIV-positive women, it appears that HPV16 is less associated with immunocompromised status than are other HPV types, and that HPV16 may be adept at side-stepping immune defenses even in healthy women.

For prevention of HIV infection, Antigenics is in phase II testing of QS-21, a triterpene glycoside vaccine adjuvant consisting of purified saponins. When added to vaccines and other immunotherapies, QS-21 may enhance immune response, increasing total vaccine-specific antibody response and T-cell response. QS-21 may also increase vaccine potency and act synergistically with other adjuvants.

In addition to new vaccines, novel antiviral agents are also entering the pipeline, especially for HIV. Achillion Pharmaceuticals is in phase II testing of elvucitabine (ACH-126,443), a new NRTI. In the laboratory, this drug has activity against hepatitis B virus (HBV) and other viruses resistant to other NRTIs, with no mitochondrial toxicity often seen with this drug class. In fact, when combined with stavudine, elvucitabine reduced the level of mitochondrial damage caused by the former drug. Its half-life of more than 24 hours allows once daily dosing. Phase II studies are underway in patients with chronic hepatitis B virus (HBV) or HIV+ infection resistant to lamivudine.

Rather than attacking the virus after it has infected a healthy cell, entry or fusion inhibitors prevent the virus from entering a healthy cell, thereby blocking viral replication. An HIV entry inhibitor in phase II development by AnorMed, AMD-070, in combination with AMD-887, a preclinical compound in preclinical development in Canada, may be an especially potent blocker of HIV replication. These drugs may also prove to be useful when combined with approved anti-HIV agents.

Another HIV entry inhibitor is BMS-488043, in phase II testing by Bristol-Myers Squibb. This orally administered drug is designed to prevent the gp120 molecule of HIV from attaching to the CD4 receptor, thereby blocking HIV infection of CD4 T-cells. In a placebo-controlled, randomized study of 30 HIV-positive individuals, BMS-488043 (800 or 1800 mg twice daily) for eight days led to a peak reduction in viral load at day 9. However, viral load slowly rebounded in most patients. Overall, the drug was well tolerated, and dose-defining studies are underway.

Bavarian Nordic is in phase II testing of MVA-BN HIV nef, which combines the MVA-F6 attenuated pox virus vector with the HIV Nef antigen in hopes of controlling HIV replication after interrupting or in conjunction with antiretroviral therapy. Extended follow-up of patients enrolled in a phase I trial suggests that MVA nef is safe and immunogenic, with 11 of 14 HIV-infected persons mounting an immune response to the Nef antigen. A phase II study is underway in 75 HIV-infected patients with CD4 counts of 250, with 50 patients receiving MVA nef vaccine and 25 patients receiving smallpox vaccine as a control.

Gene therapy is a novel approach to block viral replication, as is the case with HGTV-43, in phase II development by Enzo Biochem. HGTV-43 uses StealthVector carrying anti-HIV-1 antisense RNA genes directed against genes directing viral replication, and it delivers the antisense genes to targeted blood cells of HIV-1 infected patients. Preclinical studies suggest that human immune cells into which antisense genes are inserted are resistant to HIV-1. In phase I trials, stem cells were collected from each patient, treated with HGTV-43 in the laboratory and reinfused. This was well tolerated; the treated cells engrafted into the bone marrow; and anti-HIV-1 antisense RNA expression continued to circulate CD4+ immune cells for up to two years.

With the explosive growth of the AIDS epidemic, and dramatically increasing prevalence of other STDs, it is imperative to develop multiple modes of attack against these diseases with significant morbidity and often mortality. This is especially true given the propensity for viruses to develop resistance. Fortunately, the pipeline is rich not only in individual agents but also in a variety of potentially complementary therapeutic strategies.

Drug	Company	Additional Information
Phase I		
TNF inhibitor (AIDS)	Advanced Biotherapy (818) 883-6716 www.advancedbiotherapy.com	TNF alpha inhibitor; HIV infection
ArV vaccine (AVX101)	AlphaVax (919) 595-0400 www.alphavax.com	vaccine using company's AVS vector VRP (VEE replicon particle); HIV infection
AMD-070	AnorMED (604) 530-1057 www.anormed.com	an HIV-entry inhibitor that targets the CXCR4 chemokine receptor; HIV infection
UC-781	Biosyn (215) 914-0900 www.biosyn-inc.com	HIV non-nucleoside reverse transcriptase inhibitor
Multikine	CEL-SCI (703) 506-9460 www.cel-sci.com	cytokine cocktail which includes interleukin-2 (IL-2), IL-b, TNF-a, Gm-CSF and an IFN-g/immuno-modulator; HIV infection
HIV vaccine	CytRx (310) 826-5648 www.cytrx.com	vaccine uses a DNA and protein technology
DNA-HIV-C/ NYVAC-HIV-C	EuroVacc +41-21-692 5856 www.eurovacc.org	designed to combat HIV subtype C, utilizes a highly attenuated recombinant vaccinia virus
HIV vaccine	GenVec (240) 632-0740 www.genvec.com	prophylactic vaccine against HIV based upon GenVec's adenovector technology
PRO-140 (CCR5 MAb)	Progenics Pharmaceuticals (914) 789-2800 www.progenics.com	fully human monoclonal antibody which selectively binds the chemokine receptor CCR5, a facilitator in HIV-1

Drug	Company	Additional Information
MVA-RN	Walter Reed Army Institute (301) 319-9000 wrair-www.army.mi	anthrax-derived polypeptide called Lethal factor (LFn), of Research (WRAIR) fused to the HIV-1 gag p24 protein; HIV infection
Phase II		
elvucitabine, (ACH-126,443)	Achillion Pharmaceuticals (203) 624-7000 www.achillion.com	reverse transcriptase (RT) inhibitor; HIV infection
AMD-070	AnorMed (604) 530-1057 www.anormed.com	CXCR4 inhibitor; HIV infection
QS-21	Antigenics (212) 994-8200 www.antigenics.com	a triterpene glycoside vaccine adjuvant consisting of purified saponins; HIV infection
antiherpes vaccine	AuRx www.aurx.com (410) 590-7610	attenuated recombinant vaccine for the prevention of herpes simplex virus (HSV)-2 infections
MVA-BN HIV nef	Bavarian Nordic +45 3326 8383 www.bavarian-nordic.com	uses an MVA-F6 attenuated pox virus vector; HIV infection; Germany
BMS-488043	Bristol-Myers Squibb (212) 546-4000 www.bms.com	oral small-molecule attachment inhibitor of HIV-1
HGTV-43	Enzo Biochem (212) 583-0100 www.enzo.com	gene therapy using StealthVector encoding with an antisense oligonucleotide; HIV infection
EP HIV-1090	Epimmune (858) 860-2500 www.epimmune.com	composed of twenty-one unique epitopes, from conserved regions of multiple HIV virus proteins
GW873140 (ONO-4128)	GlaxoSmithKline (888) 825-5249 www.gsk.com	allosteric CCR5 receptor antagonists; HIV infection
GW-640385, VX-385	GlaxoSmithKline (888) 825-5249 www.gsk.com	HIV protease inhibitor
Cervarix (MEDI-517)	GlaxoSmithKline (888) 825-5249 www.gsk.com	combination vaccine consisting of self-assembling, virus-like particles (VLPs); HPV (Phase III in the U.K.)
Ampligen (polyl:poly C12U)	Hemispherx Biopharma (215) 988-0080 www.hemispherx.net	intravenous therapeutic composed of polyribo-nucleotide and synthetic nucleic acid, HIV infection
Immunitin (HE2000)	Hollis-Eden Pharmaceuticals (858) 587-9333 www.holliseden.com	inhibits HIV replication by manipulating host cellular factors
IR103	Immune Response Corporation (760) 431-7080 www.imnr.com	HIV-1 Immunogen with Amplivax, an immuno-stimulatory oligonucleotide adjuvant
DPC-817 (D-D4FC, Reverset)	Immune Response Corporation (760) 431-7080 www.imnr.com	oral nucleoside reverse transcriptase inhibitor; HIV infection

Drug	Company	Additional Information
HPV-16	Novavax/National Cancer Institute (NCI) (301) 854-3900 www.novavax.com	recombinant HPV-16 virus-like particle (VLP) vaccine for the potential prevention of papillomavirus-induced infection
PSI-5004 (Racivir)	Pharmasset (678) 395-0050 www.pharmasset.com	oral nucleoside reverse transcriptase inhibitor; HIV infection
PRO 542	Progenics Pharmaceuticals (914) 789-2800 www.progenics.com	fusion protein containing CD4 and antibody sequences that binds to HIV gp120
Anticort (procaine, SP-01, SP-01A)	Samaritan Pharmaceuticals (702) 735-7001 www.samaritanpharma.com	anti-cortisol steroidogenesis inhibitor; HIV infection
TNX-355	Tanox (713) 578-4000 www.tanox.com	monoclonal antibody designed to bind to the CD4 receptor on host cell surfaces; HIV infection
VRX496	VIRxSYS (301) 987-0480 www.virxsys.com	lentiviral HIV-based vector encoding anti-HIV antisense envelope sequences
PA-457	V.I. Technologies (617) 926-1551 www.vitechnologies.com	maturation inhibitor, blocks the last step in HIV maturation, as the virus buds from infected cells.
Phase III		
glyminox	Biosyn (215) 914-0900 www.biosyn-inc.com	broad-spectrum microbicide that displays activity against enveloped viruses; STD prevention
WF10	Dimethaid Research (905) 415-1446 www.dimethaid.com	intravenous formulation of tetra-chlorodecaoxide; HIV infection
interferon alfa-n3 (oral)	Hemispherx/ Interferon Sciences (215) 988-0080 www.hemispherx.net	derived from human leukocytes and contains at least 14 alpha interferon molecules; HIV infection
Simplirix	GlaxoSmithKline (888) 825-5249 www.gsk.com	gD2 subunit of herpes virus together with GSK's SBAS4, an adjuvant containing Corixa's MPL adjuvant; United Kingdom
Remune (HIV-1 immunogen)	Immune Response Corporation (760) 431-7080 www.imnr.com	immune-based therapy designed to restore HIV-specific immune responses lost early on in HIV infection
PRO 2000	Indevus Pharmaceuticals (781) 861-8444 www.interneuron.com	antimicrobial gel, prevents STD pathogens from attaching to and entering target cells
Ushercell	Polydex Pharmaceuticals (410) 516-7260 www.reprotect.com	high molecular weight cellulose sulfate gel compound; HIV prevention
AIDSVAX	VaxGen (650) 624-1000 www.vaxgen.com	genetically engineered, aluminum-adjuvanted subunit vaccine cloned from a protein (gp120) found on the surface of the HIV virus

Stroke

By Laurie Barclay, M.D.
Published September 2005

Stroke, or cerebrovascular accident, refers to localized brain damage resulting from interruption of blood flow. The three main types of stroke are ischemic, in which a blood vessel is gradually occluded or stenosed by atherosclerotic build-up; embolic, in which a blood vessel is suddenly blocked by a fragment of clot traveling from the heart or from a larger vessel; and hemorrhagic, in which a blood vessel ruptures and bleeds into the brain tissue, often in association with high blood pressure.

In the U.S., someone has a stroke every 45 seconds, and someone dies of stroke every three minutes, according to the American Stroke Association. The American Heart Association cites an incidence of 731,100 first or recurrent strokes in the U.S. in 1996, with over 4.4 million Americans estimated to be stroke survivors. Stroke is the third leading cause of death in the U.S., and is the leading cause of long-term disability. In 2004, direct and indirect costs of stroke in the U.S. were estimated to be $53.6 billion.

Risk factors for cerebrovascular disease include hypertension, cardiovascular disease, diabetes, smoking, family history of stroke, atherosclerosis and cardiac arrhythmias.

As with heart attack, acute stroke is an emergency that must be diagnosed and treated promptly, because "time is tissue." Warning signs such as weakness, paralysis or numbness of one side of the body or face or of one or more limbs; problems with speech, balance, vision or swallowing; or loss of consciousness mandate immediate intervention.

Stroke prevention focuses on control of risk factors, and antiplatelet agents or anticoagulants in some patients. If patients are seen within three or possibly up to six hours of symptom onset, intravenous recombinant tissue plasminogen activator, (rt-PA) may limit stroke damage. Surgery and/or rehabilitation may be indicated in some patients, but estimates suggest that fewer than 10% of stroke patients are eligible for currently available therapies, and that fewer than 5% actually receive treatment.

CenterWatch has identified a pipeline of 23 drugs in various phases of development for stroke. These include anticoagulants, neuroprotective agents, and therapies designed to restore function in patients with fixed deficits.

Actelion Pharmaceuticals is in phase III development of Clazosentan (AXV-343434), a competitive endothelin ET-A receptor antagonist. This drug is designed to prevent vasospasm, or contraction of blood vessels causing ischemia and neurological deficits three to 10 days after subarachnoid hemorrhage (SAH) caused by ruptured aneurysm.

Clazosentan has shown promising results in the prevention and treatment of vasospasm in preclinical models of SAH. In phase I trials in healthy volunteers, clazosentan infusions were well tolerated, without affecting blood pressure or other vital signs. In patients with SAH, those given clazosentan had fewer cases of vasospasm, less severe vasospasm, and fewer new cerebral infarcts than did those given placebo.

A global phase IIb/III development program began in late 2004 with the placebo-controlled, dose-finding CONSCIOUS-1 study in prevention of vasospasm following SAH. Trial results are anticipated by mid-2006.

Forest Laboratories is in phase III testing of desmoteplase, an anticoagulant plasminogen activator derived from the saliva of the vampire bat. Compared with tissue plasminogen activator (TPA), desmoteplase is much more potent and has the potential to triple the current stroke treatment window without increasing the risk of additional brain damage. Animal studies suggest that desmoteplase breaks down fibrin underlying blood clots, but unlike rt-PA, without affecting two brain receptors that can promote brain damage. In Europe, Asia and Australia, desmoteplase is being tested up to nine hours after stroke onset in patients.

Neurobiological Technologies has completed phase II testing of Viprinex (ancrod), a fibrinogen-depleting agent derived from the venom of the Malaysian pit viper. In U.S. and European trials enrolling more than 2,000 patients, Viprinex appeared potentially to have doubled the available treatment window after the onset of ischemic stroke symptoms. Phase III trials are planned for late 2005, pending FDA approval.

Disufenton (NXY-059, Cerovive), is in phase III testing by AstraZeneca for acute ischemic stroke. This N-tert-butyl-alpha-phenyl-nitrone (PBN) derivative is given by intravenous infusion over 72 hours started within six hours of symptom onset. By trapping damaging free radicals, it may protect brain tissue. It is still unknown whether disufenton can be safely given without prior CT scanning. If so, it may be more widely applicable than TPA and may eventually be considered for use even by paramedics.

Another neuroprotectant thought to have multiple mechanisms of action is CerAxon (citicoline), in phase III development by IVAX. It is thought to stabilize cell membranes long enough to reduce stroke-related brain cell injury.

In a trial enrolling nearly 400 patients in 33 U.S. centers, CerAxon showed no statistically significant difference from placebo in rates of full recovery and mortality or in neurological and cognitive function. However, CerAxon did appear to be more effective than placebo in a subset of patients with moderate to severe strokes.

Prasugrel (CS-747) is a platelet inhibitor in phase III development by Eli Lilly/Sankyo. In three early-phase trials, this P2Y adenosine diphosphate (ADP) receptor antagonist resulted in significantly higher and more consistent inhibition of platelet aggregation than did placebo or clopidogrel (Plavix), the current standard of care. Currently, the drug is being tested primarily in acute coronary syndrome.

A novel approach to inhibiting platelet clumping is ReoPro (abciximab, c7E3), in phase II testing by Centocor for reperfusion after acute ischemic stroke. This fragment (Fab) of a monoclonal antibody binds to the glycoprotein (IIb/IIIa) platelet receptor, thereby preventing platelet adhesion.

Medicure is in phase III testing of MC-1, a vitamin B6 metabolite and purinergic receptor antagonist that may also protect damaged cells in the heart or brain. In phase I clinical studies, MC-1 had a high degree of safety for human use.

Idraparinux (SanOrg 34006), in phase III development by Sanofi-Synthelabo, is a new member of the synthetic oligosaccharide family of anticoagulant drugs. After successful dose-finding phase II trials, idraparinux is being evaluated in over 10,000 patients for the treatment and secondary prevention of venous thromboembolism (VTE), and for prevention of thromboembolic events caused by atrial fibrillation.

The mechanism of action of idraparinux is selective inhibition of coagulation Factor Xa. Its potency and long duration of action allow administration as a single weekly injection. Unlike oral anticoagulants such as warfarin, idraparinux does not appear to interact with foods or drugs.

Neurochem has completed phase II testing of Cerebril, an oral sulfated glycosaminoglycan (GAG) mimetic. By inhibiting amyloid beta fibrillogenesis, this drug may be useful in patients with intracranial hemorrhage caused by cerebral amyloid angiopathy. No safety concerns have been identified thus far.

For acute stroke, D-Pharm is in phase II development of DP-b99, a neuroprotectant prodrug of the known calcium chelator BAPTA. In two phase I clinical trials enrolling 70 volunteers, DP-b99 was well tolerated both in single and multiple dosing, with the only major adverse effect reported being reversible irritation at the injection site. A pilot phase II trial in 34 patients with acute ischemic stroke confirmed that the drug was generally safe and showed a strong trend for improvement in neurological stroke outcome compared with placebo. At 20 medical centers in Europe and Israel, an ongoing phase II trial of efficacy will enroll 150 patients with acute stroke.

KAI Pharmaceuticals is in phase II testing of KAI-9803, an isozyme-selective, delta-protein kinase C inhibitor being tested primarily in acute myocardial infarction. Because it is designed to reduce ischemia and reperfusion injury, it may also be useful in acute stroke.

For the treatment of stroke, deep-vein thrombosis and other conditions associated with antibody-mediated thrombosis (antiphospholipid syndrome), La Jolla Pharmaceutical is in phase II development of LJP-1082, which is designed to reduce the production of disease-causing antibodies without affecting the defensive capabilities of the immune system.

The target of these antibodies causing excessive thrombosis is a small region on the beta 2-glycoprotein I blood protein, which is implicated in about 90% of patients with antibody-mediated thrombosis, in about 50% of all stroke victims under age 50, and in about 10% to 15% of the general stroke population.

In a phase I/II clinical trial, LJP 1082 was well-tolerated at all five dose levels, with an elimination half-life of at least 12 hours following intravenous injection. After treatment with a single 50 mg or 200 mg dose, some patients had reduced antibodies to LJP 1082. All adverse events were mild to moderate, and similar to those in placebo-treated groups. In the 20 patients studied, there was an apparent dose-dependent response in antibody reduction.

An interesting approach potentially offering hope to stroke survivors with fixed neurological deficits is LBS-Neurons, or cultured human neuronal cells, in phase II testing by Layton BioScience. These neurons are intended to be transplanted into a patient's brain to improve the function of neurons injured by stroke. The ability of LBS-Neurons to be frozen, transported to clinical centers for transplan-

tation, thawed and implanted may improve the feasibility of this therapy.

The LBS-Neurons are derived from a cell line of human teratocarcinoma initially developed in the mid-1980s and further manipulated in tissue culture and in animal models to become fully differentiated, non-dividing neurons. Animal models suggest that grafted LBS-Neurons will either restore the function of impaired host neurons, or replace host neurons destroyed by stroke. In a clinical trial, a single surgery was used to implant two million neurons divided among three sites within and surrounding stroke-damaged tissue, where it is hoped they will integrate with existing tissue and restore brain function.

Proglia (ONO-2506), in phase II development by Ono Pharmaceutical/Merck, is a neuroprotectant and neurotropic agent. This drug modulates astrocyte function by regulating uptake capacity of glutamate transporters and expression of GABA receptors and various astrocytic factors. Although U.S. phase II studies in acute ischemic stroke were discontinued in May 2005, they are ongoing in Japan.

Boston Life Sciences has filed an Investigational New Drug Application for the nerve growth factor Axosine (inosine), intended to facilitate recovery of motor function after stroke. Animal models have been encouraging. A proposed phase I, dose-escalation study may treat 27 patients with moderate to severe stroke patients with Axosine administered via an implantable subcutaneous pump and catheter system.

For optimal outcome following stroke, it is still vital to control risk factors and to seek immediate medical attention at the first sign of symptoms, because prevention is more successful than cure, and because "time is tissue" when it comes to preserving brain cells. However, it is encouraging that new drugs in the pipeline may extend the therapeutic window of opportunity after acute stroke, and that neurotrophic or neural transplant approaches even have the potential to reverse fixed deficits.

Drug	Company	Additional Information
IND Filed		
Axosine (inosine)	Boston Life Sciences (617) 425-0200 www.bostonlifesciences.com	a nerve growth factor
Phase I		
E-2051	Eisai Co Ltd (201) 692-1100 www.eisai.com	neuron-selective calcium channel blocker
INO-1001	Inotek Pharmaceuticals (978) 232-9660 www.inotekcorp.com	a PARS (poly ADP ribose inhibitor
NS-1209	NeuroSearch A/S +45 4460 8000 www.neurosearch.com	a glutamate antagonist with possible effectiveness as a neuroprotective agent
CI-1034	Pfizer (212) 733-2323 www.pfizer.com	a novel dopamine agonist
Phase II		
ReoPro (abciximab, c7E3)	Centocor (888) 874-3083 www.centocor.com	a fragment (Fab) of a monoclonal antibody that binds to the glycoprotein (IIb/IIIa) receptor of platelets and inhibits their clumping together
DP-b99	D-Pharm 972-8-9300794 www.dpharm.com	a neuroprotectant prodrug of the known calcium chelator BAPTA, (Phase II Israel)
argatroban	Encysive Pharmaceuticals (713) 796-8822 www.encysive.com	a non-protein, arginine-related thrombin inhibitor
KAI-9803	KAI Pharmaceuticals (650) 244-1100 www.kaipharmaceuticals.com	a delta-protein kinase C inhibitor
LJP-1082	La Jolla Pharmaceutical (858) 452-6600 www.ljpc.com	a designed to reduce the production of disease-causing antibodies, without affecting the disease-fighting ability of the immune system
LBS-neurons	Layton BioScience (408) 616-1000 www.laytonbio.com	a cultured human neuronal cells being tested for the treatment of fixed neurological deficits resulting from stroke
Proglia (ONO-2506)	Ono Pharmaceutical/Merck +81 06-6263-5670 www.ono.co.jp	a neurotropic agent that modulates astrocyte function
traxoprodil	Pfizer (212) 733-2323 www.pfizer.com	an intravenous, selective NMDA receptor antagonist
CPC-211	Questcor (510) 400-0700 www.questcor.com	an activator of pyruvate dehydrogenase
Phase II Complete		
Viprinex (ancrod)	Neurobiological Technologies (510) 262-1730 www.ntii.com	a fibrinogen-depleting agent derived from the venom of the Malaysian pit viper

Drug	Company	Additional Information
Cerebril	Neurochem (510) 262-1730 www.ntii.com	an oral sulfated glycosaminoglycan (GAG) mimetic that inhibits amyloid beta fibrillogenesis

Phase III

Drug	Company	Additional Information
clazosentan (AXV-343434)	Actelion Pharmaceuticals + 41 61 487 45 45 www.actelion.com	a competitive endothelin ET-A receptor antagonist
disufenton (NXY-059, Cerovive)	AstraZeneca (781) 839-4000 www.astrazeneca.com	an N-tert-butyl-alpha-phenyl-nitrone (PBN) derivative free-radical-trapping agent
Prasugrel (CS-747)	Eli Lilly/Sankyo (800) 545-5979 www.lilly.com	a P2Y ADP receptor antagonist with anti-platelet activity
desmoteplase	Forest Laboratories (212) 421-7850 www.frx.com	an anti-clotting plasminogen activator derived from the saliva of the vampire bat
CerAxon (citicoline)	IVAX (305) 575-6000 www.ivax.com	a neuroprotectant believed to have multiple mechanisms of action
MC-1	Medicure (204) 487-7412 www.medicure.com	a vitamin B6 metabolite
idraparinux (SanOrg 34006)	Sanofi-Synthelabo (33) 1 53 77 4000 www.sanofi-aventis.com	a synthetic idraparinux sodium molecule with anticoagulant action

Type 1 Diabetes

By Laurie Barclay, M.D.
Published January 2005

Type 1 diabetes is an autoimmune disease in which the beta cells of the pancreas do not produce sufficient insulin, causing high blood glucose, which must be treated with exogenous insulin. Unlike type 2 diabetes, type 1 diabetes, often termed juvenile or insulin-dependent diabetes, usually begins during childhood or early adulthood.

In the U.S., about 15.7 million people, or 5.9% of the population, have diabetes of either type. Although about 10.3 million have been diagnosed, about 5.4 million people are unaware that they have diabetes. The annual incidence of type 1 diabetes, which affects more than 700,000 Americans, is 3.7 to 20 per 100,000. Healthcare costs and costs of lost productivity related to diabetes are between $98 billion and $138 billion annually.

Diabetes is the seventh leading cause of death in the U.S., the leading cause of new cases of blindness in adults 20 to 74 years of age and the leading cause of end-stage renal disease, accounting for about 40% of new cases. Other complications include peripheral neuropathy, affecting about 60% to 70% of patients.

Diabetes is the most common cause of non-traumatic lower limb amputations, and it increases the risk of leg amputation 15- to 40-fold. Heart disease is present in 75% of diabetes-related deaths, and having diabetes doubles to quadruples the risk of heart disease. Most of these complications are related to changes in the microvasculature, with thickening of capillary walls resulting in local ischemia.

In type 1 diabetes, lack of insulin causes glucose to accumulate in the bloodstream instead of entering the cells. Because this glucose cannot be used for energy, symptoms include hunger, fatigue and weight loss despite increased appetite. Hyperglycemia causes frequent urination and excessive thirst. Complete destruction of beta cells and cessation of insulin production typically occurs within five to 10 years. Other symptoms may include nausea, vomiting, abdominal pain and amenorrhea.

Tests used to diagnose diabetes include fasting blood glucose of at least 126 mg/dL, urinalysis positive for glucose and ketone bodies, and low or undetectable level of insulin or C-peptide, a by-product of insulin production. Glycosylated hemoglobin (HbA1c) should be measured two to four times each year to evaluate overall glucose control.

Currently available treatment includes insulin, injected once to four times daily and adjusted based on self-testing of blood glucose; diet and weight control; exercise; and foot care. Insulin preparations differ in their onset and duration of action, and more than one type may be mixed together in an injection for optimal glucose control.

Complications include diabetic ketoacidosis, caused by breakdown of fat as an alternate fuel, and hypoglycemia related to excessive insulin use. Hypoglycemia usually responds to eating sugar, but in severe cases associated with confusion, seizures or unconsciousness, an injection of glucagon may be needed. Diabetic ketoacidosis needs to be treated immediately, or coma and even death may ensue.

CenterWatch has identified a pipeline of 19 drugs in various stages of development for diabetes treatment and monitoring. Most of these are novel formulations of insulin.

Amylin Pharmaceuticals has submitted a new drug application for Symlin (pramlintide), a synthetic injectable analog of the human hormone amylin. This hormone is normally secreted by the beta cells and works synergistically with insulin and glucagon to maintain normal glucose concentrations.

In six phase III clinical trials, Symlin has been associated with improved blood glucose control and reduced HbA1c levels in patients treated with insulin alone, or insulin plus one or more oral medications, without causing weight gain. More than 5,000 patients have been treated with Symlin in these studies, earlier trials and long-term open-label safety trials.

During treatment for 26 or 52 weeks, there were no adverse effects on lipids or blood pressure. The most common adverse effects were nausea, anorexia and vomiting. These were generally mild to moderate, dose-related and tended to resolve over time.

Pfizer in collaboration with Sanofi-Aventis has completed phase III development of Exubera, an inhaled, short-acting, fine dry-powder insulin preparation with rapid onset of action. If approved, Exubera could eliminate the need for meal-time insulin injections and improve treatment compliance. However, concerns about long-term pulmonary safety have delayed filings for regulatory approval in Europe and the U.S., pending additional safety data.

More than 2,000 patients have been treated with Exubera in worldwide clinical trials to date, some for as long as five years. Phase III clinical trials suggest that Exubera may be as effective as injected insulin and better than oral hypoglycemic agents in lowering blood glucose. In a phase III study of 328 patients, glucose control was similar in patients receiving Exubera before meals plus two daily insulin injections to that in patients receiving four daily insulin injections. Further-more, the patients receiving Exubera had greater reductions in fasting plasma glucose levels and in two-hour postprandial glucose. Compared with the insulin-only group, the Exubera group was more satisfied with overall treatment and had greater improvements in symptoms and in cognitive function.

Although the frequency and nature of adverse events were similar in the Exubera and insulin-only groups, mild to moderate cough was more common early in Exubera treatment, and there was a small, non-progressive reduction in pulmonary function.

Another pulmonary delivery system for insulin is the AERx diabetes management system, in phase III development by Aradigm and Novo Nordisk. The AERx Strip dosage form contains a disposable nozzle allowing superior aerosol performance with each inhalation, as well as adjustment for various treatment requirements to regulate the particle size and thus the primary deposition area of the medication.

Alkermes is also developing an inhaled insulin formulation, AIR-insulin, now in phase II testing. Based on positive results in preliminary trials, Alkermes is developing short-acting formulations for mealtime, and long-acting formulations to be administered once to twice daily from small, simple inhalers. The company's

proprietary AIR pulmonary drug delivery technology is based on the concept that relatively large, low-density drug particles can be inhaled into the lungs with high efficiency from simple inhaler devices.

Emisphere Technologies has completed phase II testing of Eligen, an oral formulation using a "carrier" molecule to keep insulin in a fat-soluble state. In a rat model where diabetes was induced with streptozotocin to destroy beta cells, Eligen reversed hyperglycemia, polydipsia (increased water consumption), weight loss and autonomic dysfunction. In primates, Eligen rapidly and significantly increased insulin levels and prolonged reduction of blood glucose.

Oralin is an oral liquid form of insulin in phase II development by Generex Biotechnology. Using a RapidMist device, this unique formulation is delivered directly into the mouth where it is rapidly absorbed into the bloodstream through the buccal mucosa. In clinical trials involving more than 250 people, insulin and blood glucose levels after Oralin administration were consistent with levels achieved by injected insulin.

An alternate approach to novel insulin formulations is encapsulated pancreatic islet cell implants, in phase II testing by Amcyte/Mylan. These proliferated insulin-secreting cells resemble islets of Langerhans and are designed to reduce the need for supplemental insulin.

Once fully developed and approved, these proliferated islets could theoretically treat patients with a simple infusion into the abdominal cavity, without the need for life-long immune suppression. A clinical safety trial showed that blood sugar control was achievable following intraperitoneal transplantation.

An approach based on the autoimmune etiology of type 1 diabetes is Diamyd rhGAD65, in phase II testing by Diamyd Medical. This recombinant human glutamic acid decarboxylase (GAD65) is designed to prevent and treat insulin-dependent diabetes in patients with GAD antibodies. In a phase I trial, no safety concerns were defined, and there was a positive outcome at one of the dose levels in a phase II trial.

Another approach targeting the immune system is TRX4, an anti-CD3 monoclonal antibody in phase II development by TolerRx. This humanized monoclonal antibody binds to the CD3 receptor found on all T cells to regulate normal T cell signaling. TRX4 is designed to block the function of T-effector cells that cause autoimmune disease, promoting immunological tolerance. Based on the results of a phase II clinical trial in Europe, TolerRx is planning further clinical trials in patients with new-onset type I diabetes after discussions with the FDA in 2005.

Insmed is in phase II development of SomatoKine (mecasermin rinfabate), a novel recombinant insulin-like growth factor (IGF-BP3) complex. In a double-blind, randomized, placebo-controlled trial, SomatoKine was safe and well tolerated, with mild, dose-dependent hypoglycemia. It improved insulin sensitivity and glycemic control, with decrease in requirements for insulin dosage by 49% (P < .01), in mean blood glucose by 23% (P < .03), in plasma insulin levels by 47% and in mean growth hormone by 72%.

Neurocrine Biosciences is in phase II testing of NBI-6024, a peptide based on insulin B chain amino acid residues 9 to 23. Safety data show that this compound is safe and well tolerated.

Also in phase II testing is AS-3201, an aldose reductase inhibitor being developed by Dainippon Pharmaceutical for diabetic complications such as cataract, neuropathy, retinopathy and nephropathy. Results of a double-blind, randomized trial published in 2004 in Diabetes Care suggest that S-3201 penetrates the sural nerve and inhibits sorbitol accumulation in patients with diabetic sensorimotor polyneuropathy. Sensory nerve conduction velocities also improved by 1 m/s (P < .05). However, additional studies are needed to determine whether AS-3201 delays progression or leads to regression of polyneuropathy.

Novel formulations of insulin by the inhaled or oral route may allow greater patient convenience and compliance. Approaches targeting the immune basis of diabetes may theoretically allow earlier intervention in the course of this disease, while drugs correcting defects in the microvasculature may help to address neuropathy, retinopathy, and other chronic complications.

Drug	Company	Additional Information
Phase I		
AT1391	Altea Therapeutics (678) 495-3100 www.alteatherapeutics.com	daily insulin skin patch formulation using its PassPort technology
NN344	Novo Nordisk +45 4444-8888 www.novonordisk.com	neutral, soluble long-acting human insulin analog

Drug	Company	Additional Information
Phase I Completed		
Islet Neogenesis	Transition Therapeutics (416) 260-7770 www.transitiontherapeutics.com	stimulates the regeneration of insulin-producing islet Therapy (I.N.T.) cells by gastrin and epidermal growth factors
Phase I/II		
Oral insulin	Nobex (919) 474-0507 www.nobexcorp.com	oral insulin
Phase II		
AIR-insulin (inhaled insulin)	Alkermes (617) 494-0171 www.alkermes.com	inhaled insulin based on the company's AIR pulmonary drug delivery technology
Encapsulated islets	Amcyte/Mylan (310) 264-7768 www.amcyte.com	encapsulated pancreatic islet cell implants
AS-3201	Dainippon Pharmaceutical (81) 6-6337-5875 www.dainippon-pharm.co.jp	aldose reductase inhibitor for diabetic complications including cataract, neuropathy, retinopathy and nephropathy
Diamyd, rhGAD65	Diamyd Medical +46(0)8-661 00 26 www.diamyd.com	recombinant human glutamic acid decarboxylase (GAD65)
AVE0277, DiaPep277	DeveloGen AG +49 (0)551-50 558 0 www.develogen.com	24-amino acid peptide formed from residues 437 to 460 of hsp60
Oralin	Generex Biotechnology (416) 364-2551 www.generex.com	oral liquid form of insulin
SomatoKine (mecasermin rinfabate)	Insmed (804) 565-3022 www.insmed.com	novel recombinant insulin-like growth factor (IGF-BP3) complex
NBI-6024	Neurocrine Biosciences (858) 658-7600 www.neurocrine.com	peptide based on insulin B chain amino acid residues 9 to 23
P93/01	Probiodrug AG +49 345 5559900 www.probiodrug.de	dipeptidyl peptidase IV (DP-IV) inhibitor
Zenapax (daclizumab)	Protein Design Labs (510) 574-1400 www.pdl.com	immunosuppressive monoclonal antibody that targets the alpha chain of the human IL-2 receptor
TRX4	TolerRx (617) 354-8100 www.tolerrx.com	an anti-CD3 monoclonal antibody
Phase II Completed		
Eligen, insulin (oral)	Emisphere Technologies (914) 347-2220 www.emisphere.com	Oral formulation that uses a "carrier" molecule that keeps insulin in a fat-soluble state

Drug	Company	Additional Information
Phase III		
AERx diabetes management system	Aradigm/Novo Nordisk (510) 265-9000 www.aradigm.com	pulmonary delivery of insulin, using Aradigm's AERx system
Phase III Completed		
Exubera	Pfizer in collaboration with Sanofi-Aventis (212) 733-2323 www.pfizer.com	inhaled insulin

Sponsors

U.S. Sites Rate Eli Lilly, Wyeth and Genentech Top Sponsors in 2005

By Paul Dewberry and Sara Gambrill
Published May 2005

Sponsors increasingly rely on their abilities to collaborate effectively with investigative sites and CROs in order to achieve drug development speed and cost advantages and, ultimately, a successful return on investment following market launch. Results from a recent Thomson CenterWatch survey of 612 investigative sites in the United States show that the quality of sponsor-site relationships has improved across the board.

Twelve of the 15 companies rated in-depth improved their scores relative to the last survey we conducted of investigative sites in the United States, in 2003. Seventy-five percent of sites rated relationships with all sponsors "Good" or "Excellent," compared with 70% previously. In fact, the lowest score from 2005 is 10% higher than the lowest in 2003, up from 61%. Sponsors and sites seem to be communicating better, which is good news in unsettled times for the industry.

The tally this year was one of the closest ever, but several companies did lead the way: Eli Lilly continued its consistent performance in the survey, with overall site ratings of "Good" or "Excellent" of 79%.

Of 27 attributes assessed, Wyeth had the highest "Good"/"Excellent" score in nine of them—five more than the company with the next nearest top scores (Lilly). Amgen improved compared with 2003 in 25 of 27 areas, including five areas that improved "Good"/"Excellent" scores by 20% or more. Genentech was rated as "Excellent" by 48% of sites, the top of any sponsor.

All 27 attributes surveyed showed improvement over 2003. The most dramatic increase came in organization and preparation, followed by the prompt payment of grants. These two areas were also among the most important to sites. In addition, the ability to work effectively with CROs is seen as "Good" or "Excellent" by three-fourths of sites, up from two-thirds in 2003.

Two observations that stand out in the ratings of the sponsors are the emergence of the biotechnology sector and the dramatic improvement in certain companies. The average score for companies increased by 5% compared with the 2003 results, although several companies showed much stronger improvement. Boehringer Ingelheim, Amgen, Sanofi-Aventis and Wyeth all made huge strides compared to their results in previous CenterWatch surveys. The results suggest these companies made an exceptional effort to improve their clinical development process. Sites have noticed. The biotechnology companies, as they continue conducting more trials, seem to be learning from the experience of their older, larger brethren in the clinical space.

"For several years, we were dismayed at where we stood in the CenterWatch survey. It's tremendous change for us.

It reflects on some of the changes that we've made in the way we work with sites. I'm delighted to see that some of the things we've done are having an impact and being recognized within the sites," said Ira Spector, vice president of clinical trial operations and vice chief of clinical development,

Wyeth. "We have paid attention to what sites have said about us in the past in [The CenterWatch] survey in the context of a much larger program that we've undertaken in the last year-and-a-half to radically change the way we conduct clinical studies called 'Clinical Breakthrough.'"

According to Duane Schmitz, director of clinical operations, U.S. Medical, Eli Lilly, "[The CenterWatch] survey means a tremendous amount to us. We work hard at being viewed as reliable and trustworthy overall as a corporation and actively listening to everyone we touch, in this case our development partners at our investigative sites. So this survey is one indication that we're succeeding at doing that."

Areas that stand out most for improvement include:

- **Flexibility.** Willingness to modify protocol or budgets was the area that received the lowest scores in the survey. On average, only 62% of sites found sponsors "Good" or "Excellent" in this area. Sites find this attribute crucial: it was rated "Very Important" by nearly two-thirds of respondents.

- **Grant payment process.** While improving overall, the grant payment process continues to be a broad category that leaves sites less than satisfied. Just two-thirds of sites find grant payments prompt.

- **Contract and budget negotiations.** Contract and budget negotiations are listed as most likely to cause delays in conducting a trial by over 50% of respondents.

- **Query handling process.** The query handling process was considered efficient by 64% of sites.

Most sponsor tallies were improved compared with 2003, but some of the companies that have faced the most trying times in the last two years saw lesser improvement than others. Merck (overall 2005 score: up 4% compared with 2003), Pfizer (down 5%) and AstraZeneca (up 3%) lagged behind the average of all sponsors, which improved 5%. This contrasts with Wyeth (up 16%), Boehringer Ingelheim (up 13%), and Amgen (up 12%).

Other findings of note included:

- **EDC.** Asked what could best help prevent future delays, 45% of sites listed electronic data capture (EDC) technologies the most of any factor.

- **Organization and preparation.** The single most important attribute to sites was organization and preparation, which saw the single greatest improvement over 2003, with 82% of respondents finding sponsors "Good" or "Excellent" at preparing their trials.

- **Patient recruitment.** While 62% found patient recruitment funding important, only 48% sought recruitment planning help from sponsors.

An aspect of the survey that was approached differently this year involved rating the importance to clinical success of all the attributes that contribute to a company's rating. The results of this are encouraging. The five most important attributes, which all were listed as "Very Important" by more than 80% of respondents, also were rated "Good" or "Excellent" by more than 80%.

Sites rated these attributes the most important to study success in 2005:

- Is organized and prepared (86% listed as "very important," 82% found sponsors "good to excellent").

- Has professional, well trained monitors/CRAs (82%, 82%).

- Maintains open communication (81%, 82%)

- Provides good overall protocol design (81%, 84%)

- Is responsive to inquiries (80%, 81%)

The companies receiving the highest percentages of "Excellent" for 2005 overall are: Genentech, Eli Lilly, Amgen, Boehringer Ingelheim and Bristol-Myers-Squibb (BMS). Boehringer and BMS were two organizations that showed significant improvement since the last survey was conducted. Investigative sites in our 2003 survey named a largely different group of top organizations: Lilly, Pfizer, Johnson & Johnson, Abbott Labs and Merck.

Survey Methodology

Thomson CenterWatch conducted the survey of investigative sites in the United States between January and March 2005. An 11-page survey was mailed, faxed or emailed to 9,500 sites conducting trials in the United States. Our survey instrument, which has been used since 1997 in both North America and in Europe, was developed with input from clinical research professionals at sponsor companies, CROs and investigative sites. A total of 612 investigative sites completed the survey, representing a 6% response rate, and the highest response ever for this CenterWatch survey. It is clear that sites want to make their voices heard.

Approximately 34% of the sample are principal investigators, with the remaining 66% describing themselves as study coordinators or administrators. Investigators had an average of 10 years of experience with clinical research. Three-quarters of researchers conduct clinical research on a full-time basis, while 25% reported part-time involvement in clinical research.

Investigators were asked to rate the sponsors that they have worked with during the past two years on a wide range of attributes and responsibilities. Investigators were also asked to provide ratings for the three companies that they have worked with most frequently and to rate these companies on more than 25 relationship attributes involving project management, personnel, workstyle, study initiation and ongoing study conduct activities. For this year's survey, sites were also asked to rate the importance of all the attributes to the success of their clinical studies.

In all, 18 major pharmaceutical and biotechnology companies are rated by investigative sites in this year's survey. These companies include Abbott Laboratories, Amgen, Sanofi-Aventis, Astra-Zeneca, Bayer, Biogen, Bristol-Myers Squibb, Boehringer Ingelheim, Eli Lilly, Genentech, Genzyme, GlaxoSmithKline, Johnson and Johnson, Merck, Novartis, Pfizer, Roche and Wyeth. The results for Sanofi-Aventis reflect a consolidation of results listing Sanofi-Aventis, Sanofi-Synthelabo, and Aventis, because of the recently completed merger of the companies. Results for Pfizer in 2003 reflected a similar consolidation of data including Pharmacia.

General Project Management

The attributes making up this category explore whether sponsors are organized and prepared, how realistic their project timelines are, sponsor responsiveness to inquiries, how realistic patient enrollment goals are, whether sponsors work effectively with CROs and how well open communication is maintained. Being organized and preparedwas rated "Very Important" by 86% of sites, the attribute to receive the highest rating of importance. It was also the single most improved score of all attributes.

Sponsors that received the highest percentages of "Excellent" ratings in this category of attributes include Genentech (51%), Eli Lilly (48%), and Amgen (47%), Bristol-Myers Squibb (44%), and Sanofi-Aventis (44%).

With regard to realistic project timelines, Eli Lilly's Schmitz said, "We did implement, three or four years ago, a tool or a metric that broke down the timelines to key milestones and then drove that accountability down into the organization with the intent of being 'real' being more important than being fast. By doing that, we got realistic timelines, which ultimately then helps you actually be higher quality and more reliable."

Study Initiation

Attributes making up this category include good protocol design, good CRF design, informative multicenter meetings, and scientific rationale aligned with good clinical practices realities. Of all these attributes, good protocol design and rationale alignment with good practices are essential attributes. More than 60% of sites rate these two areas "Very Important" to success.

The top rated companies—and the percentage of sites rating these companies as "Excellent" in this category include—Amgen (49%), Eli Lilly (46%), Genentech (44%), Boerhinger (41%) and Merck (39%).

"[Ensuring that we have good scientific rationale in our protocols] is really a line throughout the culture," said Eli Lilly's Schmitz. "We were the first company to roll out 'Principles of Medical Research' throughout our organization. That is communicated throughout, all the way from sales to early research and across the board. What we really focus on and emphasize is that we conduct research solely to answer relevant scientific questions. That's gotten a lot of support from senior management on down."

Ongoing Study Conduct

The attributes of good drug availability, good support of patient recruitment, good funding for patient recruitment, the use of technology to improve efficiency, ongoing support, low monitor turnover and an efficient query handling process comprise the category of ongoing study conduct.

Something worth noting with regard to patient recruitment: while adequate funding for patient recruitment was considered "Very Important" by 62% of sites, only 48% thought that patient enrollment planning and assistance was "Very Important." Sites made clear on the survey that they have their own preferred methods for recruitment, needing only funding to succeed.

Top companies receiving "Excellent" ratings in this category include Boehringer Ingelheim (48%), Genentech (46%), Eli Lilly (42%) and Bristol-Myers Squibb, Johnson & Johnson, and Amgen (all three 41%).

Staff Professionalism

More than 80% of sites consider the professionalism of clinical research associates (CRAs) to be a critical success factor and slightly more than 60% ranked the professionalism of M.D./scientific staff as essential. This is the category that received the highest percentages of "Excellent" ratings from investigative sites, suggesting an area of strength for most sponsor companies. The average score for sponsors is 50%, 10 points higher than any other category.

Companies receiving the highest ratings of "Excellent" performance include Genentech (59%), Johnson & Johnson (59%), Boehringer (57%), Eli Lilly (57%), and Amgen (56%). The professionalism category is the only one of the survey in which a majority of sites rate the sponsors they work with as "Excellent."

Workstyle

The attributes in this category are sponsor flexibility, supportive culture and the ability to create a collaborative team environment. Site ratings of workstyle attributes are mixed. Slightly more than one in four investigative sites give sponsors a top rating in terms of their flexibility—or willingness to modify protocols and budgets. Of all attributes surveyed, this had the lowest average rating. Companies that received the highest percentage of sites giving them "Excellent" ratings are Genentech (49%), Johnson & Johnson (45%), Amgen (43%), and Wyeth (40%).

"We've made some major changes in the way we work with sites. The first being the contract itself. Our site contract two years ago was 17 pages long and fairly difficult to read unless you had a legal background. We put together a team of people who work with sites as well as our contract people, our medical people and our legal people and we revamped that agreement. It is now a 12-page document that is fairly easy to read," said Wyeth's Spector.

"We adopted a completely different way of working with sites, which, essentially, instead of approaching an individual site with an individual negotiation and having fairly protracted negotiation site by site, we basically go out with what we believe is a much more fair package up front.

In exchange for that we look for less negotiation, so more upfront fee but less backend negotiation. In general what we've done is try to go from a highly negotiated environment to a much more standardized environment with our relationships with sites," added Wyeth's Spector.

Grant Payment Process

The grant payment process is made up of several attributes including fair grant payment amounts, realistic grant payment schedules and promptness of grant payments. Fair grant payment amounts are considered by sites to be one of the most essen tial factors, with just under three-quarters of sites rating it as such.

In this category, sponsors typically receive low ratings. Grant Payment was the area that saw some of the improvement, but remains the lowest category score. These results imply that sponsors are doing a better job of setting reasonable grant payment schedules and in paying grants more promptly than they did in 2003. Top companies receiving "Excellent" ratings for their support of the grant payment process include Eli Lilly (41%), Genentech (39%), and Amgen (37%).

Looking Ahead

With sponsors under increasing pressure to cut costs and at the same time refill drug pipelines, the key area where they can make improvements—and show results—is in clinical development. Wyeth clearly needed to leap forward—and did.

"Wyeth's pipeline is pretty robust with a new compound entering development track every month now for four years.

The number of sites we've been using has increased as well. The number of active sites is almost doubled from 2003 to 2005. We've had to change our organization structure to be able to manage that to provide enough coverage for sites.

"I'm delighted to see that Wyeth has moved up in the ratings. This is a great checkpoint along the way, but it's also something we expect to continue to work on and to evolve in the next couple of years," said Spector.

A number of conclusions can be drawn from the results of the 2005 Thomson CenterWatch Investigative Site Survey.

Several sponsors have made a clear and successful effort to improve the quality of their relationships with investigative sites, particularly Boehringer Ingelheim, Wyeth, and Amgen.

Biotechs have done an excellent job of moving into the clinical development mainstream, demonstrated by increasing numbers of sites rating them, and rating them well.

Differentiation seems to be declining, as the range of average scores in 2003 was 18%, and in 2005, 8%. The highest score is one point lower than in 2003, but the lowest score has increased from 61% to 71%.

Some of the traditional leaders (Merck, AstraZeneca, Pfizer) that have had difficulties in the last two years showed little or no improvement compared with 2003. While only AstraZeneca showed actual decline in ratings, the followers from previous surveys have improved to the point of meeting or exceeding the leaders.

Eli Lilly had the top score for the third time of the eight years this survey has been conducted. While other leaders have faltered in continuing to increase quality of relations with sites, Lilly has consistently pursued excellence in this critical area for the industry.

5.01

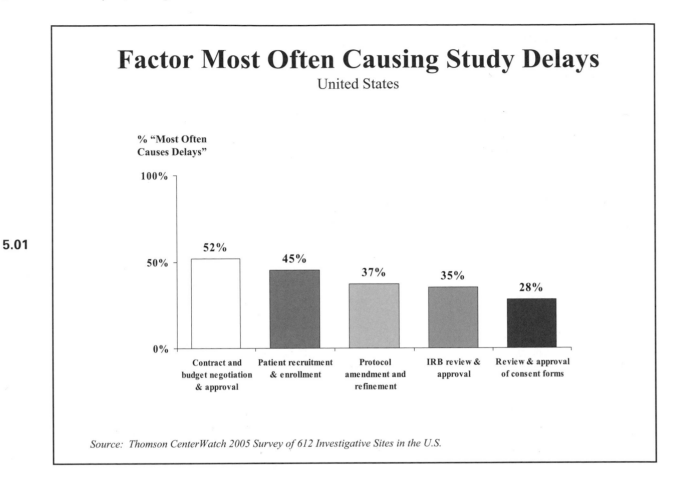

5.02

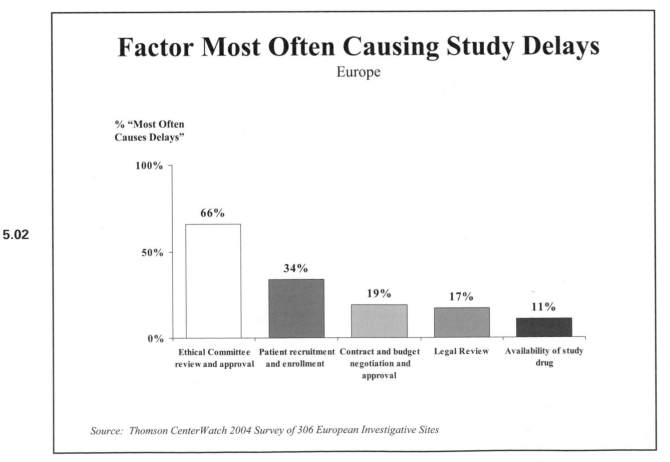

Factors That Could Best Prevent Future Delays
United States

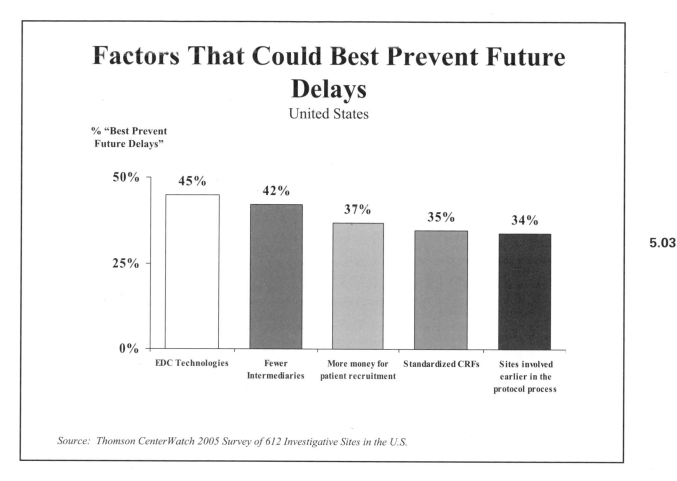

% "Best Prevent Future Delays"

Source: Thomson CenterWatch 2005 Survey of 612 Investigative Sites in the U.S.

5.03

Most Important Qualifications
Top Skills Desired Among New Hires, by Industry Sub-Sector

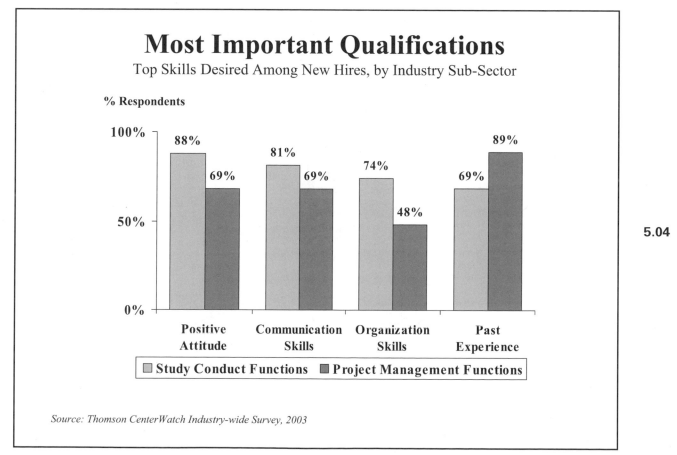

% Respondents

Source: Thomson CenterWatch Industry-wide Survey, 2003

5.04

5.05

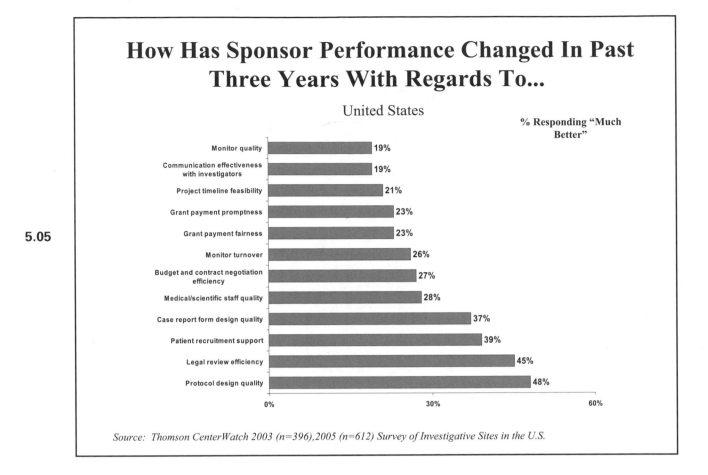

How Has Sponsor Performance Changed In Past Three Years With Regards To...

United States

% Responding "Much Better"

Monitor quality	19%
Communication effectiveness with investigators	19%
Project timeline feasibility	21%
Grant payment promptness	23%
Grant payment fairness	23%
Monitor turnover	26%
Budget and contract negotiation efficiency	27%
Medical/scientific staff quality	28%
Case report form design quality	37%
Patient recruitment support	39%
Legal review efficiency	45%
Protocol design quality	48%

Source: Thomson CenterWatch 2003 (n=396),2005 (n=612) Survey of Investigative Sites in the U.S.

5.06

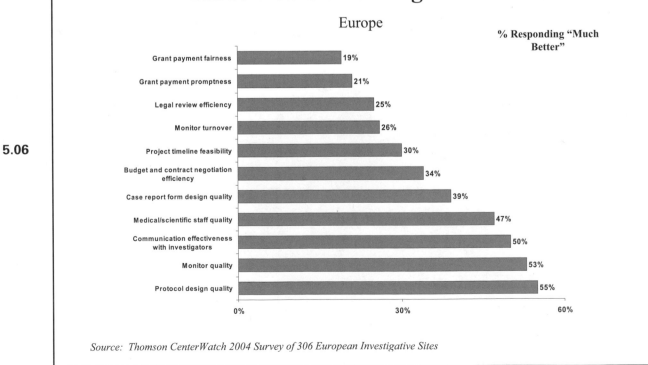

How Has Sponsor Performance Changed In Past Three Years With Regards To...

Europe

% Responding "Much Better"

Grant payment fairness	19%
Grant payment promptness	21%
Legal review efficiency	25%
Monitor turnover	26%
Project timeline feasibility	30%
Budget and contract negotiation efficiency	34%
Case report form design quality	39%
Medical/scientific staff quality	47%
Communication effectiveness with investigators	50%
Monitor quality	53%
Protocol design quality	55%

Source: Thomson CenterWatch 2004 Survey of 306 European Investigative Sites

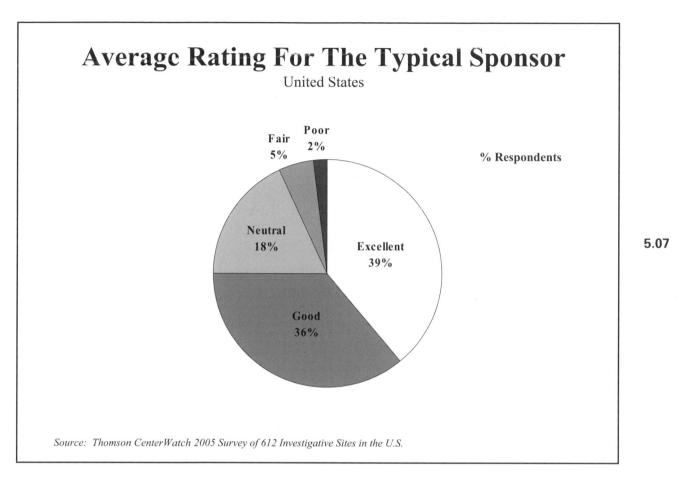

Average Rating For The Typical Sponsor
United States

% Respondents

Poor
2%

Fair
5%

Neutral
18%

Excellent
39%

Good
36%

5.07

Source: Thomson CenterWatch 2005 Survey of 612 Investigative Sites in the U.S.

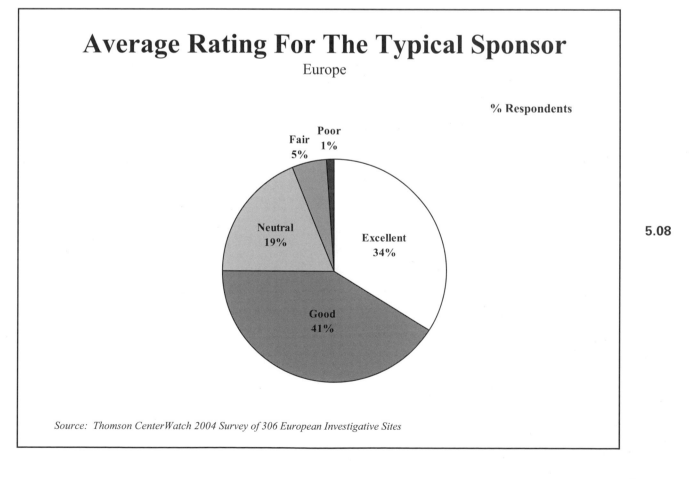

Average Rating For The Typical Sponsor
Europe

% Respondents

Poor
1%

Fair
5%

Neutral
19%

Excellent
34%

Good
41%

5.08

Source: Thomson CenterWatch 2004 Survey of 306 European Investigative Sites

5.09

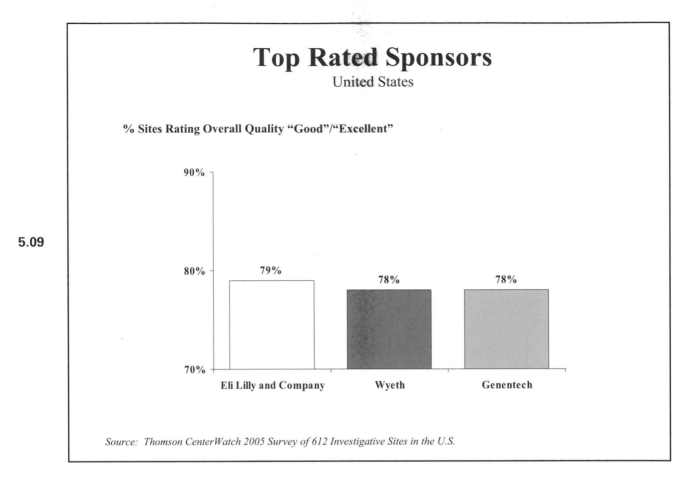

5.10

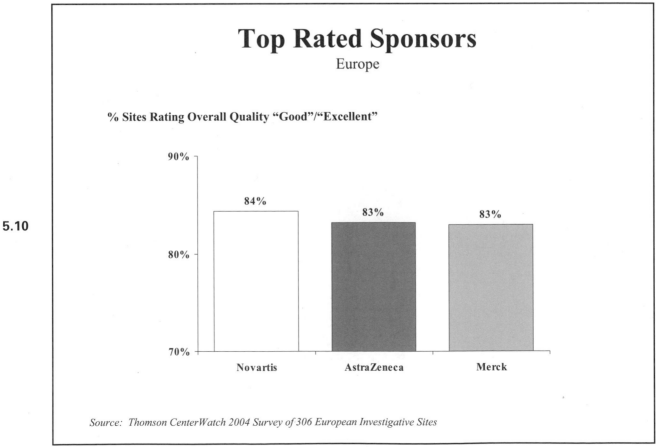

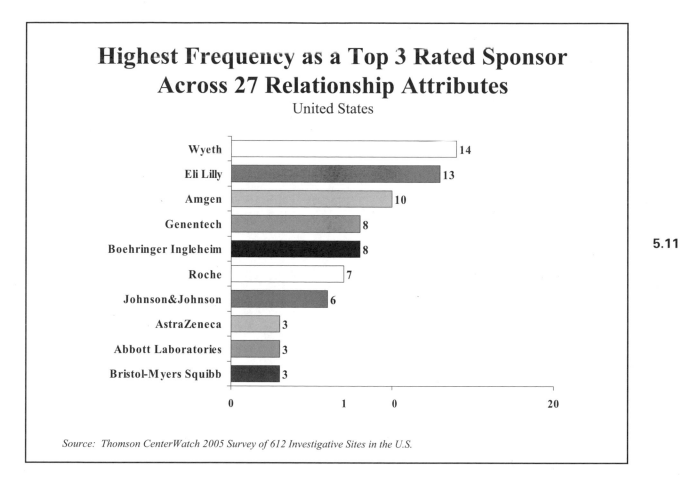

Highest Frequency as a Top 3 Rated Sponsor
Across 27 Relationship Attributes
United States

5.11

Source: Thomson CenterWatch 2005 Survey of 612 Investigative Sites in the U.S.

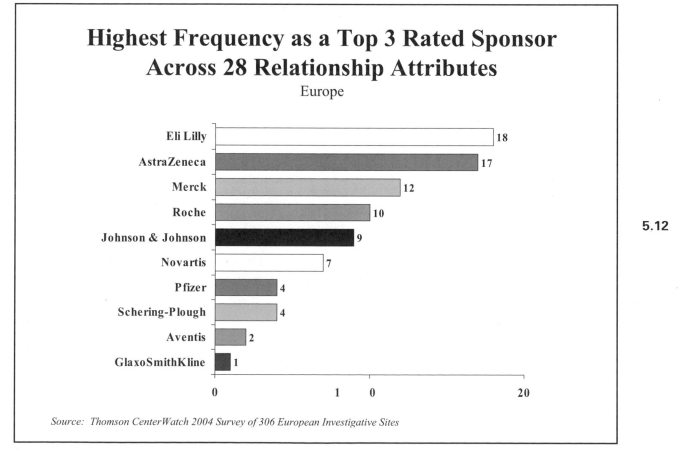

Highest Frequency as a Top 3 Rated Sponsor
Across 28 Relationship Attributes
Europe

5.12

Source: Thomson CenterWatch 2004 Survey of 306 European Investigative Sites

5.13

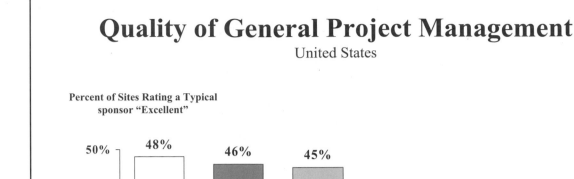

Quality of General Project Management
United States

**Percent of Sites Rating a Typical
sponsor "Excellent"**

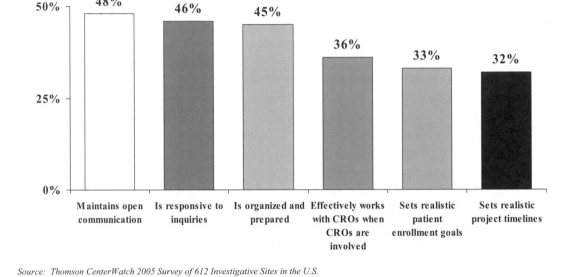

48%	46%	45%	36%	33%	32%
Maintains open communication	Is responsive to inquiries	Is organized and prepared	Effectively works with CROs when CROs are involved	Sets realistic patient enrollment goals	Sets realistic project timelines

Source: Thomson CenterWatch 2005 Survey of 612 Investigative Sites in the U.S.

5.14

Quality of General Project Management
Europe

**Percent of Sites Rating a Typical
sponsor "Excellent"**

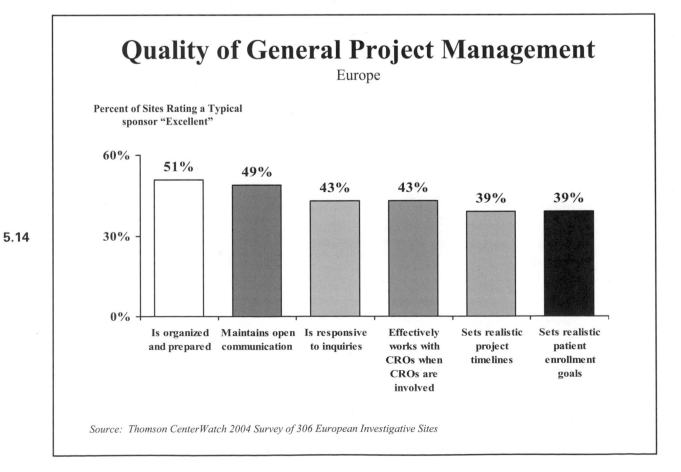

51%	49%	43%	43%	39%	39%
Is organized and prepared	Maintains open communication	Is responsive to inquiries	Effectively works with CROs when CROs are involved	Sets realistic project timelines	Sets realistic patient enrollment goals

Source: Thomson CenterWatch 2004 Survey of 306 European Investigative Sites

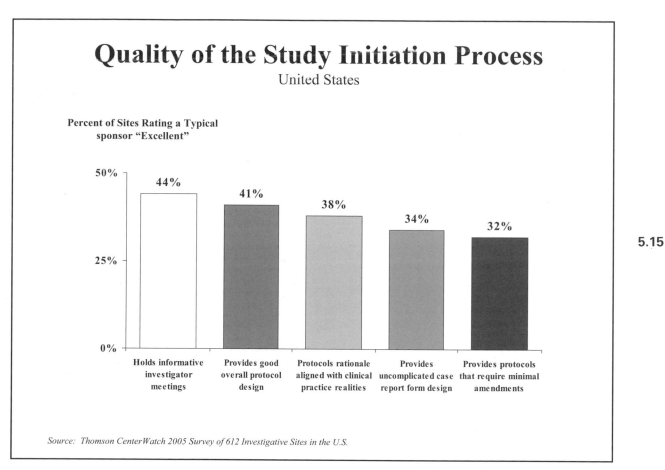

Quality of the Study Initiation Process
United States

Percent of Sites Rating a Typical sponsor "Excellent"

- 44% — Holds informative investigator meetings
- 41% — Provides good overall protocol design
- 38% — Protocols rationale aligned with clinical practice realities
- 34% — Provides uncomplicated case report form design
- 32% — Provides protocols that require minimal amendments

Source: Thomson CenterWatch 2005 Survey of 612 Investigative Sites in the U.S.

5.15

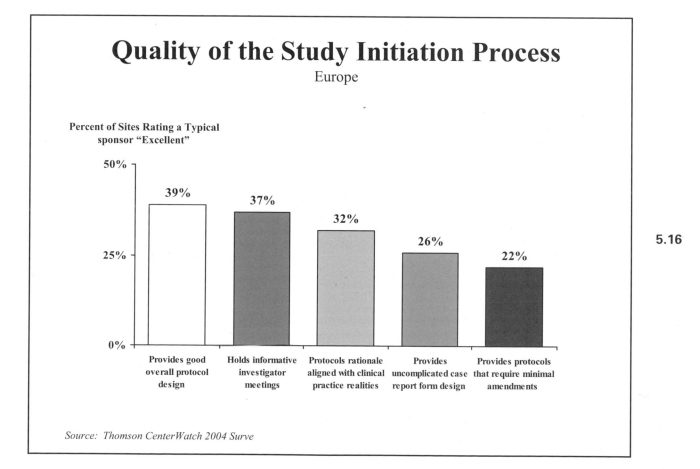

Quality of the Study Initiation Process
Europe

Percent of Sites Rating a Typical sponsor "Excellent"

- 39% — Provides good overall protocol design
- 37% — Holds informative investigator meetings
- 32% — Protocols rationale aligned with clinical practice realities
- 26% — Provides uncomplicated case report form design
- 22% — Provides protocols that require minimal amendments

Source: Thomson CenterWatch 2004 Surve

5.16

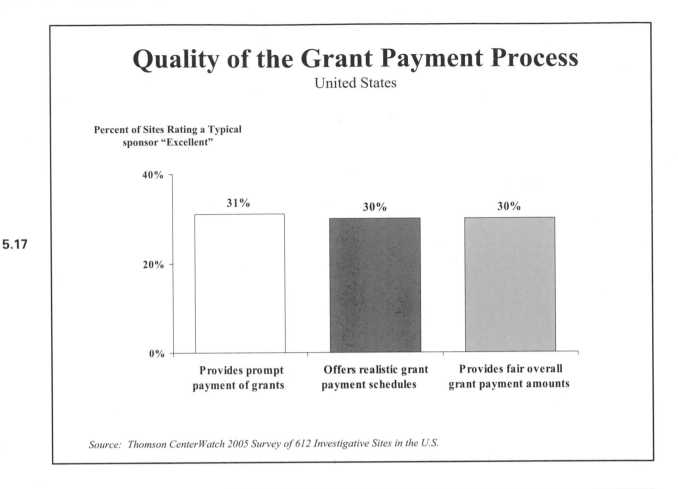

5.17

Quality of the Grant Payment Process
United States

Percent of Sites Rating a Typical
sponsor "Excellent"

31%	30%	30%
Provides prompt payment of grants	Offers realistic grant payment schedules	Provides fair overall grant payment amounts

Source: Thomson CenterWatch 2005 Survey of 612 Investigative Sites in the U.S.

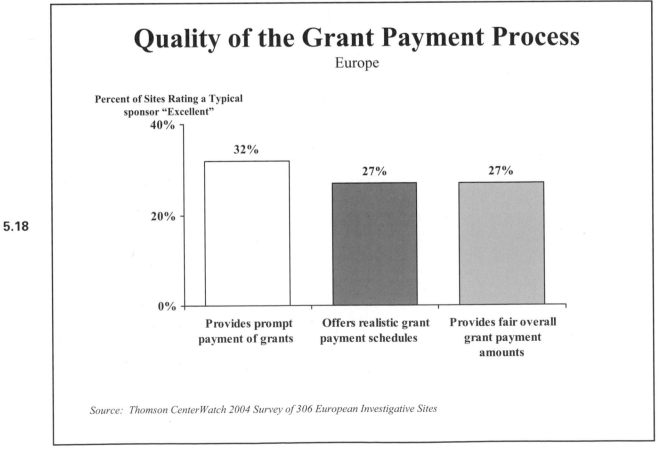

5.18

Quality of the Grant Payment Process
Europe

Percent of Sites Rating a Typical
sponsor "Excellent"

32%	27%	27%
Provides prompt payment of grants	Offers realistic grant payment schedules	Provides fair overall grant payment amounts

Source: Thomson CenterWatch 2004 Survey of 306 European Investigative Sites

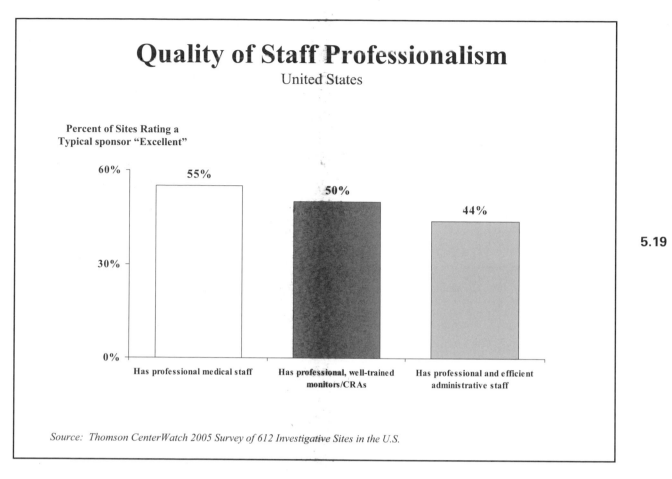

Quality of Staff Professionalism
United States

Percent of Sites Rating a
Typical sponsor "Excellent"

Source: Thomson CenterWatch 2005 Survey of 612 Investigative Sites in the U.S.

5.19

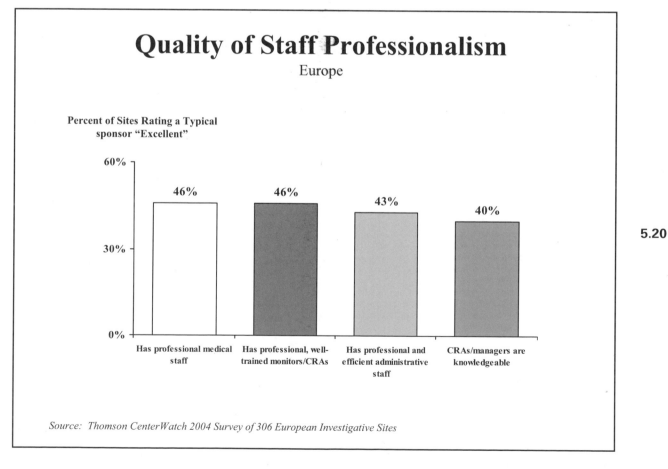

Quality of Staff Professionalism
Europe

Percent of Sites Rating a Typical
sponsor "Excellent"

Source: Thomson CenterWatch 2004 Survey of 306 European Investigative Sites

5.20

5.21

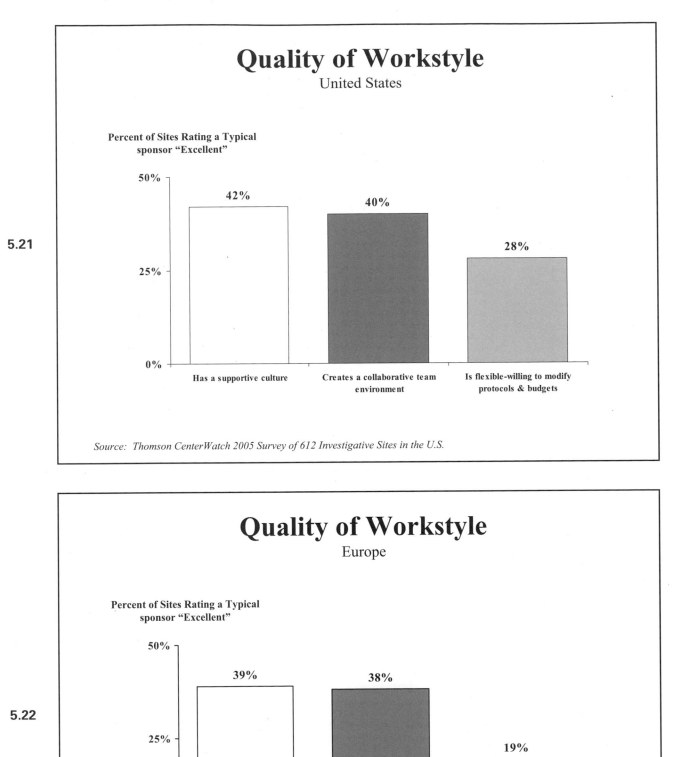

Quality of Workstyle
United States

Percent of Sites Rating a Typical sponsor "Excellent"

42% — Has a supportive culture

40% — Creates a collaborative team environment

28% — Is flexible-willing to modify protocols & budgets

Source: Thomson CenterWatch 2005 Survey of 612 Investigative Sites in the U.S.

5.22

Quality of Workstyle
Europe

Percent of Sites Rating a Typical sponsor "Excellent"

39% — Creates a collaborative team enviornment

38% — Has a supportive culture

19% — Is flexible - willing to modify protocols and budgets

Source: Thomson CenterWatch 2004 Survey of 306 European Investigative Sites

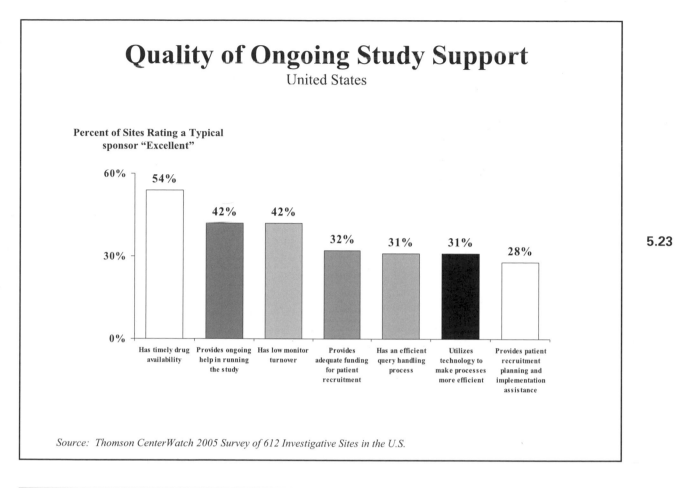

Quality of Ongoing Study Support
United States

Percent of Sites Rating a Typical sponsor "Excellent"

5.23

Source: Thomson CenterWatch 2005 Survey of 612 Investigative Sites in the U.S.

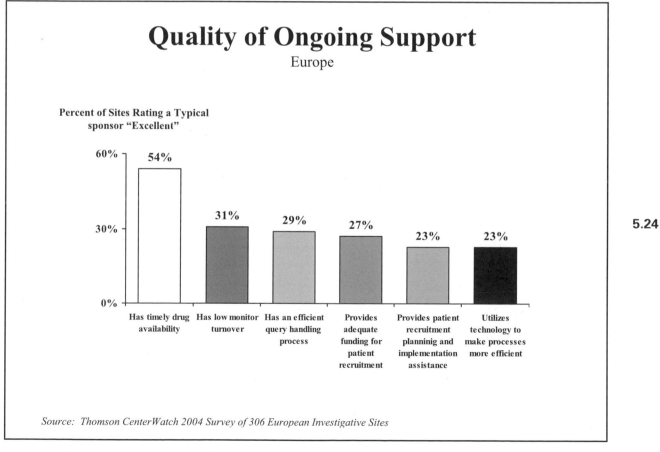

Quality of Ongoing Support
Europe

Percent of Sites Rating a Typical sponsor "Excellent"

5.24

Source: Thomson CenterWatch 2004 Survey of 306 European Investigative Sites

General Project Management Evaluated
United States

5.25

GENERAL PROJECT MANAGEMENT	2001	2003	2005
Is organized and prepared	43%	38%	45%
Sets realistic project timelines	30%	28%	32%
Is responsive to inquiries	43%	39%	46%
Sets realistic patient enrollment goals	35%	32%	33%
Effectively works with CROs when CROs are involved	28%	32%	36%
Maintains open communication	*	41%	48%

Question not asked in this year

Percent of Sites Rating a Typical Sponsor "Excellent"

Source: Thomson CenterWatch 2001 (n=405), 2003 (n=396),2005 (n=612) Survey of Investigative Sites in the U.S.

General Project Management Evaluated
Europe

5.26

GENERAL PROJECT MANAGEMENT	2000	2002	2004
Is organized and prepared	42%	*	46%
Sets realistic project timelines	28%	31%	33%
Is responsive to inquiries	41%	40%	40%
Sets realistic patient enrollment goals	29%	29%	32%
Effectively works with CROs when CROs are involved	28%	37%	37%
Maintains open communication	*	*	44%

Percent of Sites Rating a Typical Sponsor "Excellent"   *Question not asked in this year*

Source: Thomson CenterWatch 2004 Survey of 306 European Investigative Sites

Project Attributes Evaluated I
United States

PROJECT ATTRIBUTES	2001	2003	2005
Provides good overall protocol design	35%	33%	41%
Has protocols where scientific rationale is aligned with clinical practice realities	*	31%	38%
Provides protocols that require minimal amendments	*	22%	32%
Provides uncomplicated case report form design	34%	24%	34%
Holds informative investigator meetings	34%	35%	44%
Has timely drug availability	44%	38%	54%
Provides adequate funding for patient recruitment	28%	25%	32%

5.27

Percent of Sites Rating a Typical Sponsor "Excellent"   *Question not asked in this year

Source: Thomson CenterWatch 2001 (n=405), 2003 (n=396),2005 (n=612) Survey of Investigative Sites in the U.S.

Project Attributes Evaluated II
United States

PROJECT ATTRIBUTES	2001	2003	2005
Provides patient recruitment planning and implementation assistance	*	21%	28%
Has low monitor turnover (monitor staff does not keep changing)	38%	33%	42%
Provides ongoing help in running the study	*	32%	42%
Provides fair overall grant payment amounts	31%	28%	31%
Offers realistic grant payment schedules	28%	22%	30%
Provides prompt payment of grants	26%	23%	30%
Utilizes technology to make processes more efficient	*	21%	31%

5.28

*Question not asked in this year

Percent of Sites Rating a Typical Sponsor "Excellent"

Source: Thomson CenterWatch 2001 (n=405), 2003 (n=396),2005 (n=612) Survey of Investigative Sites in the U.S.

Project Attributes Evaluated I

Europe

5.29

PROJECT ATTRIBUTES	2000	2002	2004
Provides good overall protocol design	32%	36%	39%
Has protocols where scientific rationale is aligned with clinical practice realities	*	*	32%
Provides protocols that require minimal amendments	*	*	22%
Provides uncomplicated case report form design	27%	31%	26%
Holds informative investigator meetings	25%	32%	37%
Has timely drug availability	48%	44%	54%
Provides adequate funding for patient recruitment	*	*	27%

*Question not asked in this year

Percent of Sites Rating a Typical Sponsor "Excellent"

Source: Thomson CenterWatch 2004 Survey of 306 European Investigative Sites

Project Attributes Evaluated II

Europe

5.30

PROJECT ATTRIBUTES	2000	2002	2004
Provides patient recruitment planning and implementation assistance	27%	27%	23%
Has low monitor turnover (monitor staff does not keep changing)	35%	34%	31%
Provides ongoing help in running the study	*	*	41%
Provides fair overall grant payment amounts	23%	27%	27%
Offers realistic grant payment schedules	23%	34%	27%
Provides prompt payment of grants	29%	38%	32%
Utilizes technology to make processes more efficient	*	*	23%

*Question not asked in this year

Percent of Sites Rating a Typical Sponsor "Excellent"

Source: Thomson CenterWatch 2004 Survey of 306 European Investigative Sites

Personnel & Work Style Evaluated
United States

PERSONNEL & WORK STYLE	2001	2003	2005
Has professional medical staff	53%	49%	55%
Has professional, well-trained monitors/CRAs	48%	44%	50%
Has professional and efficient administrative staff	41%	34%	44%
Is flexible - willing to modify protocols and budgets	27%	23%	28%
Has a supportive culture	37%	32%	42%
Creates a collaborative team environment	36%	31%	40%

5.31

Percent of Sites Rating a Typical Sponsor "Excellent"

Source: Thomson CenterWatch 2001 (n=405), 2003 (n=396),2005 (n=612) Survey of Investigative Sites in the U.S.

Personnel & Work Style Evaluated
Europe

PERSONNEL & WORK STYLE	2000	2002	2004
Has professional medical staff	40%	48%	46%
Has professional, well-trained monitors/CRAs	42%	46%	46%
CRAs/managers are knowledgeable	*	*	40%
Has professional and efficient administrative staff	31%	35%	43%
Is flexible - willing to modify protocols and budgets	18%	18%	19%
Has a supportive culture	34%	34%	38%
Creates a collaborative team environment	32%	38%	39%

5.32

*Question not asked in this year

Percent of Sites Rating a Typical Sponsor "Excellent"

Source: Thomson CenterWatch 2004 Survey of 306 European Investigative Sites

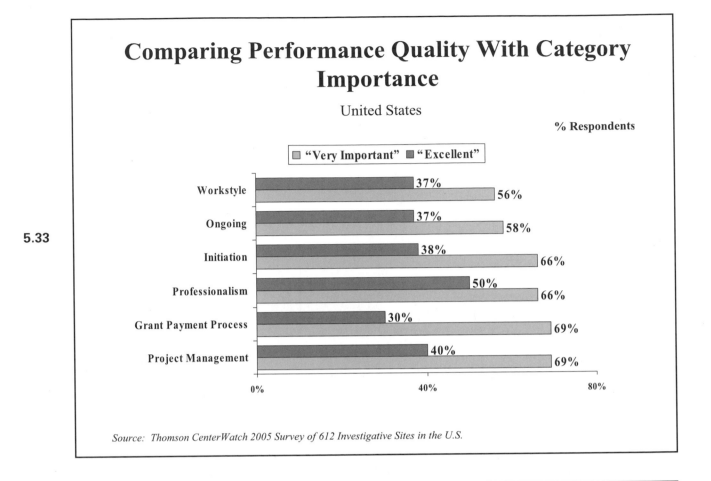

5.33

Comparing Performance Quality With Category Importance

United States

% Respondents

□ "Very Important" ■ "Excellent"

- Workstyle: 37% / 56%
- Ongoing: 37% / 58%
- Initiation: 38% / 66%
- Professionalism: 50% / 66%
- Grant Payment Process: 30% / 69%
- Project Management: 40% / 69%

Source: Thomson CenterWatch 2005 Survey of 612 Investigative Sites in the U.S.

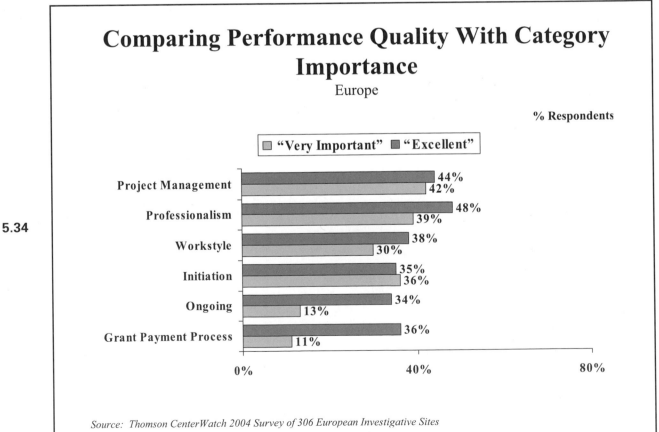

5.34

Comparing Performance Quality With Category Importance

Europe

% Respondents

□ "Very Important" ■ "Excellent"

- Project Management: 44% / 42%
- Professionalism: 48% / 39%
- Workstyle: 38% / 30%
- Initiation: 35% / 36%
- Ongoing: 34% / 13%
- Grant Payment Process: 36% / 11%

Source: Thomson CenterWatch 2004 Survey of 306 European Investigative Sites

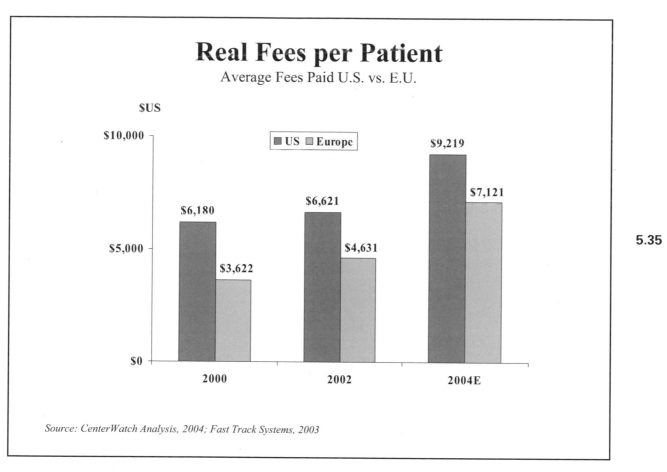

Real Fees per Patient
Average Fees Paid U.S. vs. E.U.

$US

Legend: ■ US □ Europe

- 2000: $6,180 / $3,622
- 2002: $6,621 / $4,631
- 2004E: $9,219 / $7,121

Source: CenterWatch Analysis, 2004; Fast Track Systems, 2003

5.35

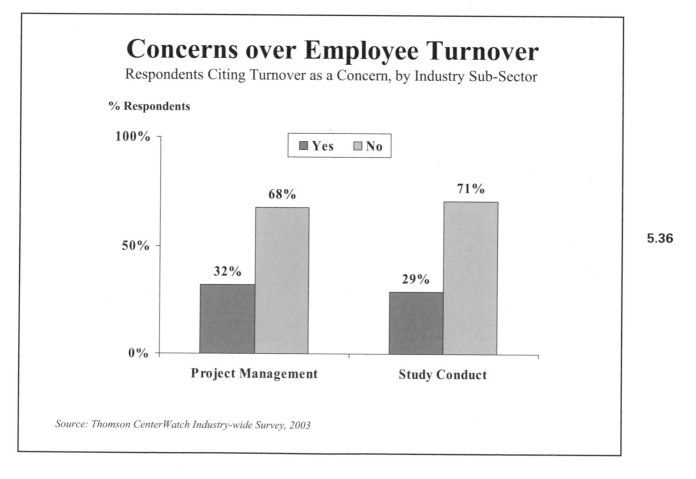

Concerns over Employee Turnover
Respondents Citing Turnover as a Concern, by Industry Sub-Sector

% Respondents

Legend: ■ Yes □ No

- Project Management: 32% / 68%
- Study Conduct: 29% / 71%

Source: Thomson CenterWatch Industry-wide Survey, 2003

5.36

5.37

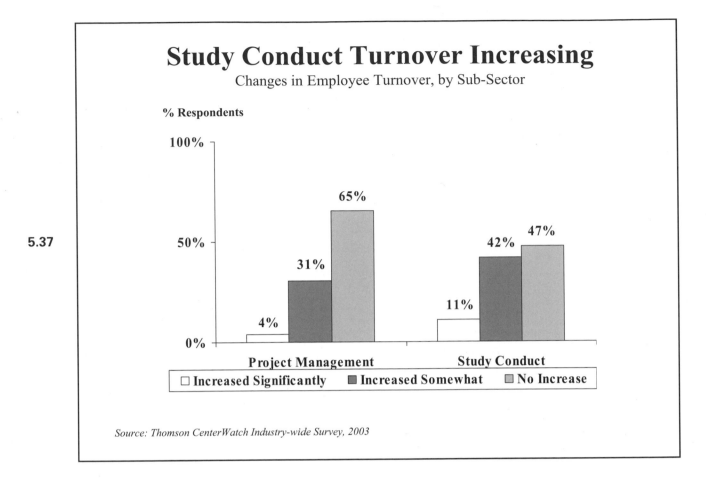

Study Conduct Turnover Increasing
Changes in Employee Turnover, by Sub-Sector

% Respondents

Source: Thomson CenterWatch Industry-wide Survey, 2003

5.38

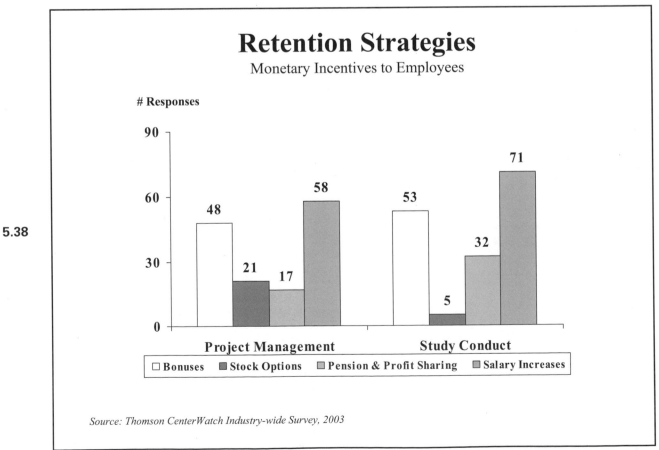

Retention Strategies
Monetary Incentives to Employees

Responses

Source: Thomson CenterWatch Industry-wide Survey, 2003

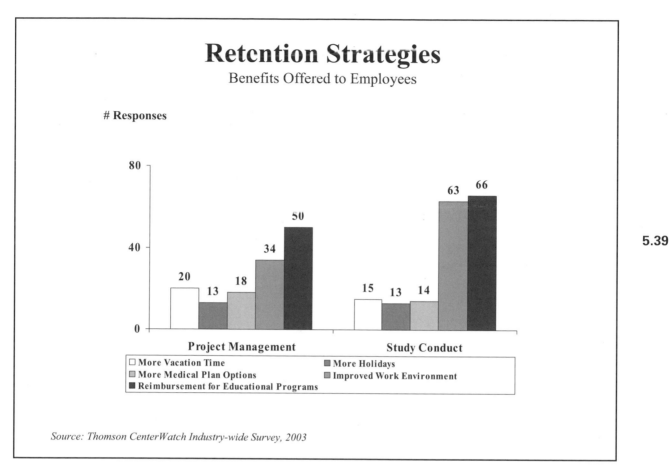

Retention Strategies
Benefits Offered to Employees

5.39

Source: Thomson CenterWatch Industry-wide Survey, 2003

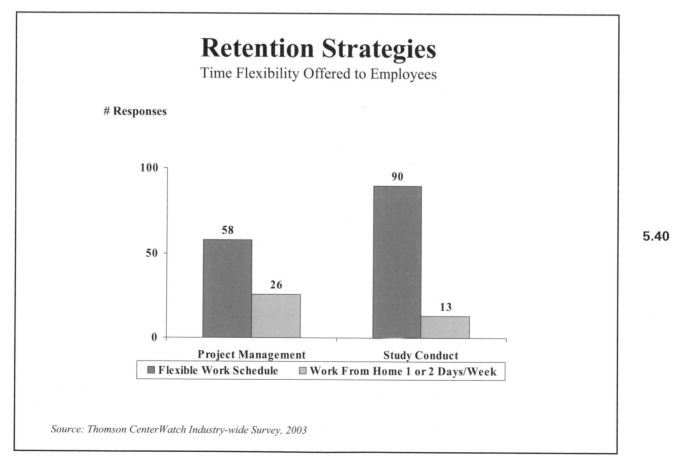

Retention Strategies
Time Flexibility Offered to Employees

5.40

Source: Thomson CenterWatch Industry-wide Survey, 2003

5.41

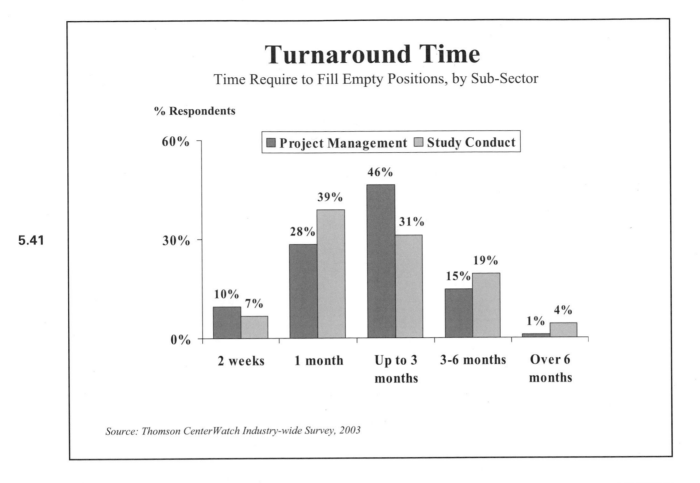

Turnaround Time
Time Require to Fill Empty Positions, by Sub-Sector

Source: Thomson CenterWatch Industry-wide Survey, 2003

5.42

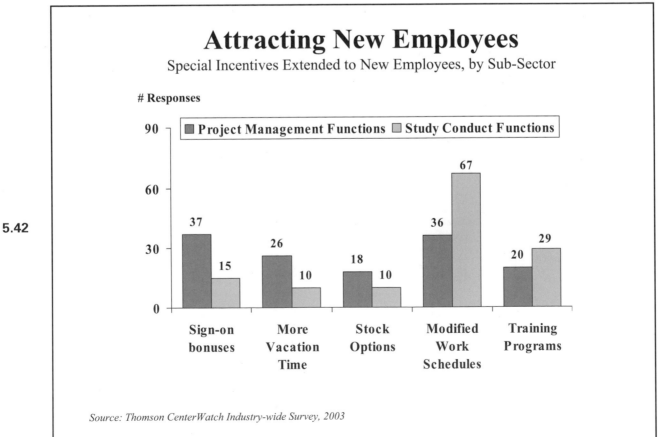

Attracting New Employees
Special Incentives Extended to New Employees, by Sub-Sector

Source: Thomson CenterWatch Industry-wide Survey, 2003

Contract Research Organizations

PharmaNet, ICON and Covance are Top CROs in 2005 CenterWatch Survey of Investigative Sites in U.S.

By Paul Dewberry and Sara Gambrill
Published June 2005

Similar to the results from Europe in the 2004 Thomson Center-Watch Site Survey, PharmaNet, which completed its merger with SFBC International in December 2004, received ratings from sites head and shoulders above the rest of CROs rated, with the highest score in 15 of 25 attributes rated, and in the top three 24 times out of 25. It is the only CRO considered "Good"/"Excellent" by three-fourths of sites. The most recent U.S. and European surveys have shown the same degree of dominance over the rest of the field.

Though it finished second, ICON's performance was remarkable because ICON's improvement was so spectacular when compared with its last place rating two years ago.

ICON was in the top three on 20 of 25 attributes, the best in six. Seventy percent of sites rated ICON "Good"/"Excellent," a 19% jump from the 2003 survey, the most recent in the United States.

The overall score for CROs increased by 4% to 65%, though the actual scores showed a considerable variance among firms. All of the top five CROs improved by better than 4%, including Parexel, while the next seven all failed to keep pace. While sponsors' ratings saw a decrease in the range of highest to lowest score to 8%, the gap between the highest and lowest rated CRO remained the same, at 18%.

Covance and Quintiles were the only other CROs to be rated "Good"/"Excellent" by more than two-thirds of sites, with Parexel coming just below (65%). Only the top five were rated "Excellent" by at least 33% of sites in any category, further evidence that there is a much clearer preference for certain CROs than for certain sponsors, according to investigators in the United States.

The following five attributes of a CRO rated as most important to study success in 2005 were termed "Essential":

- Is organized and prepared (87% listed as "Very Important," 74% found CROs "Good"/"Excellent").

- Has professional, well trained monitors/CRAs (84%, 68%).

- Maintains open communication (82%, 73%)

- Is responsive to inquiries (82%, 71%)

- Provides good overall protocol design (80%, 84%)

PharmaNet led in three of these "Essential" categories. ICON led in being organized and prepared, as well as for the professional nature of their monitors and CRAs.

Thomas Newman, M.D., executive vice president, American Operations, Pharma-Net, said, "The core of our business is working with investigators to recruit and retain patients and produce high quality data. To do that effectively, we have to be able to partner with investigative sites and study coordinators. We have talked about past [CenterWatch] survey results that have been favorable to PharmaNet, and we're very proud of that and very proud of our employees. [The Center-

Watch survey] is absolutely critical. We were anxious to hear the results. This is really important work that CenterWatch does."

John Hubbard, Ph.D., president and chief operating officer, U.S., ICON, added, "We are very, very pleased that we did well on the survey this year. We do believe it's important. [The CenterWatch survey] came up at one of our proposal defense meetings. Obviously, the person who asked me the question had read it and asked me to comment on it. We know people are reading [the CenterWatch survey]."

The Survey Methodology

Thomson CenterWatch conducted the survey of investigative sites in the United States between January and March 2005.

An 11-page survey was mailed, faxed or emailed to 9,500 sites conducting trials in the United States. Our survey instrument, which has been used since 1997 in both North America and in Europe, was developed with input from clinical research professionals at sponsor companies, CROs and investigative sites. A total of 612 investigative sites completed the survey, representing a 6% response rate.

Approximately 34% of the sample are principal investigators, with the remaining 66% describing themselves as study coordinators or administrators. Investigators had an average of 10 years of experience with clinical research. Three-quarters of researchers who responded conduct clinical research on a full-time basis, while 25% reported part-time involvement in clinical research.

Investigators were asked to rate the CROs that they have worked with during the past two years on a wide range of attributes and responsibilities. Investigators were also asked to provide ratings for the three companies that they have worked with most frequently and to rate these companies on more than 25 relationship attributes involving project management, personnel, workstyle, study initiation and ongoing study conduct activities. For this year's survey, sites were also asked to rate the importance of all the attributes to the success of their clinical studies.

Investigative sites rate only those CROs with which they have worked in the last two years. In total, 12 CROs were rated across 25 specific responsibilities. The 25 attributes comprise the following categories:

- General project management

- Personnel professionalism

- Workstyle

- Study initiation

- Ongoing study support

- Grant payment process

Of these individual attributes, the sites indicated which areas represent those most essential to study success as well as their assessments of the companies. Attribute ratings by company, and their perceived importance, have been consistent across all CenterWatch surveys conducted since 1997.

In the 2005 CenterWatch relationship quality survey, investigative sites evaluated 15 CRO companies including: Covance, Quintiles, Parexel, MDS Pharma, ICON, PPD, PharmaNet/SFBC, Charles River/Inveresk, Kendle, Omnicare, Ingenix/I3 and PRA.

Detailed Highlights

The incidence of positive ratings for CROs across all attributes is lower than that of sponsor companies by an average of 11 percentage points. Overall, three-fourths of sites rate their relations with sponsors as "Good"/"Excellent," while CROs are so regarded by two-thirds. This gap has stayed fairly consistent over time. (Sponsor ratings from the 2005 CenterWatch relationship quality survey were published in the May issue.)

The widest variability between CROs and sponsors lies in the area of staffing. While 56% of investigators listed sponsors' medical staff professionalism as "Excellent," only 38% so described the CROs, and for the ability to limit monitor turnover, sponsors scored 43% versus 27% for the CROs. Both sponsors and CROs received their worst scores in the area of flexibility in willingness to modify protocols and budgets, only being rated "Excellent" 29% and 22% of the time, respectively.

General Project Management

This area of the survey includes organization and preparation, realism of project timelines, responsiveness to inquiries, and maintaining open communications. On average, 34% of sites found CROs "Excellent" in this area. Maintaining open communications, one of the "Essential" attributes, found CROs "Excellent" 40% of the time, also the highest aggregate "Excellent" score. PharmaNet was best in this area, with 43% finding excellence, followed by ICON (42%) and Covance (38%). Organization and preparation was the most "Essential" attribute according to the sites, with 87% finding this "Very Important" to study success.

ICON's Hubbard said, "What we've done as a routine part of the project now is develop a communication plan, which identifies all of the relevant parties both on the sponsor side as well as on our side, so when there are issues, they get escalated appropriately and at the right level, so that the people who can deal with the problem or issue the best are the people who are actually working on the project. And if those things are not getting understood or addressed in a timely manner, then there's a clear escalation pathway both in our organization as well as in the sponsor's organization. And we found that really helps a lot because then people know who to go to in order to get questions answered and to get things addressed in a very quick manner."

William Taafe, president of corporate development, U.S., ICON, added, "We don't wait until a problem happens. We also agree with a client up front how a change of scope can be managed, and we've created a process where we inform them on a regular basis. We work on a proactive process where there are regular notifications with a change order log, which is signed off by both ICON and the sponsor."

Professionalism

Professionalism is prized by investigators in their relationships with both CROs and sponsors. All three attributes in this area were rated similarly in importance between CROs and sponsors. Professionalism of CRAs is one of the "Essential" attributes to study success. It receives a high rating of "Excellent" among all attributes for CROs, 36%. Professionalism of medical staff was the highest rated attribute, with 38% rating "Excellent" (also the highest rating for sponsors). Whatever else they may think of CROs, sites do appreciate the professionalism with which studies are conducted. PharmaNet (42%), ICON (41%), Quintiles (37%), and Covance (36%) were rated highest in this area.

PharmaNet's Newman said, "Over the past couple of years, we've been diligent about having new hires—even if they say they have monitoring experience—go through a co-monitoring program with an experienced PharmaNet, usually senior, CRA. We do that for pre-study visits, routine monitoring visits, closeout visits. There's a checklist of things that the co-monitor is grading the new monitor on and making sure they know how to do things. Until the new hire demonstrates, on the basis of the work experience and these monitoring checklist scores, that they're competent to do the visit, they do not go out on their own. We also provide CRAs with a lot of support, so when they're in the field they're encouraged to call data management if there's a question about how certain data should be captured to avoid queries and further hassling of the sites. A project manager is always available to help the CRA by phone."

Workstyle

The attributes that make up the workstyle category include flexibility on budget and protocol matters, maintaining a supportive culture, and creating a team atmosphere. ICON was highest rated in the area, with 38% "Excellent." PharmaNet, Covance, and Quintiles were the other three CROs to score above 33% "Excellent" in this area.

ICON's Hubbard said, "We use a continuous improvement process. We survey our sites, as well as our clients, on every study. Surveys come back to me and Bill [Taafe] for review, so we see it right when it comes back as to how did we handle issues at the site, were we courteous, knowledgeable, did we provide service for the site?"

Study Initiation

Areas of study initiation improved in this survey. Providing uncomplicated CRFs and holding informative investigator meetings improved by 9% and 10%, respectively over the 2005 survey. This still remains an improvement area for sites, with 31% of sites finding CRO excellence overall. ICON, PharmaNet, Covance, and Quintiles are the leaders in Study Initiation.

Ongoing Study Conduct

This area includes patient enrollment assistance and support, low turnover of monitors, ongoing help in running the study, efficiency of the query handling process, and the use of technology to make processes more efficient. Overall, only about a quarter of sites found CROs "Excellent" in this regard (27%). This is a considerable improvement over the 2003 figure of 19%. One of the more interesting aspects of this area is in the efficient use of technology. While only 43% of sites thought this an important attribute for sponsors, 68% found it critical in CRO performance. No other attribute showed such a swing. PharmaNet, ICON, and Covance led this area.

PharmaNet's Newman said, "One of the things we're just about to come out with is a couple of laminated pages that are oriented toward study coordinators that describe in some detail how to fill out certain aspects of the case report form, with the idea of getting it right the first time and avoiding queries. We take a very proactive approach from both clinical and data management. We also have a good electronic data capture system that we're using on some studies. That provides immediate feedback to the site of course in

terms of edit checks built into to it so if there's a mistake made, we'll fire right back while the person's on the computer and the correction can be made right there."

Grant Payment Process

The grant payment process is the toughest area on CROs, less than a quarter of sites seeing excellence on CRO performance. This was still a 6% improvement over 2003. Several recent Thomson CenterWatch surveys have indicated how important the grant and budget process is to sites, and these results indicate the lack of satisfaction felt. Only PharmaNet and ICON were rated "Excellent" by more than 30% of sites.

Impressions

Investigative sites have an excellent perspective to rate CRO performance. Of the responses in the 2005 Thomson CenterWatch Site Survey, more than one-third had worked with at least eight of the top 12 CROs in the last two years. Perhaps this is why such a clear layering was displayed. Five companies—PharmaNet, ICON, Covance, Quintiles and Parexel were clearly preferred as partners in conducting studies. No other company was found "Excellent" by sites more than one-third of the time in any category.

Worth noting are two findings in particular from this year's survey regarding what sites believe hurts and helps the efficiency of study conduct. As a factor that most often causes delays, "contract and budget negotiation and approval" is listed by 52% of respondents. Forty-five percent of sites rated "EDC Technologies" as having the best potential to prevent delays in the future.

PharmaNet's back-to-back top rankings in both the 2004 Thomson CenterWatch European Investigative Site Survey and this year's Thomson CenterWatch U.S. Investigative Site Survey indicate that this CRO is clearly number one in the field, but they cannot afford to be complacent. ICON's huge gains over its 2003 survey ranking—last—serves to illustrate that a CRO can improve its relationship with sites dramatically if the task is undertaken seriously and carefully. Both CROs have demonstrated that a proactive, rather than a reactive, approach to working with sites serves both parties well. CROs would do well to continue to consider what sites are telling them, since sponsors certainly are.

6.01

Worldwide CRO Market
Historical and Projected Distribution, by Region

% World Market Share

Source: Thomson CenterWatch Analysis, 2004; Frost & Sullivan, 2004

6.02

Worldwide CRO Market
CRO Market Size and Growth Rate, 2004-2009E

$ US in Billions

% World Market Share

Source: Goldman Sachs, 2005

Number of Clinical CROs
CROs in Europe and North America

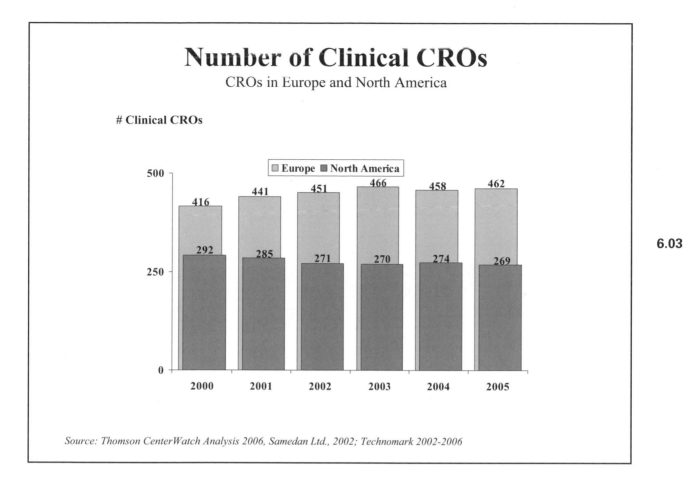

 # Clinical CROs

Source: Thomson CenterWatch Analysis 2006, Samedan Ltd., 2002; Technomark 2002-2006

6.03

Shifting Share of Clinical Projects
Share of Industry-Sponsored Projects

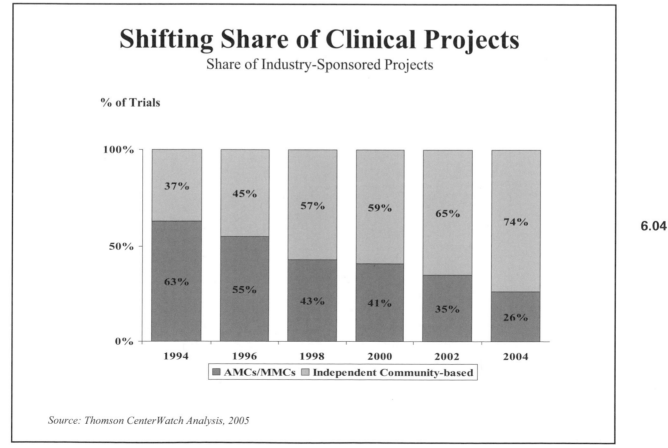

% of Trials

Source: Thomson CenterWatch Analysis, 2005

6.04

6.05

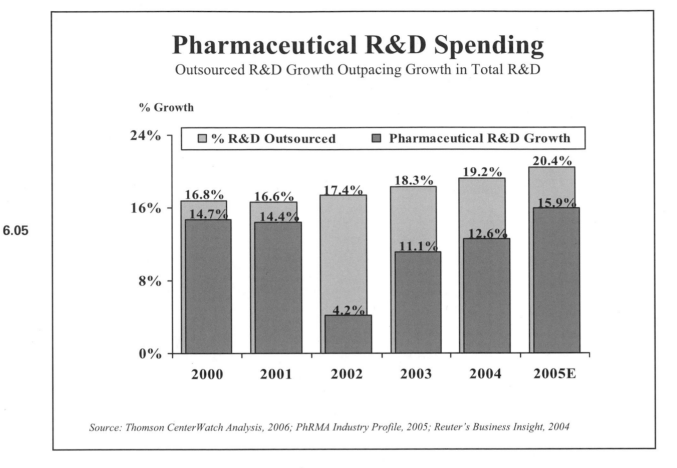

Pharmaceutical R&D Spending
Outsourced R&D Growth Outpacing Growth in Total R&D

% Growth

□ % R&D Outsourced   ■ Pharmaceutical R&D Growth

Source: Thomson CenterWatch Analysis, 2006; PhRMA Industry Profile, 2005; Reuter's Business Insight, 2004

6.06

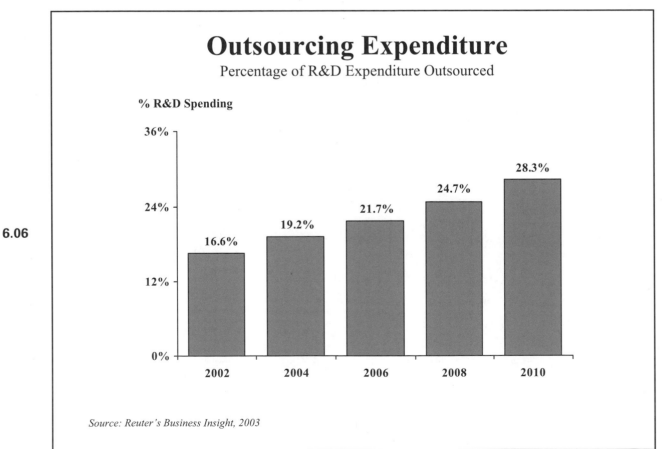

Outsourcing Expenditure
Percentage of R&D Expenditure Outsourced

% R&D Spending

Source: Reuter's Business Insight, 2003

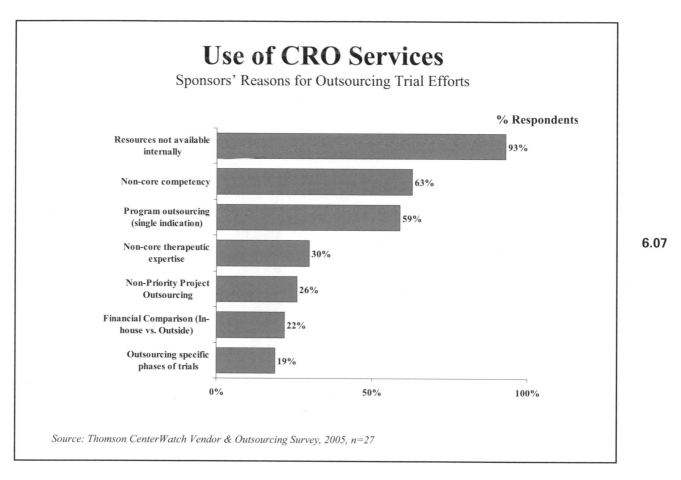

Use of CRO Services
Sponsors' Reasons for Outsourcing Trial Efforts

% Respondents

Resources not available internally	93%
Non-core competency	63%
Program outsourcing (single indication)	59%
Non-core therapeutic expertise	30%
Non-Priority Project Outsourcing	26%
Financial Comparison (In-house vs. Outside)	22%
Outsourcing specific phases of trials	19%

Source: Thomson CenterWatch Vendor & Outsourcing Survey, 2005, n=27

6.07

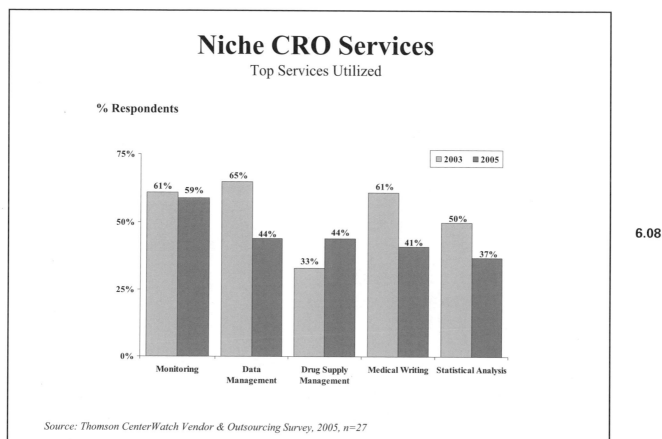

Niche CRO Services
Top Services Utilized

% Respondents

Legend: 2003, 2005

Service	2003	2005
Monitoring	61%	59%
Data Management	65%	44%
Drug Supply Management	33%	44%
Medical Writing	61%	41%
Statistical Analysis	50%	37%

Source: Thomson CenterWatch Vendor & Outsourcing Survey, 2005, n=27

6.08

6.09

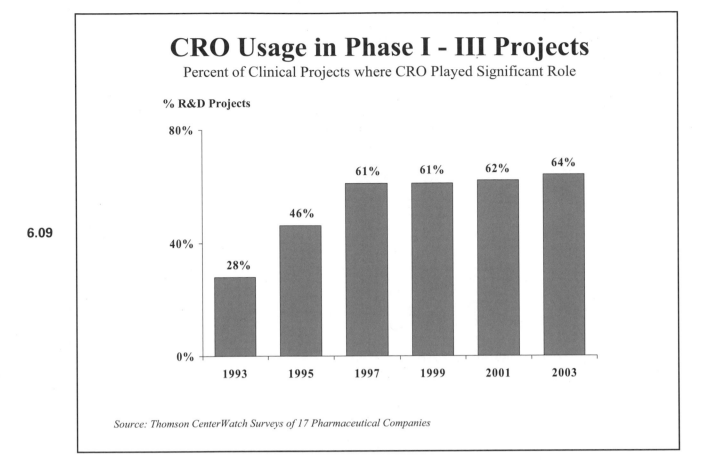

CRO Usage in Phase I - III Projects
Percent of Clinical Projects where CRO Played Significant Role

% R&D Projects

Source: Thomson CenterWatch Surveys of 17 Pharmaceutical Companies

6.10

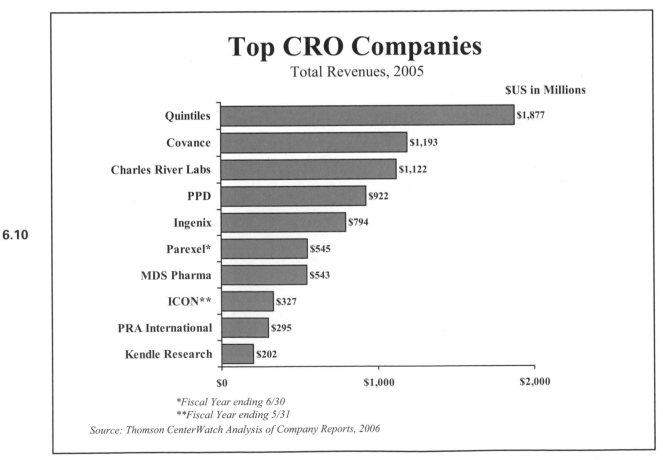

Top CRO Companies
Total Revenues, 2005

$US in Millions

*Fiscal Year ending 6/30
**Fiscal Year ending 5/31
Source: Thomson CenterWatch Analysis of Company Reports, 2006

CRO Sector Metrics
Selected Figures, Top 6 Public CROs

$US in Millions

	2000	2001	2002	2003	2004
Total Revenues	$2,065	$2,460	$2,930	$3,350	$3,829
Income from Operations	$254	$277	$306	$330	$413
Total Net Income	$146	$192	$126	$185	$229
Operating Margin	12.8%	10.6%	6.6%	8.9%	9.7%
% Growth Total Revenue	--	25.8%	20.5%	15.6%	14.7%

Aggregate figures from the 6 largest public CROs (2004) - Covance, Parexel, PPD, Charles River, Kendle, and Icon

Source: Thomson CenterWatch Analysis of Company Reports, 2006

6.11

Top 5 CROs Taking Share
Market Share, by Year

% Market Share

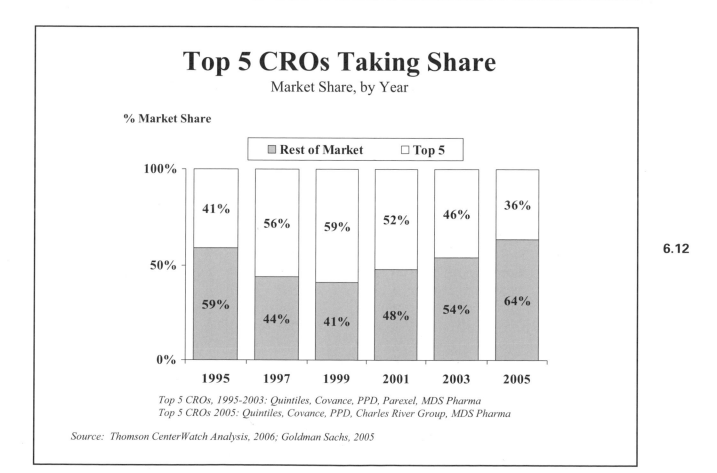

Top 5 CROs, 1995-2003: Quintiles, Covance, PPD, Parexel, MDS Pharma
Top 5 CROs 2005: Quintiles, Covance, PPD, Charles River Group, MDS Pharma

Source: Thomson CenterWatch Analysis, 2006; Goldman Sachs, 2005

6.12

6.13

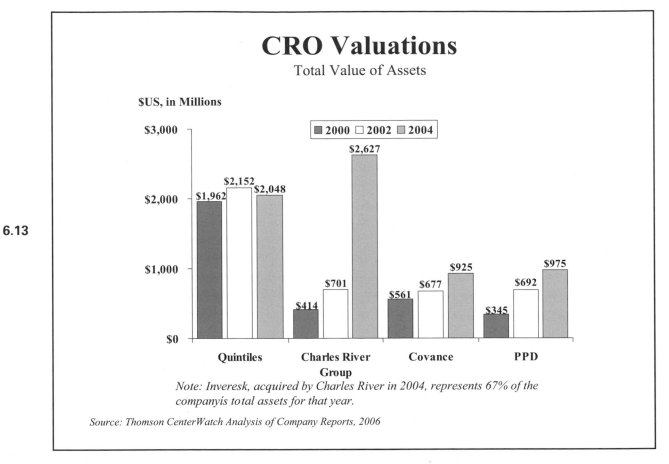

CRO Valuations
Total Value of Assets

$US, in Millions

Legend: ■ 2000 □ 2002 ■ 2004

Quintiles: $1,962 / $2,152 / $2,048
Charles River Group: $414 / $701 / $2,627
Covance: $561 / $677 / $925
PPD: $345 / $692 / $975

Note: Inveresk, acquired by Charles River in 2004, represents 67% of the companyís total assets for that year.

Source: Thomson CenterWatch Analysis of Company Reports, 2006

6.14

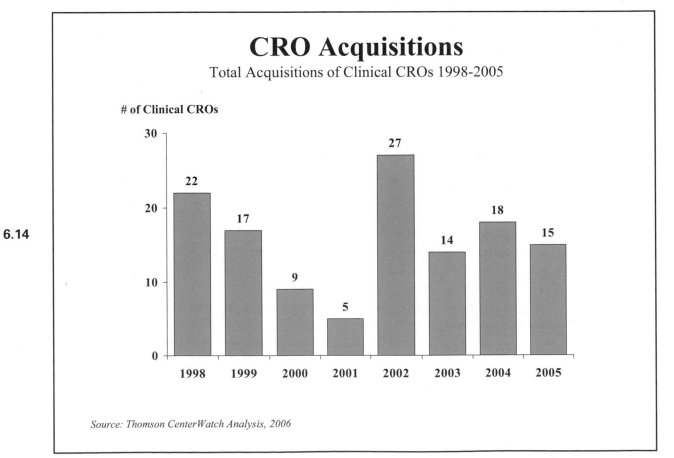

CRO Acquisitions
Total Acquisitions of Clinical CROs 1998-2005

of Clinical CROs

1998: 22
1999: 17
2000: 9
2001: 5
2002: 27
2003: 14
2004: 18
2005: 15

Source: Thomson CenterWatch Analysis, 2006

Select CRO Acquisitions, 2005

Acquirer	Acquiree	Primary Services Purchased
Omnicare	Clinimetrics Research	Biotechnology
Bionomics	Neurofit	CNS Trials/European Clinical
ICON	Biomines Research Solutions	Indian Clinical
West Pharmaceutical Services	Monarch Analytical Laboratories	Central Lab
MedTrials	DataMedix	Data Management
Paragon Biomedical	InDatum	Global Clinical
PRA	RxCCI	Regulatory
PRA	GMG BioBusiness	Regulatory
i3 Research	SKM Oncology	Global Clinical
Covance	Sternberger Monoclonals	Laboratory Services
Parexel	QdotPharma	Early Global Clinical
Covance	GFI Clinical Services	Early Clinical
Premier Research Group	PharmData	Data Management
Jubilant Organosys	Target Research Associates	Global Clinical
Battelle	CareStat	Clinical

Source: Thomson CenterWatch Analysis, 2006

6.15

CRO Performance

Sites Rating CRO Services "Very Important" and "Excellent"

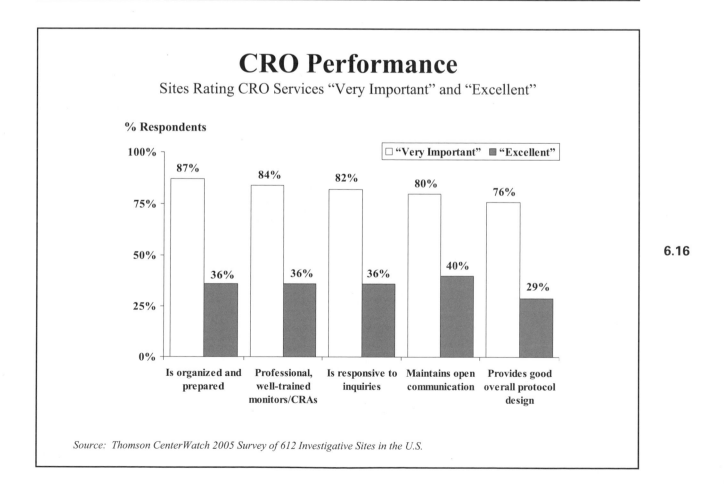

6.16

Source: Thomson CenterWatch 2005 Survey of 612 Investigative Sites in the U.S.

6.17

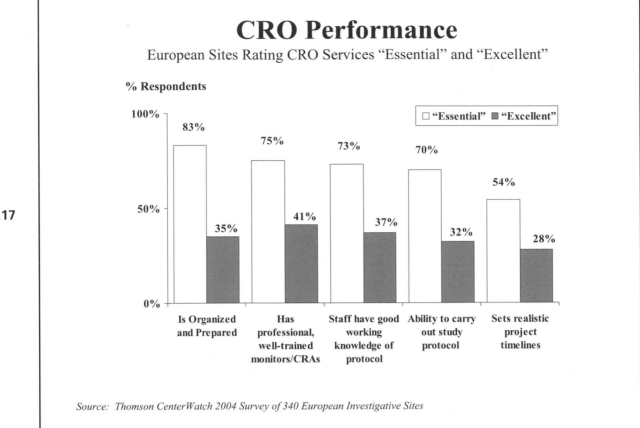

CRO Performance
European Sites Rating CRO Services "Essential" and "Excellent"

% Respondents

Legend: ☐ "Essential" ■ "Excellent"

- Is Organized and Prepared: 83% / 35%
- Has professional, well-trained monitors/CRAs: 75% / 41%
- Staff have good working knowledge of protocol: 73% / 37%
- Ability to carry out study protocol: 70% / 32%
- Sets realistic project timelines: 54% / 28%

Source: Thomson CenterWatch 2004 Survey of 340 European Investigative Sites

6.18

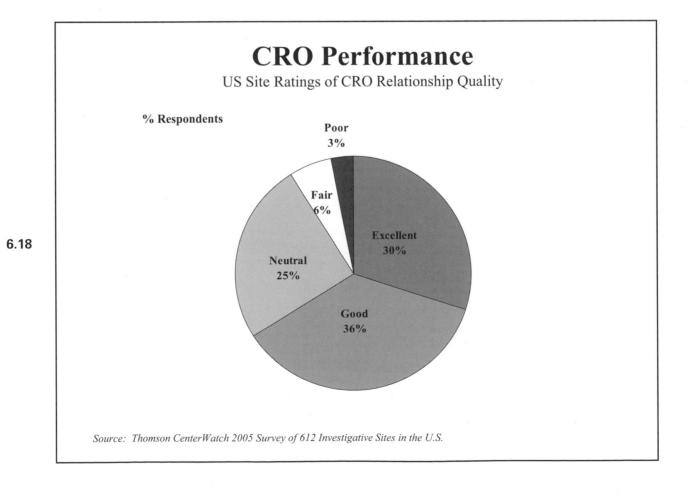

CRO Performance
US Site Ratings of CRO Relationship Quality

% Respondents

- Poor 3%
- Fair 6%
- Neutral 25%
- Excellent 30%
- Good 36%

Source: Thomson CenterWatch 2005 Survey of 612 Investigative Sites in the U.S.

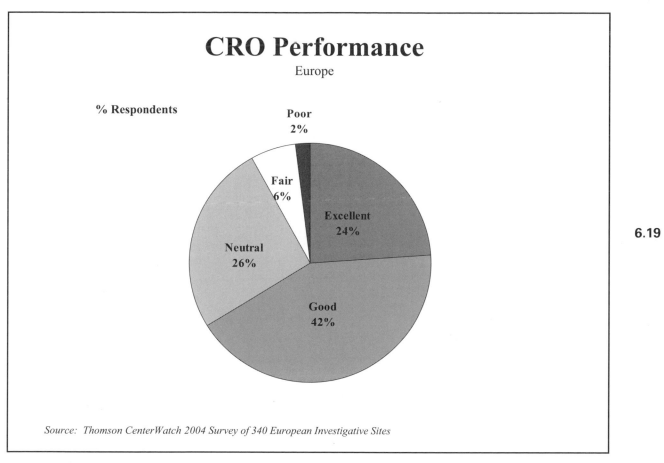

CRO Performance
Europe

% Respondents

- Poor 2%
- Fair 6%
- Excellent 24%
- Neutral 26%
- Good 42%

Source: *Thomson CenterWatch 2004 Survey of 340 European Investigative Sites*

6.19

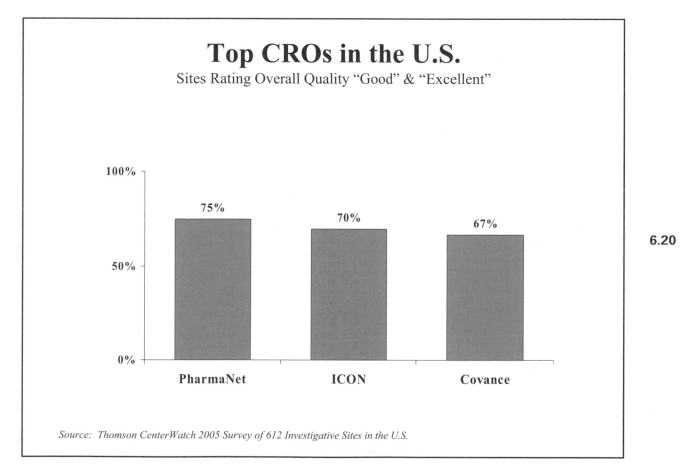

Top CROs in the U.S.
Sites Rating Overall Quality "Good" & "Excellent"

- PharmaNet 75%
- ICON 70%
- Covance 67%

Source: *Thomson CenterWatch 2005 Survey of 612 Investigative Sites in the U.S.*

6.20

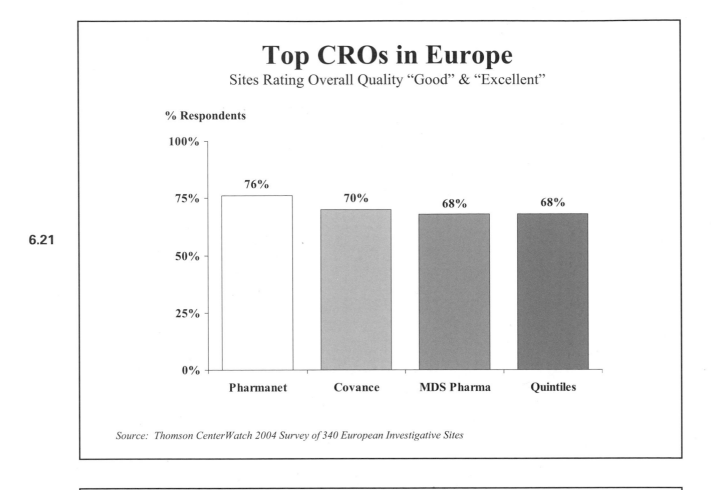

6.21

Top CROs in Europe
Sites Rating Overall Quality "Good" & "Excellent"

Source: Thomson CenterWatch 2004 Survey of 340 European Investigative Sites

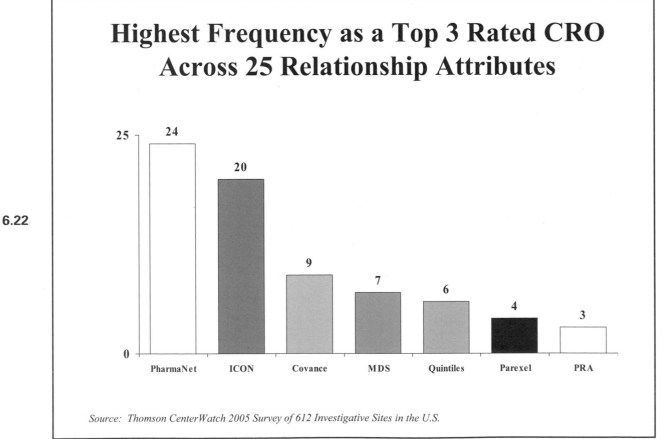

6.22

Highest Frequency as a Top 3 Rated CRO Across 25 Relationship Attributes

Source: Thomson CenterWatch 2005 Survey of 612 Investigative Sites in the U.S.

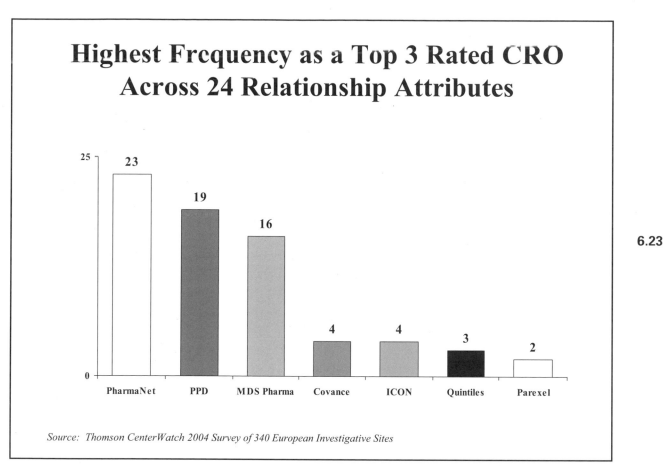

Highest Frequency as a Top 3 Rated CRO Across 24 Relationship Attributes

Source: Thomson CenterWatch 2004 Survey of 340 European Investigative Sites

6.23

CRO Project Management
United States

General Project Management	2001	2003	2005
Is organized and prepared	28%	28%	36%
Sets realistic project timelines	19%	21%	28%
Is responsive to inquiries	28%	28%	36%
Sets realistic patient enrollment goals	20%	21%	29%
Effectively works with sponsors	26%	27%	36%
Maintains open communication	*	32%	40%

Percent of Sites Rating a Typical CRO "Excellent"   ** Question not asked in this year*

Source: Thomson CenterWatch 2005 Survey of 612 Investigative Sites in the U.S.

6.24

CRO Project Management
Europe

6.25

Project Management	2000	2002	2004
Organized and Prepared	37%	29%	35%
Realistic Project Timelines	26%	20%	28%
Responsive to Inquiries	34%	26%	32%
Realistic Patient Enrollment Goals	22%	18%	n/a
Effectively Works with Sponsor	32%	32%	35%
Maintains Open Communication	*	*	34%

Percent of Sites Rating a Typical CRO "Excellent"   ** Question not asked in this year*

Source: Thomson CenterWatch 2000, 2002, 2004 Survey of 355, 545, 340 European Investigative Sites, respectively

CRO Professionalism & Workstyle
United States

6.26

Professionalism & Work Style	2001	2003	2005
Has professional medical staff	30%	31%	38%
Has professional, well-trained monitors/CRAs	31%	30%	36%
Has professional and efficient administrative staff	24%	26%	32%
Is flexible - willing to modify protocols and budgets	15%	17%	22%
Has a supportive culture	22%	24%	32%
Creates a collaborative team environment	23%	25%	34%

Percent of Sites Rating a Typical CRO "Excellent"

Source: Thomson CenterWatch 2005 Survey of 612 Investigative Sites in the U.S.

CRO Professionalism and Workstyle

Europe

Professionalism and Workstyle	2000	2002	2004
Professional Medical Staff	32%	31%	35%
Professional Monitors/CRAs	37%	37%	41%
Professional Administrative Staff	26%	24%	29%
CRAs/Managers are Knowledgeable	*	*	32%
Willing to Modify Protocols and Budgets	16%	14%	16%
Supportive Culture	22%	20%	27%
Collaborative Team Environment	20%	20%	27%

Percent of Sites Rating a Typical CRO "Excellent"   ** Question not asked in this year*

Source: Thomson CenterWatch 2000, 2002, 2004 Survey of 355, 545, 340 European Investigative Sites, respectively

6.27

CRO Project Initiation & Grant Payment

United States

Project Initiation & Grant Payment Process	2001	2003	2005
Provides good overall protocol design	20%	22%	29%
Provides uncomplicated case report form design	21%	20%	29%
Holds informative investigator meetings	22%	24%	34%
Provides fair overall grant payment amounts	16%	19%	22%
Offers realistic grant payment schedules	16%	16%	22%
Provides prompt payment of grants	16%	14%	22%

Percent of Sites Rating a Typical CRO "Excellent"

Source: Thomson CenterWatch 2005 Survey of 612 Investigative Sites in the U.S.

6.28

CRO Project Initiation & Grant Payment
Europe

6.29

Project Initiation & Grant Payment Process	2000	2002	2004
Good Protocol Design	22%	27%	32%
Provides uncomplicated case report form design	18%	26%	*
Informative Multicenter Meetings	17%	18%	26%
Fair Grant Payments	16%	21%	21%
Realistic Grant Payments	12%	21%	23%
Prompt Grant Payments	4%	24%	21%

Percent of Sites Rating a Typical CRO "Excellent"   *Question not asked in this year*

Source: Thomson CenterWatch 2000, 2002, 2004 Survey of 355, 545, 340 European Investigative Sites, respectively

CRO Ongoing Study Conduct
United States

6.30

Ongoing Study Conduct	2001	2003	2005
Provides patient recruitment planning and implementation assistance	18%	16%	23%
Has low monitor turnover (monitor staff does not keep changing)	21%	18%	27%
Provides ongoing help in running the study	*	32%	31%
Utilizes technology to make processes more efficient	*	21%	22%
Has timely drug availability	23%	28%	38%
Has an efficient query handling process	17%	18%	24%

Percent of Sites Rating a Typical CRO "Excellent"   *Question not asked in this year*

Source: Thomson CenterWatch 2005 Survey of 612 Investigative Sites in the U.S.

CRO Ongoing Study Conduct
Europe

Ongoing Study Conduct	2000	2002	2004
Efficient Contract and Budget Negotiations	15%	16%	*
Good Drug Availability	28%	35%	*
Good Patient Recruitment Support/Assistance	8%	19%	17%
Low Monitor Turnover	12%	19%	28%
Efficient Query Handling Process	4%	18%	24%

Percent of Sites Rating a Typical CRO "Excellent"   ** Question not asked in this year*

Source: Thomson CenterWatch 2000, 2002, 2004 Survey of 355, 545, 340 European Investigative Sites, respectively

6.31

CRO Performance:
European Site Ratings of CROs

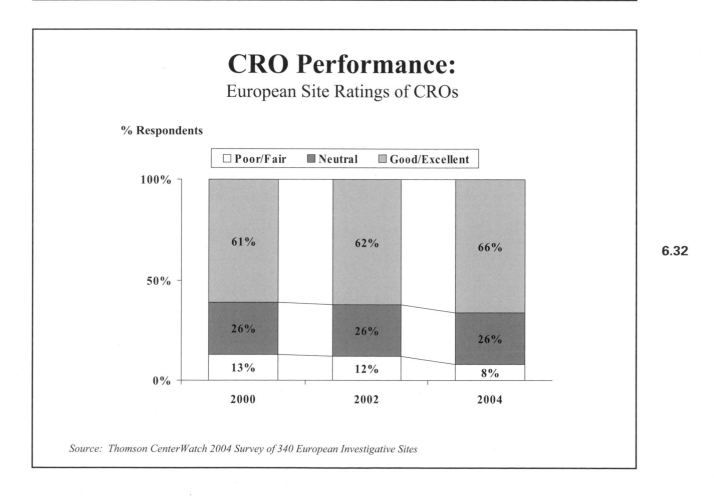

% Respondents

□ Poor/Fair   ■ Neutral   ▨ Good/Excellent

Source: Thomson CenterWatch 2004 Survey of 340 European Investigative Sites

6.32

6.33

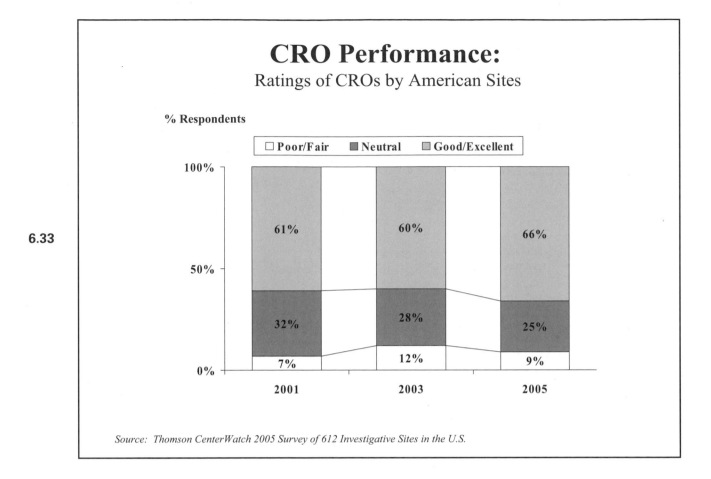

CRO Performance:
Ratings of CROs by American Sites

% Respondents

Legend: ☐ Poor/Fair ■ Neutral ▨ Good/Excellent

	2001	2003	2005
Good/Excellent	61%	60%	66%
Neutral	32%	28%	25%
Poor/Fair	7%	12%	9%

Source: Thomson CenterWatch 2005 Survey of 612 Investigative Sites in the U.S.

6.34

Top Rated CROs in the U.S.
Select Project Attributes

Attribute	Top Three Companies
Is organized and prepared	MDS Pharma, Covance, PPD
Has Professional, Well-trained Managers/CRAs	Pharmanet, Kendle Intíl, MDS Pharma
Is Responsive to Inquiries	Pharmanet, MDS Pharma, Kendle Intíl
Maintains Open Communication	Pharmanet, Kendle Intíl, Covance
Has Good Protocol Design	MDS Pharma, Ingenix, Covance

Source: Thomson CenterWatch, 2003 Survey of 396 U.S. Investigative Sites

Top Rated CROs in Europe
Select Project Attributes

Attribute	Top Three Companies
Is organized and prepared	Pharmanet, PPD, Covance
Sets realistic project timelines	Covance, Quintiles, ICON
Effectively works with a study sponsor	Pharmanet, MDS Pharma, Parexel
Has professional medical staff	Pharmanet, PPD, Quintiles
Is flexible - when responsible for budget negotiations	Pharmanet, PPD, MDS Pharma
Staff have good working knowledge of protocol	Pharmanet, ICON, MDS Pharma

Source: Thomson CenterWatch 2004 Survey of 340 European Investigative Sites

6.35

CRO Performance
Attributes Rated More Important for CROs than Sponsors, 2005

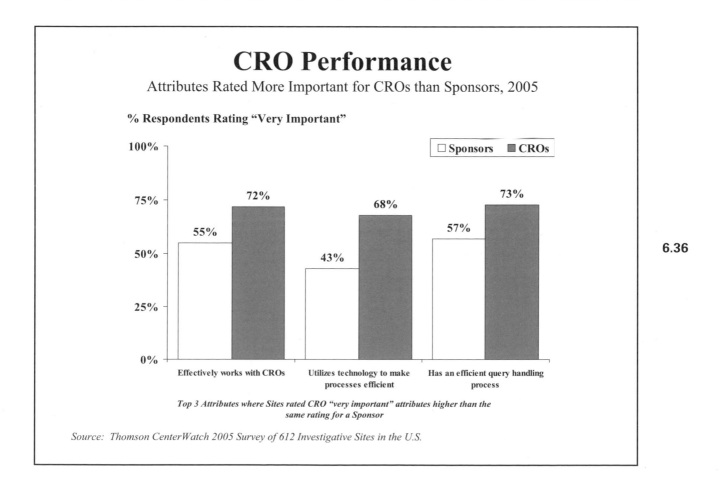

% Respondents Rating "Very Important"

Legend: □ Sponsors ■ CROs

- Effectively works with CROs: Sponsors 55%, CROs 72%
- Utilizes technology to make processes efficient: Sponsors 43%, CROs 68%
- Has an efficient query handling process: Sponsors 57%, CROs 73%

Top 3 Attributes where Sites rated CRO "very important" attributes higher than the same rating for a Sponsor

Source: Thomson CenterWatch 2005 Survey of 612 Investigative Sites in the U.S.

6.36

Industry Profiles
Select Trial Management Organizations

6.37

Company	Type	Studies	Sites	Founded	HQ
Research Solutions	SMO	172	196	1999	Little Rock, AK
Research Strategies	Site Support Services	100+	18	1996	Pasadena, CA
Clinical Research Consultants	CRO	60	7	1987	Hoover, AL
New Mexico Cancer Care Alliance	Charitable Organization	48	N/A	2002	Albuquerque, NM

Source: Thomson CenterWatch Analysis, 2006

SMO Market Size
Worldwide Total Sales of SMO Services, 1996-2004

6.38

$US in Millions

- 1996: $85
- 1998: $160
- 2000: $210
- 2002: $235
- 2004E: $282

Source: Thomson CenterWatch Analysis, 2004

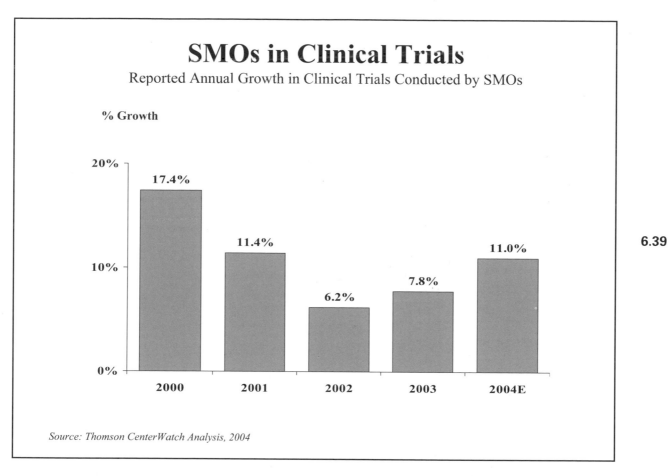

SMOs in Clinical Trials
Reported Annual Growth in Clinical Trials Conducted by SMOs

% Growth

- 2000: 17.4%
- 2001: 11.4%
- 2002: 6.2%
- 2003: 7.8%
- 2004E: 11.0%

Source: Thomson CenterWatch Analysis, 2004

6.39

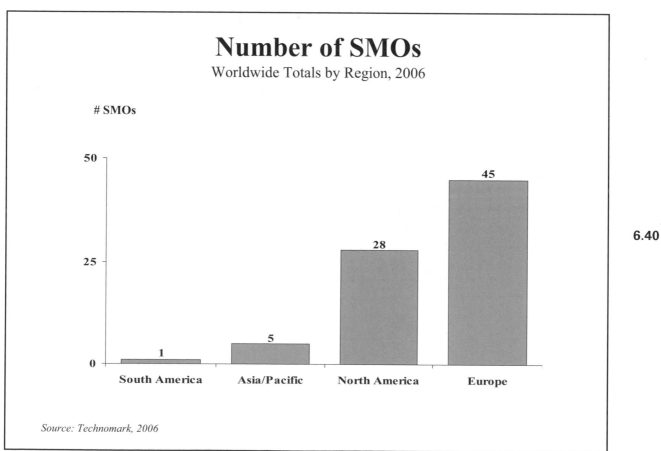

Number of SMOs
Worldwide Totals by Region, 2006

SMOs

- South America: 1
- Asia/Pacific: 5
- North America: 28
- Europe: 45

Source: Technomark, 2006

6.40

6.41

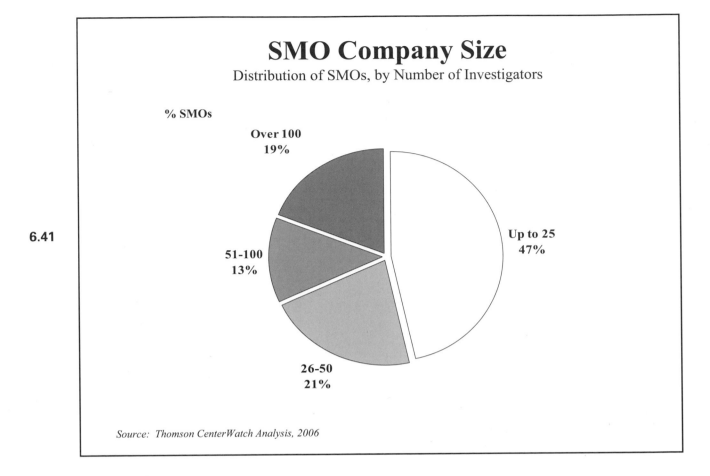

6.42

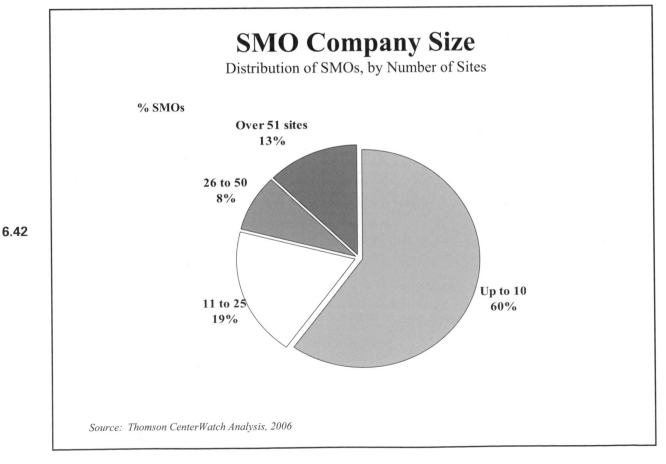

SMO Announcements
Major Developments in the SMO Industry, 2003

2/03	Research Solutions allies with Digestive Health Network of Cincinnati
3/03	Radiant Research buys two CNS sites from Canadian Medical Laboratories
3/03	Radiant Research buys rival Protocare
4/03	Internationally-focused NMI improves US coverage with new sites
5/03	Information technology company iGate buys Pittsburg SMO PCRN
6/03	Aremel begins operations with a single site in France
7/03	Canadian SMO Sound Medical Research closes down
7/03	PCTI adds 4th site affiliation, the Childrenís Medical Center of Dayton
8/03	AmericasDoctor launches Essential Patient Recruitment services
9/03	Synexus opens 11th site in the UK
10/03	Intercern closes SMO business, refocuses on phase I staffing
11/03	AmericasDoctor Cuts site network by 20%, to 138 total sites
12/03	PPS Clinical Research launched in St. Louis

6.43

Source: Thomson CenterWatch, 2004

SMO Announcements
Major Developments in the SMO Industry, 2004

3/04	Welsh, Cason, Anderson & Stowe makes $1.7B bid for US Oncology
4/04	AmericasDoctor spins off Essential Group, Inc., a niche CRO business
4/04	Synexus opens 12th site in Glasgow, Scotland
5/04	Pioneer Behavioral Health acquires Pivotal Research Centers
5/04	Radiant expands phase I capabilities with plans for 300 beds at 10 facilities
5/04	Research Solutions announces three new site alliances
6/04	Profiad expands UK network with 12 secondary care sites
7/04	Research Solutions acquires Arkansas Research Medical Testing
9/04	Radiant Research raises $26M to fund phase I expansion
11/04	Research Solutions announces new alliance with Kingís Daughters Clinic

6.44

Source: Thomson CenterWatch, 2005

6.45

SMO Announcements
Major Developments in the SMO Industry, 2005

2/05	Accelovance acquires nTouch Research
2/05	Pioneer Behavioral Healthís Q2 revenue jumps 24%
3/05	Odyssey Research invited by Chinese SFDA to train investigators
3/05	Research Solutions adds 9 new site alliances in 4 states
5/05	Radiant Research opens new 120-bed phase I unit in Texas, and adds 24-36 phase I/IIa beds at four existing units
5/05	Benchmark Research opens site in New Orleans
5/05	Accelovance opens office in Beijing, China; additional sites planned
9/05	Pioneer Behavioral Healthís Q4 up 22.3%; revenue from trial services up 51%
11/05	Accelovance opens office in Shanghai, China
12/05	Synexus opens office in Mumbai, India

Source: Thomson CenterWatch, 2006

Outsourcing

Wyeth,RPS Shift Outsourcing Model

Faced with an enviable problem of having more than 200 new and ongoing studies and a new compound entering development each month for the next four years, Wyeth wanted a new way to meet its growing regional field operation needs. The sponsor didn't see the value in paying hourly rates for monitors from $110 to $150, or about $300,000 a year.

So Wyeth forged a strategic partnership with RPS. In the first year alone, the initiative shifted Wyeth's outsourcing model from 80% use of CROs to 20%. In years to come, Wyeth expects to continue this dramatic outsourcing shift. The success of the initiative will be closely watched by sponsors and CROs—which could see its business model threatened.

Wyeth,RPS Shift Outsourcing Model

By Karyn Korieth
Published June 2005

Wyeth Pharmaceuticals, which signed a groundbreaking deal with Accenture two years ago to outsource its entire clinical data management operations, has begun a strategic alliance with Research Pharmaceutical Services (RPS) to handle its clinical monitoring operations in the United States, Canada and Latin America. The initiative, expected to save Wyeth millions of dollars in outsourcing costs, may signal changes in the drug development sector, which has begun to look for new ways to manage clinical trial conduct in the face of rising drug development costs.

Executives at Wyeth and RPS say their partnership, which involves a long-term contract, differs from the staff-augmentation or functional insourcing models adopted at other major pharmaceutical companies. The initiative represents more of a business process outsourcing approach, which means sponsors don't relinquish control of the function, but rather they form a business partnership with the provider. The Wyeth-RPS model, which required a complete re-structuring of Wyeth's internal field operations, merges the clinical operations expertise, management, infrastructure and support of both organizations.

The partners share common goals and rewards to complete studies. And the initiative not only addresses higher efficiencies and lower cost points, but also provides flexibility for Wyeth to manage studies as its pipeline changes in the future. "It is different from other types of models in that it is truly strategic. It is set up to marry two clinical operations groups to come up with the overall process," said Samir Shah, vice president of Strategic Development at RPS, who engineered the deal at RPS along with chief executive officer Daniel Perlman and chief operating officer Janet Brennan.

"Our model is sustainable with years to come in terms of being able to change as Wyeth changes. We see that their pipeline is growing dramatically. As a result of that, their operations will change," Shah added.

The success of the strategic alliance, which has created a buzz in the CRO and biopharmaceutical sectors, will be closely watched by both sponsors and CROs. While the companies haven't announced specific cost savings, Wyeth expects to save millions of dollars by decreasing its dependency on outsourcing to CROs, while at the same time improving quality and speed of its clinical monitoring operations. In the first year alone, the initiative changed Wyeth's outsourcing model from 80% use of CROs to 20%. In years to come, Wyeth expects to dramatically shift its outsourcing paradigm; cost savings from the initiative will be rolled back into development and pipeline growth.

Monitoring Solution Needed

The Wyeth-RPS partnership follows a much talked about strategic alliance that gave consulting giant Accenture responsibility for Wyeth's entire clinical data management operation. As part of the agreement, which Forrester Research called the first of its type in the life sciences industry, Accenture received a 10-year contract to provide clinical data management services for Wyeth R&D worldwide; the company acquired 175 of Wyeth's employees and much of its clinical data management infrastructure. Accenture also agreed to meet highly specific performance criteria designed to improve the data management process. The arrangement, reached two years ago, grew out of a partnership between the two companies formed to re-structure Wyeth's clinical research and development operations. Results from the partnership have been impressive, including a 400% increase in drug discovery productivity during the past three years, an 80% reduction in clinical trial cycle times and a 30% reduction in contracted costs.

After the success of its Accenture deal, Wyeth turned its attention to its regional field operations. Wyeth, one of the world's largest research-driven pharmaceutical and health-care product companies, was faced with an enviable problem: Because it has such a dynamic pipeline, with more than 200 new and ongoing studies and a new compound entering development track each month for four years, the company wanted a new way to meet the growing regional field operation needs.

An executive team looked at the cold, hard facts: The number of studies they needed to get started, the number of monitors available and their budget. "If we looked at the traditional model for using a CRO, even if we negotiated tremendous rates, we'd be paying hourly rates for monitors anywhere from $110 to $150. That's $220,000 to $300,000 a year per CRA. We had to find a creative solution to use our money wiser and leverage our purchasing power," said David Bartholomew, senior director/department head of clinical trial logistics at Wyeth Research, who led the initiative with RPS along with James Kirwin, assistant vice president of clinical trial operations, and Walter Young, associate director of the clinical contracts and outsourcing group.

In the past, Wyeth heavily relied on outsourcing for its monitoring work. In phases II and III, the company did about 50% of the work internally; for phase IV and vaccine studies, 90% of the work was outsourced. Wyeth had already narrowed its list of service providers from approximately 45 CROs down to five preferred providers in order to improve efficiencies and cost. But Wyeth needed greater savings and efficiencies. "Large companies have a lot of infrastructure. When we bring in a CRO or another vendor, we still have management capacity inside to review the reports and to help oversee the project. Where does the CRO model flourish? In a small company that needs project help. They need the clinical, the training departments and people to write the reports, which Wyeth does not. This initiative will eliminate such overlapping redundancies and streamline service deliverables," Bartholomew said.

What Wyeth wanted was a creative solution that could address efficiencies, flexibility and pricing not obtainable by traditional outsourcing methods. The executive team outlined their ideas, understanding it would require a re-design of the entire field operations group to support a new model. Their proposal was sent to Wyeth's key providers, big vendors and RPS. So RPS proposed a solution outside of the traditional outsourcing model. "Some of the bids that came back from the big vendors were generic, not creative," said Bartholomew. "RPS pulled out a clean, fresh pad of paper and said, 'How we can work this out?' Between the two companies, we found a very clear, harmonized way to do this. It's truly a partnership. This initiative will redefine the traditional vendor/sponsor roles and create a truly transparent relationship."

The deal developed between Wyeth and RPS merges the clinical operations expertise, management, infrastructure and support of both organizations. Rather than designing a short-term, gap-filling structure, the initiative incorporates a strategic vision of Wyeth's future and allows the company flexibility in managing their pipeline. "This is truly an outside-of-the-box deal," said Shah. "We are taking a look at the entire clinical process and bringing together two strong operations groups—both Wyeth and RPS—and coming up with a new way of working and a way that is outside their current process. It forces a re-engineering to come up with a better process. You change the organization, you change the matrix. But you do that [with] two organizations that can come together and provide an overall model that is not only sustainable, but is flexible and can grow as their needs grow. That is what we designed."

Internal Change

Under the initiative, which was launched in January, RPS has become an integral part of the Wyeth Americas Research Operations (ARO) organization. Through this strategic relationship, Wyeth looks to RPS to provide not only monitoring capabilities, but operational support, expertise and process improvement. The two companies jointly are responsible for planning, training and clinical monitoring services. "Combining the strong clinical and operational abilities of both companies has allowed our partnership to achieve a total capability that is new to this industry," said Perlman.

The initiative gives RPS joint responsibility for Wyeth's monitoring in the United States, Canada and Latin America. Growth in Latin America, in particular, has become a critical area for Wyeth. In order to meet Wyeth's clinical monitoring needs in Latin America, last September RPS formed an exclusive alliance with LatinTrials, a full-service CRO based in Argentina, to conduct clinical development programs under joint operations throughout the Americas.

In order for the initiative to be fully implemented, internal change at Wyeth was necessary to create a more efficient, standardized monitoring organization.

The relationship required a re-design of Wyeth's field ARO organization, which is Wyeth's monitoring organization in Canada, United States and Latin America led by Jean-Paul St. Pierre, M.D., assistant vice president of Americas Research Operations. An infrastructure was established to incorporate the additional RPS monitors; processes and training were standardized for monitors at both companies.

The reorganization allowed Wyeth to re-align its teams throughout the entire organization by therapeutic areas, which was a key part of Wyeth's "Clinical Breakthrough," a program designed to radically change the way the company conducts clinical studies. "We want to have monitors who have a chance to specialize and grow with their careers," Bartholomew said. "The model will be set up in such a way that it will be seamless—that the site can go from phase II to phase III to marketing studies using the same team monitor and the same team to manage all the way through. The consistency is wonderful for the sites. They get to know the people and to understand the product, the company and the person."

Measuring Progress

The design of the contract also will drive efficiencies in Wyeth's site monitoring process, which is one of the ways the deal differs from the functional provider model more commonly adopted by big pharma. "Functional provider models are set up to augment staff only. With this model, we brought in the management as well as the staff; we wanted to bring in a partner and use their expertise," said Bartholomew. "It will help us raise the bar on quality, raise the bar on being able to meet the demands of our studies."

Shah added, "One of the biggest differentiators about this relationship unlike other models is that it was not a staff augmentation model that just added bodies to the equation, but an entire clinical re-engineering utilizing expertise of both organizations, Wyeth and RPS, to come up with a new way of working. Wyeth recognized that there is a world outside of themselves and looked at a partner that could complement their clinical operations group and bring together overall process improvement."

The governance structure developed for the initiative includes three levels. At the top, a steering committee, which includes executives from both Wyeth and RPS, meets quarterly to review metrics and discuss high-level status of progress and challenges. Next, senior management from both companies hold monthly operational meetings to review the day-to-day of overall operations, resolve issues and view strategic operations. In addition, weekly team meetings are held to review resource capacities, review of study start timelines, and discussion of day-to-day operations management. "We have meetings as a team to review common metrics and monitor the initiative's progress together," said Bartholomew.

To measure progress, the contract defines 15 points of measurement, with the four main components involving speed, quality, customer service and cost. "We put together common metrics. Our metrics set turnaround times and expectations that we both have to abide by," Bartholomew said. "If we meet all of our criteria and our studies are successful, RPS will profit. At the same return, if Wyeth misses a goal or timeline, RPS will not benefit. We have common goals and common rewards to get the studies completed."

Executives from both Wyeth and RPS agree that one of the most important elements of the strategic alliance is its flexibility. "We're looking to make decisions quickly on our pipeline; we want to be able to start studies, stop studies and make decisions on studies quickly. We needed a vendor that could meet those needs. With a CRO, it takes time and money to get trials started because of the intense startup efforts and training. If for some reason you have to stop the study, the rampdown period is as exhaustive as the startup," Bartholomew said. "What we are looking to do is create a pool. These people are full-time employees of RPS. They are 100% dedicated to Wyeth. The beauty of the initiative is being able to scale up and down, handling the ebb and flow of the workload. RPS knows our pipeline. They know when studies are going to start and when they are going to end so they can start planning their staffing around our pipeline."

The agreement also allows for expanding the partnership into other functional areas in the future. "As Wyeth looks at other initiatives, we have the ability to be cross-functional in design," said Shah. "If they want to go into other areas for similar types of initiatives, whether it be clinical trial operations or statistics programming, we are set up to do that. We are an organization that has internal operations management in place so they are not talking to multiple vendors. Some organizations have moved to a labor arbitrage model by going from a CRO to a staffing type model. That gives you some immediate cost savings, but it doesn't address the overall needs of what will be a sustainable model from years to come. It's more a short-term gap-filling. If you have

five or six of these short-term gap fillings, then all of a sudden you need another organization to be able to manage all of them."

Deal Signals Industry Shift

Wyeth's deals with both Accenture and RPS may signal a shift in an industry looking for new ways to develop drugs faster without sacrificing quality. More often than not, the pharmaceutical industry has outsourced on a project-by-project basis in order to solve a specific problem, such as a need for statisticians, rather than investing in long-term relationships with CROs or other vendors. While CROs want to offer full-service contracts, and have taken significant steps to sell bundled services in order to give sponsor companies better deals, much of their work has been piecemeal, especially from the major pharmaceutical companies.

The notion of so-called functional outsourcing began to appear in the drug development industry during the past five years. With this concept, sponsors first identify an activity that they feel is "non-core," meaning it doesn't define the company's competitive advantage in the marketplace. This non-core activity becomes a good candidate for outsourcing across all projects, allowing the company to focus internal resources on core competencies. "Functional outsourcing is more strategic in nature," said John Vogel, Ph.D., founder of John R. Vogel Associates, a drug development consultancy that works with pharmaceutical companies and pharmaceutical service providers on outsourcing issues. "It requires the sponsor to decide what is a non-core activity that they are willing to minimize or eliminate in-house in order to benefit by getting it off their books, moving it outside, and giving it to someone else who can do it just as well or even more efficiently."

While other industries have outsourced strategically for more than a decade in order to improve their competitive position and financial performance, pharmaceutical companies have been slower to adopt the model; drug companies traditionally consider all activities as integral to their organizations and have resisted defining any of their functions as non-core. Yet many see a shift in this thinking. Pharmaceutical companies are under intense pressure to fill their pipelines with blockbuster drugs; yet they also face rising development costs and a slowdown in sales. "There is a tremendous amount of pressure on the bottom line for the pharmaceutical industry and they have fewer products in the pipeline to work with. They've got to start looking at re-tooling the way that they do things. Functional outsourcing may be the outcome of some of that re tooling," Vogel said.

Five years ago, one of the first functional outsourcing relationships began when Kforce Clinical Research was selected by a leading global biopharmaceutical company to provide regional monitoring services; the relationship is characterized by a mix of permanent employees and outsourced resources. Since then, Kforce has partnered with three additional major biopharmaceutical companies in a similar fashion. While other pharmaceutical companies and vendors have formed strategic alliances, which involve contracts that share risks and rewards, the deal between Wyeth and Accenture for clinical data management was considered groundbreaking in the industry because it was the first to turn over an entire function to the provider. The initiative between Wyeth and RPS represents yet another variant on traditional outsourcing models in that the two companies formed a business partnership, which involved setting mutual goals to improve clinical trial monitoring.

Sponsors and CROs alike will watch the success of these strategic partnerships during the next couple of years. "If these outsourcing deals can be demonstrated to yield significant benefits, other large sponsors may follow suit," said Vogel. "If these deals demonstrate tremendous advantages—and the advantages have to be in lower cost and faster drug development— that could create problems for traditional full-service CROs because the big money is with the big sponsors. If you take an entire function, like clinical monitoring, out of the equation for all projects at a sponsor, a full-service CRO has less to deal with. Take away several functions, like monitoring, data management and biostatistics, across all projects at a sponsor, and there won't be a need for a full-service CRO."

CROs, many of which struggle with issues of high infrastructure costs and turnover, are aware that the pharmaceutical industry is undergoing changes that give competitive advantage to companies that improve operating performance and reduce costs.

"My view is that the full-service CROs have made a significant investment in integrating activities and selling bundled services on a project-by-project basis. Functional outsourcing essentially un-bundles the services. CROs can continue trying to sell the value proposition of drug development expertise, but large pharma traditionally does its own program and protocol development," Vogel said. "It's a little early to start manning the lifeboats. But I think that these deals could potentially catch the interest of other large sponsors. My sense is that these kinds of discussions are going on at large companies at least to the extent of looking and saying, 'Are there some things that we are staffing and doing here that someone else could do as well, maybe even better?' That's a real change in philosophy."

7.01

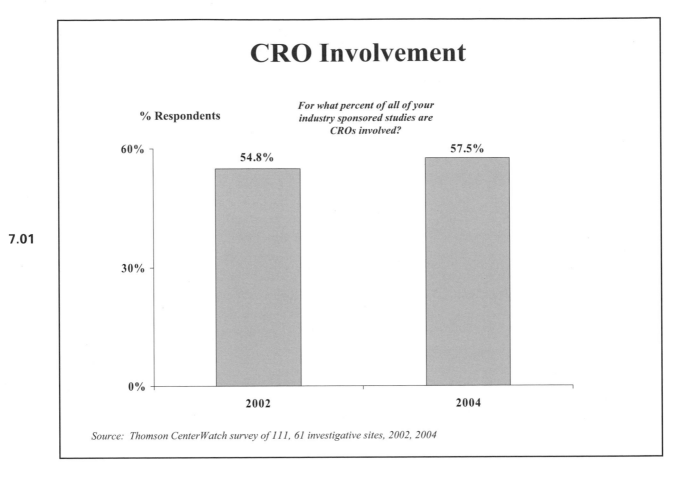

CRO Involvement

% Respondents

For what percent of all of your industry sponsored studies are CROs involved?

54.8% — 2002
57.5% — 2004

Source: Thomson CenterWatch survey of 111, 61 investigative sites, 2002, 2004

7.02

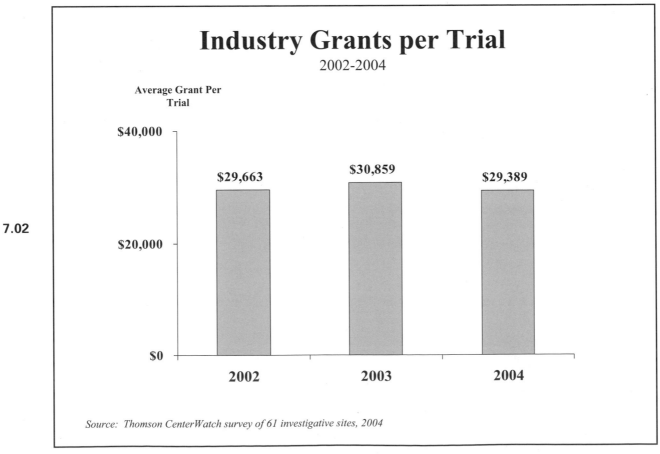

Industry Grants per Trial
2002-2004

Average Grant Per Trial

$29,663 — 2002
$30,859 — 2003
$29,389 — 2004

Source: Thomson CenterWatch survey of 61 investigative sites, 2004

Selecting Countries for Multinational Trials

Key Criteria Used by Sponsors

Average Score

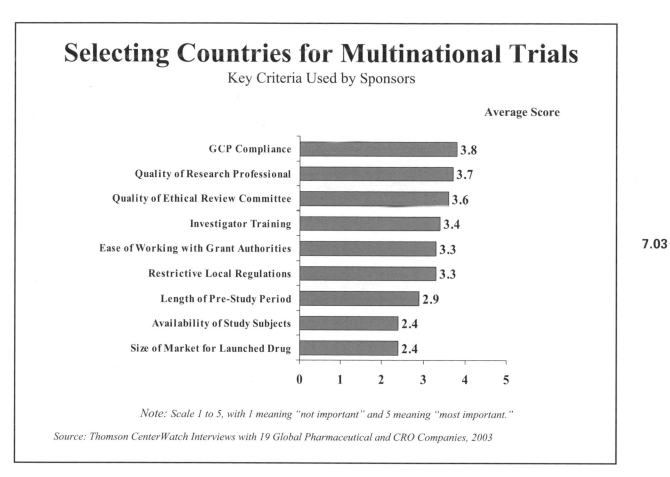

GCP Compliance — 3.8
Quality of Research Professional — 3.7
Quality of Ethical Review Committee — 3.6
Investigator Training — 3.4
Ease of Working with Grant Authorities — 3.3
Restrictive Local Regulations — 3.3
Length of Pre-Study Period — 2.9
Availability of Study Subjects — 2.4
Size of Market for Launched Drug — 2.4

0 1 2 3 4 5

7.03

Note: Scale 1 to 5, with 1 meaning "not important" and 5 meaning "most important."

Source: Thomson CenterWatch Interviews with 19 Global Pharmaceutical and CRO Companies, 2003

Investigative Site Operating Concerns

Most Frequent Responses

% Respondents

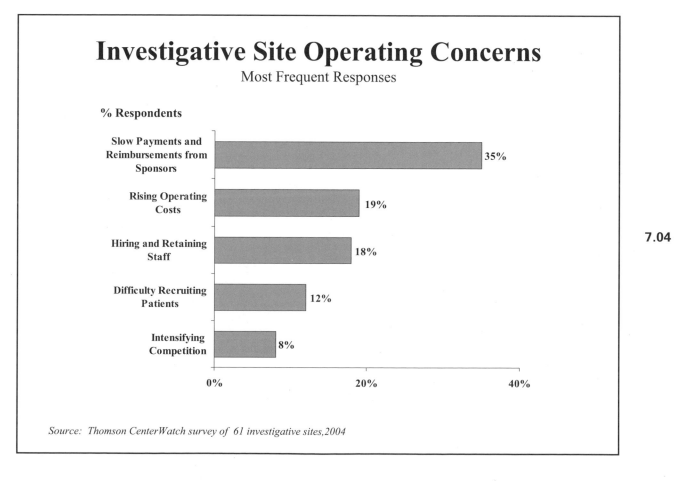

Slow Payments and Reimbursements from Sponsors — 35%
Rising Operating Costs — 19%
Hiring and Retaining Staff — 18%
Difficulty Recruiting Patients — 12%
Intensifying Competition — 8%

0% 20% 40%

7.04

Source: Thomson CenterWatch survey of 61 investigative sites, 2004

What is the biggest challenge you face today?

7.05

2002	
Slow Reimbursements from Sponsors	35%
Rising Operating Costs	19%
Hiring and Retaining Staff	18%
Difficulty Recruiting Patients	12%
Intensifying Competition	8%

2004	
Finding / competing for appropriate studies	25%
Budget doesnít cover hidden costs	21%
Difficulty Recruiting Patients	10%
Increased EDC requirements	9%
Negotiations of Contracts	9%

Source: Thomson CenterWatch survey of 111, 61 investigative sites, 2002, 2004

CRO Impact on Study Profits

7.06

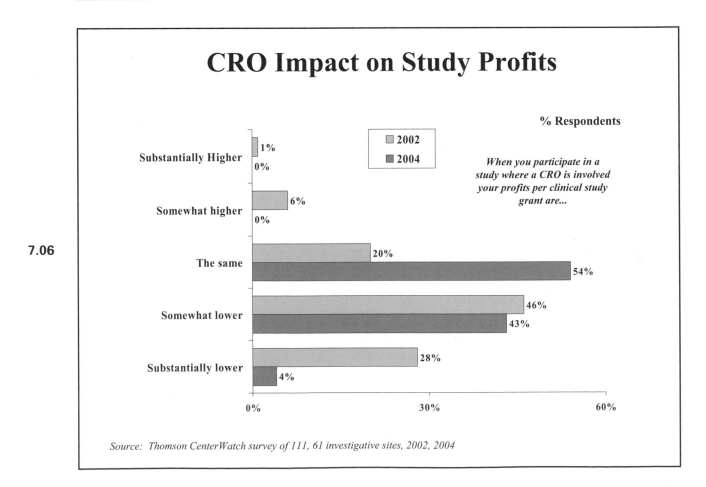

Source: Thomson CenterWatch survey of 111, 61 investigative sites, 2002, 2004

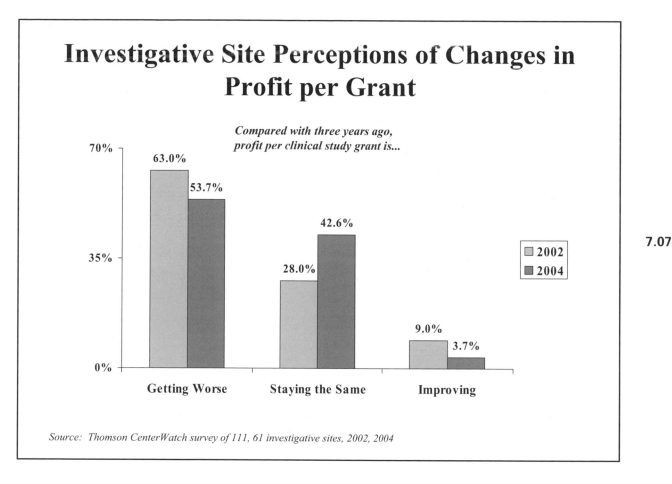

Investigative Site Perceptions of Changes in Profit per Grant

Compared with three years ago, profit per clinical study grant is...

- 2002
- 2004

Getting Worse: 63.0% (2002), 53.7% (2004)
Staying the Same: 28.0% (2002), 42.6% (2004)
Improving: 9.0% (2002), 3.7% (2004)

Source: Thomson CenterWatch survey of 111, 61 investigative sites, 2002, 2004

7.07

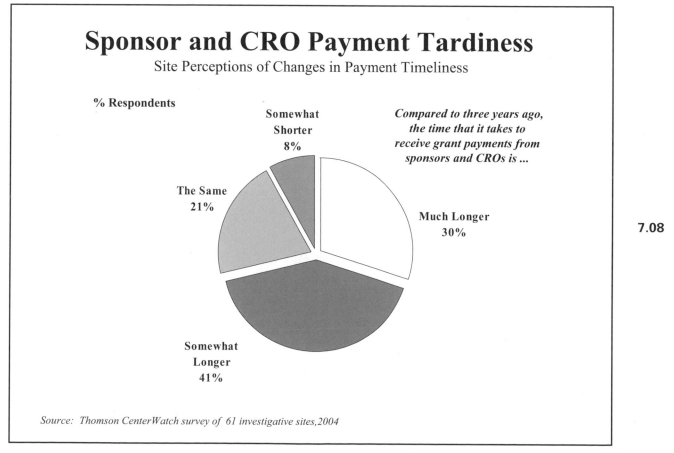

Sponsor and CRO Payment Tardiness
Site Perceptions of Changes in Payment Timeliness

% Respondents

Compared to three years ago, the time that it takes to receive grant payments from sponsors and CROs is ...

- Somewhat Shorter 8%
- The Same 21%
- Much Longer 30%
- Somewhat Longer 41%

Source: Thomson CenterWatch survey of 61 investigative sites, 2004

7.08

7.09

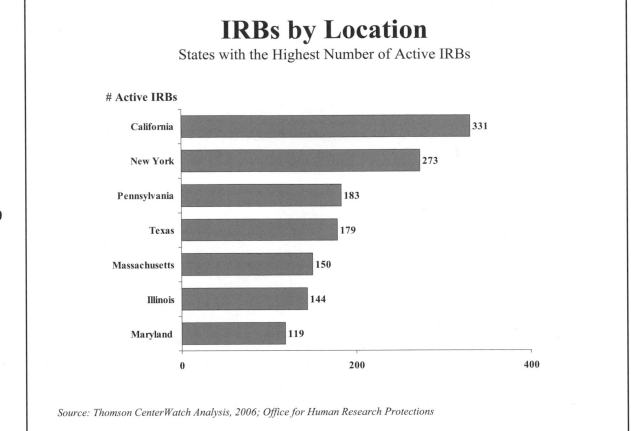

IRBs by Location
States with the Highest Number of Active IRBs

Active IRBs

State	# Active IRBs
California	331
New York	273
Pennsylvania	183
Texas	179
Massachusetts	150
Illinois	144
Maryland	119

Source: Thomson CenterWatch Analysis, 2006; Office for Human Research Protections

7.10

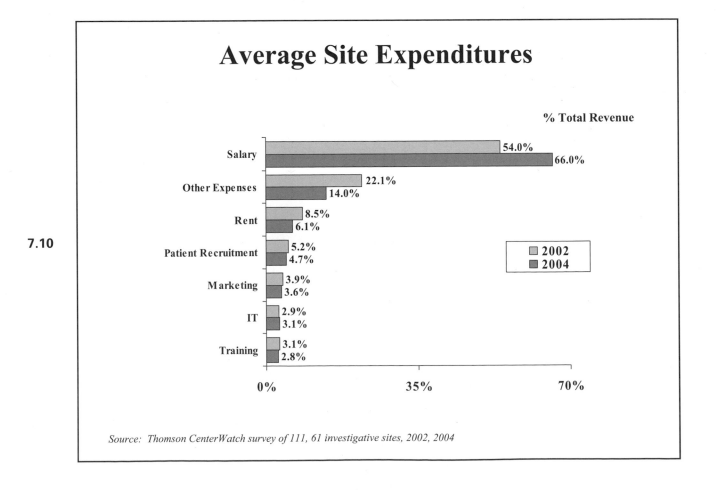

Average Site Expenditures

% Total Revenue

	2002	2004
Salary	54.0%	66.0%
Other Expenses	22.1%	14.0%
Rent	8.5%	6.1%
Patient Recruitment	5.2%	4.7%
Marketing	3.9%	3.6%
IT	2.9%	3.1%
Training	3.1%	2.8%

Source: Thomson CenterWatch survey of 111, 61 investigative sites, 2002, 2004

Site Revenue Benchmarks

Independent Investigative Site Mean Annual Revenues

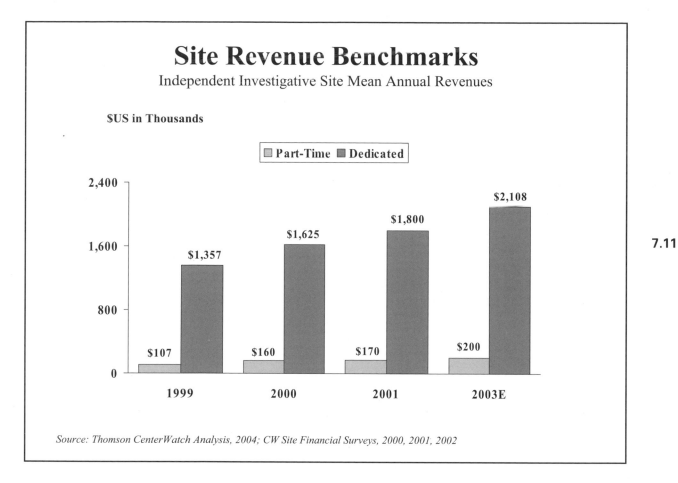

$US in Thousands

Legend: ▢ Part-Time ▦ Dedicated

Year	Part-Time	Dedicated
1999	$107	$1,357
2000	$160	$1,625
2001	$170	$1,800
2003E	$200	$2,108

Source: Thomson CenterWatch Analysis, 2004; CW Site Financial Surveys, 2000, 2001, 2002

7.11

Typical Investigative Site Revenue Allocation

2004

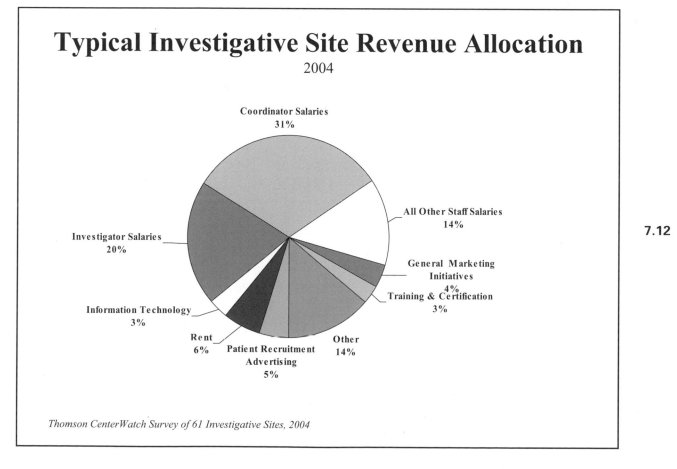

- Coordinator Salaries 31%
- All Other Staff Salaries 14%
- General Marketing Initiatives 4%
- Training & Certification 3%
- Other 14%
- Patient Recruitment Advertising 5%
- Rent 6%
- Information Technology 3%
- Investigator Salaries 20%

Thomson CenterWatch Survey of 61 Investigative Sites, 2004

7.12

7.13

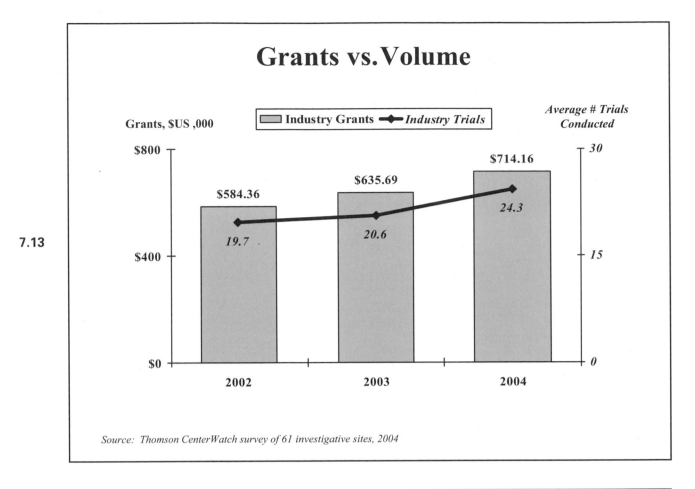

Grants vs. Volume

Grants, $US ,000

☐ Industry Grants ◆ Industry Trials

Average # Trials Conducted

- $800
- $584.36
- $635.69
- $714.16
- 19.7
- 20.6
- 24.3
- $400
- $0
- 2002
- 2003
- 2004
- 30
- 15
- 0

Source: Thomson CenterWatch survey of 61 investigative sites, 2004

7.14

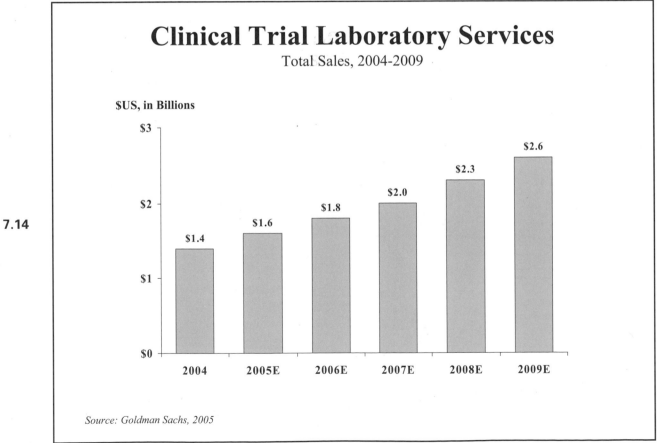

Clinical Trial Laboratory Services
Total Sales, 2004-2009

$US, in Billions

- $3
- $2.6
- $2.3
- $2.0
- $1.8
- $1.6
- $1.4
- $2
- $1
- $0
- 2004
- 2005E
- 2006E
- 2007E
- 2008E
- 2009E

Source: Goldman Sachs, 2005

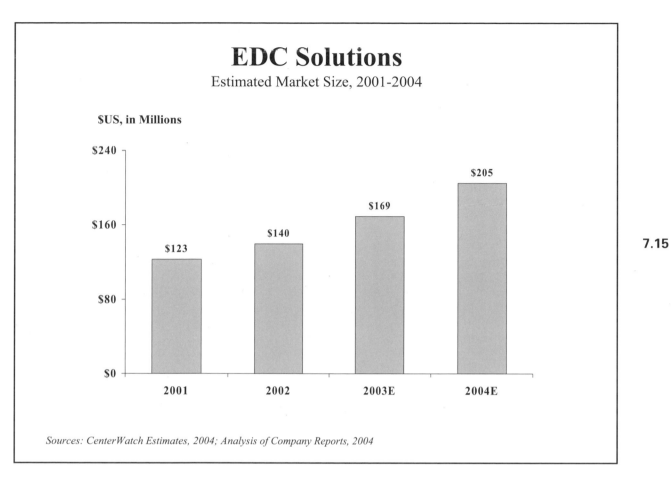

EDC Solutions
Estimated Market Size, 2001-2004

$US, in Millions

Sources: CenterWatch Estimates, 2004; Analysis of Company Reports, 2004

7.15

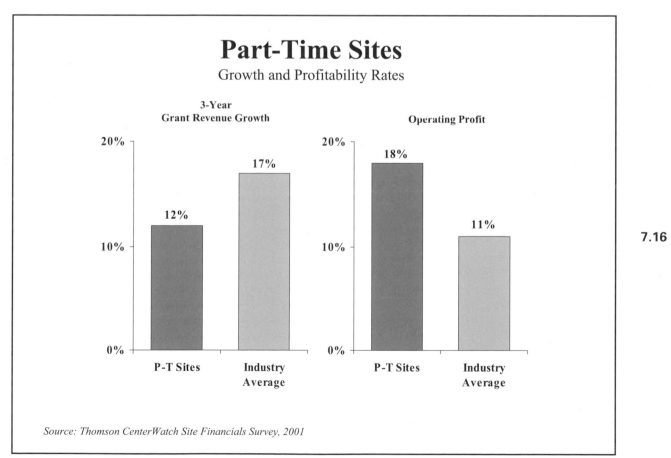

Part-Time Sites
Growth and Profitability Rates

3-Year Grant Revenue Growth

Operating Profit

Source: Thomson CenterWatch Site Financials Survey, 2001

7.16

7.17

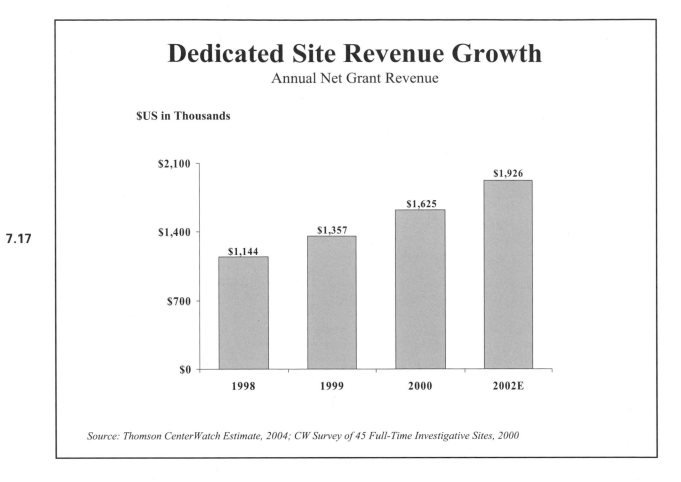

Dedicated Site Revenue Growth
Annual Net Grant Revenue

$US in Thousands

Source: Thomson CenterWatch Estimate, 2004; CW Survey of 45 Full-Time Investigative Sites, 2000

7.18

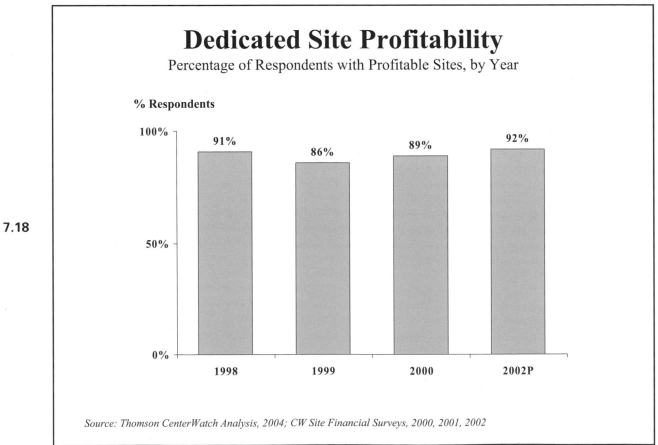

Dedicated Site Profitability
Percentage of Respondents with Profitable Sites, by Year

% Respondents

Source: Thomson CenterWatch Analysis, 2004; CW Site Financial Surveys, 2000, 2001, 2002

Highest Degree Attained by Outsourcing Department Personnel

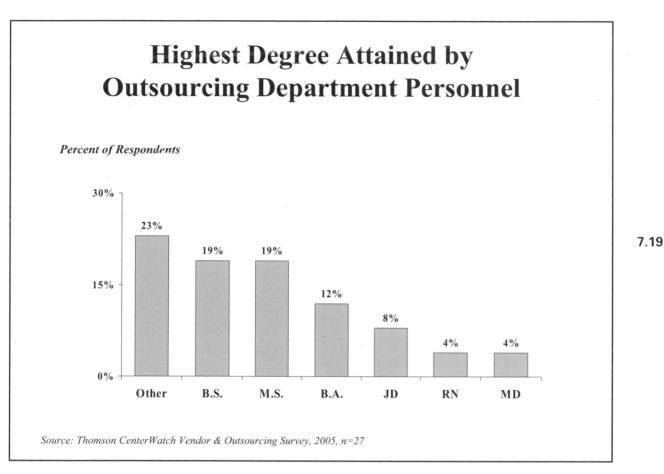

Percent of Respondents

Source: Thomson CenterWatch Vendor & Outsourcing Survey, 2005, n=27

Outsourcing Department Reporting Structure

Division	% Respondents
Clinical Functions	43%
R&D	23%
Project Management	12%
Finance	12%
Other	10%

Source: Thomson CenterWatch Vendor & Outsourcing Survey, 2005, n=27

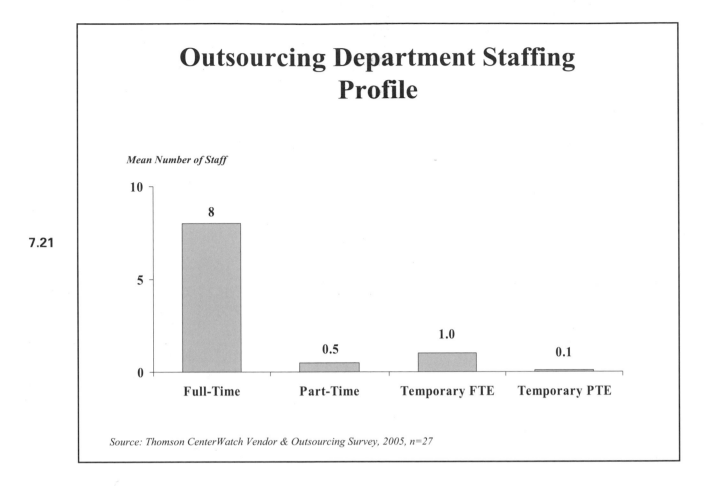

Outsourcing Department Staffing Profile

Mean Number of Staff

7.21

Source: Thomson CenterWatch Vendor & Outsourcing Survey, 2005, n=27

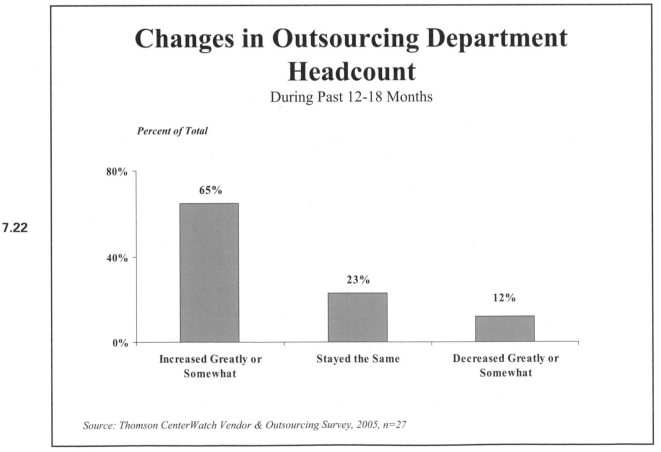

Changes in Outsourcing Department Headcount

During Past 12-18 Months

Percent of Total

7.22

Source: Thomson CenterWatch Vendor & Outsourcing Survey, 2005, n=27

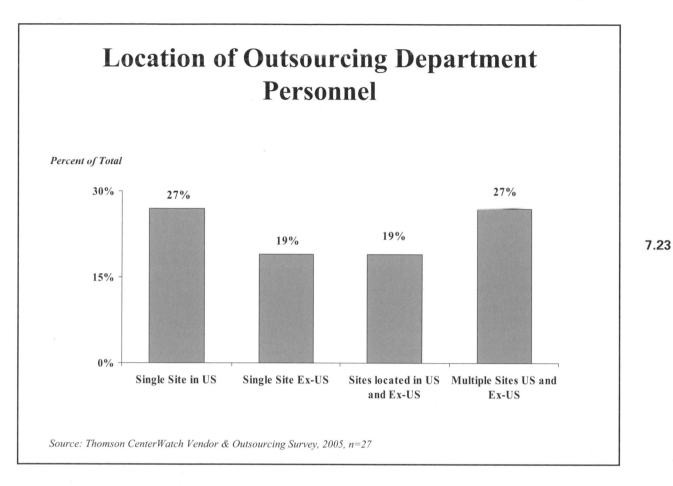

Location of Outsourcing Department Personnel

Percent of Total

Source: Thomson CenterWatch Vendor & Outsourcing Survey, 2005, n=27

7.23

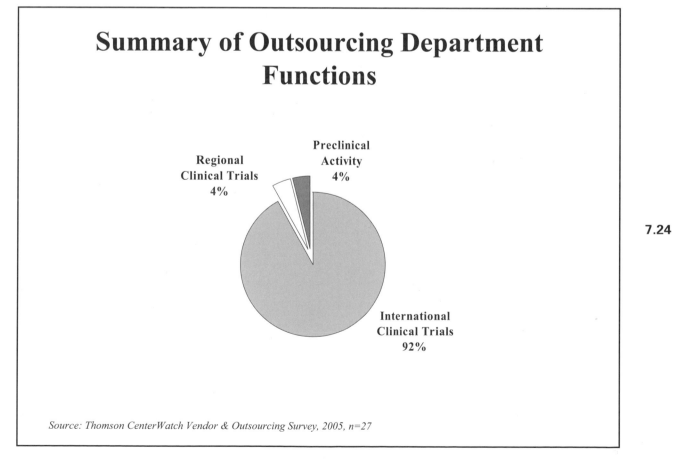

Summary of Outsourcing Department Functions

Source: Thomson CenterWatch Vendor & Outsourcing Survey, 2005, n=27

7.24

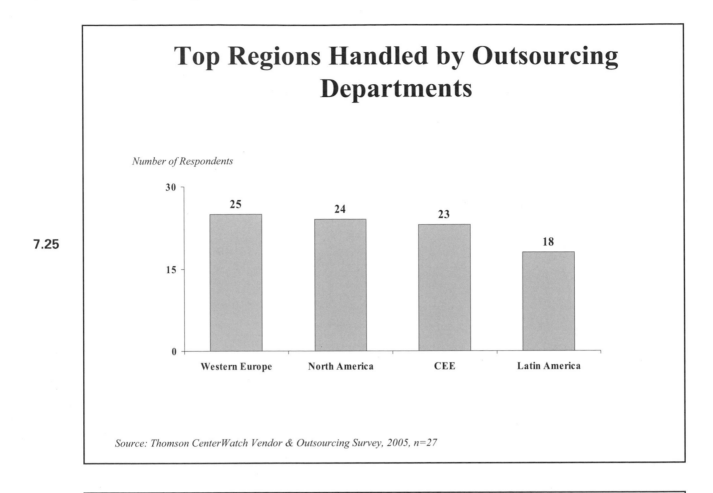

7.25

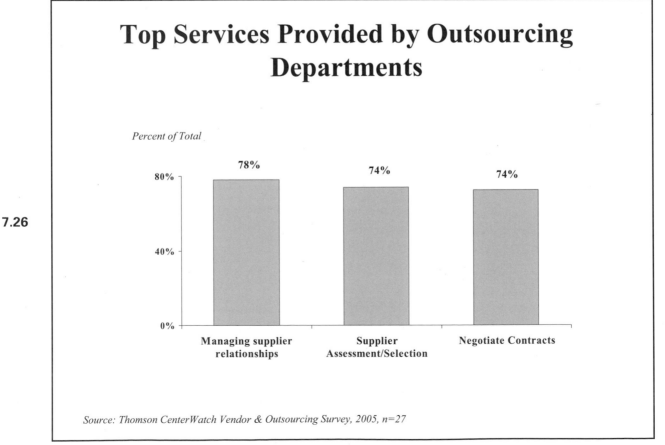

7.26

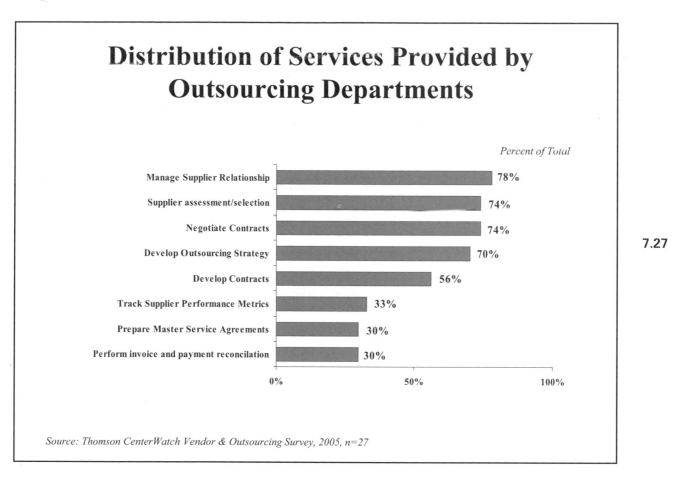

Distribution of Services Provided by Outsourcing Departments

Percent of Total

Service	Percent
Manage Supplier Relationship	78%
Supplier assessment/selection	74%
Negotiate Contracts	74%
Develop Outsourcing Strategy	70%
Develop Contracts	56%
Track Supplier Performance Metrics	33%
Prepare Master Service Agreements	30%
Perform invoice and payment reconcilation	30%

Source: Thomson CenterWatch Vendor & Outsourcing Survey, 2005, n=27

7.27

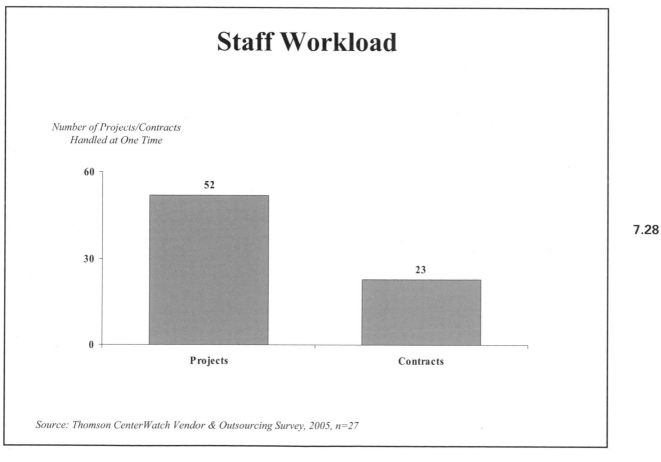

Staff Workload

Number of Projects/Contracts Handled at One Time

	Number
Projects	52
Contracts	23

Source: Thomson CenterWatch Vendor & Outsourcing Survey, 2005, n=27

7.28

How Department is Initially Engaged

7.29

Contact Initiator	Percent of Respondents
Project Leader	46%
Clinical Operations Personnel	25%
Department Personnel Requesting Outsourcing	21%
Project Team Member	8%

Source: Thomson CenterWatch Vendor & Outsourcing Survey, 2005, n=27

Top Three Department Responsibilities

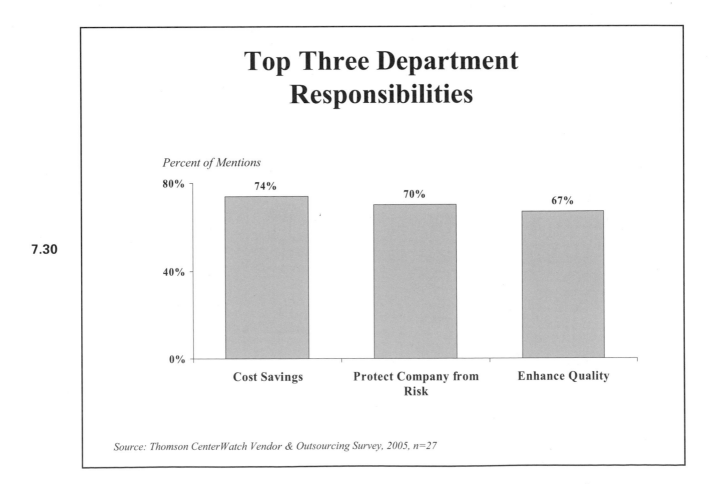

7.30

Percent of Mentions

- Cost Savings: 74%
- Protect Company from Risk: 70%
- Enhance Quality: 67%

Source: Thomson CenterWatch Vendor & Outsourcing Survey, 2005, n=27

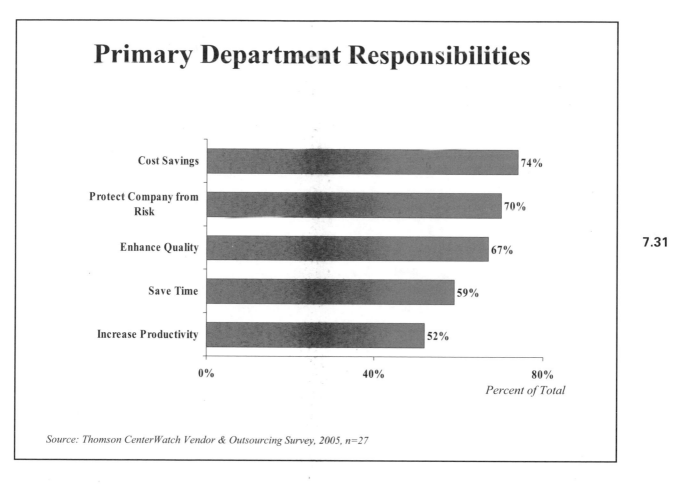

Primary Department Responsibilities

Source: Thomson CenterWatch Vendor & Outsourcing Survey, 2005, n=27

7.31

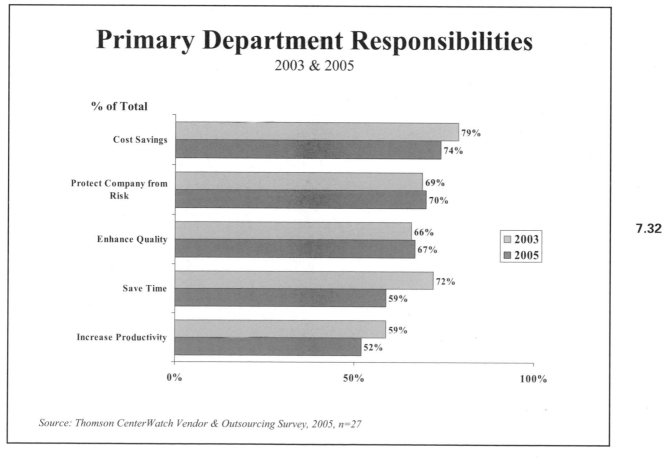

Primary Department Responsibilities
2003 & 2005

Source: Thomson CenterWatch Vendor & Outsourcing Survey, 2005, n=27

7.32

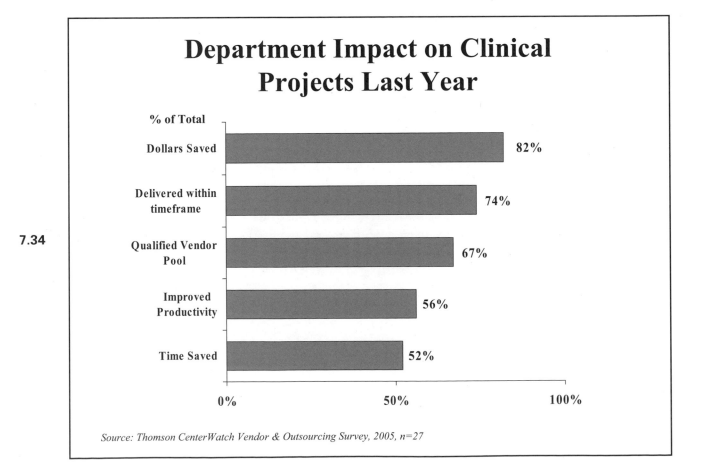

7.33

Criteria Used to Measure Outsourcing Department Effectiveness

% of Total

- Customer Satisfaction — 62%
- Cost Savings — 23%
- Contract Turnaround Time — 12%
- Contract Volume — 4%

Source: Thomson CenterWatch Vendor & Outsourcing Survey, 2005, n=27

7.34

Department Impact on Clinical Projects Last Year

% of Total

- Dollars Saved — 82%
- Delivered within timeframe — 74%
- Qualified Vendor Pool — 67%
- Improved Productivity — 56%
- Time Saved — 52%

Source: Thomson CenterWatch Vendor & Outsourcing Survey, 2005, n=27

Impact on Clinical Projects
2003 & 2005

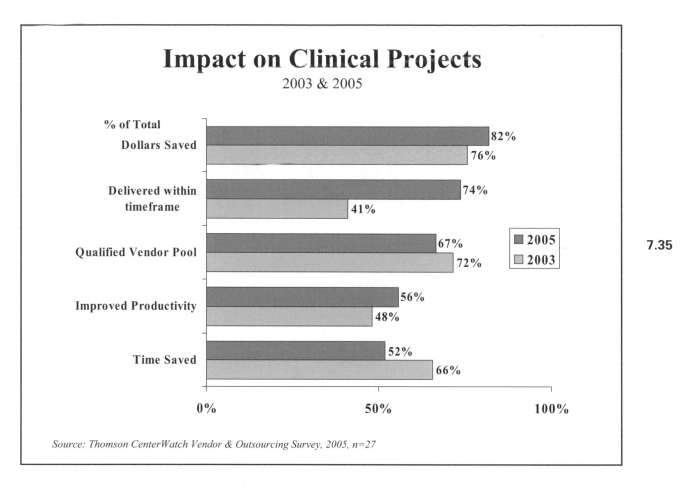

Source: *Thomson CenterWatch Vendor & Outsourcing Survey, 2005, n=27*

7.35

Frequency of Preparing Justification

Prepares Justification	Percent of Respondents
Quarterly	43%
Every Six Months	14%
Annually	43%

7.36

Source: *Thomson CenterWatch Vendor & Outsourcing Survey, 2005, n=27*

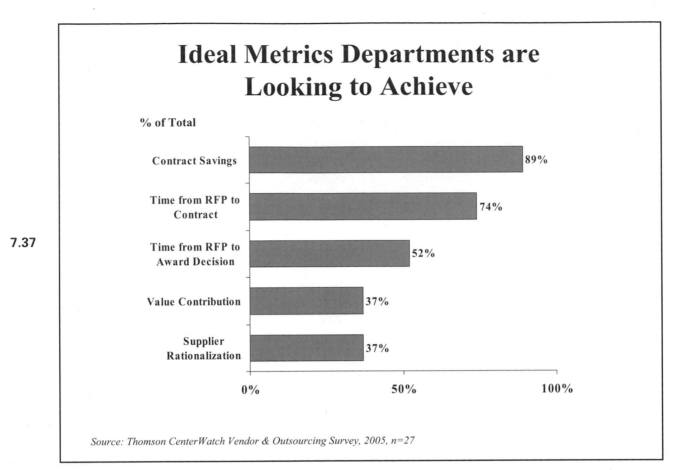

7.37

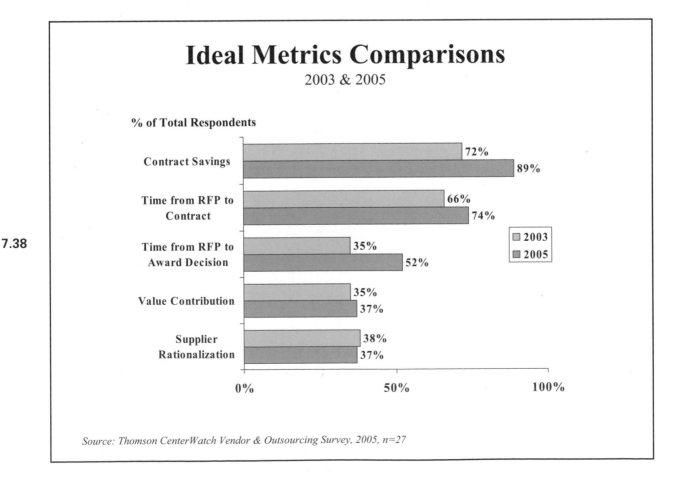

7.38

Types of Contracts Responsible For

CRO Contracts	96%
Central Lab Agreements	93%
Central ECG	85%
Consultant Agreements	78%
Electronic Data Capture (EDC) agreements	70%
Medical Imaging Contracts	70%
Agreements with Phase I Units	67%
Confidentiality Agreements	63%
Agreement with Patient Recruitment Providers	63%
SMO Agreements	52%

Source: Thomson CenterWatch Vendor & Outsourcing Survey, 2005, n=27

7.39

Top Factors Rated Important When Selecting a Vendor

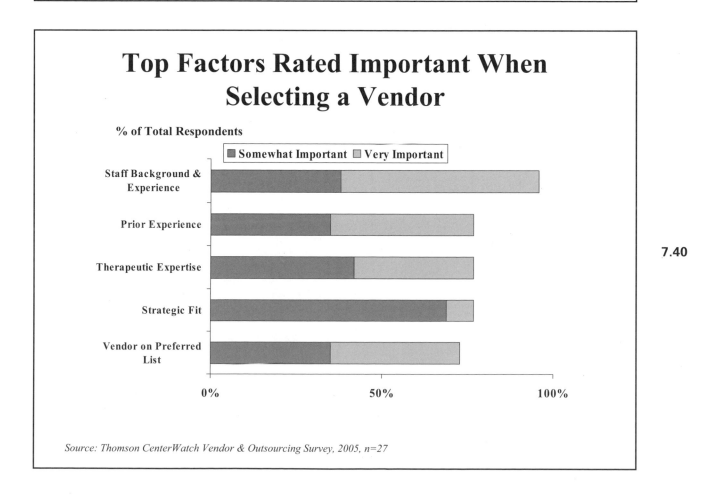

Source: Thomson CenterWatch Vendor & Outsourcing Survey, 2005, n=27

7.40

Importance of Vendor Selection Criteria

7.41

	Percent Rate	
	<u>"Very Important"</u>	<u>"Somewhat Important"</u>
Personnel Background and Experience	58%	38%
Prior Experience Working with CRO (vendor)	42%	35%
Therapeutic Expertise	35%	42%
CRO on Preferred List	38%	35%
Recommended by Clinical Team	27%	31%
Geographic Location	19%	38%
Cultural Fit	19%	38%
Price	12%	31%
Timeliness of Proposal Response	8%	31%
Strategic Fit	8%	59%
Ease of Integration into Project	8%	60%
Staff Turnover Rate	8%	38%
CRO organizational structure	4%	31%
Experience with EDC	4%	15%
Capability to offer special services (e.g., IVRS, etc.)	0	27%

Source: Thomson CenterWatch Vendor & Outsourcing Survey, 2005, n=27

Top Niche CRO Services Utilized

7.42

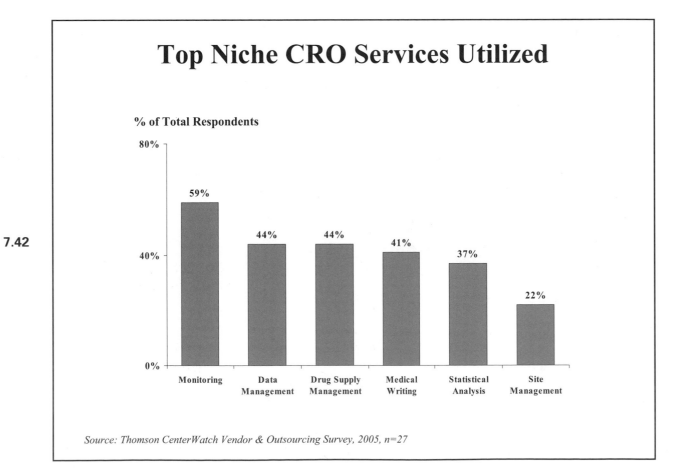

Source: Thomson CenterWatch Vendor & Outsourcing Survey, 2005, n=27

Top Niche CRO Services Utilized

2003 & 2005

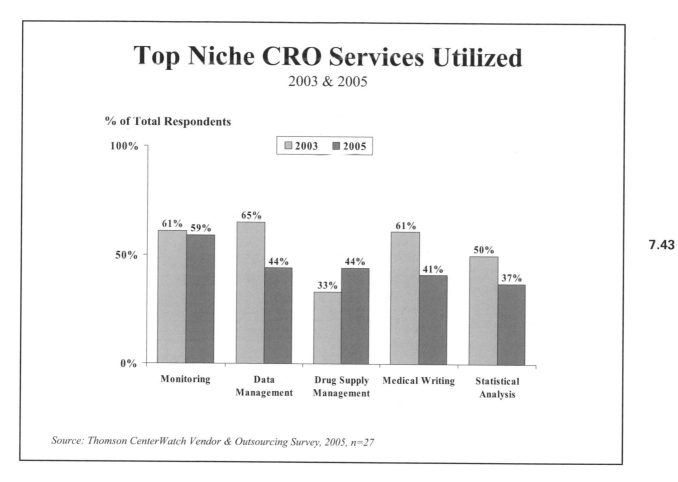

% of Total Respondents

Legend: 2003, 2005

- Monitoring: 61% (2003), 59% (2005)
- Data Management: 65% (2003), 44% (2005)
- Drug Supply Management: 33% (2003), 44% (2005)
- Medical Writing: 61% (2003), 41% (2005)
- Statistical Analysis: 50% (2003), 37% (2005)

Source: Thomson CenterWatch Vendor & Outsourcing Survey, 2005, n=27

7.43

Full-Service and Niche Vendor Selection Criteria

Percent Rate "Very Important"

	Full Service	Niche Service
Personnel Background and Experience	58%	43%
Prior Experience Working with CRO	42%	50%
CRO on Preferred List	38%	19%
Therapeutic Expertise	35%	38%
Recommended by Clinical Team	27%	29%
Geographic Location	19%	19%
Cultural Fit	19%	29%
Price	12%	10%
Timeliness of Proposal Response	8%	5%
Strategic Fit	8%	19%
Ease of Integration into Project	8%	19%
Staff Turnover Rate	8%	19%
Experience with EDC	4%	5%

7.44

Source: Thomson CenterWatch Vendor & Outsourcing Survey, 2005, n=27

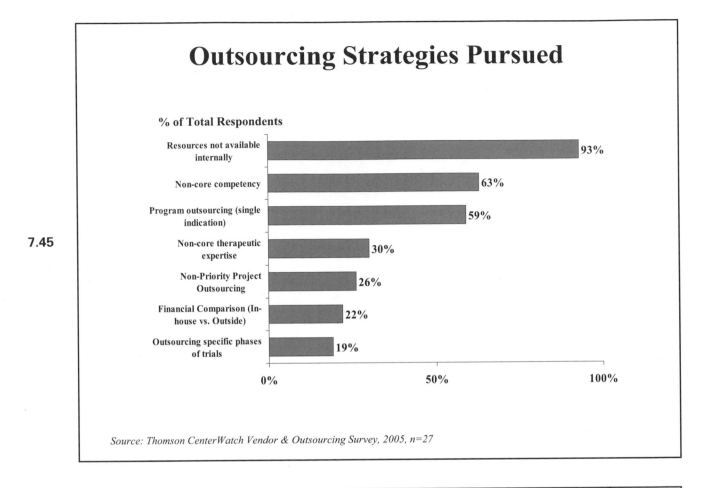

7.45

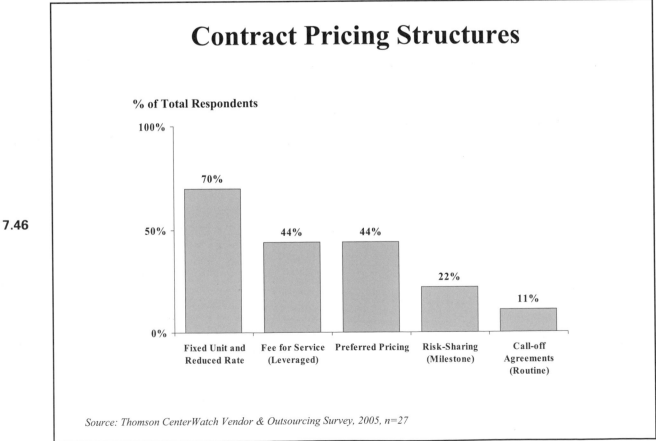

7.46

Financial Incentives Utilized

	Number of Companies
Financial bonuses to project team	2
Financial bonuses to company	7
For:	
Meeting timelines early	6
Meeting or beating patient enrollment goals	6
Coming in or below budget	3
Quality of deliverables	2
Low project team turnover	2

Note:11% of contracts incorporates performance incentives

Source: Thomson CenterWatch Vendor & Outsourcing Survey, 2005, n=27

7.47

Financial Penalties Utilized

	Number of Companies
Withdrawal of future business	7
Withhold payments, decrease payments	6
Financial penalties	5
For:	
Missing timelines	7
Poor deliverables quality	6
Study delays	5
Not meeting patient enrollment goals	4
Over budget	2

Note: 17% of contracts incorporates performance penalties

Source: Thomson CenterWatch Vendor & Outsourcing Survey, 2005, n=27

7.48

7.49

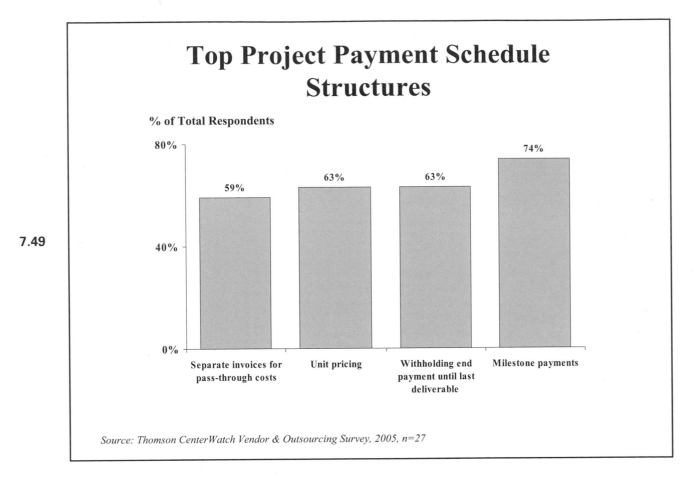

Top Project Payment Schedule Structures

% of Total Respondents

Source: Thomson CenterWatch Vendor & Outsourcing Survey, 2005, n=27

7.50

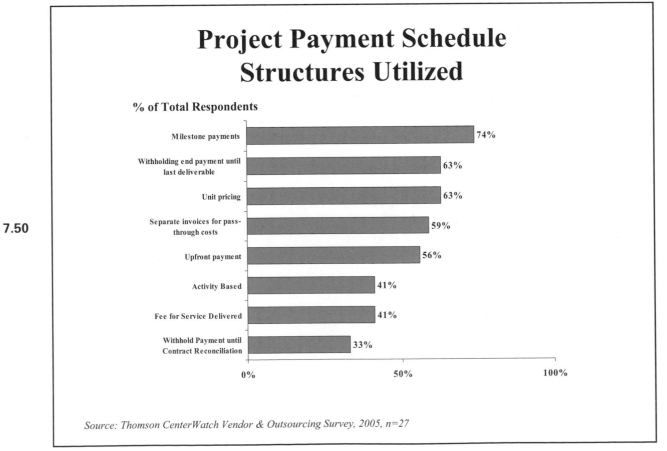

Project Payment Schedule Structures Utilized

% of Total Respondents

Source: Thomson CenterWatch Vendor & Outsourcing Survey, 2005, n=27

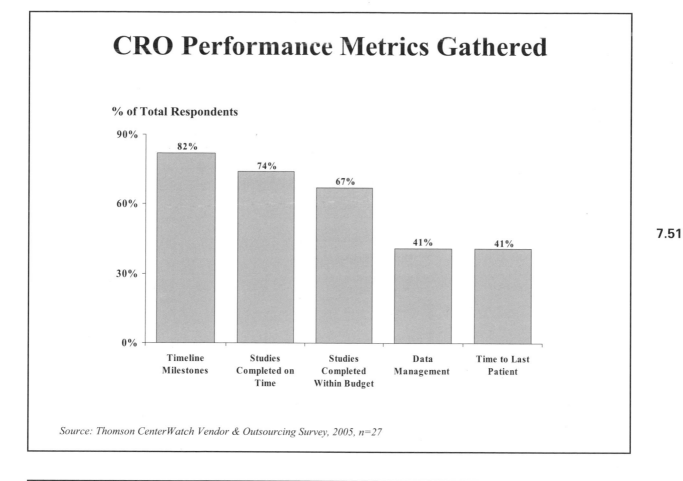

CRO Performance Metrics Gathered

% of Total Respondents

Source: Thomson CenterWatch Vendor & Outsourcing Survey, 2005, n=27

7.51

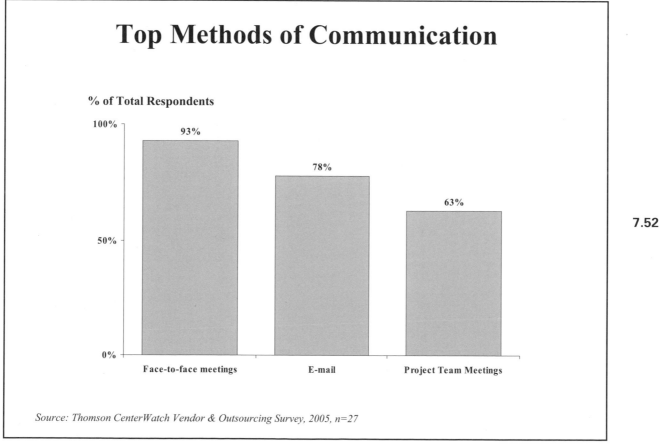

Top Methods of Communication

% of Total Respondents

Source: Thomson CenterWatch Vendor & Outsourcing Survey, 2005, n=27

7.52

7.53

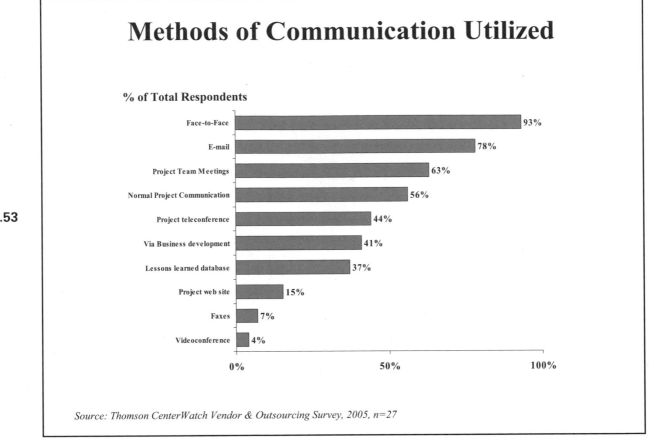

Methods of Communication Utilized

% of Total Respondents

Method	%
Face-to-Face	93%
E-mail	78%
Project Team Meetings	63%
Normal Project Communication	56%
Project teleconference	44%
Via Business development	41%
Lessons learned database	37%
Project web site	15%
Faxes	7%
Videoconference	4%

Source: Thomson CenterWatch Vendor & Outsourcing Survey, 2005, n=27

7.54

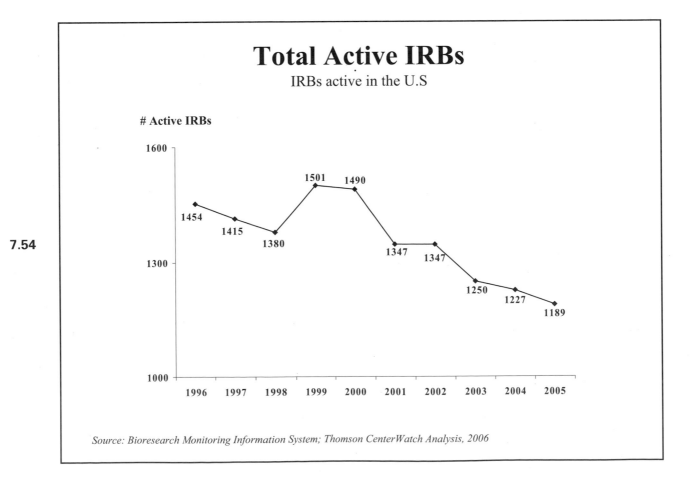

Total Active IRBs

IRBs active in the U.S

 # Active IRBs

Year	# Active IRBs
1996	1454
1997	1415
1998	1380
1999	1501
2000	1490
2001	1347
2002	1347
2003	1250
2004	1227
2005	1189

Source: Bioresearch Monitoring Information System; Thomson CenterWatch Analysis, 2006

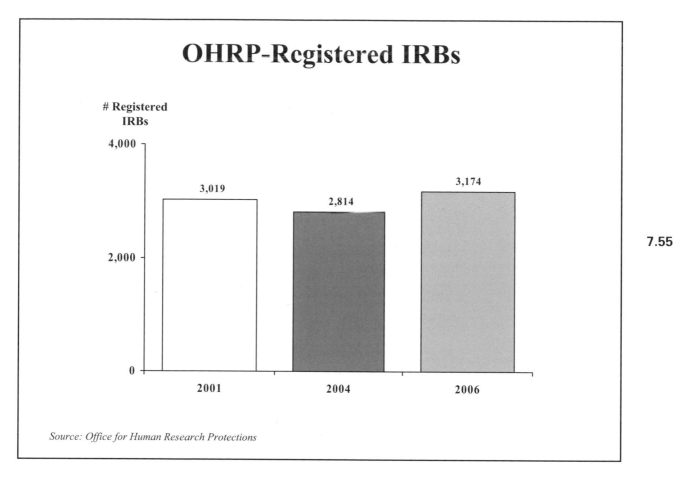

OHRP-Registered IRBs

Registered
IRBs

Source: Office for Human Research Protections

7.55

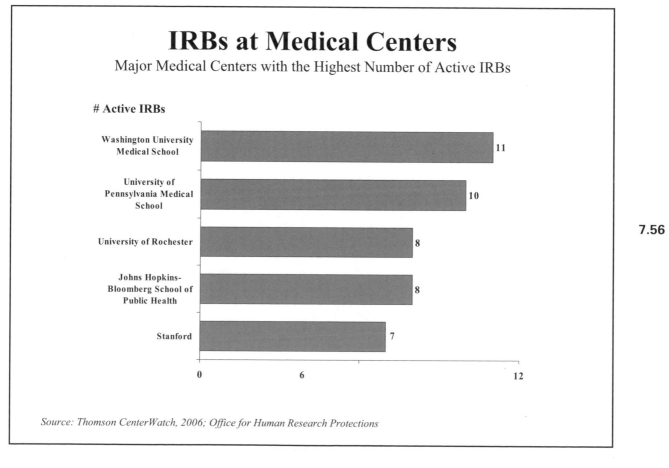

IRBs at Medical Centers

Major Medical Centers with the Highest Number of Active IRBs

Active IRBs

Source: Thomson CenterWatch, 2006; Office for Human Research Protections

7.56

7.57

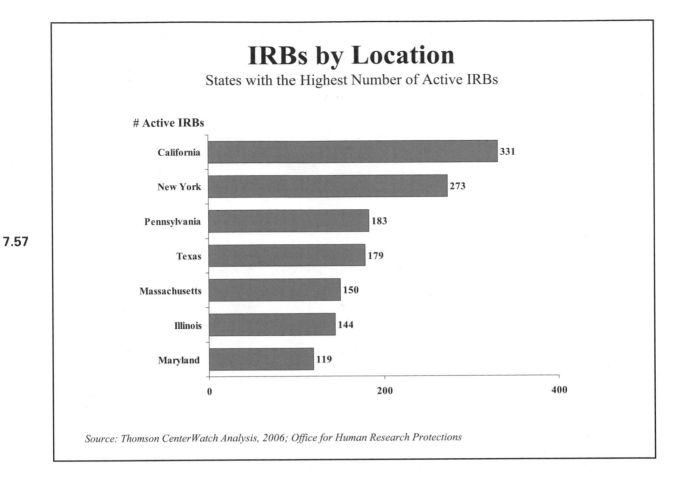

IRBs by Location

States with the Highest Number of Active IRBs

 # Active IRBs

State	# Active IRBs
California	331
New York	273
Pennsylvania	183
Texas	179
Massachusetts	150
Illinois	144
Maryland	119

Source: Thomson CenterWatch Analysis, 2006; Office for Human Research Protections

## CHAPTER EIGHT

Investigative Site Infrastructure and Operations

Contract and Budget Process Top Cause of Study Delay

By Sara Gambrill
Published October 2005

The Thomson CenterWatch 2005 Survey of Investigative Sites in the U.S. revealed, surprisingly, that sites rate the contract and budget negotiation and approval process as the number one factor most often causing study delays—edging out the oft-cited patient recruitment and enrollment process. Delays in the contract and budget negotiation and approval process have broad implications for the drug development process, including holding up the patient recruitment and enrollment process. Sites' attempts to speed the process before signing a contract by completing regulatory packets without receiving an upfront fee often backfire costing sponsors and sites time and money. Accepting unfavorable terms can lead to a site's dangerously cutting corners on the informed consent process or to insolvency.

Investigative sites have been trying to address the problem areas—low fees, rotating and/or ill-informed sponsor contract personnel, no industry-wide standardized contract and indemnification clauses—for years, but for some they have only gotten worse, in fact, the worst problem for sites in terms of study delay.

There have been numerous industry estimates of how much money is lost by sponsors per day due to study delays. No matter which estimate is applied, it is clear that study delays are extremely expensive to sponsors. The clinical research industry has focused for so long on time reductions in the patient recruitment and enrollment process, according to industry insiders, that it has lost sight of the fact that the unnecessarily difficult and protracted contract and budget negotiation and approval process causes major delays in the patient recruitment and enrollment process. But, investigative sites see concrete and immediate ways that the contract and budget negotiation and approval process could be improved, which, in turn, could improve cycle times for the patient recruitment and enrollment process.

Poor Timing

"The first thing [sponsors ask is], 'Are you going to be able to meet your enrollment goal?'" said Michelle Sowell, clinical research director, Clinical Research Atlanta, an Atlanta, Ga.-based site founded in 1993.

Sites argue that another well-timed question from sponsors would be more helpful to speeding the drug development process. "They could ask, 'What are your main concerns in your budget and contract?' said Lona Sheeran, managing director, Midwest Research Specialists, a Milwaukee, Wisc.-based site founded in 1995. "When they come out to do their pre-study site visit, that may be something that they should ask off the bat. 'What types of things do you want to see in a contract and budget? What will you as a site negotiate on and what will you absolutely not negotiate on?' Because if I say, 'I absolutely will not negotiate on screen fails. This is how I want it.' They can say right away, 'There's no way we can do that, so I'll just move to another site.' Neither one of us has wasted any time. But if I think they're going to budge on it, we could waste up to three weeks going back and forth. I've never had anybody ask me those questions, but I think that would really help because I have the same arguments over and over again."

Marion Stamp-Cole, senior director of clinical research, ProMed Healthcare, a Portage, Mich.-based investigative site network founded in 1994, added, "A budget is provided after you've had site selection, when in fact it should happen way before. Even if we have the patient population, the principal investigator is interested, and we know we have patients who would qualify, we need to know from a business perspective if it's the right business decision to conduct this study, based on the budget. And it really puts the site in a very difficult situation to make a business decision on their viability of doing research at such short notice, which oftentimes it is."

Delaying Patient Recruitment

The poor timing of the contract and budget negotiation and approval process and the prolonged haggling over fees and terms comes at a price: the patient recruitment and enrollment process is held up.

"When it comes to enrollment and recruitment, that gets a little hung up because you're relying on that execution for the starting of all your things you've got lined up. You've got these patients lined up, you have a list, you're waiting for your IRB approvals and you want to do your direct mail. Well, you can't do that until that contract's been signed. I think quite often the two just go hand-in-hand. The contract folks don't always realize that everything, all the regulatory documents are done. This is the one outstanding thing we're waiting for until we can start the recruitment process," said Stamp-Cole.

Lauri Adams, director of clinical research, University Clinical Research, a dedicated Deland, Fla.-based site founded in 1998, added, "Our process is when the site contracts and the studies come in that we start looking for potential patients at

that time. And what happens sometimes is that we have the patients ready and we're waiting. And drug, in most cases, cannot be released until contract is executed. Therefore we're waiting. And in some cases, this causes delays. We have to reschedule patients."

Sites Addressing Delays

In order to speed study startup time, some sites turn around regulatory documentation before getting a signed contract or an agreed upon budget, usually at the behest of the sponsor company or the site management organization (SMO). But sites can be left holding the bag if the contract comes in and is unsatisfactory to them.

"The request is can we have a fast turnaround on regulatory documentation, so we're asked to actually complete reg packs prior to even signing a contract or agreeing on a budget, which means that we have an expense up front without a signed contract. There was a time when we took a stance of we can't start regulatory documents until we receive a contract to ensure that everything is okay, and that held us up even further. So now we vacillate and we try to find a happy medium for the sponsor and for our staff, but it is something that we struggle with," said Adams.

Sheeran has found her site in the same bind, "As a site, I'm really hesitant to move forward until the [contract/budget] is finalized and discussed. What happens a lot of times is sponsors and even SMOs tend to push IRB submissions prior to budget and contract negotiation just so that they don't waste time. What happens at that point is that if you do push through the IRB and all of a sudden you become approved, but you don't have the contract signed, now you have an open study at the IRB that now you must go through a closing and the sponsor is upset because they just paid for your IRB submission."

One of the reasons that the contract and budget negotiation and approval process is so prolonged is because every sponsor company has its own contract, each one very different. In addition, sites must negotiate the same points over and over with the same sponsor company sometimes because different sponsor company contract personnel work with the same sites. Communication within sponsor companies about how a contract with a site was handled in the past does not occur, so sites are left to re-invent the wheel. While sites can get good at this, there are limits.

Debbie Fridman, clinical research director, Pacific Coast Hematology/Oncology, a site based in Fountain Valley, Calif., founded in 1979, has had success dealing with sponsors' different contracts—with help. "One of the things that we have that is very different is an in-house attorney. When I started here, we set up our own standardized contract with each [sponsor] company because we found that each company used the same contract, regardless of the study," Fridman said. "Initially [the attorney] and I reviewed all of the contracts that came through, went through anything we had issues with. That helped a lot. I'm not a legal person, so it's nice to have legal help. The majority of the issues that we have come down to money— when they're going to pay us, how much they're going to pay us, IRB costs. We started direct billing for IRB costs to the drug company. That works really well. It saves us a lot of time with these $700 charges that we don't have to track."

But other sites have had difficulty trying to standardize contracts. Stamp-Cole said, "What we have been trying to do as a strategy for ProMed Healthcare is to move forward toward a master agreement with preferred pharmaceutical sponsors that we do business with on a regular basis. This has helped immensely. On the same side, it is amazing the amount of sponsors that will not consider a master agreement, even with continued regular business done with them and the fact that it can speed things up."

Another approach to solving delays in the contract and budget negotiation and approval process is to get one's site International Organization for Standardization [ISO]-certified. While it is a costly and long undertaking—about two to three years— it was worth it for Wichita, Kansas-based PriVia, an investigative site founded in 1988. Kristin Forret, research business operations leader, Privia, said, "Part of one of our ISO policies is that when we're negotiating the budget and contract we get together as a management team along with whoev-

er the study coordinator is going to be on a particular study. And we discuss everything as far as recruitment, enrollment, advertising, the budget and contract. That was something that was not happening before. We were getting budgets that we don't even think we realized how expensive they were going to be cost-wise. And that was causing delays as well."

PriVia is also a member of the Model Agreement Group Initiative, a group comprising sites, contract research organizations (CROs) and sponsors trying to come up with a model agreement together. "Last year, when we first started there weren't as many sites and sponsors on board. It was mostly just sites, and now I'm seeing more sponsors and more CROs involved in that as well and I've actually seen more contracts where I'm seeing very similar language or the exact language that's in our model agreement," Forret said.

Forret keeps the lines of communication open with sponsor companies, telling them what her timeline is—when she is submitting to the IRB, when she would like the contract and budget finalized. She then asks the sponsor if it's acceptable, and most of the time it is, according to her. But even the best attempts at reducing delays can be foiled. "There are cases I've come across where the budget's been accepted but the contract hasn't yet and that person went on vacation. Then it became a case where we weren't able to continue with that until he arrived back."

Stamp-Cole has been able to achieve success negotiating the budget and contract with one person at a sponsor company only to find out that she is working with another the next time and starting from scratch. "If there was more sharing of language within the organization, I think that would be a real plus on speeding things up. It's amazing that some groups will not talk to others about that," said Stamp-Cole.

One of the biggest problems at the site level may be that the contract and budget negotiation process is left to the clinical research coordinator, who may be the only coordinator at the site. In recent years, sites have hired coordinators dedicated to only one activity such as patient recruitment, regulatory or contracts. Coordinators have begun to specialize. But there are plenty of sites—the majority perhaps—that have a coordinator who does everything. "I think a part of the problem also is that you have centers where there's single coordinators, so that one coordinator who's responsible for seeing all the patients is also responsible for doing all of the regulatory, which includes contracts and budgets. And because they're so busy just trying to get patient care done and get the paperwork done, probably the least of their worries is looking at a contract," said Fridman.

Informed Consent Process Suffering?

Delays in the drug development process are not the only—nor the most serious—possible ramifications of a contentious contract and budget negotiation and approval process. Much worse is the potential failure to execute requirements properly because of poor budget amounts. Sites that accept inadequate budgets because they are inexperienced or they have only one overburdened coordinator may find themselves cutting corners in very important areas such as the informed consent process.

In the 2004 Thomson CenterWatch Survey of Study Volunteer Experience, 20% of respondents said that no one reviewed the informed consent form with them. Another 6% said that a family member reviewed it with them, which means that more than one-quarter of respondents did not give a truly informed consent. A startling statistic. It is not clear whether insufficient reimbursement to the sites was at fault; however, sponsor companies should consider very seriously how much money they are paying sites to carry out this process according to Good Clinical Practices.

Clinical Research Atlanta's Sowell said, "People who are in the offices negotiating these trials don't have a clue what it takes to go through an informed consent with an individual. If you're going to go by ICH-GCP guidelines and you're going to give all eight elements of that informed consent to that patient, have time to ask questions, etc., it's going to take more than 10 minutes. And I'm hoping more sites are taking that time because they'll send me a budget that pays me $50 for the informed consent. I don't accept that budget. My charge is $150 for an informed consent. That

means I'm reviewing the elements, I'm giving them their options and that they're voluntary—everything. You can't do that in 10 minutes."

Indemnification: The Deal Breaker

Where inexperienced sites can get into trouble—and insolvency—is accepting a contract in which they agree to indemnify the sponsor. More experienced sites conjecture that if less experienced sites truly understood what they were signing off on, they wouldn't, and the practice of sponsors trying to get sites to indemnify them would cease. As the situation stands now, indemnification for a sponsor is a deal breaker for experienced sites and must be negotiated—another needless delay on the sponsor company's part. It is arguably the simplest problem a sponsor can eliminate.

"Every several contracts we will receive a contract that has a reverse indemnification clause and absolutely puts the brakes on the contracting process until we can come to an agreement that the verbiage is removed from the contracts," said Adams.

Added Sowell, "How am I going to cross-indemnify [a pharmaceutical company]? I'm not. They can take everything I have, and I'm still not going to have enough money. That's the number one problem I see."

Sometimes sites must just walk away. "Indemnification is always a big issue. Most malpractice carriers do not allow a site to indemnify a drug company. That's a major, major battle with drug companies. We've actually had companies that said, 'Sorry, then we can't work with you.' That's just a risk you have to take because you've got to protect yourself too. Most companies are more than willing to work with us on it," said Fridman.

What Can Sponsors Do?

Clearly, it's going to take work on both the sponsor and site sides to make the contract and budget negotiation and approval process run more smoothly. Inexperienced sites must become more savvy about what they need from a contract and budget, and sponsors must listen.

Wyeth, which had received low ratings from sites in past Thomson CenterWatch surveys of U.S.

sites, shot to second place in the rankings this year and the company gives credit to its finding out what sites want, studying the problems and attempting to fix them.

In May, Ira Spector, vice president of clinical trial operations and vice chief of clinical development, Wyeth, described to The CenterWatch Monthly how Wyeth had approached issues surrounding the contract and budget negotiation and approval process. "We have paid attention to what sites have said about us in the past in [The CenterWatch] survey in the context of a much larger program that we've undertaken in the last year-and-a-half to radically change the way we conduct clinical studies, called 'Clinical Breakthrough.' Our site contract two years ago was 17 pages long and fairly difficult to read unless you had a legal background. We put together a team of people who work with sites as well as our contract people, our medical people and our legal people, and we revamped that agreement. It is now a 12-page document that is fairly easy to read," said Spector.

Wyeth has adopted a completely new way of negotiating with sites, according to Spector. "Instead of approaching an individual site with an individual negotiation and having a fairly protracted negotiation site by site, we basically go out with what we believe is a much more fair package up front. In exchange for that we look for less negotiation, so more upfront fee but less back-end negotiation. In general what we've done is try to go from a highly negotiated environment to a much more standardized environment with our relationships with sites," added Spector.

Wyeth's dramatic rise to number two in the 2005 Thomson CenterWatch Survey of Investigative Sites in the U.S. from a number 13 ranking in 2003 speaks for itself. Other sponsor companies may need to make a similar exceptional effort and do something "radical" to fix the problem.

CenterWatch will study the progress that sponsor companies have made in its next Survey of U.S. Sites and continue to monitor new attempts to ameliorate the confounding problem of the contract and budget negotiation and approval process, both in CenterWatch's upcoming Survey of Investigative Sites in Europe next year and in the next iteration of the Survey of Investigative Sites in the U.S. in 2007.

8.01

8.02

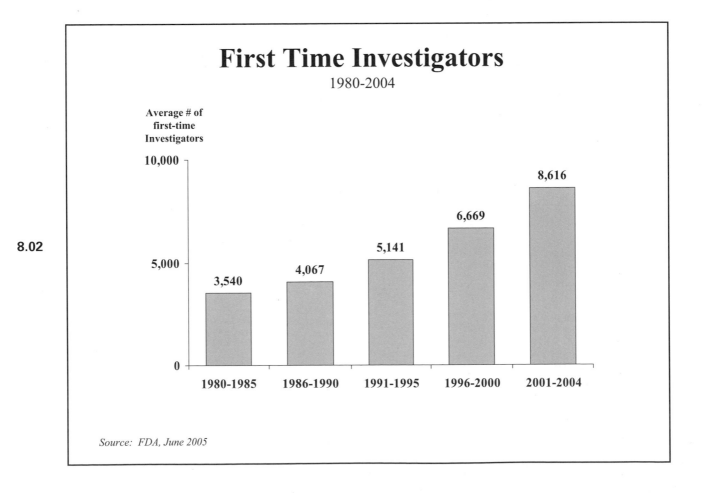

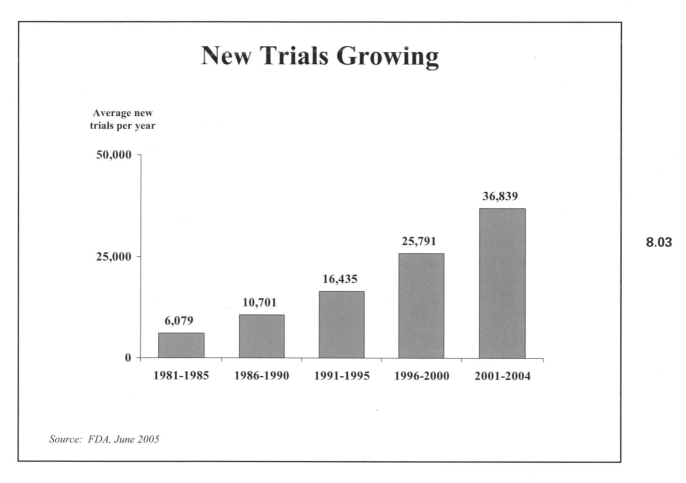

New Trials Growing

Average new
trials per year

8.03

Source: FDA, June 2005

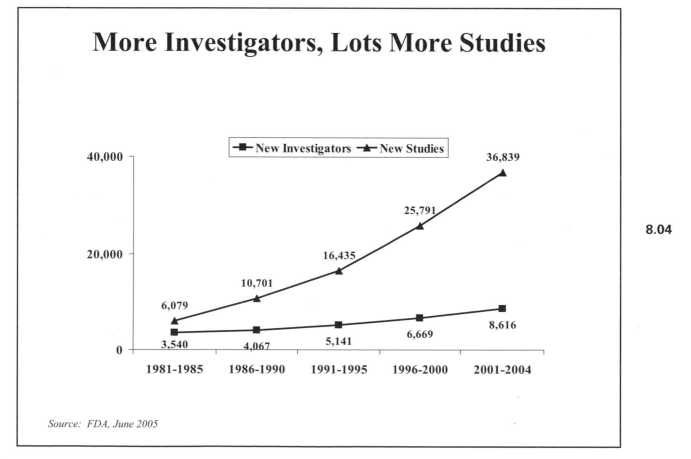

More Investigators, Lots More Studies

8.04

Source: FDA, June 2005

8.05

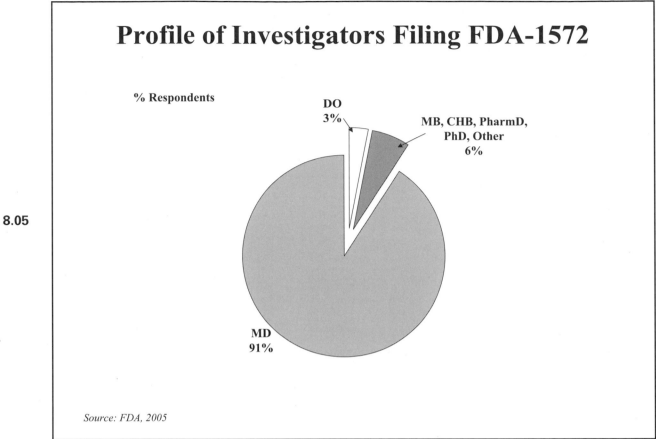

Profile of Investigators Filing FDA-1572

% Respondents

DO
3%

MB, CHB, PharmD,
PhD, Other
6%

MD
91%

Source: FDA, 2005

8.06

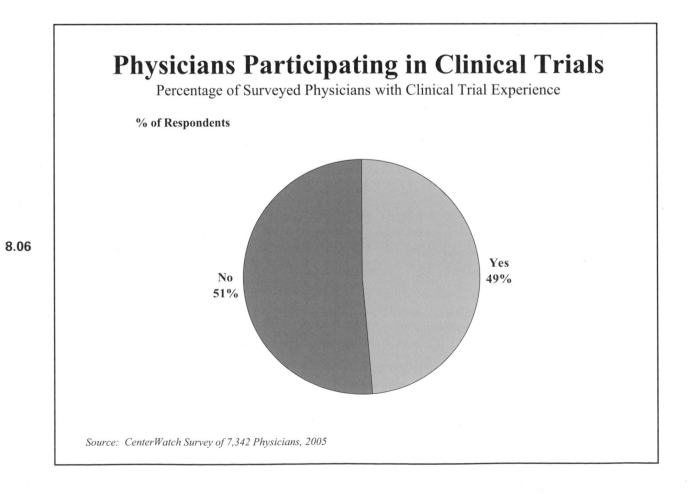

Physicians Participating in Clinical Trials
Percentage of Surveyed Physicians with Clinical Trial Experience

% of Respondents

No
51%

Yes
49%

Source: CenterWatch Survey of 7,342 Physicians, 2005

Aging Investigators

NIH Traditional Grant Recipients by Age, 1980-2001

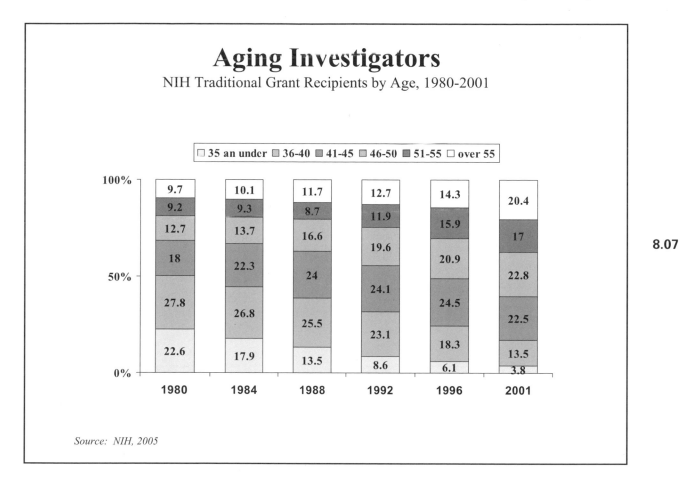

Source: NIH, 2005

8.07

Investigator Age

NIH Grant Recipients

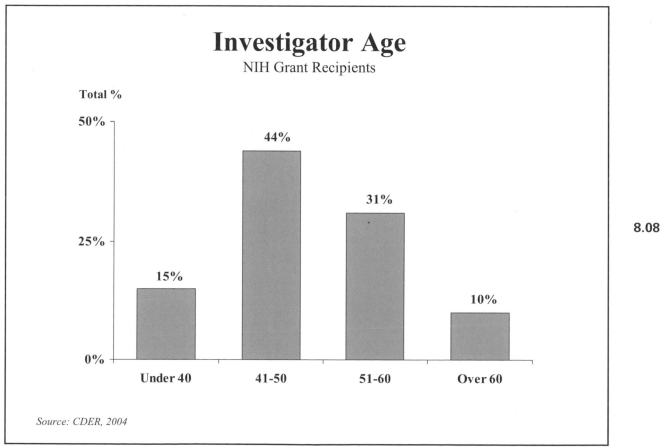

Source: CDER, 2004

8.08

8.09

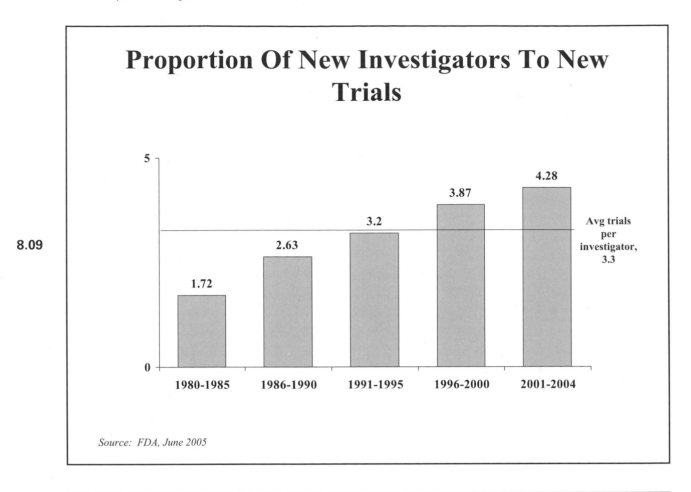

Proportion Of New Investigators To New Trials

Source: FDA, June 2005

8.10

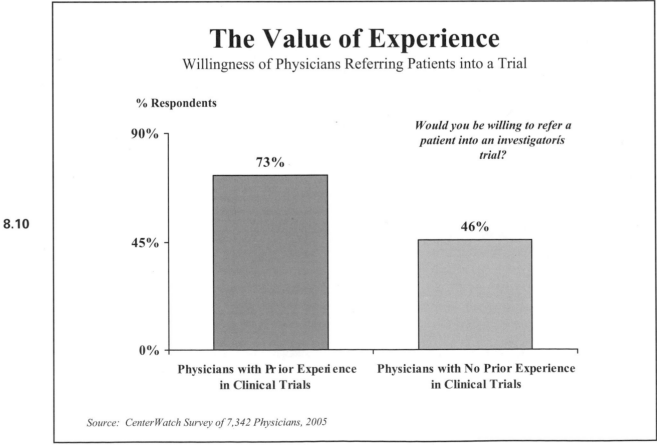

The Value of Experience
Willingness of Physicians Referring Patients into a Trial

Source: CenterWatch Survey of 7,342 Physicians, 2005

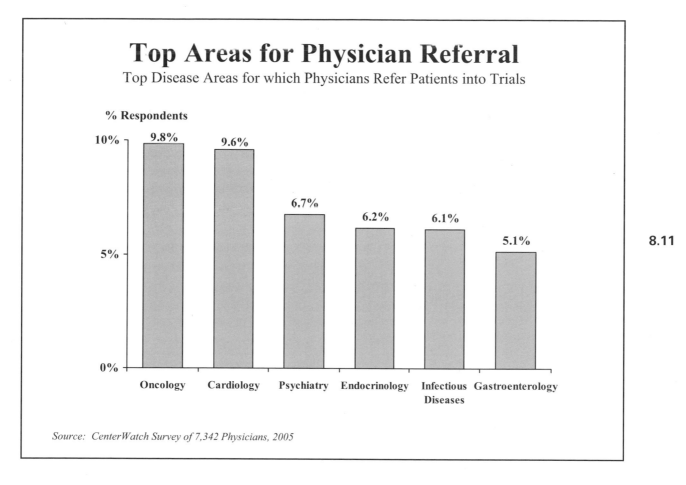

Top Areas for Physician Referral

Top Disease Areas for which Physicians Refer Patients into Trials

% Respondents

Source: CenterWatch Survey of 7,342 Physicians, 2005

8.11

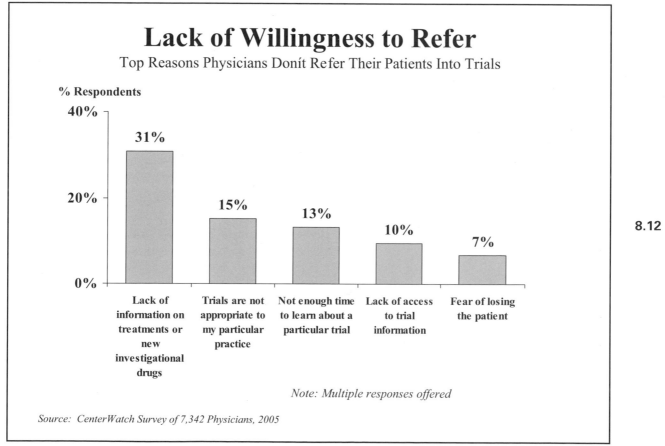

Lack of Willingness to Refer

Top Reasons Physicians Donít Refer Their Patients Into Trials

% Respondents

Note: Multiple responses offered

Source: CenterWatch Survey of 7,342 Physicians, 2005

8.12

Physician Comfort with Participation
Factors Increasing Willingness to Participate

8.13

Factor	% Indicating
Information	47.4%
Easier Process	36.1%
Compensation	7.2%
Need For Communication with Researchers	9.3%

Note: Based on Open-Ended Responses

Source: Thomson CenterWatch Survey of 244 Physicians, 2004

Clinical Research Personnel
Distribution of Personnel by Specialty

8.14

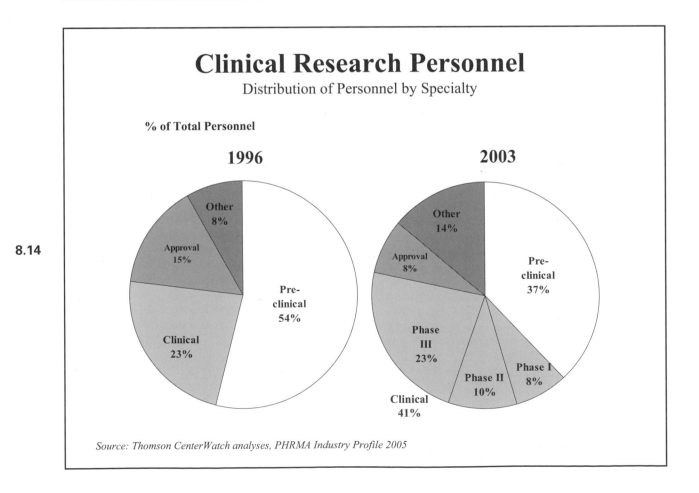

% of Total Personnel

1996

Other 8%
Approval 15%
Pre-clinical 54%
Clinical 23%

2003

Other 14%
Approval 8%
Pre-clinical 37%
Phase III 23%
Phase II 10%
Phase I 8%
Clinical 41%

Source: Thomson CenterWatch analyses, PHRMA Industry Profile 2005

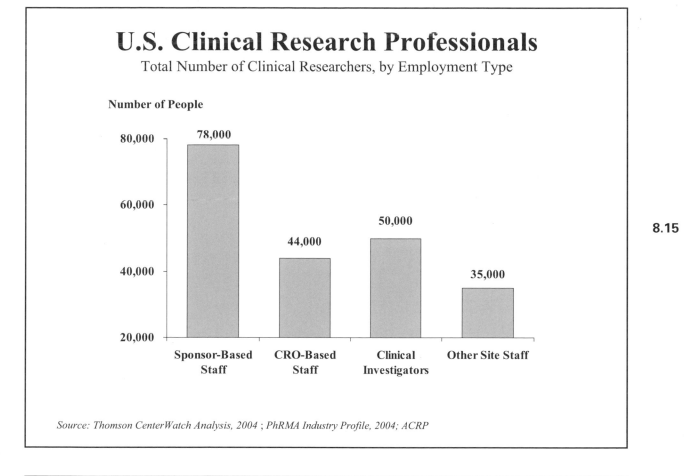

U.S. Clinical Research Professionals
Total Number of Clinical Researchers, by Employment Type

Number of People

8.15

Source: Thomson CenterWatch Analysis, 2004 ; PhRMA Industry Profile, 2004; ACRP

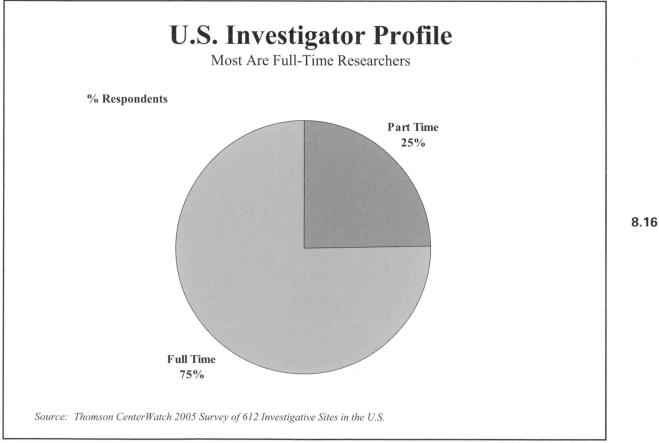

U.S. Investigator Profile
Most Are Full-Time Researchers

% Respondents

8.16

Source: Thomson CenterWatch 2005 Survey of 612 Investigative Sites in the U.S.

8.17

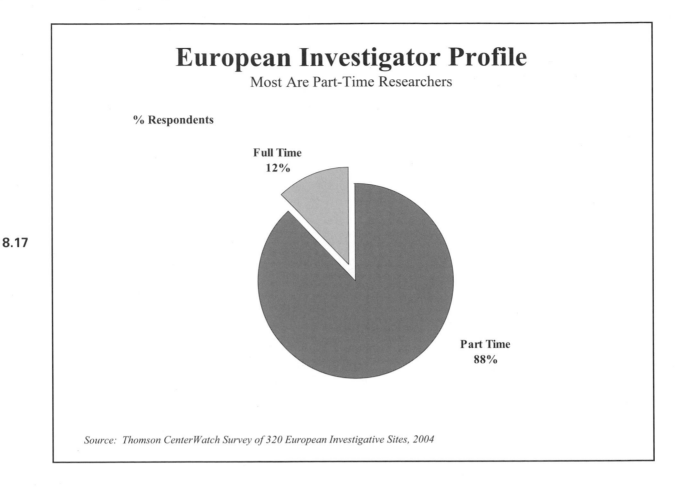

European Investigator Profile
Most Are Part-Time Researchers

% Respondents

Full Time
12%

Part Time
88%

Source: Thomson CenterWatch Survey of 320 European Investigative Sites, 2004

8.18

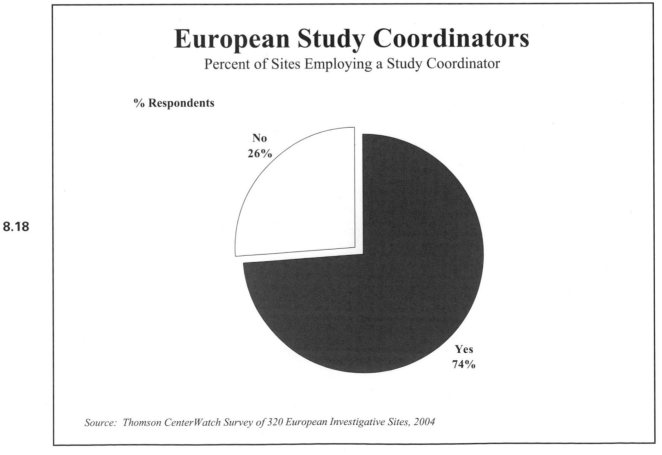

European Study Coordinators
Percent of Sites Employing a Study Coordinator

% Respondents

No
26%

Yes
74%

Source: Thomson CenterWatch Survey of 320 European Investigative Sites, 2004

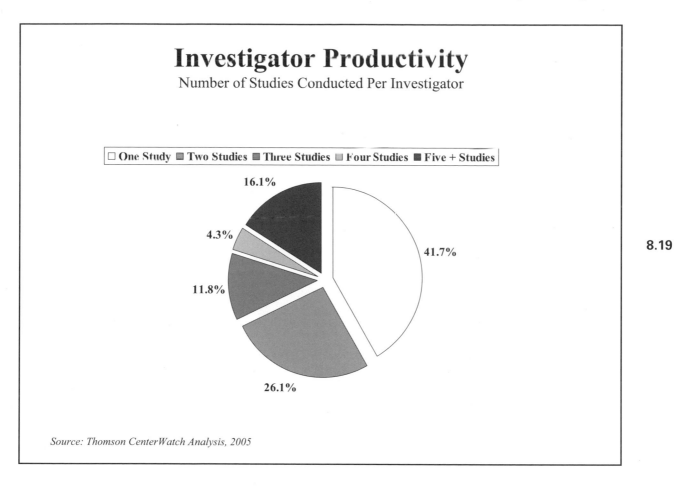

Investigator Productivity
Number of Studies Conducted Per Investigator

☐ One Study ▨ Two Studies ▨ Three Studies ▨ Four Studies ■ Five + Studies

16.1%

4.3%

11.8%

41.7%

26.1%

Source: Thomson CenterWatch Analysis, 2005

8.19

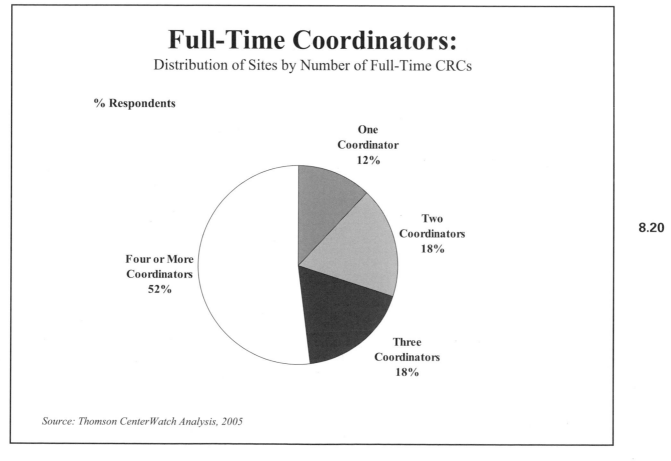

Full-Time Coordinators:
Distribution of Sites by Number of Full-Time CRCs

% Respondents

One
Coordinator
12%

Two
Coordinators
18%

Four or More
Coordinators
52%

Three
Coordinators
18%

Source: Thomson CenterWatch Analysis, 2005

8.20

8.21

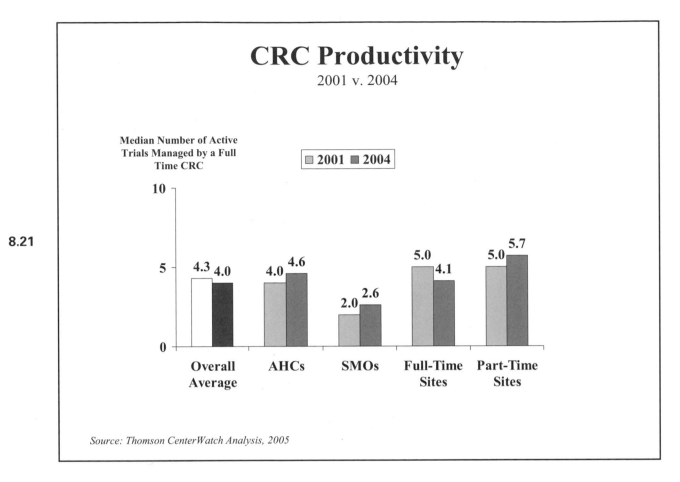

8.22

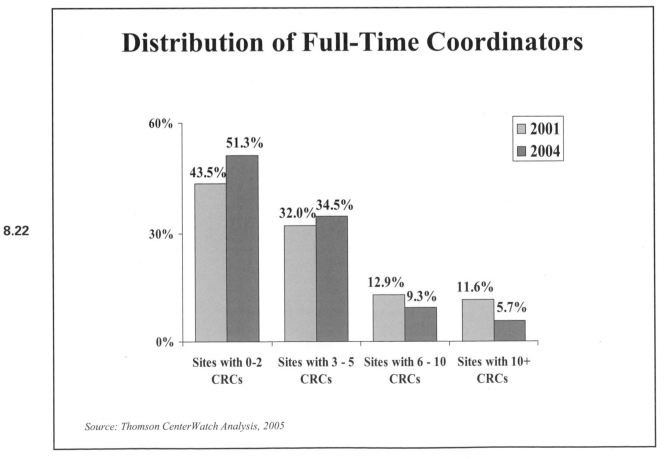

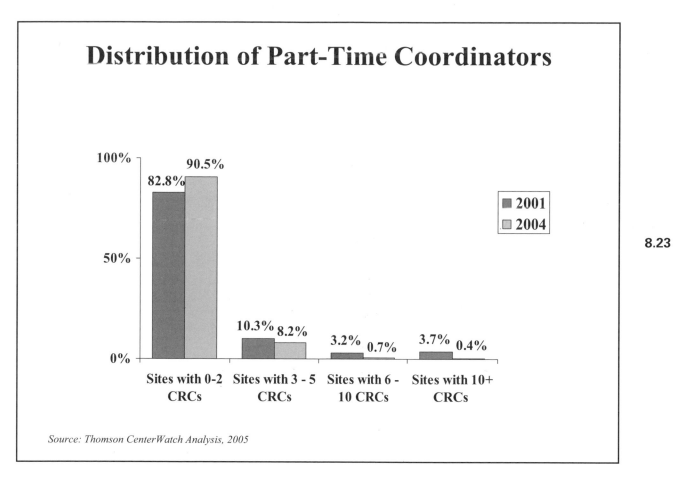

Distribution of Part-Time Coordinators

8.23

Source: Thomson CenterWatch Analysis, 2005

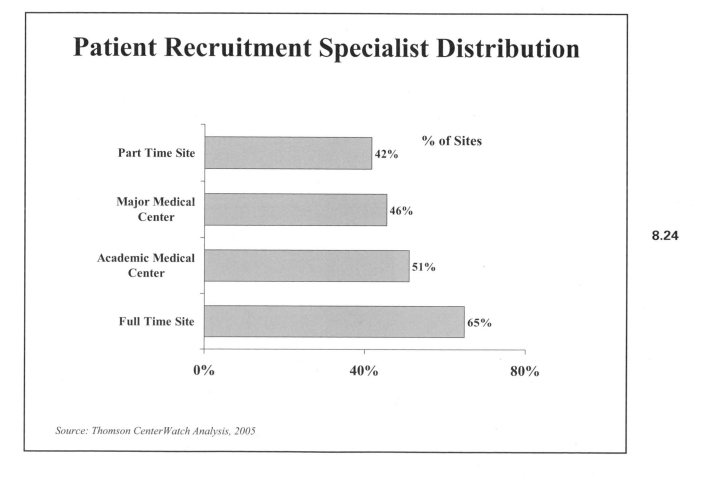

Patient Recruitment Specialist Distribution

8.24

Source: Thomson CenterWatch Analysis, 2005

8.25

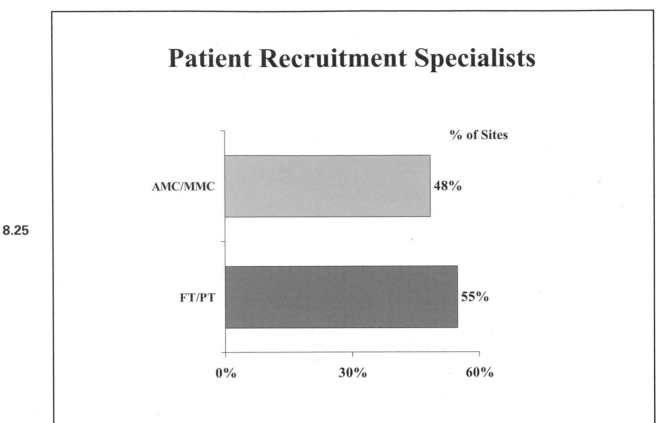

Patient Recruitment Specialists

% of Sites

AMC/MMC — 48%

FT/PT — 55%

0%   30%   60%

Source: Thomson CenterWatch Analysis, 2005

8.26

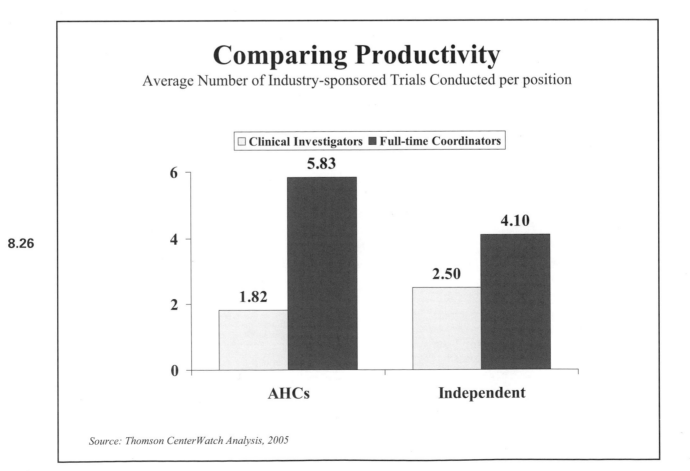

Comparing Productivity

Average Number of Industry-sponsored Trials Conducted per position

☐ Clinical Investigators ■ Full-time Coordinators

AHCs: 1.82, 5.83

Independent: 2.50, 4.10

Source: Thomson CenterWatch Analysis, 2005

Comparing Productivity

Average Number of Industry-sponsored Trials Conducted per position

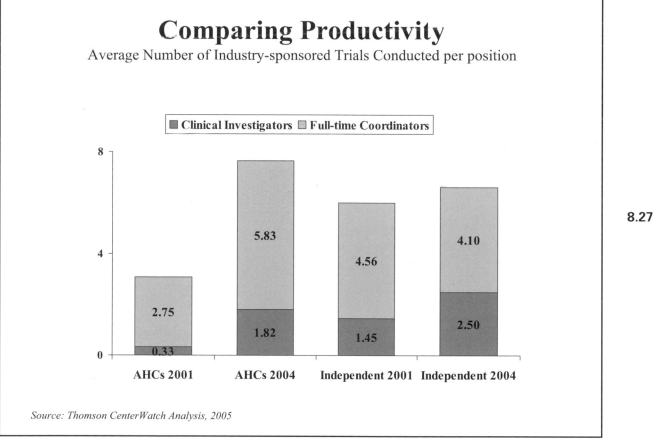

■ Clinical Investigators ■ Full-time Coordinators

Source: Thomson CenterWatch Analysis, 2005

8.27

Years of Experience

Major Clinical Research Positions

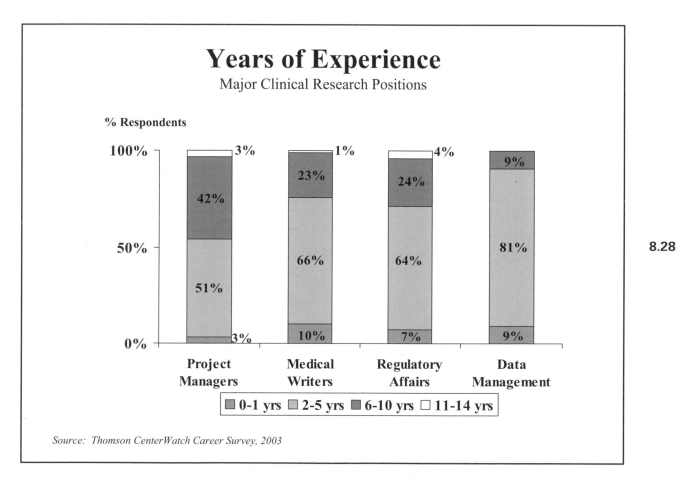

% Respondents

■ 0-1 yrs □ 2-5 yrs ■ 6-10 yrs □ 11-14 yrs

Source: Thomson CenterWatch Career Survey, 2003

8.28

8.29

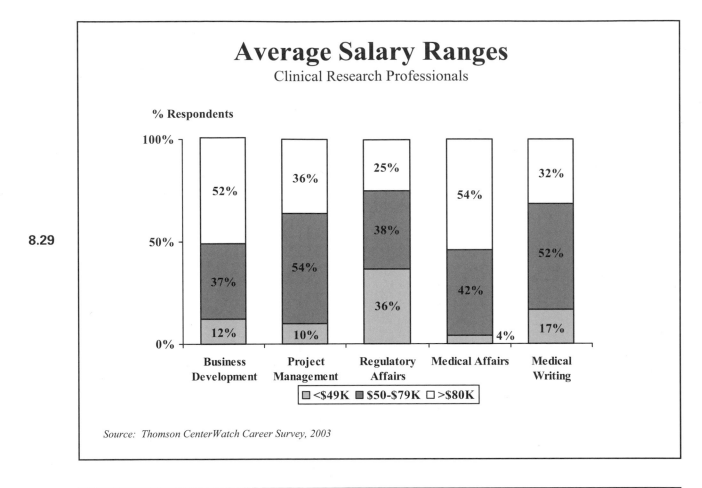

Average Salary Ranges
Clinical Research Professionals

% Respondents

Legend: ☐ <$49K ▨ $50-$79K ☐ >$80K

Source: Thomson CenterWatch Career Survey, 2003

8.30

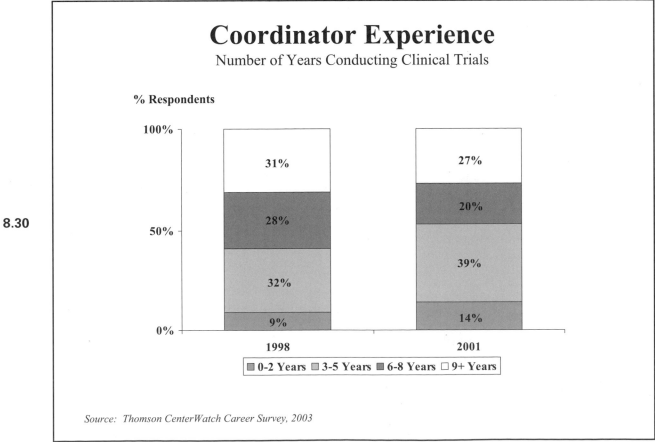

Coordinator Experience
Number of Years Conducting Clinical Trials

% Respondents

Legend: ▨ 0-2 Years ☐ 3-5 Years ▨ 6-8 Years ☐ 9+ Years

Source: Thomson CenterWatch Career Survey, 2003

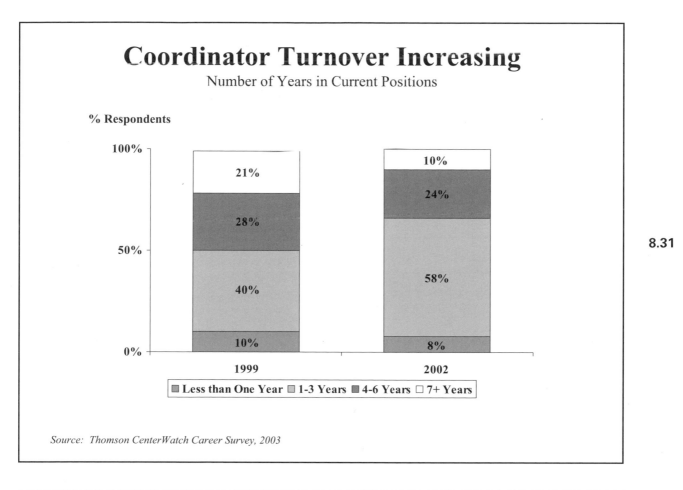

Coordinator Turnover Increasing
Number of Years in Current Positions

% Respondents

8.31

Source: *Thomson CenterWatch Career Survey, 2003*

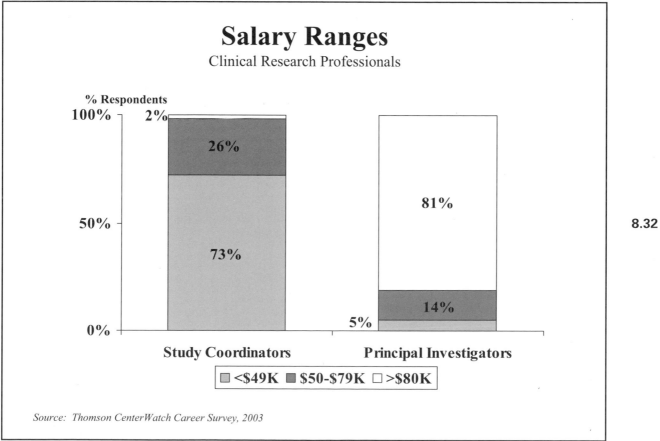

Salary Ranges
Clinical Research Professionals

% Respondents

8.32

Source: *Thomson CenterWatch Career Survey, 2003*

8.33

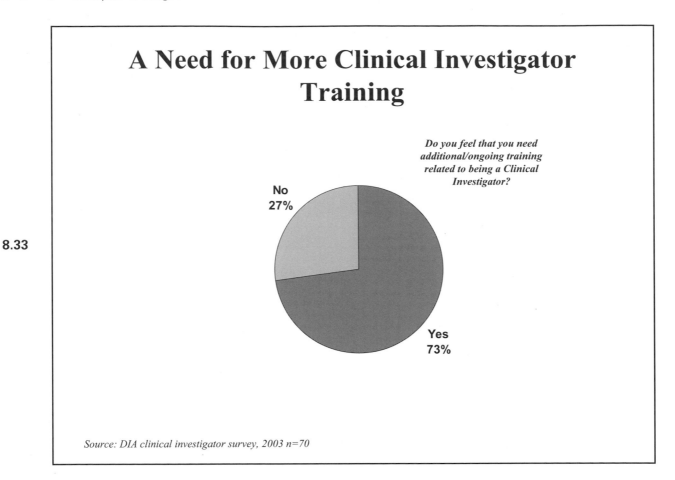

8.34

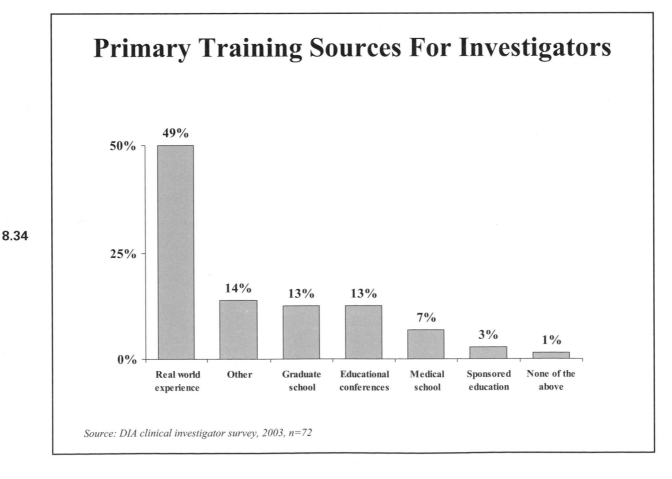

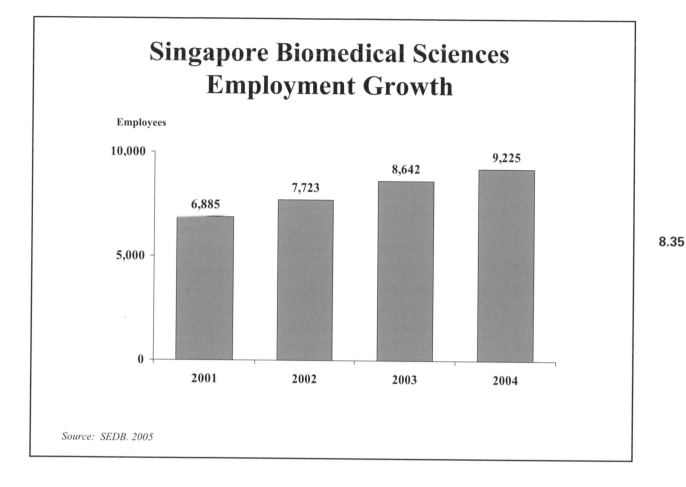

Singapore Biomedical Sciences Employment Growth

Employees

Source: SEDB. 2005

8.35

Study Volunteers

Anticipated by CenterWatch's first ever study of the investigator demographic in 2001, a shortage of clinical research investigators has indeed come to pass in 2005. In an effort to address the problem, some trial management organizations and site support service companies are training and empowering new, eager physicians in rural areas of the United States to become successful clinical research investigators.

As a result of broadening the investigator base, large patient pools—including minority and treatment-naïve patients—are being recruited in these untapped, rural regions of the United States as well. Trial management organizations and site support service companies that are pushing into these underserved areas are experiencing both healthy growth and excellent patient retention numbers.

The New Frontier: Tapping Into Rural U.S.

Addressing the Investigator Shortfall

By Karyn Korieth & Sara Gambrill
Published July 2005

As sponsor companies send clinical trials overseas to markets that offer well-educated physicians and large numbers of treatment-naïve patients, in the United States an increasing number of trial management organizations are finding untapped resources closer to home. They are developing clinical trials resources in both medium-sized communities and rural areas outside of the major metropolitan areas where drug trials have been conducted in the past. Among the prime locations they are targeting are multi-specialty clinics and physician's offices in non-urban communities across the country such as Jonesboro, Ark.; Chagrin Falls, Ohio; or Albuquerque, N.M.

In these non-urban and rural communities, trial management organizations (TMOS) and site support service companies (SSSCs) have found physicians eager to participate in clinical research; large patient pools, including minority and treatment-naïve patients; and underserved, sometimes uninsured, patients who want access to cutting edge treatments. Many companies working in non-metropolitan areas have grown during the past five years, not only adding sites and investigators, but also attracting greater numbers of industry-sponsored studies.

TMOs and SSSCs are expanding their research capabilities into previously underdeveloped areas at a time when CenterWatch had predicted a shortfall in the number of investigators available to handle sponsor demand. CenterWatch research estimates that 37.8% of the clinical investigators in 2001 were age 50 or older, compared with only 3.8% under the age of 35. The gap between the number of active investigators and the number of active clinical trials may continue to widen during the next decade as active investigators retire.

"Pharmaceutical companies will have to decide to start using sites they've never used before or else they will run out of sites," said Nadina Jose, M.D., president and chief executive officer of the Pasadena, Calif.-based Research Strategies, a site support services company that bases its business model on recruiting and training investigators from geographical areas undeveloped in terms of clinical research opportunities. "There may be investigator shortages in the bigger cities. But in the areas where we are, there is not a shortage. They are just starting to get involved."

David Jones, president and chief executive officer of Little Rock, Ark.-based Research Solutions, a TMO, sees the non-metropolitan areas as a great underdeveloped clinical trials resource for both investigators and patients. "A lot of studies are sent overseas, but there continues to be a shortage of quality investigators in this country," said Jones. "We are attempting to bring some of the larger physician institutional organizations in this country into the process to allow them to utilize their patient census, their expertise and their communities to participate in clinical studies. There is certainly a challenge to get the numbers of patients needed to get involved in the process in this country. But it allows a tremendous opportunity for people who are interested in participating in studies."

Some site management organizations that feature experienced investigators and extensive training programs may see their experience as an advantage compared with companies that have inexperienced investigators.

Yet when bringing clinical trials into a new geographical area, especially to rural or underserved communities, site management organizations face unique challenges. National studies have documented that rural patients, in particular, have limited knowledge about clinical trials and often share a widespread fear and distrust of the medical care system; this skepticism has increased in recent months due to highly publicized concerns about the safety of marketed drugs. Many fear being treated like "guinea pigs" or are skeptical about the quality of care provided in a clinical trial. In addition, patients in rural areas may have difficulty getting back and forth from a clinical site; those with low incomes may find it hard to take time off work or find appropriate childcare.

TMOs and SSSCs working in non-urban areas are sensitive to the unique patient recruitment challenges posed by cultural and financial factors in these communities. These organizations place a strong emphasis on education, not just through the informed consent process, but also by conducting outreach and advocacy programs to support recruitment efforts, such as attending health fairs, providing free health screenings at community centers and speaking at churches and community groups. At the same time, these organizations develop strong relationships with local physicians because in many non-urban communities, a recommendation from a trusted doctor could help a patient decide whether or not to participate in a clinical trial.

By taking clinical research into non-urban community settings, TMOs and SSSCs have found new investigators and patient populations for their studies. Yet at the same time, the organizations have helped raise the level of healthcare in these communities by offering higher standards of treatment and access to cutting edge therapies. "For someone who has a chronic disease, who has tried everything that is out there, this is something new

and cutting edge that they would otherwise not have access to," said Julie Stover, chief operating officer of Research Solutions. "In certain situations, the patients may not be able to afford the medications otherwise. It's a real bonus for both the patients and the clinic." Untapped areas in the U.S. can mimic areas of the developing world where clinical trials offer similar opportunities.

In this article, CenterWatch profiles organizations representing a variety of perspectives, including non-profit and academic organizations that are developing clinical trials resources in non-urban and rural communities that have no prior clinical trials experience. Organization leaders discuss their motivation and success, as well as offer insight about the special challenges faced when working in these untapped areas.

Targeting Untapped Areas

Research Solutions began conducting studies six years ago in Arkansas and Louisiana after discovering the area had been largely overlooked for clinical research. In fact, the company found that many communities with populations anywhere from 100,000 to 300,000, and even those with larger statistical market areas, had never been developed in terms of the clinical trials process. "During our research we had seen there just wasn't a huge concerted effort to bring research to patients in this area," said Stacie Wickliffe, executive vice president and director of marketing at Research Solutions. "We did an analysis of where research was being conducted and it's all been in the larger metropolitan areas. There was a huge black hole in this area."

The company, which now has several hundred investigators at 55 sites in 12 states, develops relationships with large multi-specialty clinics or group practices that haven't been involved with clinical research in the past. In many cases, these multi-specialty clinics or large group practices provide healthcare for about 75% of the community's population. "Ultimately, we are working with midrange communities with large statistical market areas that in many cases reach 500,000 to a million people. Generally speaking, the focal point is a large multi-specialty clinic that takes care of healthcare needs for a significant number of people," said Jones. "We are trying to bring large physician groups that have large patient populations into the clinical trials process."

For example, Research Solutions partners with a multi-specialty group of 50 physicians in Morristown, Tenn., which has a statistical market area close to 500,000 people; the practice never had clinical studies offered to them in the past. Another multi-specialty clinic in Texas treats patients from 10 surrounding counties. "We are trying to develop relationships with larger multi-specialty clinics. In most cases, they are not necessarily sitting in large cities; in fact, some of the larger cities have large group practices, but not large multi-specialty practices," said Jones. "The practices that sit in some of the smaller communities of this country are a huge reservoir of untapped patient resources that actually are clamoring to be involved in clinical studies."

Working with multi-specialty groups also helps Research Solutions involve additional investigators and patients in future studies. The organization initially works with the family practice or internal medicine physicians as their key investigators and then offers studies to specialists within the group, such as dermatologists or urologists. "We are continually offering different types of therapeutic studies to other physicians within that multi-specialty group who may not have participated in clinical studies up to that particular point in time. We encourage other physicians in the group to get more involved in the clinical research process," Jones said. "Because we have coordinators on their campus on an ongoing basis, we are in a position to be able to have access to the full patient population that they have within their clinic. It's a real win-win situation because it gives us access to the patient population not only from the internal medicine practices, but from all of the therapeutic areas that are in the clinic."

Research Solutions, which has 290 active studies, finds it can generate greater publicity about clinical studies underway in its communities than trial management organizations typically find in large metropolitan areas. "We usually put out a press release to local publications in the communi-

ty talking about the various studies their clinics have been awarded," Jones said. "If one of their larger clinics gets accepted to participate in a clinical study, it's a really big deal. We've seen front-page headlines in some of the local newspapers—and they are not necessarily small newspapers, but the major newspapers in the communities—bragging about the fact that their facilities have been approved for doing these cutting-edge medicine clinical studies. It helps the whole process in terms of getting patients involved, getting patients excited about participating in the studies and making themselves really proud of the fact that their local physicians have been chosen, much like some of the more prestigious locations around the country, to participate in these studies."

Training New Investigators

Since its launch in 1996, Research Strategies, a site support services company based in Pasadena, Calif., has identified, trained, developed and maintained clinical investigative sites that had no prior clinical trial experience. When the company began, its first major project involved enrolling investigators, who lacked clinical research experience, for a urology trial in Southeast Asia. "We did all the training for the investigators and research coordinators. When we got back to the United States, we realized it could be done here as well," said Jose, the president and CEO of Research Strategies. "It was like the light at the end of the tunnel opening up our business to a place that was uncharted territory."

Research Strategies, which began with one site and now has 18, seeks out sites with untapped populations and untapped geography for clinical trials; for example, the company has contracts with sites in Greenwood, Ind.; Reno, Nev.; and Chagrin Falls, Ohio. "We look for sites that have no experience. We look for sites that are on the grass-roots level," said Jose. "We try to approach these sites and really understand them—know the politics involved in the area, what kinds of practices and traditions are being followed in the community—before we decide whether we want to do clinical trials there. We do a lot of assessment of

312

Study Volunteers
The New Frontier: Tapping Into Rural U.S.

the area before ascertaining that it's a good place to do a study."

When looking for physicians to become involved in clinical research, Jose first visits sites to determine the site's capabilities, including the physical plant, the profile of their data set and the composition of their research team. The physician's philosophy and attitude towards patient care and healthcare delivery also are an important factor. "I have to make sure that they are willing to commit themselves to doing this," Jose said. "Every investigator I look for has told me, 'I have the patients, I have the practice and I want to learn.' It has to come from them."

The rigorous investigator and site selection process makes it easier to enroll patients once trials begin since Research Strategies already understands the physician, patient base and level of commitment to doing clinical research. "It's a lot easier for us to figure out what types of studies will work," said Jose, whose company has more than 100 open studies. "If, from the very beginning, we've been able to establish the culture and the mentality about why they want to do clinical trials, when studies come across our table, we can say, 'This is good for this site because it's what they do.'"

Growth and Patient Retention

Clinical Research Consultants, an Alabama-based research support company formed five years ago, manages seven research centers in the greater Birmingham-Hoover area; the sites are located in medical centers and physician offices in inner-city and rural areas. The company, which has 60 studies open at seven locations, finds it easier to recruit patients for studies in its rural areas; its largest producing center is located at the fringes of an urban area, where most of the patients recruited for those studies are from rural areas. "We tend to find more patients who are willing to participate in trials from these rural areas," said James Kilgore, Ph.D., president and chief executive officer of Clinical Research Consultants.

The company's greatest growth has been in the rural areas, where the lack of adequate healthcare has resulted in large populations of treatment-naïve patients. Pharmaceutical companies want to include these treatment-naïve patients in clinical trials, in particular for studies testing erectile dysfunction, hypercholesterolemia and hypertension drugs. "You have to go outside the urban or inner city areas to find these naïve patients. Our greatest enrollment in studies, across the board, has been in our rural clinics versus inner city or urban areas," said Kilgore, whose company has completed more than 12,500 patient visits during the past four years.

When conducting clinical studies in rural areas, as compared with urban or inner-city areas, Kilgore's company uses different recruitment strategies. Recruitment activities such as Internet or newspaper advertisements, which routinely are used to recruit patients in metropolitan areas, don't work well in rural areas. The key to recruiting patients in rural areas, Kilgore said, is developing a good relationship with physicians. "There seems to be a bit more skepticism about Internet or newspaper advertising in the rural areas. There seems to be much more of a commitment and a trust between the physician and the patient. We don't see a lot of physician shopping in the rural areas compared to the inner city or the urban areas," Kilgore said. "A lot of their patients will participate because of that trust that they have with the investigator-physician because he's probably taken care of them, and their families, for years."

This strong relationship between physicians and their patients can also translate to higher clinical trial retention rates; Kilgore finds that a high percentage of rural volunteers complete their studies. If a patient fails to show up for visit and Clinical Research Consultants has a hard time reaching that patient, someone from the doctor's staff makes a call and the patient generally comes in. "Our loss to follow-up is extremely low in our rural clinic as compared to our urban clinics," Kilgore said. "We lose very, very few patients from those types of studies."

When conducting studies in rural areas, organizations need to be careful about the types of studies they place, Kilgore said. Urban patients are willing to enroll in short-term studies such as for pharyngitis or bronchitis; yet in rural areas, studies for chronic illnesses such as osteoarthritis or hypertension are more successful. While patients in urban areas may live or work 20 minutes away from a doctor's office, in rural areas, patients routinely drive an hour or more to be involved in a study. "In rural areas, patients have to drive for longer distances and don't want to come every week for a month," Kilgore said. "In these areas, we tend to do better and attract patients who are willing to stay in a long-term study, where they only have to come in once a month or once every three months, because of the distances involved."

Another challenge related to distance involves the reluctance of some trial monitors to drive more than an hour from the airport to a rural location. "Monitors seem to be carrying a heavier and heavier load and are under more time constraints. They generally don't want to be too far away from an airport," Kilgore said. "If you are in an area where you only have one or two patients, there is a cost-benefit issue. If you do recruit from a rural area, with a physician in that area, you've got to make sure that there can be a high enough enrollment to justify the cost of driving the distance to that office. For example, we are doing a lipid study and since we have more than 100 patients who are basically all untreated, which you might not find in an urban area, they are willing to come and do that review."

Making Trials Affordable

The cost of conducting clinical trials in rural communities, especially in sparsely populated areas, can be higher on a cost-per-patient basis; sites in rural communities may have fewer patients enrolled in any given clinical trial, but the sites still require research staff.

The non-profit site network New Mexico Cancer Care Alliance (NMCCA) was incorporated in 2002 to make opening cancer studies easier for both physician-investigators and sponsors by providing a central location to organize the process and complete paperwork. NMCCA staff located at a central site in Albuquerque performs all administrative procedures required for its participants to open a cancer trial such as contracting, budgeting, submitting the institutional review board (IRB) application and managing the adverse

event reports. "We are trying to become more efficient to make it less costly and more desirable for the rural parts of our state to participate in research," said Teresa Stewart, executive director of the NMCCA. "By centralizing some of the functions for research, we were able not only to continue providing research in areas where we already had it in our state, but also to make sure that clinical trials are available to all of the state of New Mexico."

The NMCCA represents about 85 cancer treatment physicians in central and northern New Mexico; this number has grown from 60 in just two years. The physicians are from five major healthcare systems in Albuquerque and Santa Fe, including the University of New Mexico Cancer Research & Treatment Center, along with multiple private practices. During the next year, the NMCCA plans to add participants from both hospitals and private practices in the southern part of New Mexico and its northwest corner. In the past two years, the alliance has brought in both physicians who have extensive experience with clinical trials and those who lack research experience except for that done in their residencies. Once physicians become an alliance participant, which means they must give the New Mexico Cancer Care Alliance the right of first refusal for any research done in their facility, participants can complete IRB training and receive a National Cancer Institute number in order to become investigators.

The NMCCA not only makes it easier for physicians to open clinical trials and trains new investigators for research studies, it improves access to cancer clinical trials for the state's largely rural population, thereby raising the level of cancer treatment available in these communities. By providing the option of participating in clinical trials, a greater number of cancer patients gain access to cutting-edge treatment and novel drugs that their treatment wouldn't otherwise include; some have access to new treatment options when standard-of-care treatment has failed. "For some patients, if they had to come all the way to Albuquerque or travel out of state, they might choose not to be treated or to not participate in research. Now there are treatment options for patients and they can stay home," Stewart said. "We believe that patients who are getting their treatment through a research trial are getting better treatment because not only do you have your physician and nurse providing chemo, or whatever the treatment is, but you also have a research nurse making sure that all of your treatment—whether standard of care or part of the protocol—is being done."

As in other largely rural areas, the NMCCA finds that when recruiting patients for its clinical trials, advertisements in newspapers or the Internet aren't effective tools. Instead, NMCCA sponsors a variety of educational programs, for both patients and medical professionals, to help make patients more comfortable about taking part in a clinical trial. "Patients have their own ideas about research. What it really takes to recruit patients is good education: face-to-face contact, talking about the studies, and educating patients about how research works," said Carmen Angel, a research nurse from New Mexico Cancer Care Associates, the NMCCA's Santa Fe participant office.

Much of the recruitment for the NMCCA's clinical trials is driven by the physician; in many cases, there is a strong trust relationship between the doctor and patient about treatment options. Because of this strong trust, patient education and ensuring trial participants fully understand the informed consent form becomes even more vital. "In our office, the physician does the initial presentation of the consent forms," said Angel. "If the patient is at all interested, I get called into the room and we all go through it together. The patient is required to take the consent form home. We never sign it the day it is presented. They take it home and talk about it with family or friends. Then we set them up with an appointment to come back and answer any questions. It can take two to three days or it can take two weeks. It depends on the patient."

In its first two years, the NMCCA has done more than 48 studies, including industry- and government-sponsored trials and investigator-initiated trials. During this time, the alliance has been successful in meeting its trial enrollment goals. And since it represents patients from multiple healthcare systems, the time spent to accrue patients to a single trial can decrease when the study is opened at multiple sites. In addition, New Mexico offers a wide range of ethnic populations available to studies, including Hispanic, Native American and White. "Part of our challenge is to overcome the fact that we're remote. We want to make it easier and more desirable for a sponsor to want to do business here," Stewart said. "Sponsors who come to New Mexico and interact with the New Mexico Cancer Care Alliance have access to a large network and they only have to do one contract with one budget. Another desirable feature of New Mexico is our ethnic mix. We have a very diverse ethnic mix, which sponsors are seeking because they need to have ethnic diversity as part of their trial."

Explaining Clinical Research

For the past three decades, the Duke Comprehensive Cancer Center has worked with its community partners to coordinate clinical trials in rural areas, offering underserved patients access to investigational treatments. The community outreach, which today is coordinated by the Duke Oncology Network (DON), has grown to include 25 clinical and research programs at partner institutions across six states throughout the southeast. At its affiliated sites within North Carolina, Duke University Medical Center physicians and fellows provide oncology services, evaluating and treating individuals with cancer. In other regional DON communities, the network helps to develop cancer care services through assistance in clinical research and professional training. In order to participate in the network, community hospitals must agree to have an infrastructure in place to support clinical trial participation.

Some facilities that partner with the Duke Oncology Network have never before participated in clinical trials and lack adequate understanding of clinical research. Network representatives first meet with the CEO or president of the organization to describe clinical research and its regulatory requirements. "We communicate the whole philosophy of how ethical behavior is carried out and put some responsibility back on the CEO for clinical research behavior within their institutions," said Jana Wagenseller, RN, Associate Director for

Research and Education, who has been instrumental in the conception and operation.

Before studies are begun, the network trains research nurses at its Duke medical facilities and meets with the pharmacists, program administrators and support staff who will participate in clinical research. For many partner institutions, DON helps develop hospital-wide policies and procedures related to clinical research; it also assists the facility in submitting its federal assurance and identifying an institutional review board.

In 2003, more than 700 patients enrolled in clinical trials through DON; the trials are either sponsored by the National Cancer Institute, pharmaceutical companies or initiated by Duke physicians. By offering access to clinical trials through rural clinics, the network can provide a level of care that patients would be unable to obtain otherwise. Many of these underserved patients lack the resources to travel to a tertiary-care medical center, yet clinics in rural areas often don't have the resources to offer specialized cancer services and clinical trial opportunities.

At the same time, participation of these rural patients benefits Duke researchers and the greater medical community. The support of research initiatives by DON affiliates allows Duke researchers to complete trials more rapidly than otherwise might be possible, according to Alison Andre, MS, PT, director of the Duke Oncology Network in Durham, N.C. Since the clinical trials are available to a greater number of patients through the network, enrollment is enhanced, potentially expediting the process for new drugs to reach the market. In addition, many pharmaceutical companies want access to a network for its studies since the data will reflect more cultural and socioeconomic diversity. "We feel we are helping to improve the standard of care for people in the community," Andre said. "There is also an advantage to Duke and cancer research as a whole."

When enrolling patients from rural communities for its studies, an important part of the network's role involves understanding the diverse cultural, religious and financial factors that may influence a patient's decision to participate in the clinical trial. For example, when the network had a study using thalidomide, they knew it would be hard to recruit patients from rural, under-educated communities who historically have had negative opinions about the drug. At the same time, some drugs provided through a clinical trial may be attractive to patients who might lack medical insurance to pay for the drug. These cultural and financial factors also are critical when obtaining informed consent from a trial participant. "Communication is important. When obtaining consent, if people don't understand clinical research, you don't just give a patient a piece of paper. You sit down and have a conversation with them, with their family members present, and help them really understand what the trial is about," Wagenseller said. "We need to have a good understanding of the community and the local context within the community. Every community is a little bit different. The culture is different. It's part of our role to understand what their values are and what culturally will be appropriate."

Many of the network's affiliated sites are in rural communities, from West Virginia to Florida, with strong faith-based initiatives. In these communities, patients may turn to their pastors for advice when offered the chance to participate in a clinical trial. In response, the network collaborates with local churches and faith-based initiatives to educate religious leaders about clinical trials and the role clinical studies play in cancer care. "We use them to advocate with patients on clinical trials," said Andre. "Patients may hear about a study in the medical office, but they may want to go back to their pastor or someone they trust in their faith-based community. If they don't completely understand it from their medical provider, they go to the source where their trust is and ask for guidance."

Duke Oncology Network and other organizations working in non-metropolitan and rural areas believe they are in a win-win situation: developing new resources to conduct clinical trials throughout the country while at the same time raising the level of healthcare in non-urban communities by offering patients access to drugs and treatment that would otherwise be unavailable.

9.01

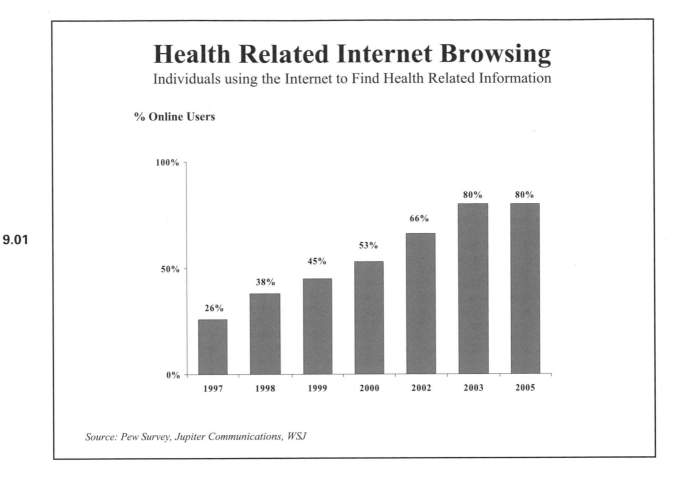

Health Related Internet Browsing
Individuals using the Internet to Find Health Related Information

% Online Users

Source: Pew Survey, Jupiter Communications, WSJ

9.02

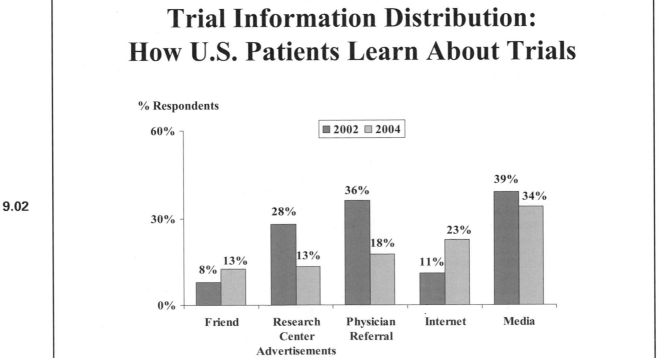

Trial Information Distribution:
How U.S. Patients Learn About Trials

% Respondents

Source: Thomson CenterWatch Surveys of 1,565; 1239 Study Volunteers, 2002, 2004

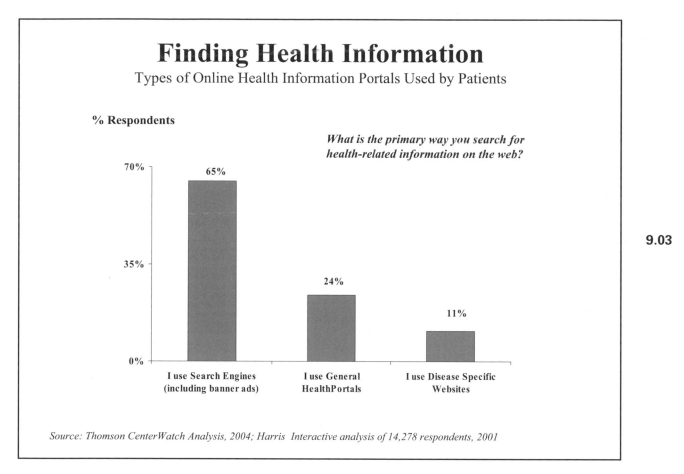

Finding Health Information

Types of Online Health Information Portals Used by Patients

% Respondents

What is the primary way you search for health-related information on the web?

65% — I use Search Engines (including banner ads)
24% — I use General HealthPortals
11% — I use Disease Specific Websites

9.03

Source: Thomson CenterWatch Analysis, 2004; Harris Interactive analysis of 14,278 respondents, 2001

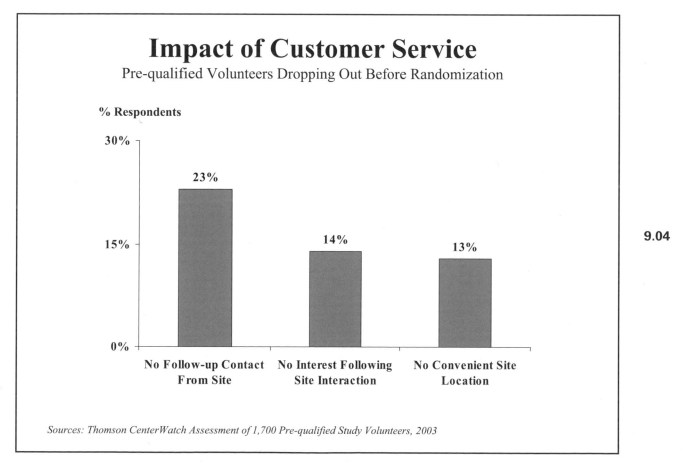

Impact of Customer Service

Pre-qualified Volunteers Dropping Out Before Randomization

% Respondents

23% — No Follow-up Contact From Site
14% — No Interest Following Site Interaction
13% — No Convenient Site Location

9.04

Sources: Thomson CenterWatch Assessment of 1,700 Pre-qualified Study Volunteers, 2003

9.05

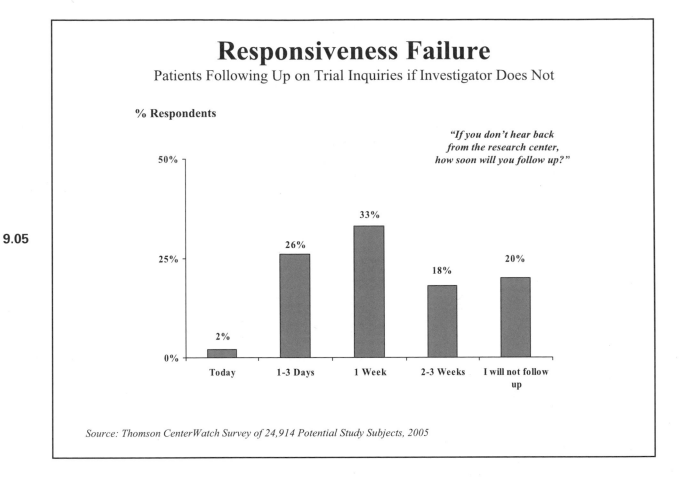

Responsiveness Failure
Patients Following Up on Trial Inquiries if Investigator Does Not

% Respondents

*"If you don't hear back
from the research center,
how soon will you follow up?"*

Source: Thomson CenterWatch Survey of 24,914 Potential Study Subjects, 2005

9.06

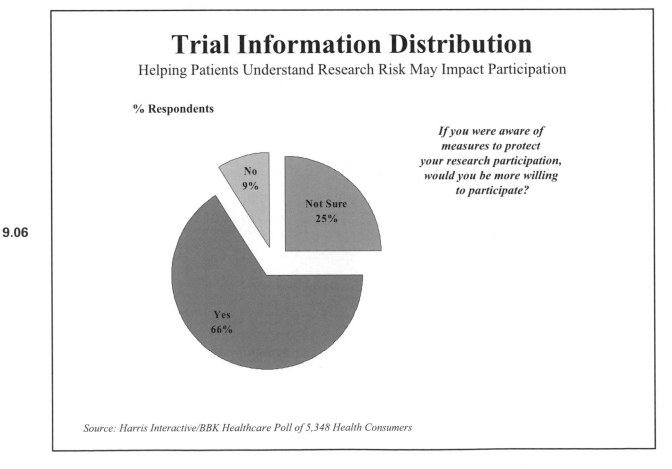

Trial Information Distribution
Helping Patients Understand Research Risk May Impact Participation

% Respondents

*If you were aware of
measures to protect
your research participation,
would you be more willing
to participate?*

Source: Harris Interactive/BBK Healthcare Poll of 5,348 Health Consumers

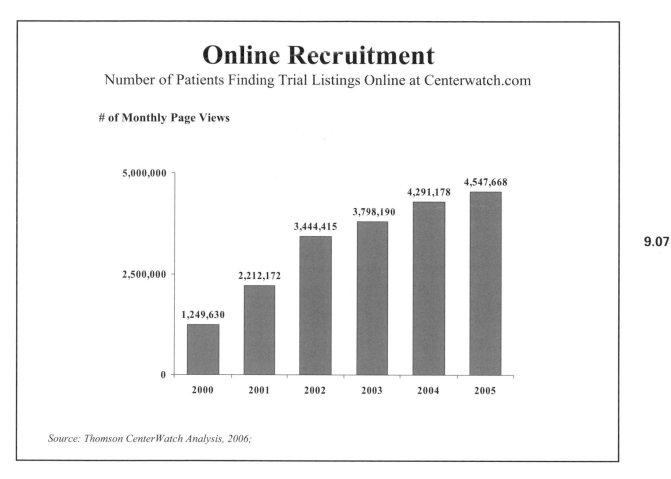

Online Recruitment

Number of Patients Finding Trial Listings Online at Centerwatch.com

# of Monthly Page Views

9.07

Source: Thomson CenterWatch Analysis, 2006;

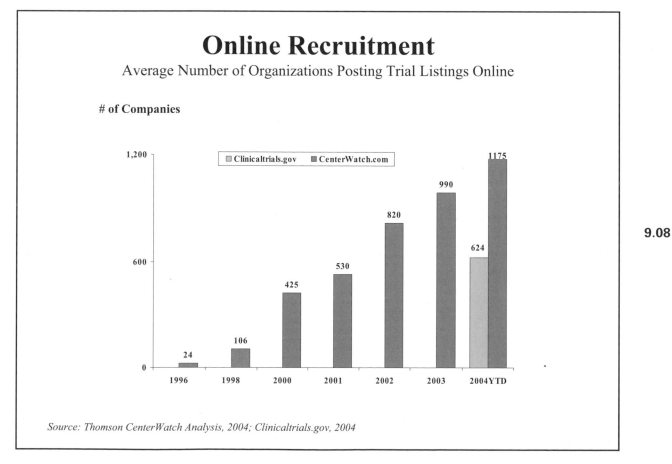

Online Recruitment

Average Number of Organizations Posting Trial Listings Online

# of Companies

9.08

Source: Thomson CenterWatch Analysis, 2004; Clinicaltrials.gov, 2004

9.09

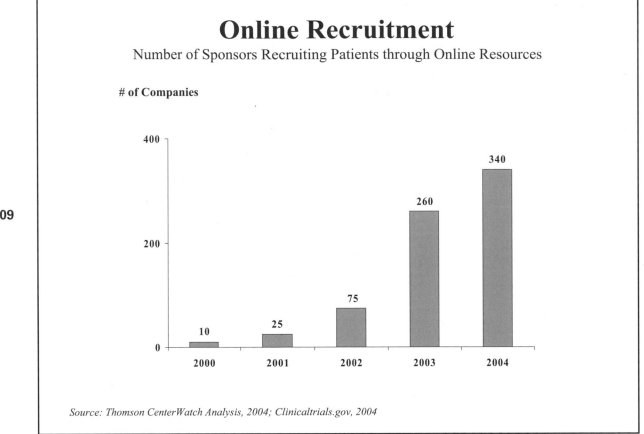

Online Recruitment
Number of Sponsors Recruiting Patients through Online Resources

of Companies

Year	#
2000	10
2001	25
2002	75
2003	260
2004	340

Source: Thomson CenterWatch Analysis, 2004; Clinicaltrials.gov, 2004

9.10

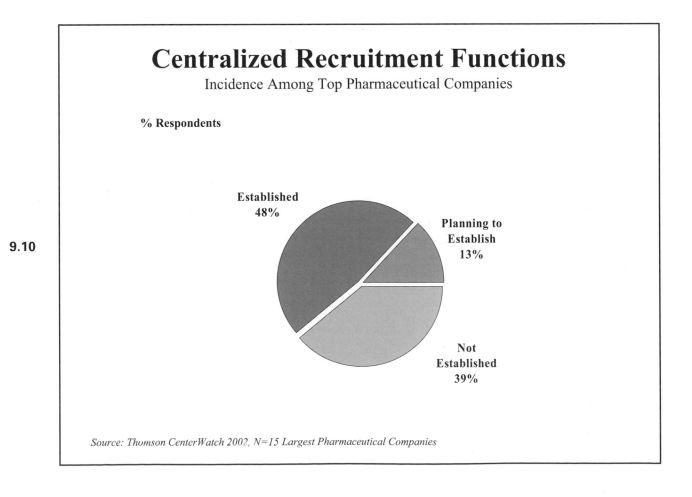

Centralized Recruitment Functions
Incidence Among Top Pharmaceutical Companies

% Respondents

- Established 48%
- Planning to Establish 13%
- Not Established 39%

Source: Thomson CenterWatch 2002, N=15 Largest Pharmaceutical Companies

Recruiting Patients Online
Majority of Sites Are Using the Internet

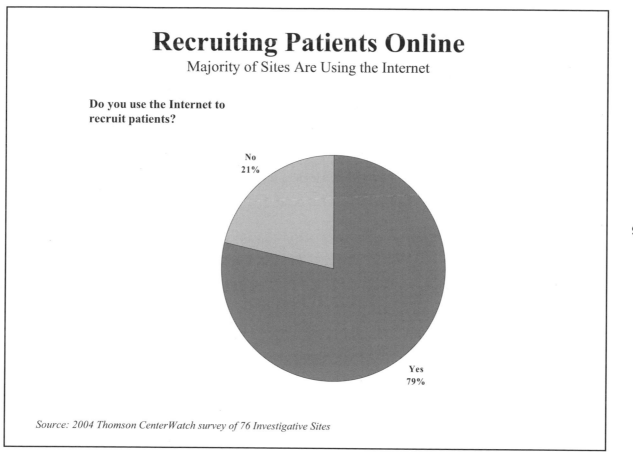

Do you use the Internet to recruit patients?

No
21%

Yes
79%

Source: 2004 Thomson CenterWatch survey of 76 Investigative Sites

9.11

Biopharma Companies Recruiting Online

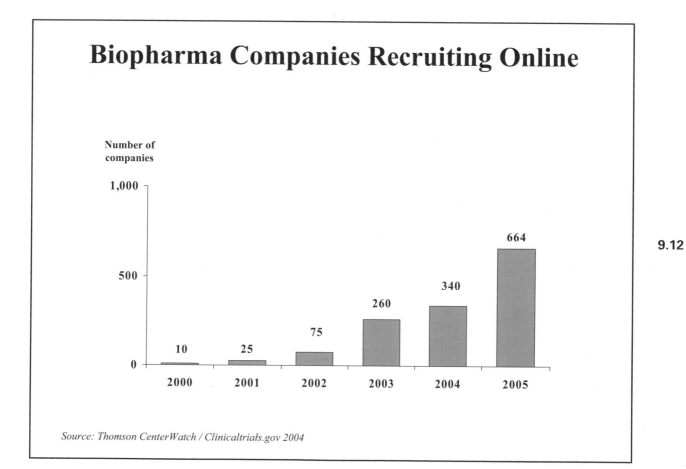

Number of companies

Source: Thomson CenterWatch / Clinicaltrials.gov 2004

9.12

9.13

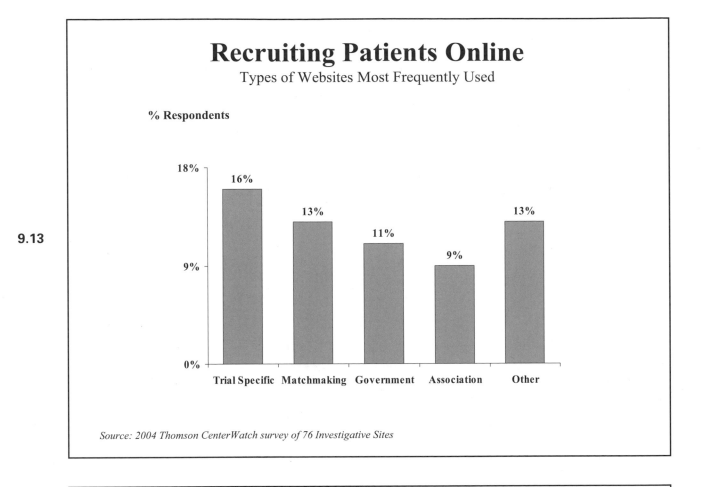

Recruiting Patients Online
Types of Websites Most Frequently Used

% Respondents

Source: 2004 Thomson CenterWatch survey of 76 Investigative Sites

9.14

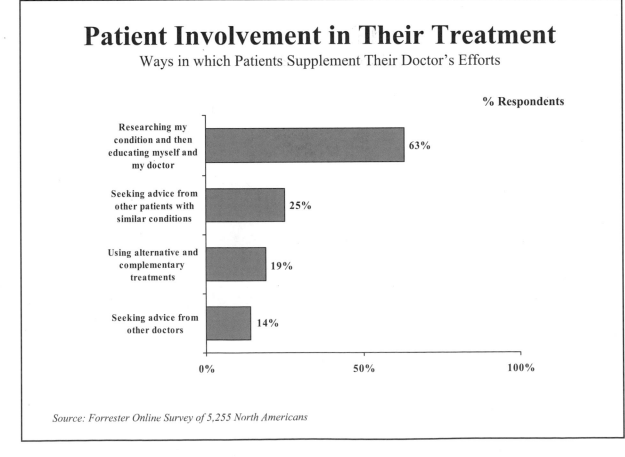

Patient Involvement in Their Treatment
Ways in which Patients Supplement Their Doctor's Efforts

% Respondents

Source: Forrester Online Survey of 5,255 North Americans

Participation in Pediatric Studies
Factors Impacting Willingness

Under what conditions would you be willing to allow your children to participate in a clinical research study?	% Respondents
Thought the drug would cure the child	75%
A child has terminal illness	73%
There were no risks involved	72%
Current treatment options no longer effective	70%
Would benefit your/someone else's child	69%
Pediatrician/Specialist Recommended it	68%
For monetary compensation	37%

Source: *The Wall Street Journal Online / Harris Interactive Health-Care Poll , 2004*

9.15

Call Center Patient Recruitment Services
Estimated Total US Market

$US, in Millions

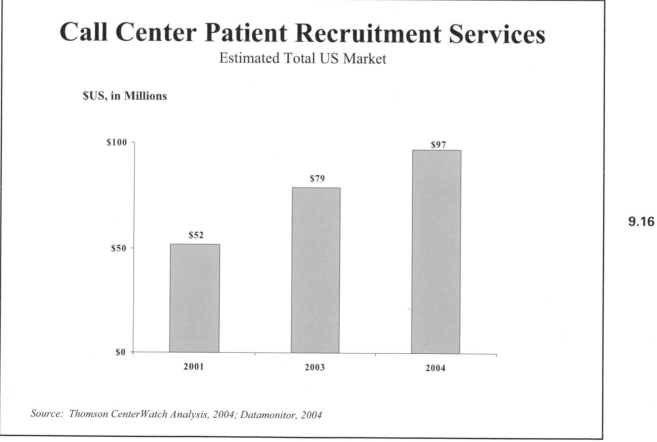

Source: *Thomson CenterWatch Analysis, 2004; Datamonitor, 2004*

9.16

9.17

Patient Recruitment Call Centers
Selected Firms with Clinical Trial Recruitment Call Centers

Call Center	Ownership
Phone Screen	American Mediconnect
Clinphone	Private (UK based)
Examination Management Services	Private
Academic Network LLC	Private
CliniCall	Private (Canada)
Integrated Marketing Concepts	Private

Source: Thomson CenterWatch, 2004

9.18

Patient Recruitment Call Centers
Firms With In-House Recruitment Centers

Firm	Ownership	Founded
Acurian	Private	1998
Matthews Media Group	Omnicom	1987
Medici Group	Private	1992
Clinical Solutions	Publicis Healthcare Communications	N/A
TrialBuilder LLC	Private	1994
PharmaTech Solutions	Private	1999
Alliance Healthcare Information	Private	1995
BBK	Private	1983
Pharmaceutical Research Plus	Private	1994

Source: Thomson CenterWatch, 2004

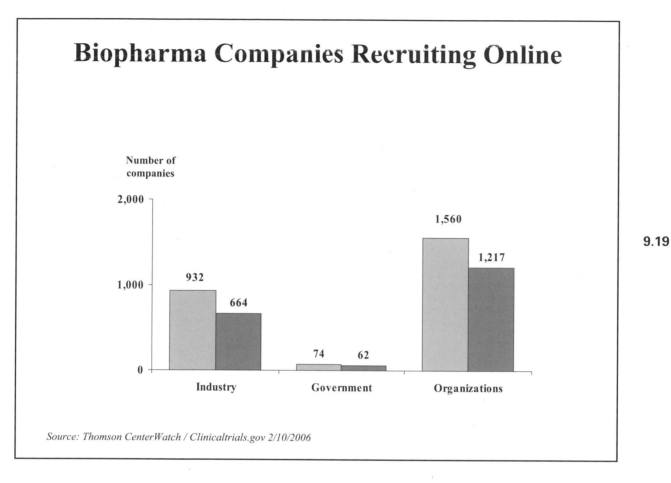

Biopharma Companies Recruiting Online

Number of
companies

Source: Thomson CenterWatch / Clinicaltrials.gov 2/10/2006

9.19

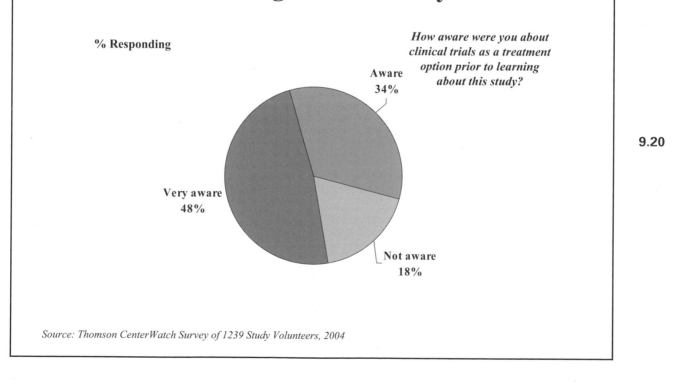

Awareness Of Clinical Trials Prior To Learning Of The Study

% Responding

How aware were you about clinical trials as a treatment option prior to learning about this study?

Aware
34%

Very aware
48%

Not aware
18%

9.20

Source: Thomson CenterWatch Survey of 1239 Study Volunteers, 2004

9.21

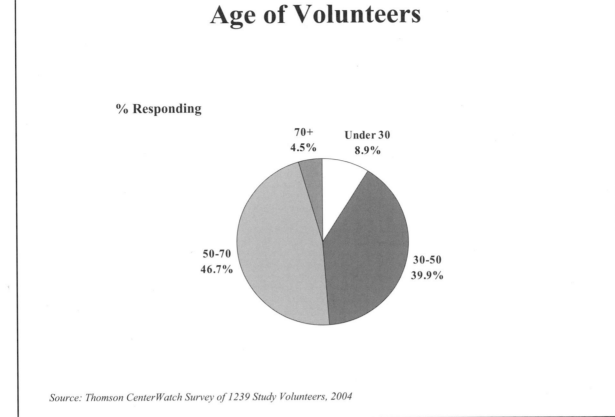

Age of Volunteers

% Responding

Source: Thomson CenterWatch Survey of 1239 Study Volunteers, 2004

9.22

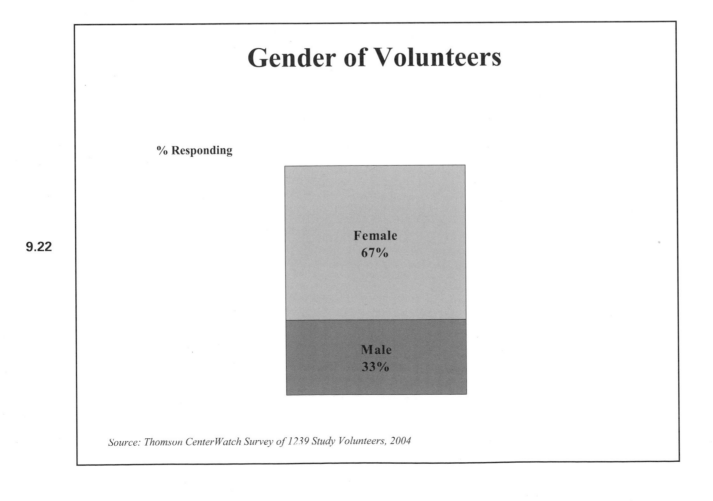

Gender of Volunteers

% Responding

Source: Thomson CenterWatch Survey of 1239 Study Volunteers, 2004

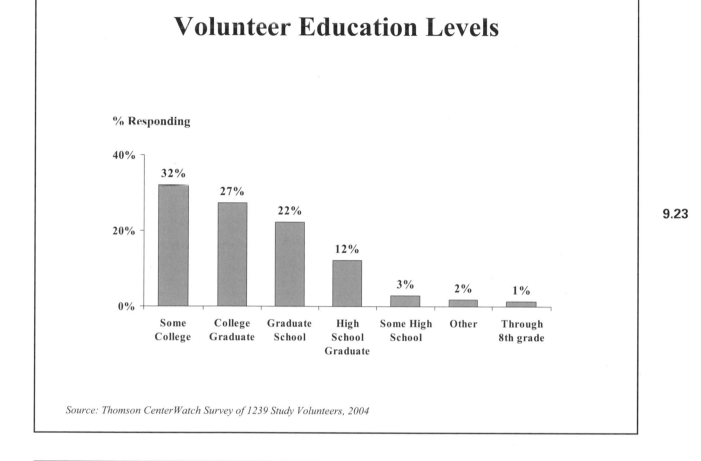

Volunteer Education Levels

9.23

Source: Thomson CenterWatch Survey of 1239 Study Volunteers, 2004

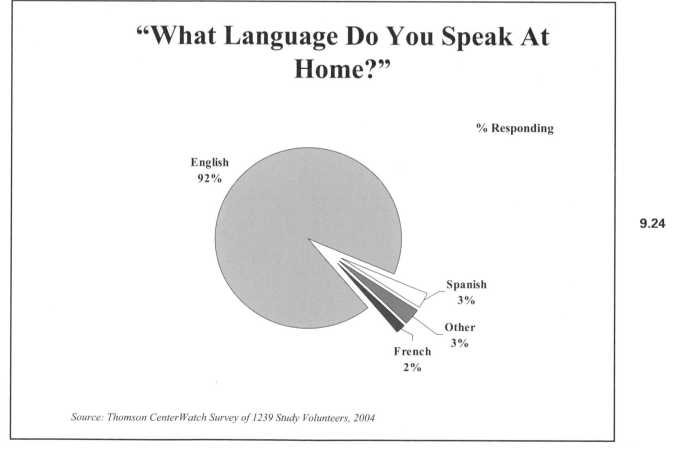

"What Language Do You Speak At Home?"

9.24

Source: Thomson CenterWatch Survey of 1239 Study Volunteers, 2004

9.25

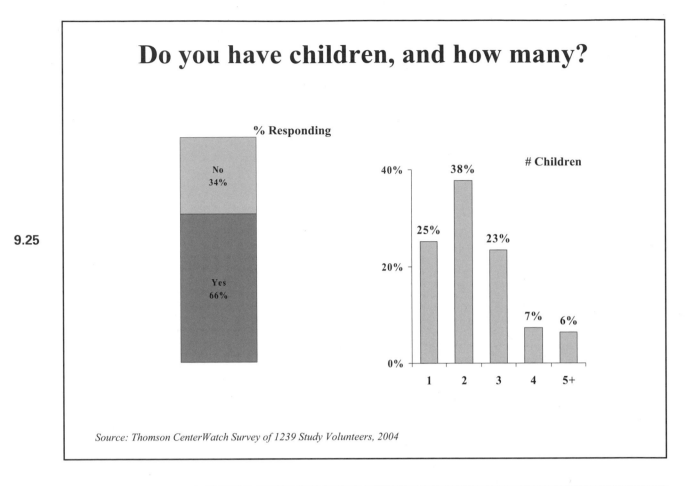

Do you have children, and how many?

% Responding

No
34%

Yes
66%

Children

Source: Thomson CenterWatch Survey of 1239 Study Volunteers, 2004

9.26

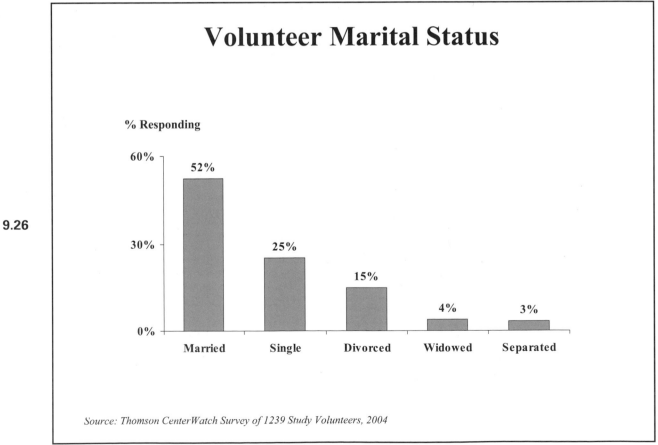

Volunteer Marital Status

% Responding

Source: Thomson CenterWatch Survey of 1239 Study Volunteers, 2004

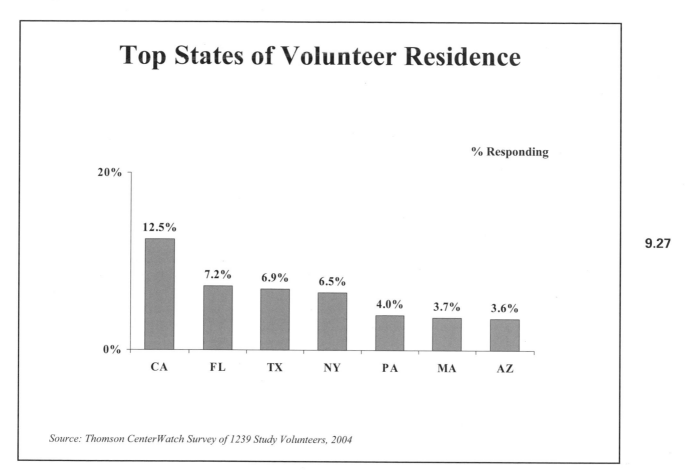

Top States of Volunteer Residence

% Responding

9.27

Source: Thomson CenterWatch Survey of 1239 Study Volunteers, 2004

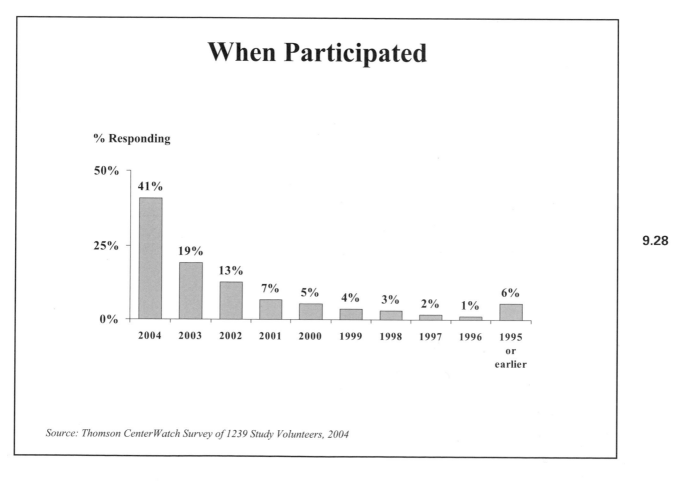

When Participated

% Responding

9.28

Source: Thomson CenterWatch Survey of 1239 Study Volunteers, 2004

9.29

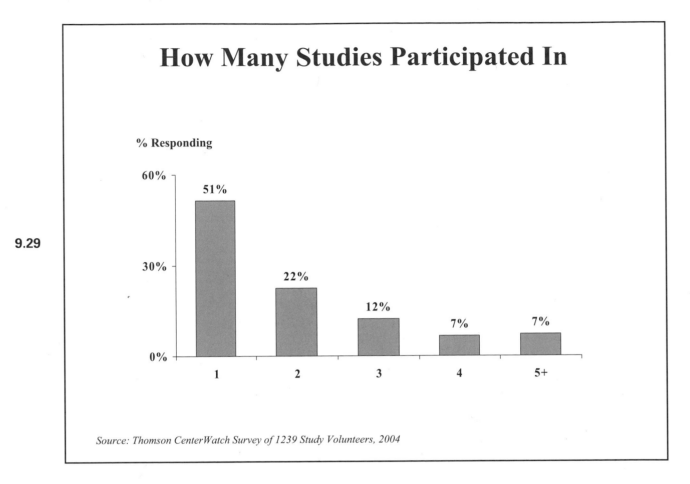

How Many Studies Participated In

% Responding

Source: Thomson CenterWatch Survey of 1239 Study Volunteers, 2004

9.30

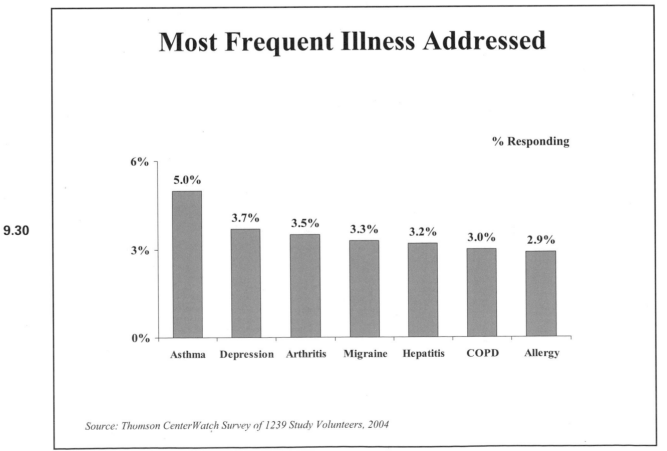

Most Frequent Illness Addressed

% Responding

Source: Thomson CenterWatch Survey of 1239 Study Volunteers, 2004

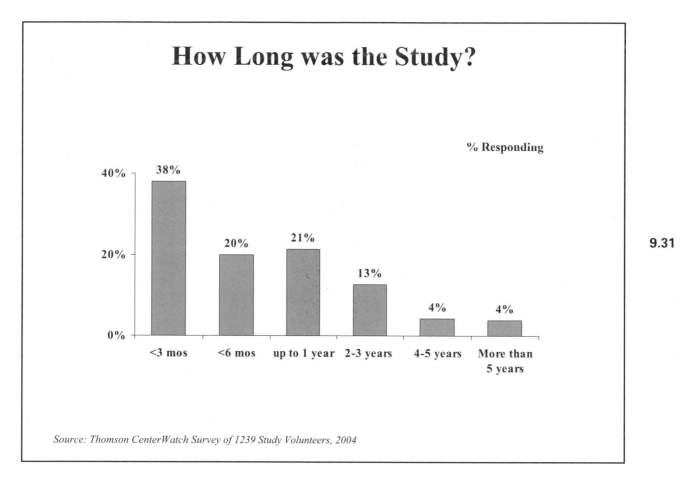

How Long was the Study?

% Responding

Source: Thomson CenterWatch Survey of 1239 Study Volunteers, 2004

9.31

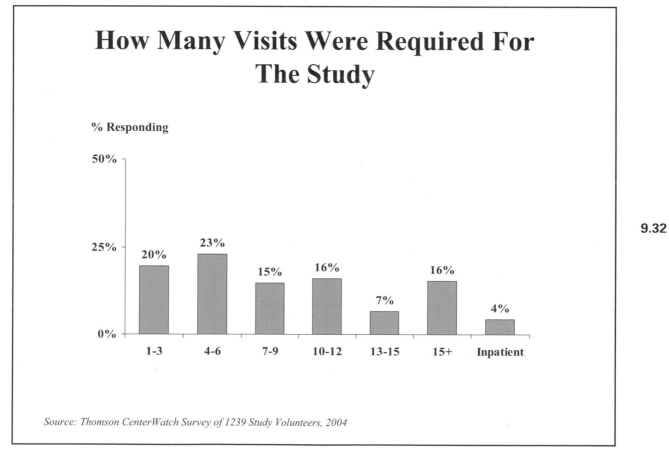

How Many Visits Were Required For The Study

% Responding

Source: Thomson CenterWatch Survey of 1239 Study Volunteers, 2004

9.32

9.33

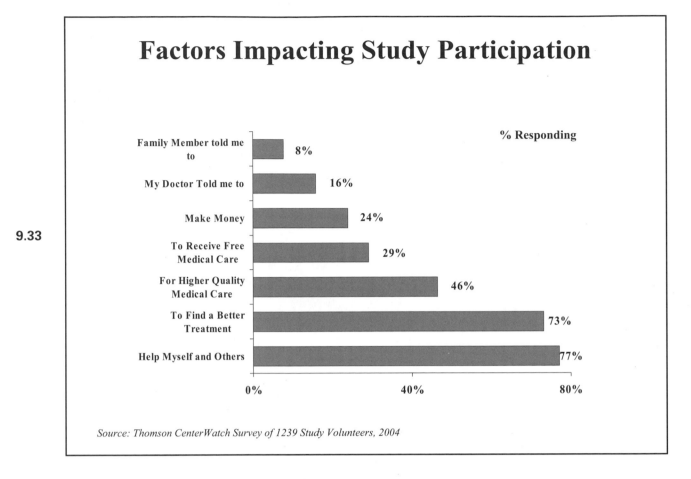

Factors Impacting Study Participation

% Responding

Family Member told me to — 8%
My Doctor Told me to — 16%
Make Money — 24%
To Receive Free Medical Care — 29%
For Higher Quality Medical Care — 46%
To Find a Better Treatment — 73%
Help Myself and Others — 77%

0%   40%   80%

Source: Thomson CenterWatch Survey of 1239 Study Volunteers, 2004

9.34

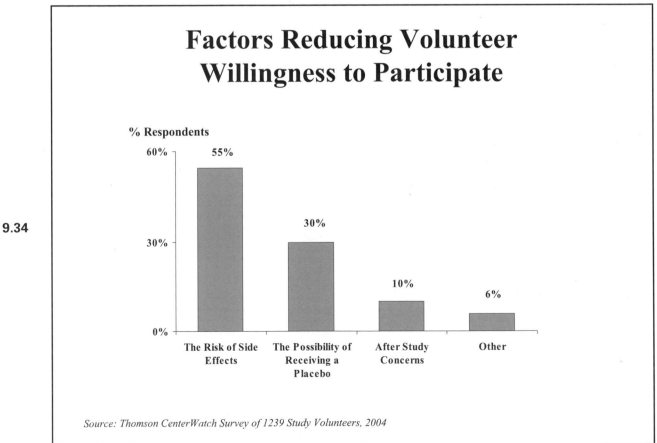

Factors Reducing Volunteer Willingness to Participate

% Respondents

60% —
55% — The Risk of Side Effects
30% — The Possibility of Receiving a Placebo
10% — After Study Concerns
6% — Other

Source: Thomson CenterWatch Survey of 1239 Study Volunteers, 2004

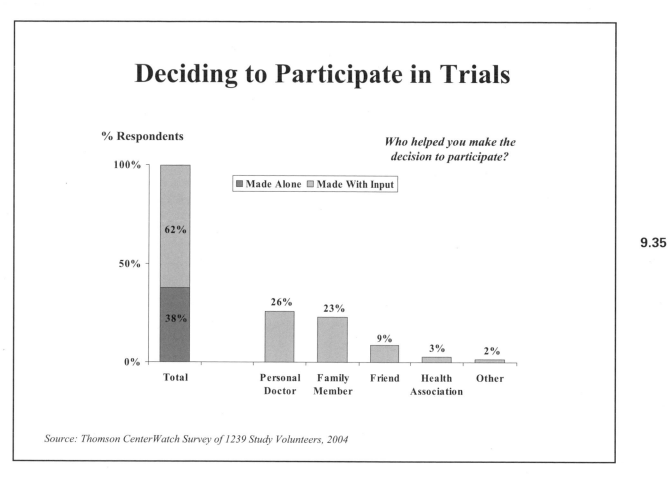

Deciding to Participate in Trials

9.35

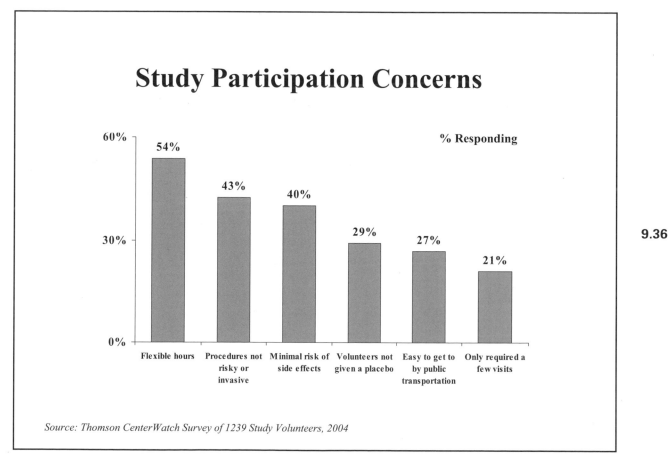

Study Participation Concerns

9.36

9.37

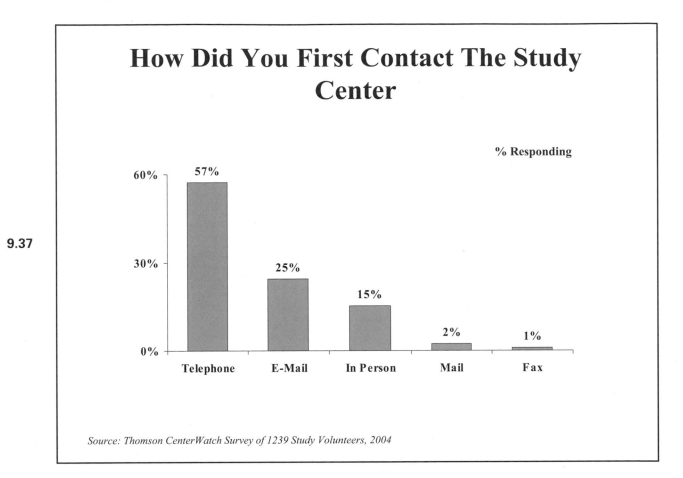

How Did You First Contact The Study Center

% Responding

Source: Thomson CenterWatch Survey of 1239 Study Volunteers, 2004

9.38

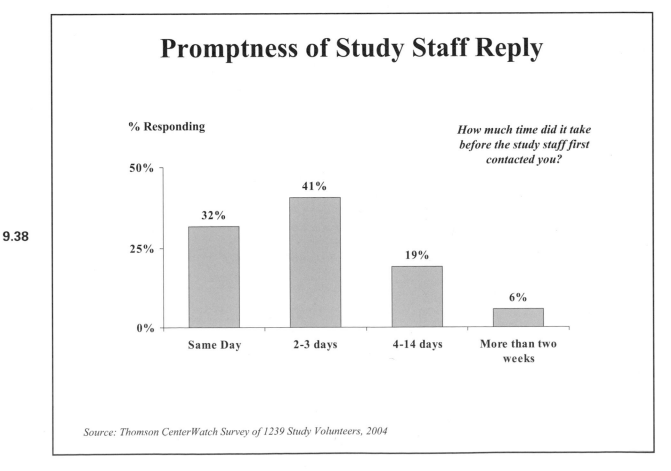

Promptness of Study Staff Reply

% Responding

How much time did it take before the study staff first contacted you?

Source: Thomson CenterWatch Survey of 1239 Study Volunteers, 2004

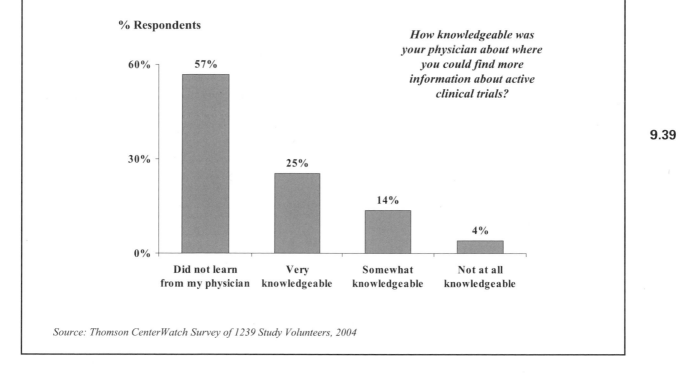

Physicians' Ability To Guide Patients To Additional Information on Trials

% Respondents

How knowledgeable was your physician about where you could find more information about active clinical trials?

Source: Thomson CenterWatch Survey of 1239 Study Volunteers, 2004

9.39

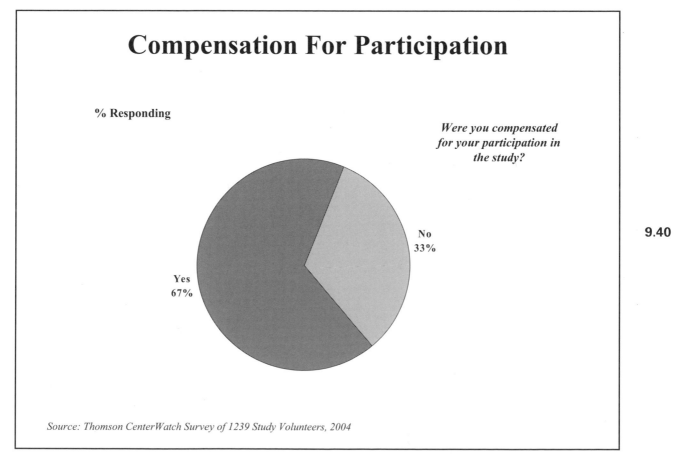

Compensation For Participation

% Responding

Were you compensated for your participation in the study?

Yes 67%

No 33%

Source: Thomson CenterWatch Survey of 1239 Study Volunteers, 2004

9.40

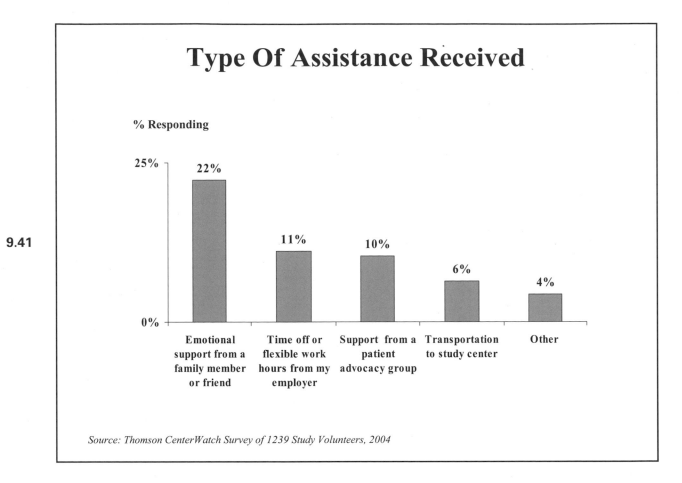

9.41

Type Of Assistance Received

% Responding

Source: Thomson CenterWatch Survey of 1239 Study Volunteers, 2004

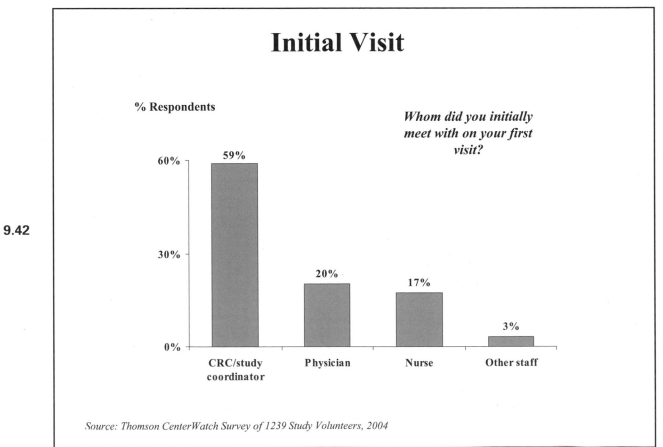

9.42

Initial Visit

% Respondents

Whom did you initially meet with on your first visit?

Source: Thomson CenterWatch Survey of 1239 Study Volunteers, 2004

Informed Consent

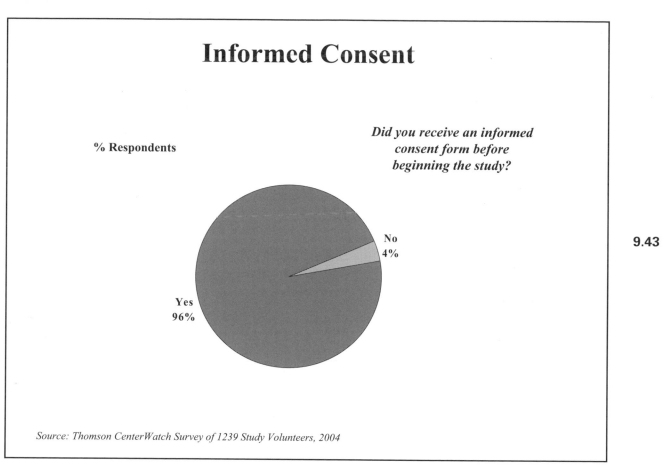

% Respondents

Did you receive an informed consent form before beginning the study?

No
4%

Yes
96%

9.43

Source: Thomson CenterWatch Survey of 1239 Study Volunteers, 2004

Understanding Informed Consent

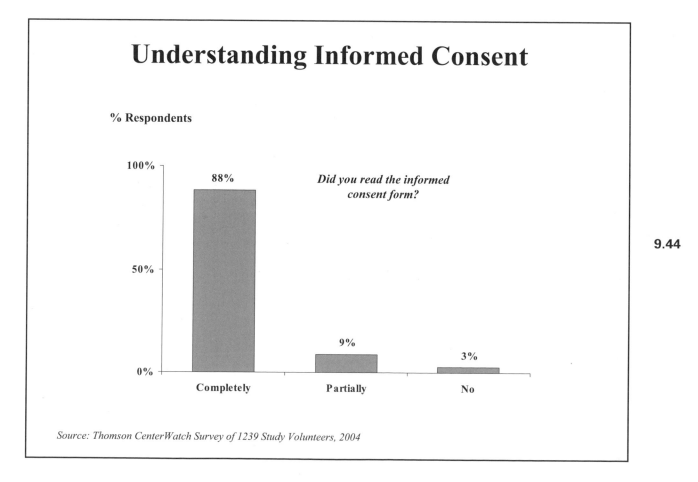

% Respondents

Did you read the informed consent form?

88%

100%

50%

0%

9%

3%

Completely   Partially   No

9.44

Source: Thomson CenterWatch Survey of 1239 Study Volunteers, 2004

9.45

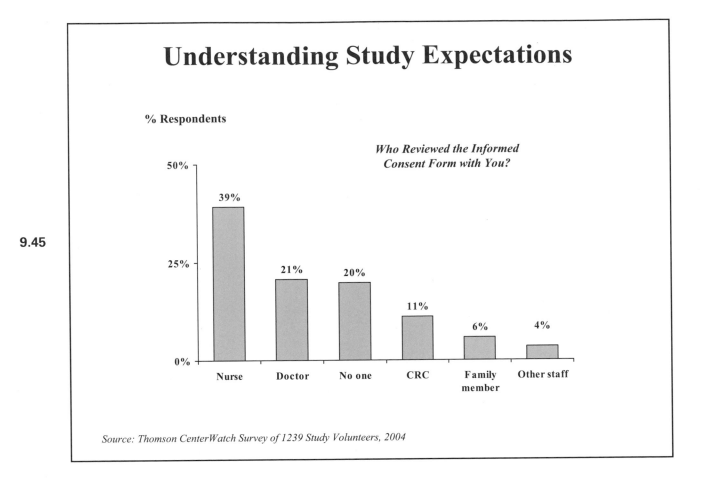

9.46

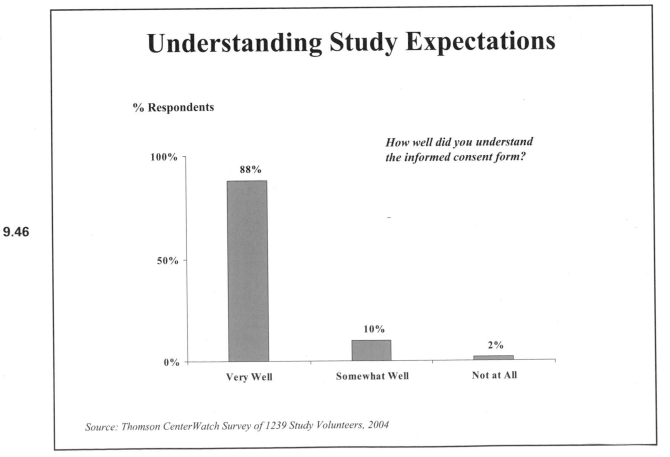

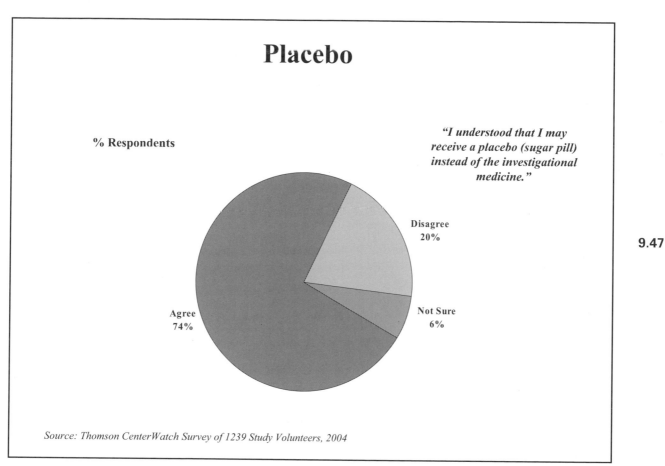

Placebo

% Respondents

"I understood that I may receive a placebo (sugar pill) instead of the investigational medicine."

Disagree 20%

Not Sure 6%

Agree 74%

Source: Thomson CenterWatch Survey of 1239 Study Volunteers, 2004

9.47

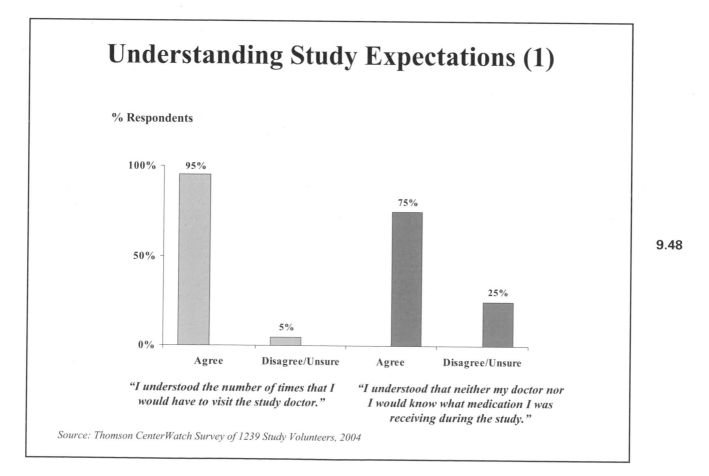

Understanding Study Expectations (1)

% Respondents

95%

75%

25%

5%

| Agree | Disagree/Unsure | Agree | Disagree/Unsure |

"I understood the number of times that I would have to visit the study doctor."

"I understood that neither my doctor nor I would know what medication I was receiving during the study."

Source: Thomson CenterWatch Survey of 1239 Study Volunteers, 2004

9.48

9.49

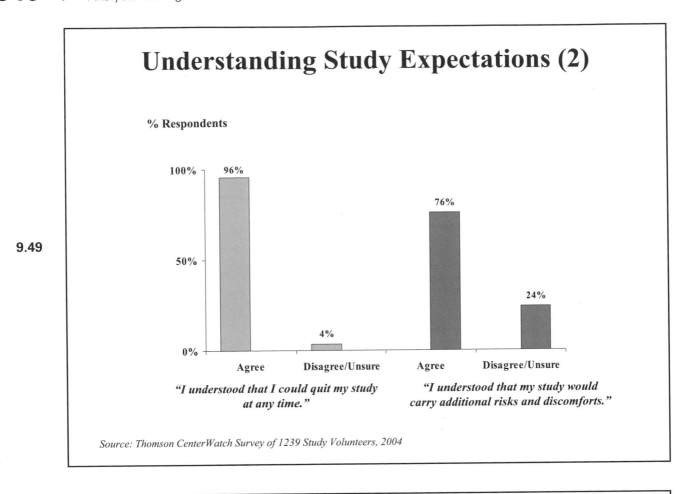

Understanding Study Expectations (2)

% Respondents

Source: Thomson CenterWatch Survey of 1239 Study Volunteers, 2004

9.50

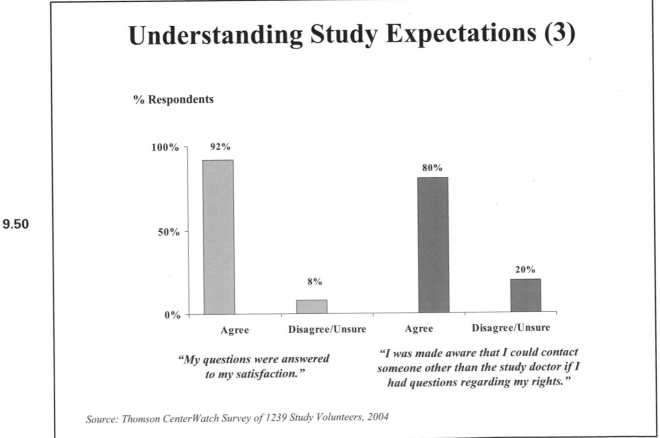

Understanding Study Expectations (3)

% Respondents

Source: Thomson CenterWatch Survey of 1239 Study Volunteers, 2004

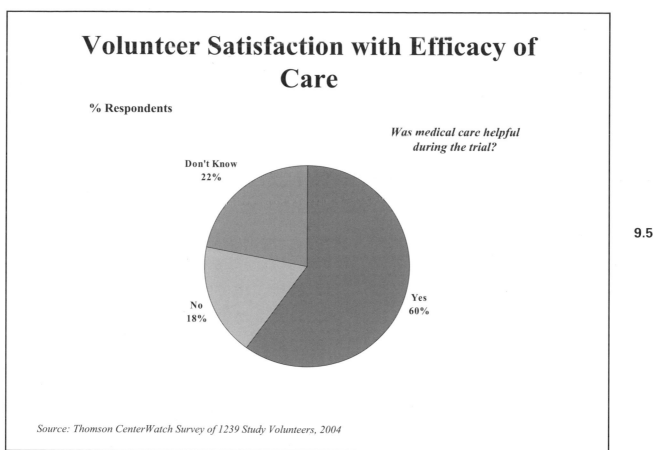

Volunteer Satisfaction with Efficacy of Care

% Respondents

Was medical care helpful during the trial?

Don't Know
22%

No
18%

Yes
60%

9.51

Source: Thomson CenterWatch Survey of 1239 Study Volunteers, 2004

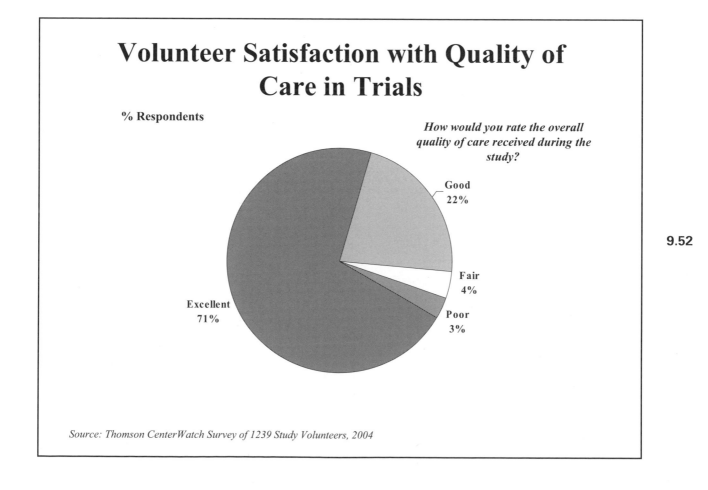

Volunteer Satisfaction with Quality of Care in Trials

% Respondents

How would you rate the overall quality of care received during the study?

Good
22%

Fair
4%

Poor
3%

Excellent
71%

9.52

Source: Thomson CenterWatch Survey of 1239 Study Volunteers, 2004

9.53

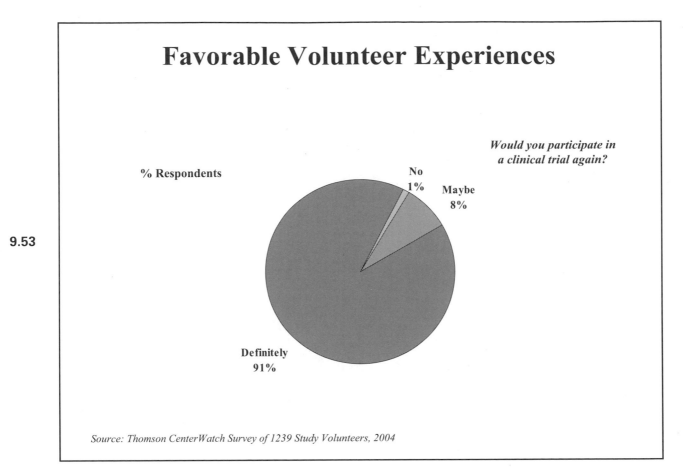

Favorable Volunteer Experiences

% Respondents

Would you participate in a clinical trial again?

No 1%

Maybe 8%

Definitely 91%

Source: Thomson CenterWatch Survey of 1239 Study Volunteers, 2004

9.54

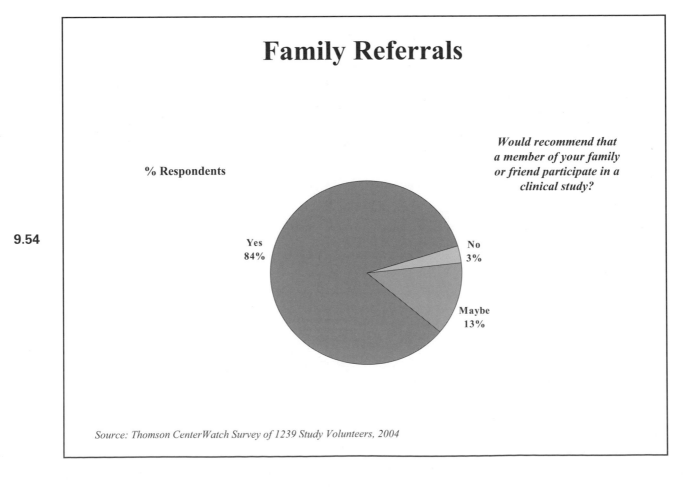

Family Referrals

% Respondents

Would recommend that a member of your family or friend participate in a clinical study?

Yes 84%

No 3%

Maybe 13%

Source: Thomson CenterWatch Survey of 1239 Study Volunteers, 2004

Clinical Trial Participation
Estimated Total Participants by Country, 2003

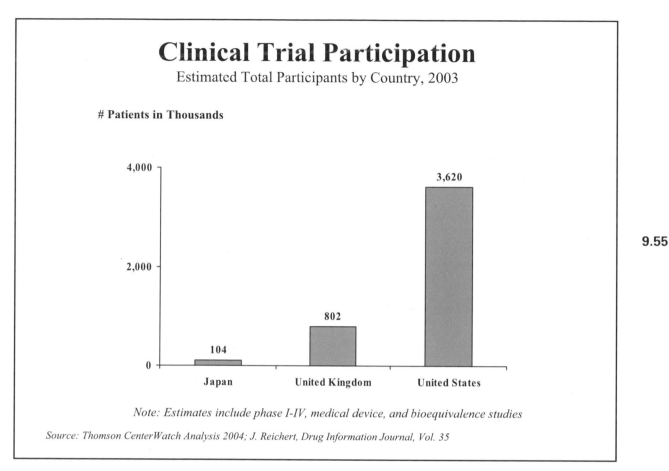

 # Patients in Thousands

Note: Estimates include phase I-IV, medical device, and bioequivalence studies

Source: Thomson CenterWatch Analysis 2004; J. Reichert, Drug Information Journal, Vol. 35

9.55

Average Number of Patients Per NDA
Number of Evaluable Patients

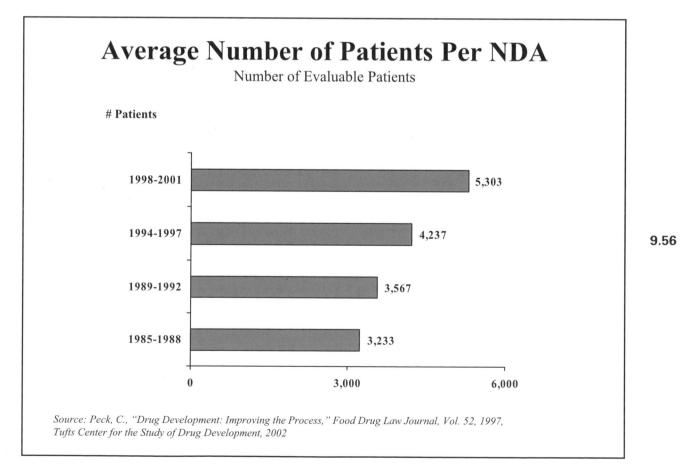

 # Patients

Source: Peck, C., "Drug Development: Improving the Process," Food Drug Law Journal, Vol. 52, 1997,
Tufts Center for the Study of Drug Development, 2002

9.56

9.57

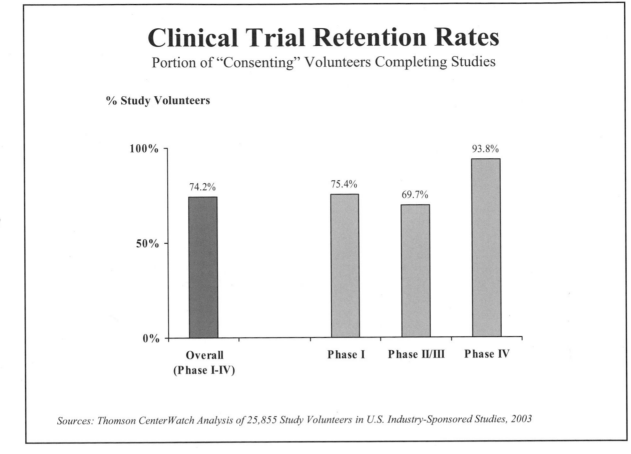

Clinical Trial Retention Rates

Portion of "Consenting" Volunteers Completing Studies

% Study Volunteers

Sources: Thomson CenterWatch Analysis of 25,855 Study Volunteers in U.S. Industry-Sponsored Studies, 2003

Regulatory

Bioequivalence Sector Breaks Out

Once considered just a subset of the phase I market, bioequivalence has grown and evolved with its own set of unique challenges. If the market continues its impressive growth, bioequivalence trial work will mature into a healthy sector in its own right. As sponsor companies continue to want to alter their products in the dynamic branded vs. generic marketplace, the BE industry will be fed a continuous supply of project opportunities.

Tied closely to the booming generic pharmaceutical industry, the companies servicing BE trials are enjoying their customers' success. A sustained growth in the global generics industry could promise continued contract opportunities in a sector already struggling to keep up with the demands of a strong phase I industry.

Bioequivalence Sector Breaks Out

By Stephen DeSantis
Published February 2006

The market for bioequivalence (BE) studies is on the rise due to recent trends in the pharmaceutical industry. Tied closely to the booming generic pharmaceutical industry, the companies servicing BE trials are enjoying their customers' success. Sustained growth in the global generics industry promises continued contract opportunities in a sector already racing to keep up with the demands of a strong phase I industry. In addition, due in part to increased generic competition, biopharmaceutical companies are developing new formulations, dosage forms and combinational products as never before, helping to create a new drug delivery sector.

The expected increase in drug candidates requiring BE testing and the entrance of biogenerics in the next few years should also contribute to an uptick in the sector.

Given recent regulatory developments in Europe, some contract research organization (CROs) are anticipating guidance in the U.S. that would require additional safety and efficacy studies for biogenerics, giving a whole new book of business to those who are prepared and experienced in the BE sector. The culmination of these industry trends may lead to a new era in what has been a modest, albeit stable, sector in clinical trials.

In fact, for many players across the clinical trial industry, from CROs to small phase I sites, central labs and information technology vendors, the BE market may just become a lot more interesting. "There is a real market out there now. It is just our estimate, but we think it is around $1 billion for all

of the bioequivalence business, which includes the clinical and bioanalytical work," Marc Lebel, Pharm.D., president of SFBC Anapharm, a CRO based in Quebec City, Quebec, Canada.

BE studies are required for any marketed chemical substance intended for human use that differs from its approved version(s), either in its mode of delivery, its manufacture or in its actual chemical make-up. To prove to regulatory authorities that the new product is equivalent to the original substance in safety and efficacy, candidates must undergo both bioanalytical testing in the laboratory, as well as clinical studies in humans. For traditional chemically based drugs, bioequivalence trials are typically short, single-dose safety studies in healthy volunteers. For most solid oral formulations, a typical testing protocol calls for a randomized, single-dose, crossover design conducted after an overnight fast, for which half of the subjects initially receive the innovator product. After a sufficient period, subjects are crossed over to receive the generic formulation. BE studies involving more complex drugs or products that deviate from the more traditional oral formulations require more extensive testing.

From a clinical perspective, BE studies closely resemble phase I trials in healthy volunteers, and research is conducted mostly by CROs with access to bioanalytical labs and plenty of beds. In the August 2004 issue of The CenterWatch Monthly, Thomson CenterWatch reported a rapid growth in the phase I market due, in part, by the need for sponsors to validate promising drug candidates earlier in the drug development process. Through running additional phase I studies, sponsors hoped to speed up the process of go/no go decision making, thereby reducing time and money spent on drug failures farther down the line. "The phase I market is pretty hot right now, and the bioequivalence industry is very similar. The generics market is putting a lot more pressure on phase I units, in a good way. The BE market is definitely cyclical, but I have never seen a sustained growth like this before. I can safely say it has probably doubled just in the last five years," said Chris Hendy, Ph.D., president and CEO of Novum Research Services. Novum is a CRO that specializes in conducting phase I and BE studies for both generic and brand pharmaceutical clients.

BE Trials and Tribulations

Those with experience managing BE trials rely heavily on their scientific experience and bioanalytical laboratory capabilities. Unlike some sponsors, generic manufacturers expect CROs to design and implement a trial protocol on their own. "Very, very few generic type companies sent us protocols," said Hendy of Novum.

The knowledge and experience in designing assays to measure a multitude of substances in the human body is an asset to a company conducting bioequivalency studies. "A lot of clinics can do the dosing. Give them a protocol, they recruit the volunteers, and they observe them and draw their blood. And you're done. Whereas with assay method, it is very drug-specific. You really have to have the scientific expertise and the technology to be able to develop an appropriate method that is acceptable to the regulators. It is a lot more critical," said Lorelei Lutter, director, business development at CanTest a Canada-based CRO that specializes in bioequivalence studies.

Because one blockbuster drug patent expiration can lead to a flood of multiple new contracts from generic clients, CROs need to be flexible with resources to ensure they can quickly come up to speed. Here, available beds can become a major issue. "A lot of generic companies are doing multiple projects in parallel, so they are looking for multi-source providers. We see a huge impact in terms of the availability of clinical space within the next three to five years. I think the demand will be much bigger than the supply out there," said Dr. Gregory Holmes, executive vice president, clinical operations for SFBC International.

Generics Drive the BE Market

Traditionally, the BE sector has been in lockstep with any rise or decline of the generic drug sector, based on the cyclical nature of drug patent expiration clusters. The modern generics industry has the Drug Price Competition and Patent Restoration Act, enacted in the U.S. in 1984, as its foundation. The law, more commonly referred to as the Hatch-Waxman Act, allowed manufacturers to submit abbreviated new drug applications (aNDAs) for generic versions of pharmaceutical products approved after 1962. The submission includes detailed manufacturing information, laboratory analysis and bioequivalence studies before proving the product was equivalent to the branded version.

"I think the spike or the dramatic increase in the number of aNDAs submitted over the past two years is partially due to the number of brand drugs coming off patent and we will see 2008 to 2009 as peak years," added Gordon Johnson, vice president for regulatory affairs for the Generic Pharmaceutical Association (GPhMA). As companies seek to submit an increasing number of aNDAs, CROs will continue to see a steady flow of outsourcing opportunities. "When a blockbuster goes off patent, there are typically 10 to 15 aNDAs approved for that product. That can lead to up to 30 studies. So when you look at multiple products going off patent, the number of bio-studies goes up substantially," stated Johnson.

Generic drugs have represented more than 50% of the overall pharmaceutical market for the past several years; yet they amount to only 12% of the overall cost of prescription drugs in 2005. These cheaper versions of proven medications offer the healthcare industry, particularly the payors, huge saving by providing cheaper alternatives. The business is one of the fastest growing sectors of the drug industry, as major blockbuster drugs marketed in the late 1990s are beginning to lose patent protection. "Our generic client base has been providing us with all of the work that we need. We have no marketing, sales or business development people. We don't need to. That is how fast the market is growing," said John Hendy, of Novum.

A Surge in Consolidations

The Hatch-Waxman Act established additional provisions in an attempt to incentivize generic drug production. The act states that the first company to submit an aNDA with the U.S. Food and Drug Administration (FDA) has the exclusive right to market the generic drug for 180 days before another approval is granted. "So that becomes the race for who gets to start the BE study first, who gets to file first, who gets approved first. Because then the reward can be really big, especially if it is a blockbuster drug," said CanTest's Lorelei. Fierce competition amongst generic companies, along with other industry pressures, has forced a recent surge in their consolidation through high profile mergers and acquisitions. The phenomenon is streamlining the process of contracting bioequivalence work to CROs.

"Because of these [generics company] consolidations, we are seeing a change in the number of actual customers. This removes a lot of the redundancies, so before...20 companies may have been working on one generic drug...now there may be half or even less," said Lutter of Cantest.

Although the generic pharmaceuticals have been the primary engine that drives the BE sector, pharmaceutical companies need to outsource bioequivalence work as well. Pharmaceutical companies, that change their branded drug's manufacturing process or facility or alter the drug's formulation or dosage must also prove equivalency through BE trials. "There is a lot of bioequivalence on the branded side as well, in their final product when they go for submission. That is a big part of our business too," said Holmes.

Even after a branded drug is approved, it may not have been clinically tested in the final form or dosage that ends up on pharmacy shelves. And because medication used in double-blind placebo-controlled trials needs to be blinded from both patient and investigator, the product is often not manufactured in its final "designer" form. In order to be consumed by patients, these final products need to be quickly tested for bioequivalence. "If you think about it, the branded version of what they put out is most definitely not what they used in all those trials. So they have to do the same tests as the generics would do," added Holmes.

Competition Is Win/Win for BE

As the worldwide generic drug market has increased, the competition between pharmaceutical companies and generic manufacturers has heated up as well. All this is good news for CROs and other companies in the clinical trial space that may benefit from the way these two sectors compete.

Typically, as the patent on branded drugs expires, a nearly identical copy has already been developed and is ready to enter the market. Under the Hatch-Waxman Act, a company can seek approval from the FDA to market a generic drug before the expiration of a patent if they can prove the patent is invalid or has not been infringed upon. The provisions have created an "arms race" of strategies designed to protect or attack a branded drugs market share. Pharmaceutical companies are incentivized to pursue dosage enhancements and formulation changes as ways to extend a product's lifespan after the original patent protection has expired. This offers prescribers, and their patients, a benefit for staying with the more expensive branded drug. "For companies that do BE it is a good thing, because you are not assaying one drug but two and this also increases the size of the contract," stated Lebel.

Developing more effective and convenient methods of delivering medicine has always been a goal of the healthcare industry. Besides the obvious patient conveniences in developing such dosage forms as extended- and controlled-release, these products can also enhance compliance and tolerability. A once daily dosage form versus a four-times daily form, for example, can reduce side effects and increase the likelihood patients will take their medications as prescribed. Each new dosage change or re-formulation submitted by the innovator pharmaceutical company requires a fresh round of bioequivalence of testing just as their generic counterparts do, adding more opportunities for companies in the space. As generic competition increases, biopharmaceutical companies will strive harder to maintain their market share through re-formulations and dosage enhancements. "The continued entry of novel formulations, combinational and biogenerics are going to come into play in the next two to five years, we know that," remarked Holmes.

Above and beyond the traditional dosage and formulation options that both generic and branded pharmaceutical companies can produce, the industry has seen a recent wave of innovation in drug delivery technologies designed to enhance a treatment's convenience, safety and even efficacy. With the influx of less conventional drug delivery methods, proving a product's equivalence can become much more challenging. "The clinical aspects of bioequivalence studies are not small; it depends on the variability of the drug. Sometimes the variability is due to the formulations. In the case of patches, for example, you have to have a very large subject population because the variability is very high. And for some combinational products you actually have to conduct two or three studies," said Lebel.

Novel Drug Delivery Systems on the Rise

In particular, the development of novel transdermal delivery systems has been a fast growing market segment for some time. By eliminating the use of painful needles or the hassles of ingesting oral tablets regularly for extended periods, delivering medication through the skin has been well received by consumers.

This type of delivery approach can be especially effective in elderly patients who do not take their medication because they have difficulty swallowing or are noncompliant due to memory loss or dementia. Pharmaceutical companies Ono Pharmaceutical and the Japanese unit of Novartis

are jointly developing the first transdermal patch for the treatment of Alzheimer's disease. The product uses the patch to deliver Exelon (rivastigmine), a drug already approved in oral formulations, and is currently in phase II trials in Japan.

This is a trend that is adding to the size and complexities of clinical trials designed to test bioequivalency. Delivering medication through the skin, instead of directly into the bloodstream, creates some unique challenges in measuring drug levels. "A good example is in dermatology trials, where you can't measure the product in the bloodstream. So how do you get those generics approved? You have to do clinical equivalency trials where you actually

have to start looking at patient populations and really do a type of efficacy trial," said Holmes.

Biogenerics

As the biotech industry prepares for the eventual arrival of generic versions of their marketed biologic products, players in the BE industry are starting to anticipate the opportunities coming their way. Dozens of marketed biologics have lost patent protection, yet there has been no biogeneric product approved in the U.S. to date. The approval of any biogeneric product in the U.S. has been stalled by the FDA's lack of regulatory guidelines, which, if created, would reduce the risk for generic companies to file. "In general the generics company comes to us four or five years in advance of the product coming into the public domain. So we know what's coming, and right now we are only getting requests from European companies. Some companies in the U.S. are looking to submit, but the FDA is late in the game," stated Lebel.

If and when a solid regulatory framework is established in the U.S., there might well be a backlog of business heading towards CROs that conduct BE studies. "I believe CROs and sites, particularly ones that do traditional phase I and bioequivalence studies, will be the first to benefit," said Alek Safarian, CEO, Novotech, an Australia-based CRO.

Marketed biological candidates currently of interest to generic companies would include such products consisting of monoclonal antibodies, synthetic proteins and therapeutic vaccines. More advanced treatments such as stem cell transplantation, gene therapy and the promises of nano-technology, paint a picture of challenges generic companies will face in the distant future. "As biologics become more of an opportunity, and as FDA provides regulatory guidance, you can assume that there will be an increase in the need for these types of studies," said Johnson of the GPhMA.

Beyond the increase in the sheer volume of products needing equivalence testing, biogenerics may alter the BE industry in other ways. Even small differences in the production of biologically based products may alter the generic drug's safety and efficacy. This makes it difficult to prove biosimilarity, and thus equivalence. Many experts predict that the approval of biogeneric drugs will require varying degrees of clinical testing, depending on differing regulatory requirements from country to country. Not only would this create an increase in the traditional clinical components associated with bioequivalence work, it could force these trials to prove equivalent efficacy as well.

Proving a generic product has the identical efficacy to the reference drug, is something most BE studies haven't needed to accomplish, because traditional small molecule pharmacology has been relatively straightforward. "The FDA is really trying to contend with whether large clinical trials are necessary or not for bioequivalence, or perhaps just with a specific group of biologics. My guess is that additional [trials] will be required for some, if not for many," said Lutter.

Given the likelihood of additional clinical testing to prove bioequivalence and an increase in clinical trial opportunities, CROs focusing on BE and others looking at the market are paying attention to how the market develops. "We've been looking into that, it is certainly something that we've already done some scientific investigation on with some of the biotech products that we think will be of particular interest to the generic industry," said Hendy.

10.01

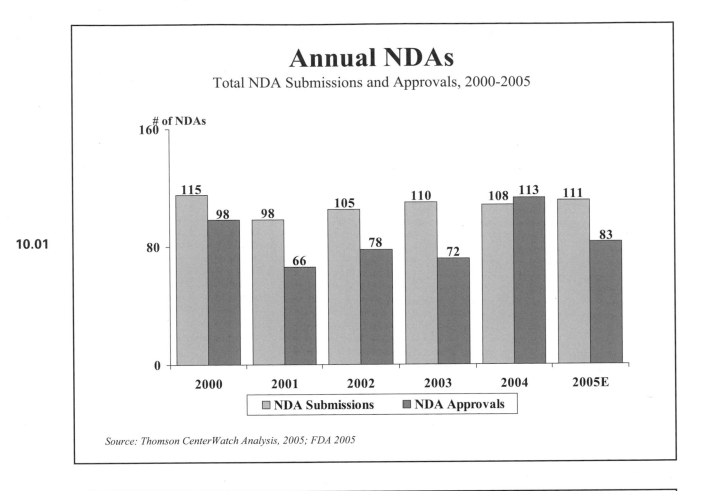

Annual NDAs
Total NDA Submissions and Approvals, 2000-2005

of NDAs

Source: Thomson CenterWatch Analysis, 2005; FDA 2005

10.02

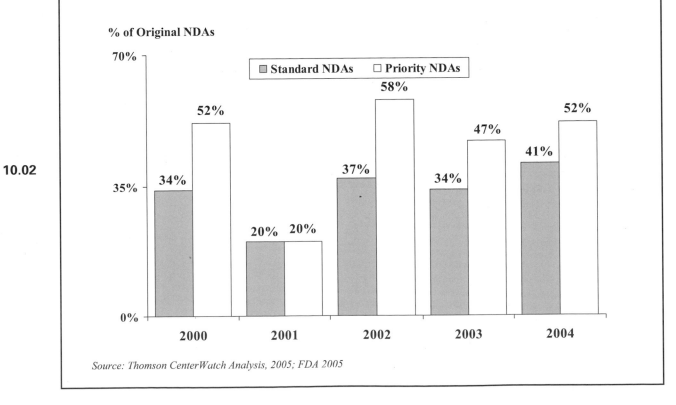

NDAs Approved by Review Status

% of Original NDAs

Source: Thomson CenterWatch Analysis, 2005; FDA 2005

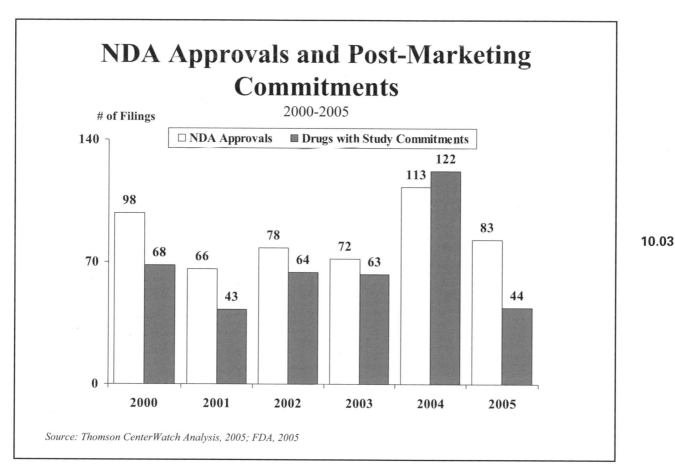

NDA Approvals and Post-Marketing Commitments
2000-2005

# of Filings

Legend: □ NDA Approvals ■ Drugs with Study Commitments

Source: Thomson CenterWatch Analysis, 2005; FDA, 2005

10.03

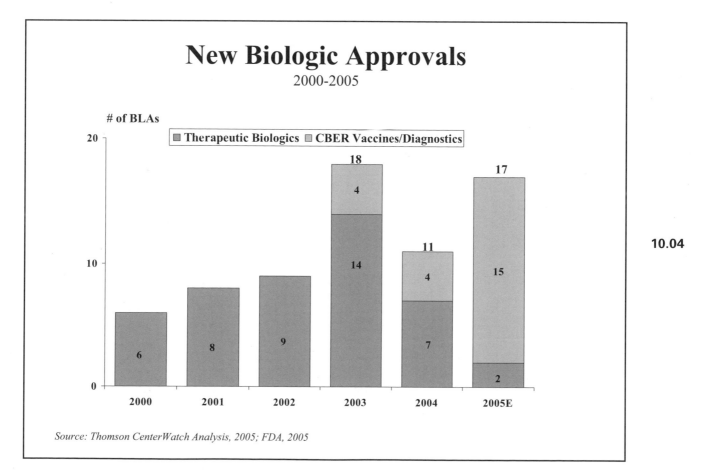

New Biologic Approvals
2000-2005

# of BLAs

Legend: ■ Therapeutic Biologics ■ CBER Vaccines/Diagnostics

Source: Thomson CenterWatch Analysis, 2005; FDA, 2005

10.04

10.05

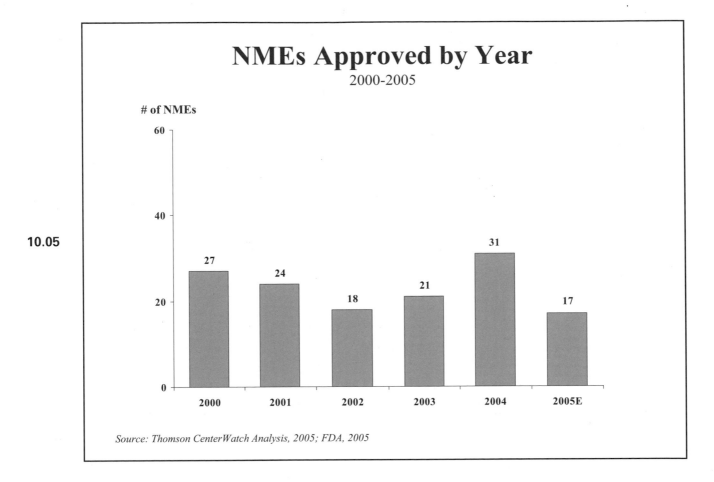

NMEs Approved by Year
2000-2005

of NMEs

Source: Thomson CenterWatch Analysis, 2005; FDA, 2005

10.06

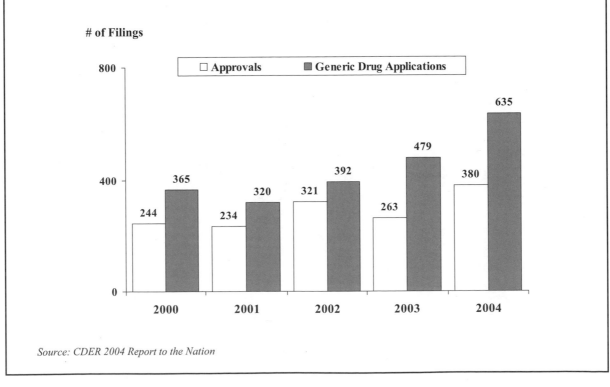

Generic Submissions and Approvals
2000-2004

of Filings

Approvals   Generic Drug Applications

Source: CDER 2004 Report to the Nation

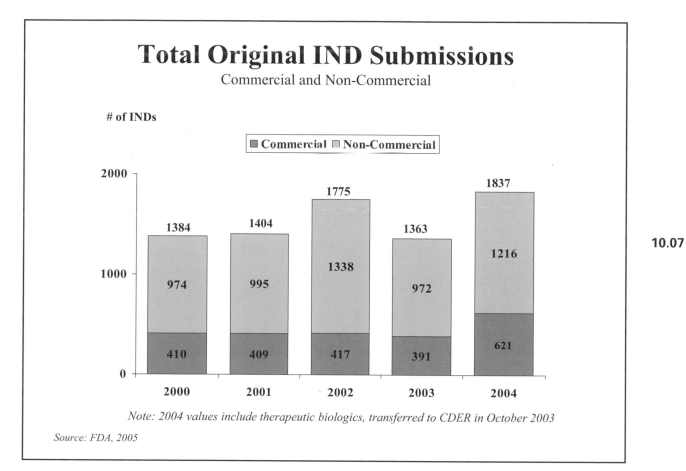

Total Original IND Submissions
Commercial and Non-Commercial

# of INDs

■ Commercial ■ Non-Commercial

Note: 2004 values include therapeutic biologics, transferred to CDER in October 2003

Source: FDA, 2005

10.07

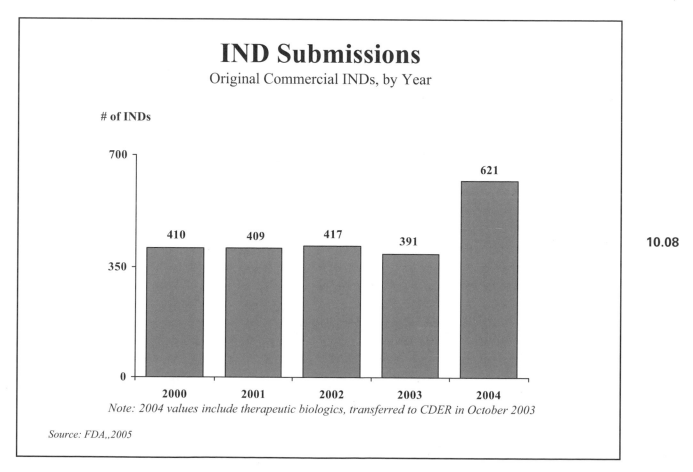

IND Submissions
Original Commercial INDs, by Year

# of INDs

Note: 2004 values include therapeutic biologics, transferred to CDER in October 2003

Source: FDA,,2005

10.08

10.09

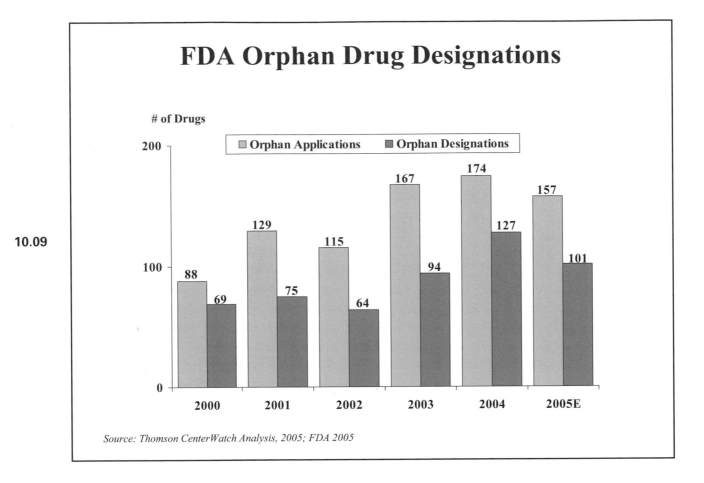

10.10

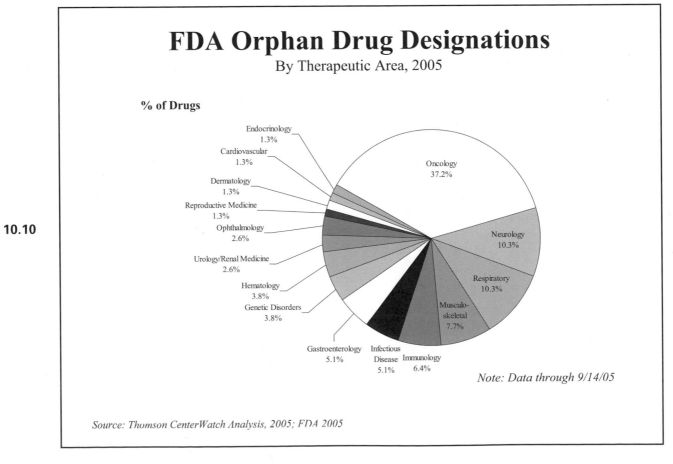

FDA Orphan Drug Designations

Designations Granted by Therapeutic Area, 2000-2005

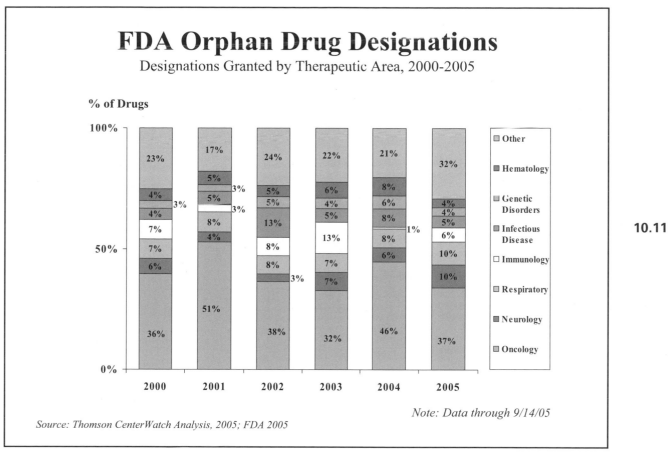

% of Drugs

Legend: Other, Hematology, Genetic Disorders, Infectious Disease, Immunology, Respiratory, Neurology, Oncology

Note: Data through 9/14/05

Source: Thomson CenterWatch Analysis, 2005; FDA 2005

10.11

FDA Fast Track Designations

Predicted Outcome of Fast Track applications, 2000-2005

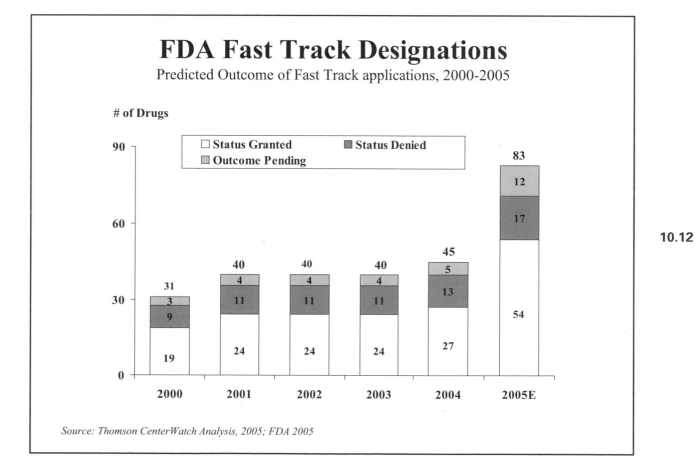

# of Drugs

Legend: Status Granted, Status Denied, Outcome Pending

Source: Thomson CenterWatch Analysis, 2005; FDA 2005

10.12

10.13

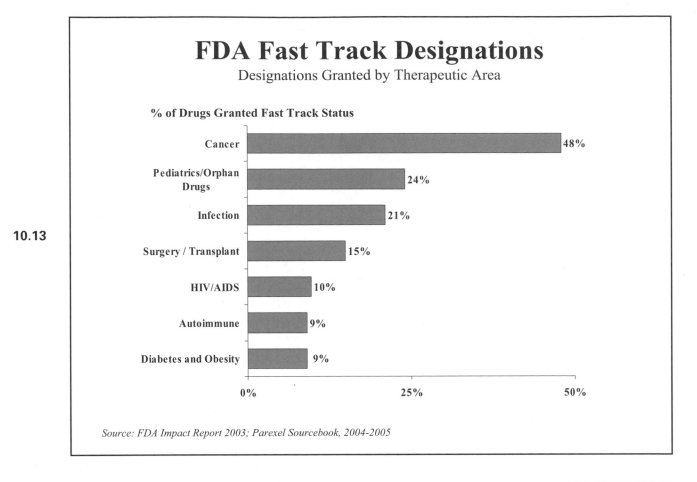

FDA Fast Track Designations
Designations Granted by Therapeutic Area

% of Drugs Granted Fast Track Status

Therapeutic Area	%
Cancer	48%
Pediatrics/Orphan Drugs	24%
Infection	21%
Surgery / Transplant	15%
HIV/AIDS	10%
Autoimmune	9%
Diabetes and Obesity	9%

Source: FDA Impact Report 2003; Parexel Sourcebook, 2004-2005

10.14

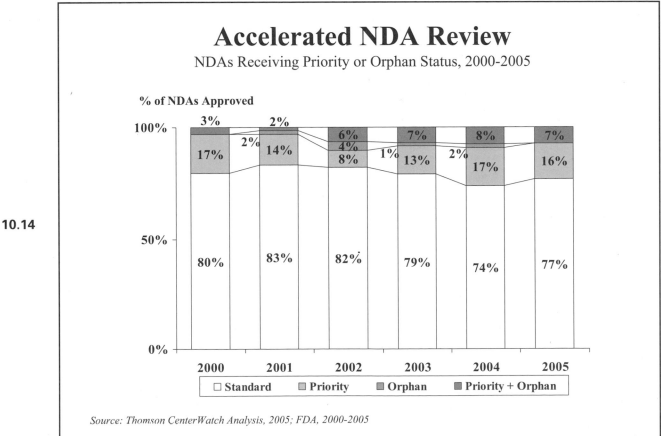

Accelerated NDA Review
NDAs Receiving Priority or Orphan Status, 2000-2005

% of NDAs Approved

	2000	2001	2002	2003	2004	2005
Priority + Orphan	3%	2%	6%	7%	8%	7%
Orphan		2%	4%			
Priority	17%	14%	8%	1%	2%	16%
				13%	17%	
Standard	80%	83%	82%	79%	74%	77%

Legend: ☐ Standard ▨ Priority ▨ Orphan ▪ Priority + Orphan

Source: Thomson CenterWatch Analysis, 2005; FDA, 2000-2005

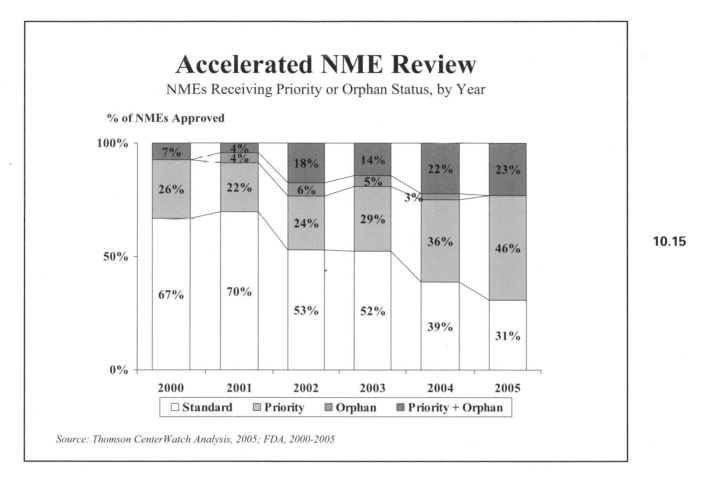

Accelerated NME Review
NMEs Receiving Priority or Orphan Status, by Year

% of NMEs Approved

10.15

Source: Thomson CenterWatch Analysis, 2005; FDA, 2000-2005

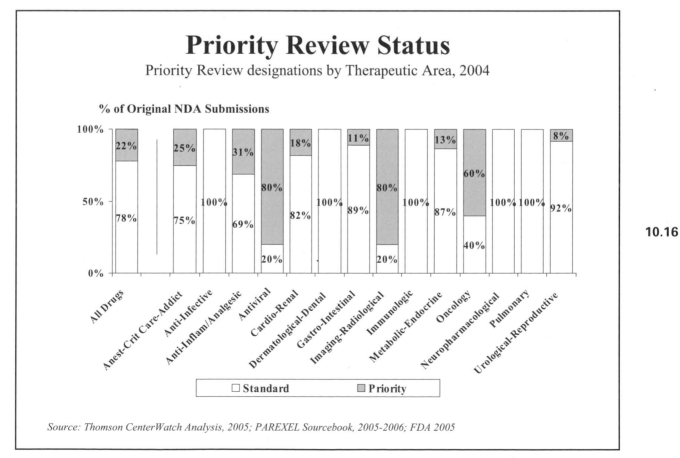

Priority Review Status
Priority Review designations by Therapeutic Area, 2004

% of Original NDA Submissions

10.16

Source: Thomson CenterWatch Analysis, 2005; PAREXEL Sourcebook, 2005-2006; FDA 2005

10.17

Priority NDA/BLA Approval Rates
Percentage Approved per 6-Month Interval, by Year of Submission

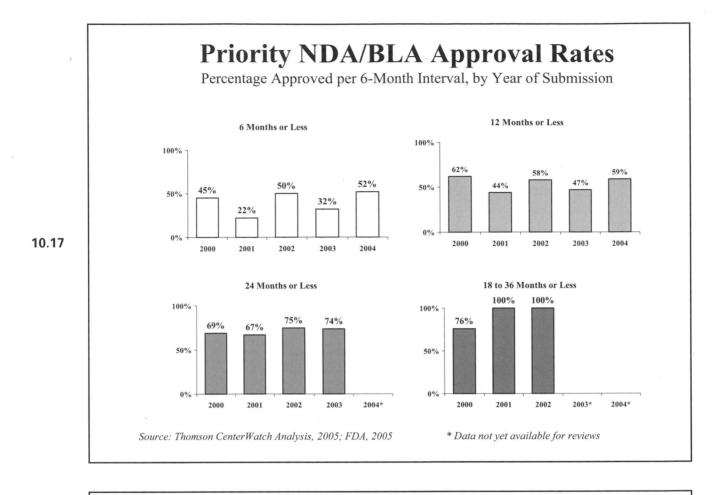

Source: Thomson CenterWatch Analysis, 2005; FDA, 2005

* Data not yet available for reviews

10.18

Results of First Review of NDAs
1998-2004

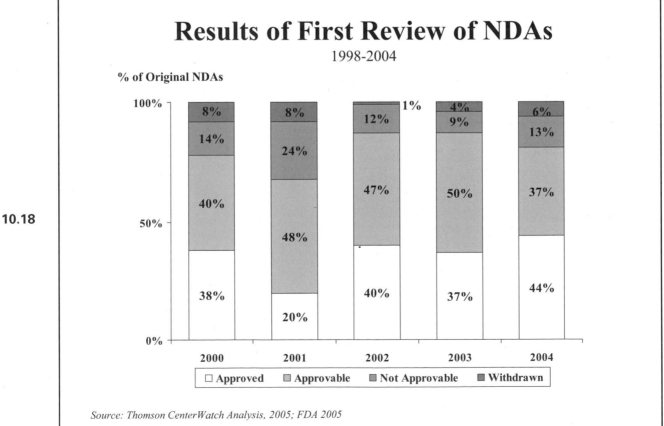

Source: Thomson CenterWatch Analysis, 2005; FDA 2005

Standard NDA/BLA Approval Rates

Percentage Approved per 6-Month Interval, by Year of Submission

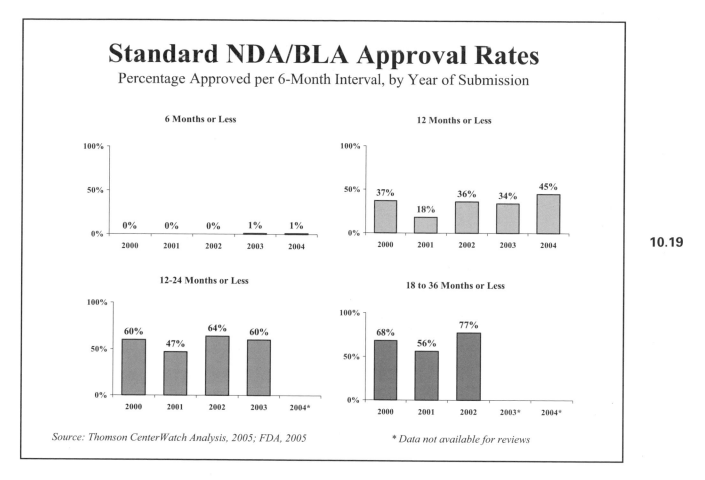

6 Months or Less

12 Months or Less

12-24 Months or Less

18 to 36 Months or Less

Source: Thomson CenterWatch Analysis, 2005; FDA, 2005

* Data not available for reviews

10.19

NMEs and Domestic R&D Expenditure

1999-2004

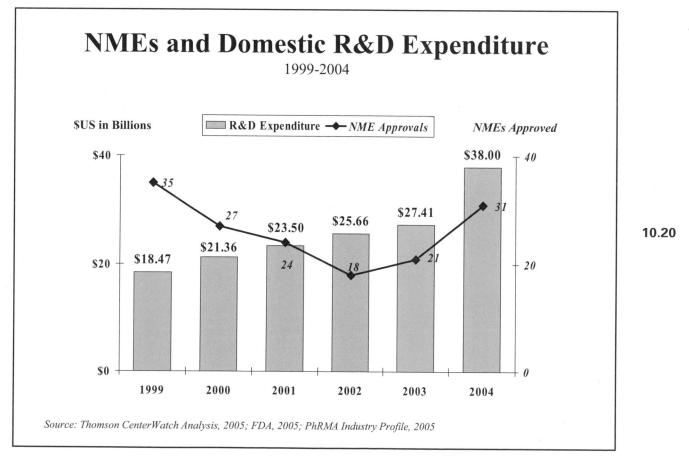

Source: Thomson CenterWatch Analysis, 2005; FDA, 2005; PhRMA Industry Profile, 2005

10.20

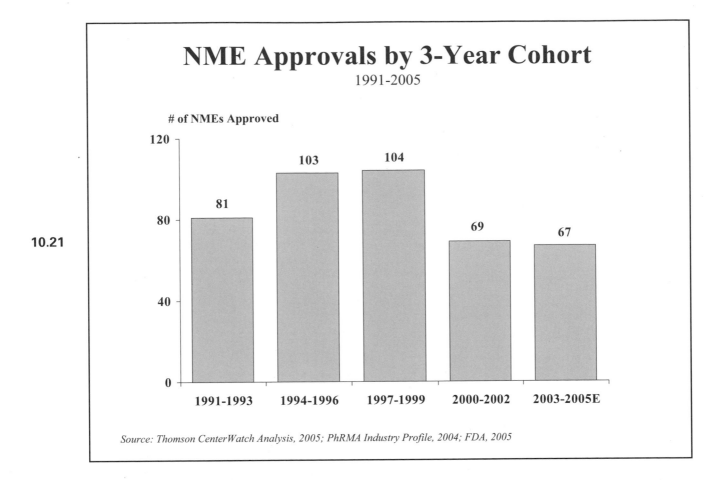

10.21

NME Approvals by 3-Year Cohort
1991-2005

of NMEs Approved

Source: Thomson CenterWatch Analysis, 2005; PhRMA Industry Profile, 2004; FDA, 2005

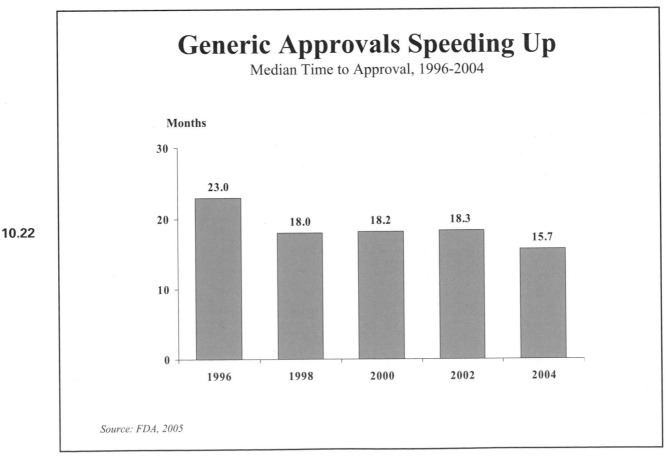

10.22

Generic Approvals Speeding Up
Median Time to Approval, 1996-2004

Months

Source: FDA, 2005

Average Exclusivity for Newly Launched Drugs

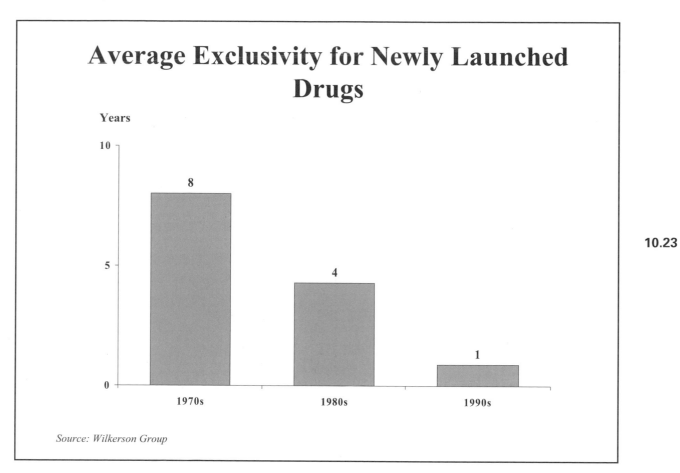

Source: Wilkerson Group

10.23

IDE Filings Submission Outcomes
2001-2004

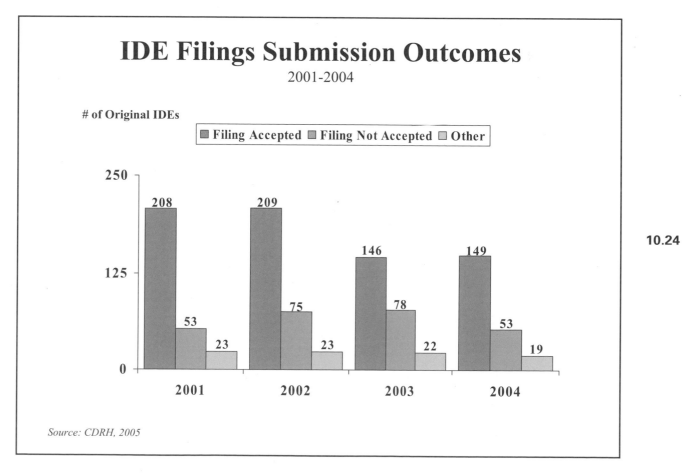

Source: CDRH, 2005

10.24

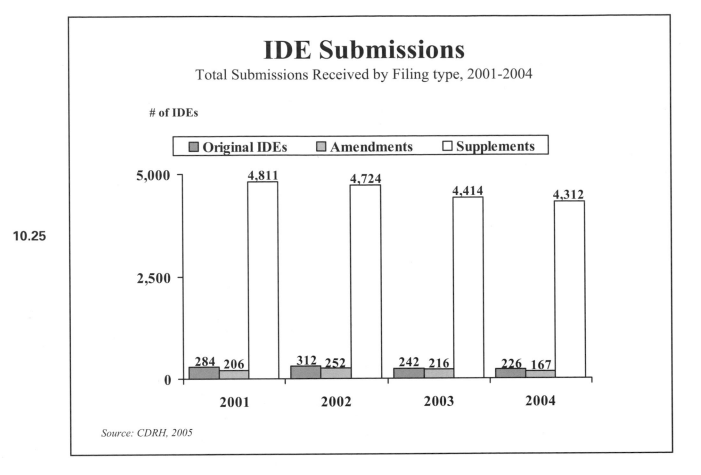

10.25

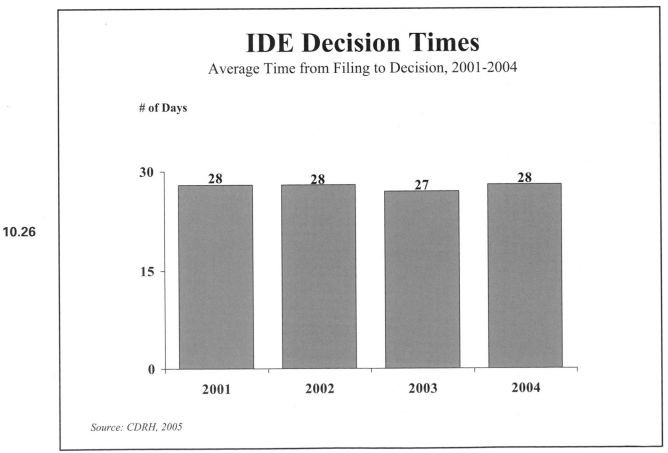

10.26

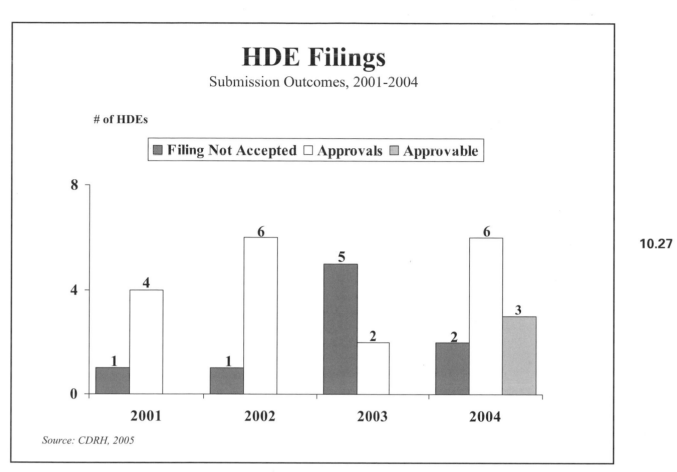

HDE Filings

Submission Outcomes, 2001-2004

# of HDEs

■ Filing Not Accepted □ Approvals ■ Approvable

Source: CDRH, 2005

10.27

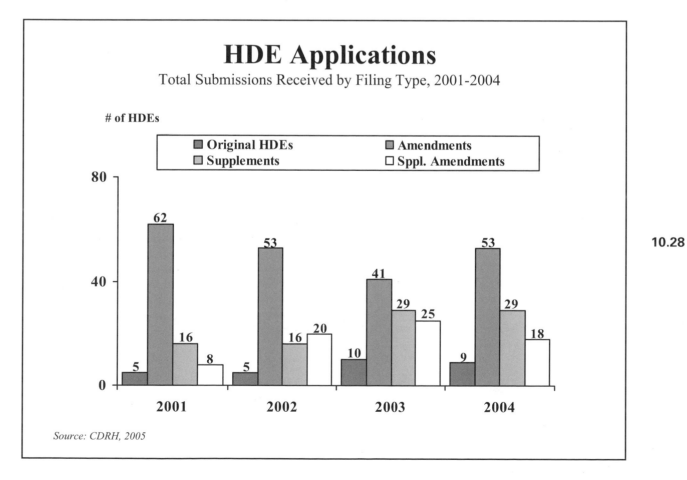

HDE Applications

Total Submissions Received by Filing Type, 2001-2004

# of HDEs

■ Original HDEs ■ Amendments
■ Supplements □ Sppl. Amendments

Source: CDRH, 2005

10.28

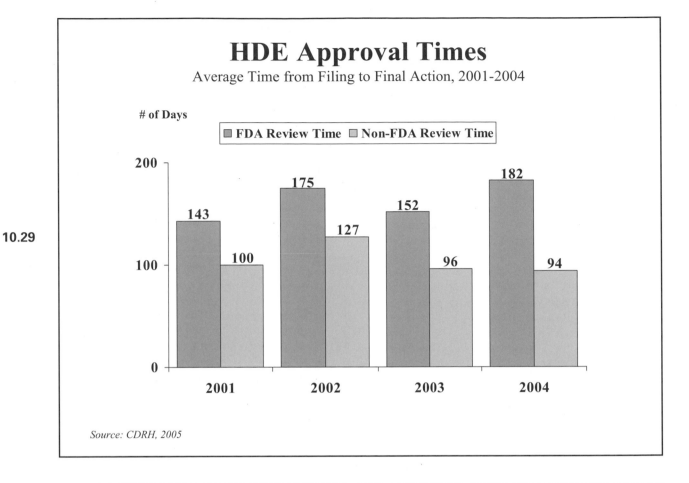

HDE Approval Times

Average Time from Filing to Final Action, 2001-2004

# of Days

■ FDA Review Time ■ Non-FDA Review Time

10.29

Source: CDRH, 2005

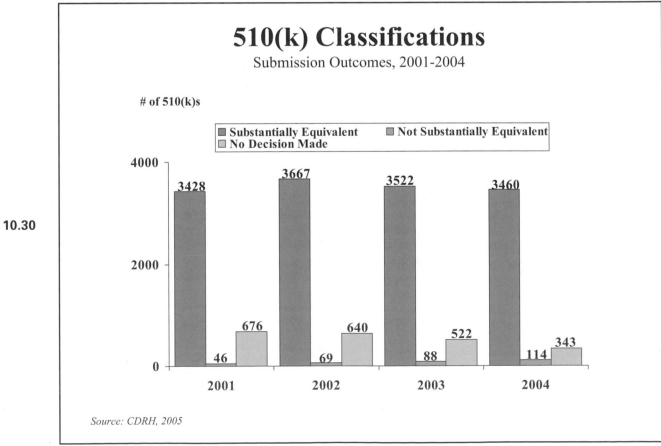

510(k) Classifications

Submission Outcomes, 2001-2004

# of 510(k)s

■ Substantially Equivalent ■ Not Substantially Equivalent
■ No Decision Made

10.30

Source: CDRH, 2005

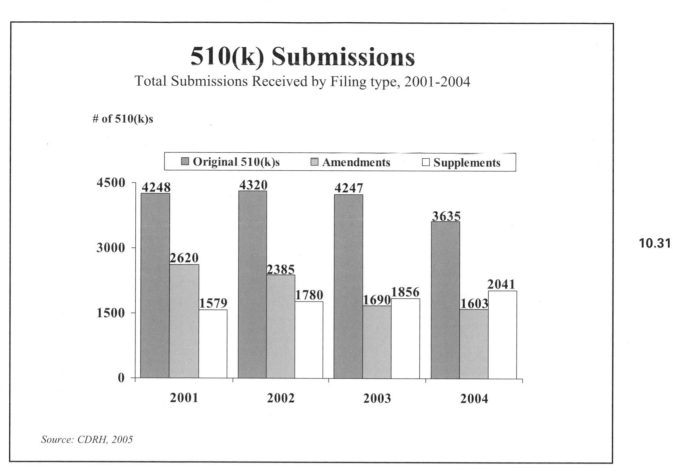

510(k) Submissions
Total Submissions Received by Filing type, 2001-2004

of 510(k)s

Original 510(k)s — Amendments — Supplements

Source: CDRH, 2005

10.31

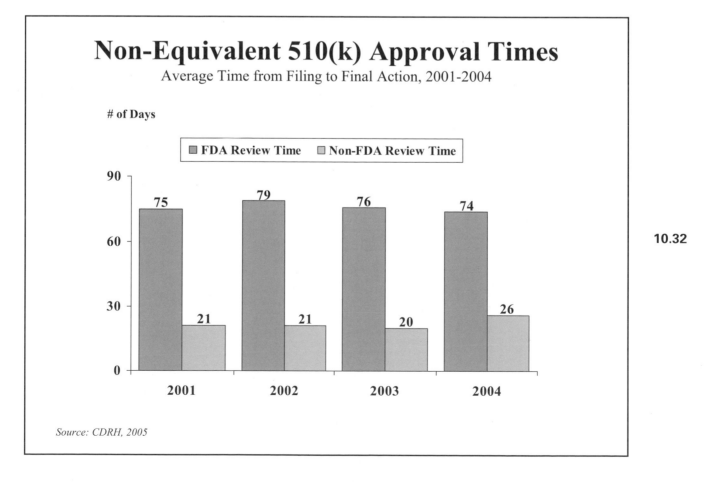

Non-Equivalent 510(k) Approval Times
Average Time from Filing to Final Action, 2001-2004

of Days

FDA Review Time — Non-FDA Review Time

Source: CDRH, 2005

10.32

10.33

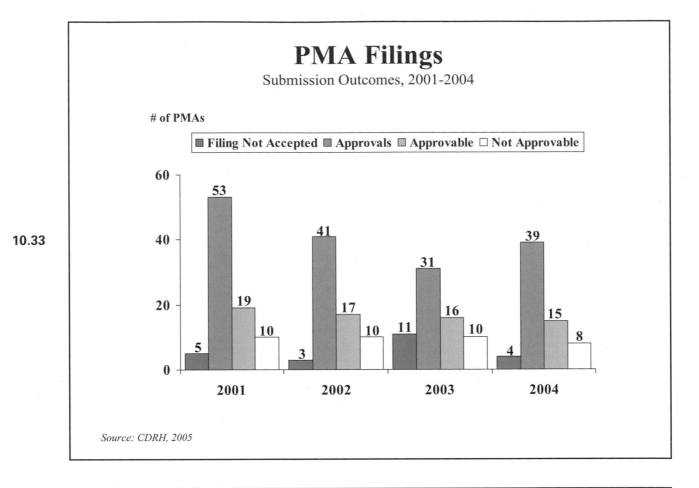

PMA Filings
Submission Outcomes, 2001-2004

# of PMAs

■ Filing Not Accepted ■ Approvals ■ Approvable □ Not Approvable

Source: CDRH, 2005

10.34

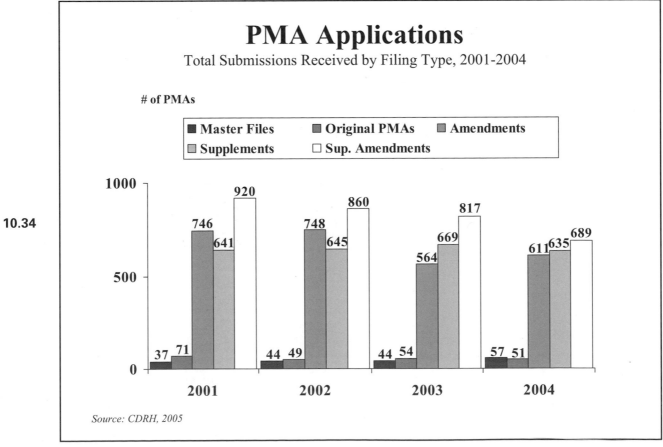

PMA Applications
Total Submissions Received by Filing Type, 2001-2004

# of PMAs

■ Master Files ■ Original PMAs ■ Amendments
■ Supplements □ Sup. Amendments

Source: CDRH, 2005

PMA Approval Times
Average Time from Filing to Final Action, 2001-2004

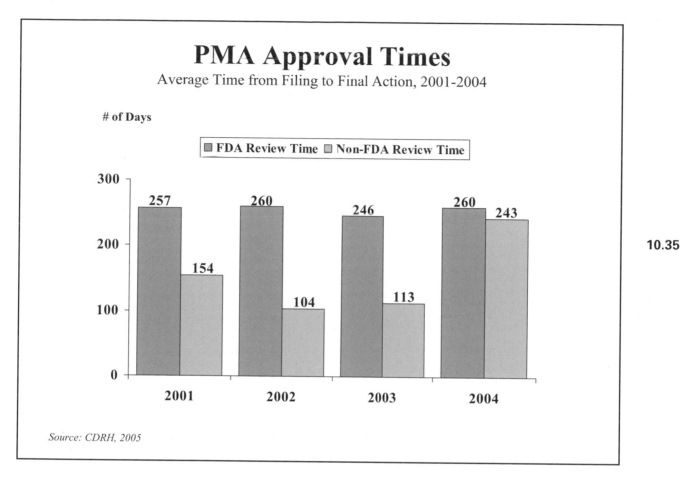

Source: CDRH, 2005

10.35

FDA Site Inspections
Site Inspections by Target, 2000-2005

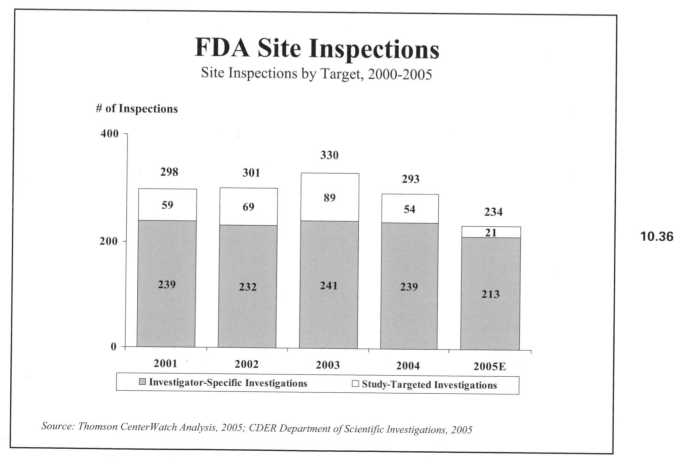

Source: Thomson CenterWatch Analysis, 2005; CDER Department of Scientific Investigations, 2005

10.36

10.37

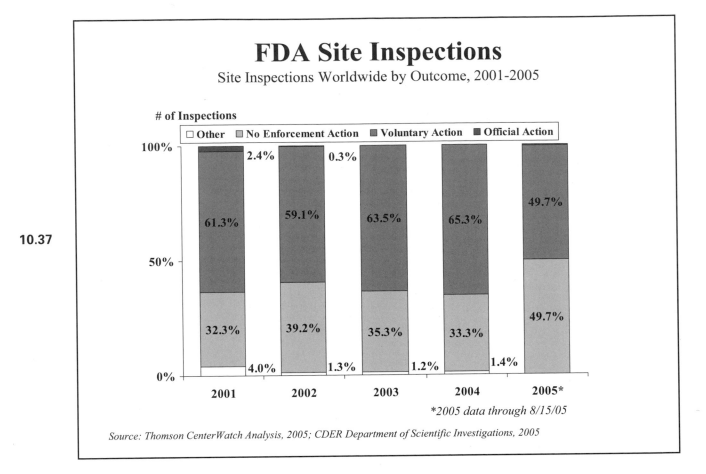

FDA Site Inspections
Site Inspections Worldwide by Outcome, 2001-2005

# of Inspections

☐ Other ▨ No Enforcement Action ▨ Voluntary Action ■ Official Action

2005 data through 8/15/05

Source: Thomson CenterWatch Analysis, 2005; CDER Department of Scientific Investigations, 2005

10.38

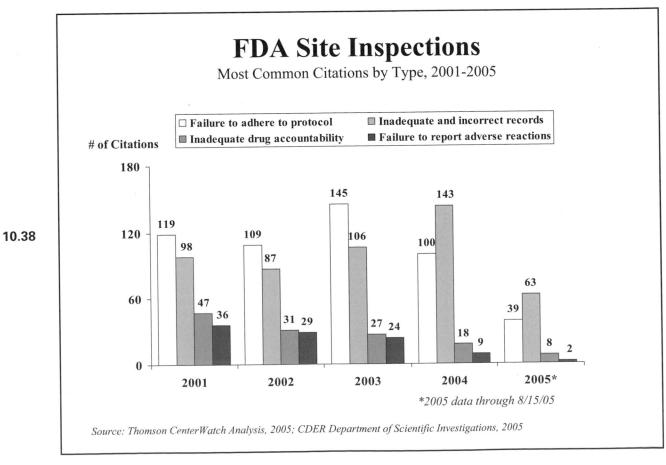

FDA Site Inspections
Most Common Citations by Type, 2001-2005

☐ Failure to adhere to protocol ▨ Inadequate and incorrect records
▨ Inadequate drug accountability ■ Failure to report adverse reactions

# of Citations

2005 data through 8/15/05

Source: Thomson CenterWatch Analysis, 2005; CDER Department of Scientific Investigations, 2005

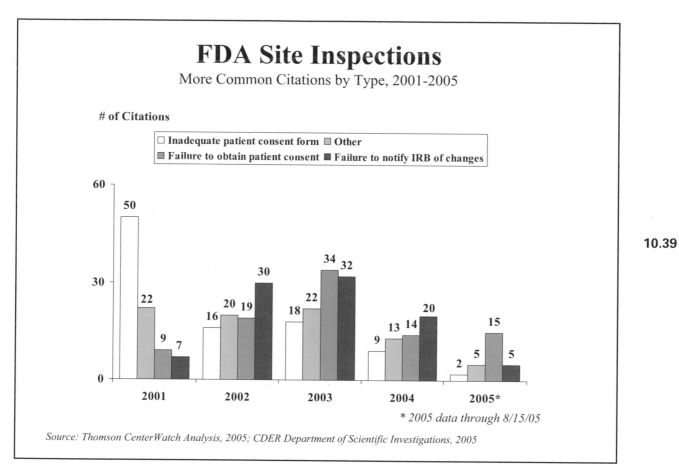

FDA Site Inspections
More Common Citations by Type, 2001-2005

of Citations

- ☐ Inadequate patient consent form
- ☐ Other
- ☐ Failure to obtain patient consent
- ■ Failure to notify IRB of changes

* 2005 data through 8/15/05

Source: Thomson CenterWatch Analysis, 2005; CDER Department of Scientific Investigations, 2005

10.39

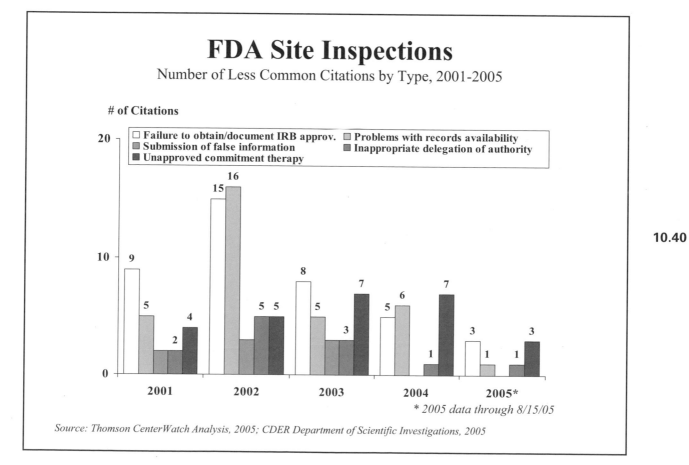

FDA Site Inspections
Number of Less Common Citations by Type, 2001-2005

of Citations

- ☐ Failure to obtain/document IRB approv.
- ☐ Problems with records availability
- ☐ Submission of false information
- ■ Inappropriate delegation of authority
- ■ Unapproved commitment therapy

* 2005 data through 8/15/05

Source: Thomson CenterWatch Analysis, 2005; CDER Department of Scientific Investigations, 2005

10.40

10.41

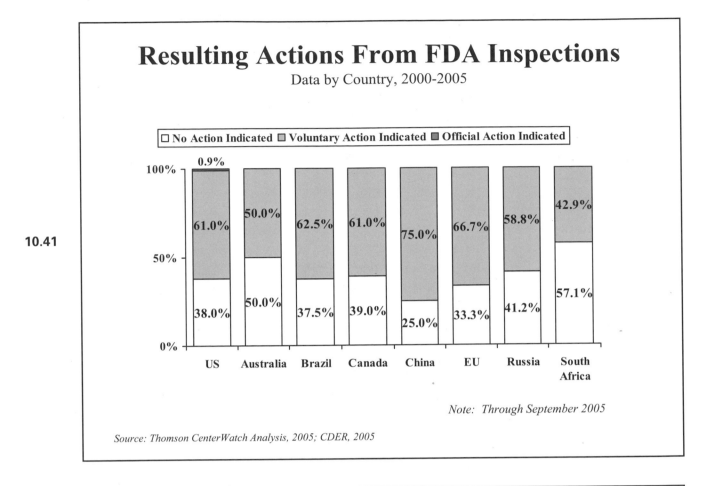

Resulting Actions From FDA Inspections
Data by Country, 2000-2005

☐ No Action Indicated ☐ Voluntary Action Indicated ■ Official Action Indicated

Note: Through September 2005

Source: Thomson CenterWatch Analysis, 2005; CDER, 2005

10.42

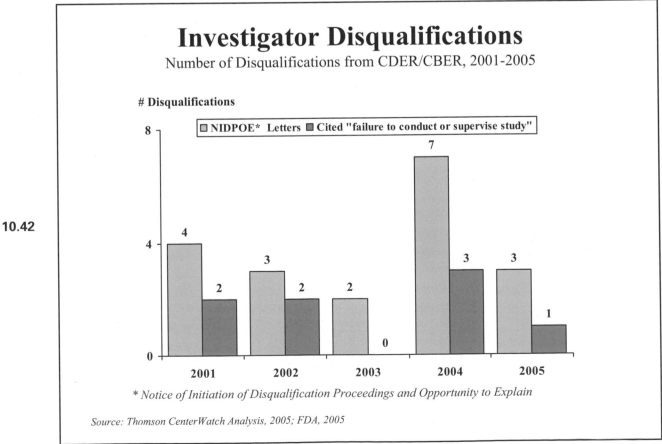

Investigator Disqualifications
Number of Disqualifications from CDER/CBER, 2001-2005

 # Disqualifications

☐ NIDPOE* Letters ■ Cited "failure to conduct or supervise study"

Notice of Initiation of Disqualification Proceedings and Opportunity to Explain

Source: Thomson CenterWatch Analysis, 2005; FDA, 2005

Responsibility for Compliance Failure
Who Investigators Believe is Responsible for Compliance Failure

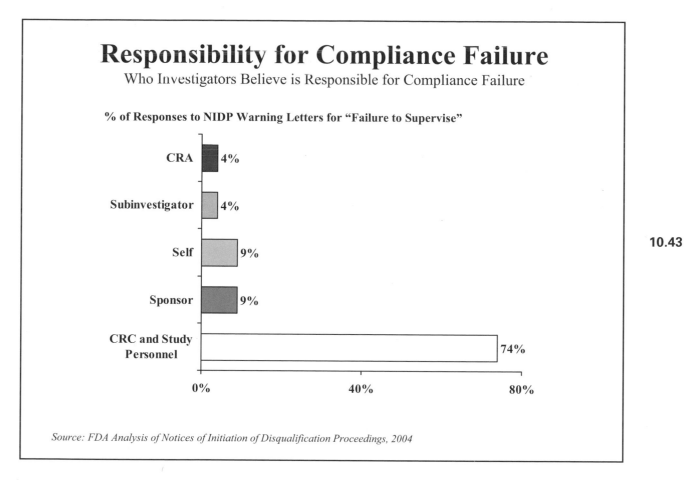

% of Responses to NIDP Warning Letters for "Failure to Supervise"

CRA — 4%
Subinvestigator — 4%
Self — 9%
Sponsor — 9%
CRC and Study Personnel — 74%

(axis: 0%, 40%, 80%)

10.43

Source: FDA Analysis of Notices of Initiation of Disqualification Proceedings, 2004

FDA Public Health Advisories
Safety Warnings Issued for Approved Drugs, 2004

10.44

Drug	Date	Indication	Safety Concern	Action
NSAIDs/ COX-2 inhibitors	12/23/2004	Chronic Pain/ Rheumatoid Arthtitis	Cardiovascular toxicity	Public Health Advisory
Bextra	12/9/2004	Rheumatoid Arthritis	Stevens-Johnson syndrome	Label Revision, Manufacturer recall
Vioxx	9/30/2004	Rheumatoid Arthritis	Cardiovascular toxicity	Public Health Advisory, Manufacturer recall
Crestor	6/9/2004	Hypercholesterol emia	serious muscle toxicity (myopathy)	Public Health Advisory, Label Revision

Source: Thomson CenterWatch Analysis; FDA, 2005

FDA Public Health Advisories
Safety Warnings Issued for Approved Drugs, 2005

Drug	Date	Indication	Safety Concern	Action
Long-Acting Beta 2-Adrenergic Agonists	11/18/05	Asthma/COPD	Exacerbation of Bronchospasm	Public Health Advisory, Label Revision
Palladone	7/23/05	Pain	Drug interaction with alcohol	Public Health Advisory, Marketing Suspended
Mifeprex/misoprostol	7/19/05	Non-surgical abortion	Bacterial Sepsis	Public Health Advisory
Duragesic	7/15/05	Pain	Opioid overdose	Public Health Advisory
Celebrex	4/7/05	Chronic Pain/Rheumatoid Arthtitis	Cardiovascular toxicity	Public Health Advisory, Label Revision
Bextra	4/7/05	Chronic Pain/Rheumatoid Arthtitis	Cardiovascular toxicity	Public Health Advisory, Marketing Suspended
Avonex	3/16/2005	Multiple Sclerosis	Liver toxicity	Label Revision
Elidel, Protopic	3/10/05	Atopic Dermatitis	Skin cancer	Public Health Advisory
Tysabri	2/28/2005	Multiple Sclerosis	Progressive multifocal leukoencephalopathy	Public Health Advisory, Marketing Suspended
Gabitril	2/18/05	Epilepsy	Seizure risk for off-label indications	Public Health Advisory
Adderall	2/9/2005	ADHD	Sudden cardiac death	Public Health Advisory (Canadian Suspension)
Viramune	1/19/2005	HIV/AIDS	Liver toxicity	Public Health Advisory

10.45

Source: Thomson CenterWatch Analysis; FDA, 2005

Approved Drugs Withdrawn from Market
1980-2005

Withdrawn Drugs	Approved	Removed	Withdrawn Drugs	Approved	Removed
Zomepirac	1980	1983	Bromfenac	1997	1998
Benoxaprofen	1982	1982	Mibefradil	1997	1998
Nomifensine	1984	1986	Grepafloxin	1997	1999
Suprofen	1985	1987	Troglitazone	1997	2000
Terfenadine	1985	1998	Cerivastatin	1997	2001
Encainide	1986	1991	Rapacuronium	1999	2001
Astemizole	1988	1999	Rofecoxib	1999	2004
Temafloxacin	1992	1992	Alosetron*	2000	2000
Flosequinan	1992	1993	Valdecoxib	2001	2004
Cisapride	1993	2000	*Returned to market in 2002 with restricted distribution*		
Dexfenfluramine	1996	1997			

10.46

Source: Thomson CenterWatch Analysis, 2005; FDA, 2005

International Regulatory Bodies
Selected Regulatory Bodies and Filing Names

Country	Regulatory Body	Clinical Trial Application	Regulatory Submission
United States	Food & Drug Administration (FDA)	Investigational New Drug Application (IND)	New Drug Application (NDA)/Biological License Application (BLA)
Canada	HealthCanada	Clinical Trial Application (CTA)/ Demandes díessais cliniques (DEC)	New Drug Submission (NDS)/ PrÈsentations de DrogueNouvelle (PDN)
European Union	European Medicines Agency (EMEA)	Clinical Trial Application (CTA)	Marketing Authorization Application (MAA)
Switzerland	SwissMedic	Clinical Trials Notification (CTN)	Marketing Authorization Application (MAA)
Australia	Therapeutic Goods Administration (TGA)	Clinical Trial Notification (CTN)/ Clinical Trial Exemption (CTX)	Submission
Russia	Ministry of Health	Clinical Trial Application	Registration Submission
India	Central Drugs Standard Control Organization (CDSCO)	Investigational New Drug Application (IND)	Import License
South Africa	Medicines Regulatory Authority (Department of Health)	Clinical Trial Application	Medicine Registration Application
Japan	Ministry of Health, Labour and Welfare (MHLW)	Clinical Trial Notification (CTN)	Japanese New Drug Application (J-NDA)
China	State Food and Drug Administration (SFDA)	Clinical Trial Application	Chinese New Drug Application (cNDA)
South Korea	Korea Food and Drug Administration (KFDA)	Investigational New Drug Application (IND)	New Drug Application (NDA)
Singapore	Health Sciences Authority (HSA)	Clinical Trial Certificate (CTC)	New Drug Application (NDA)

Source: Thomson CenterWatch Analysis; FDA, 2005

10.47

Canadian Regulatory Review
NDSs Submitted and Approved, 2000-2004

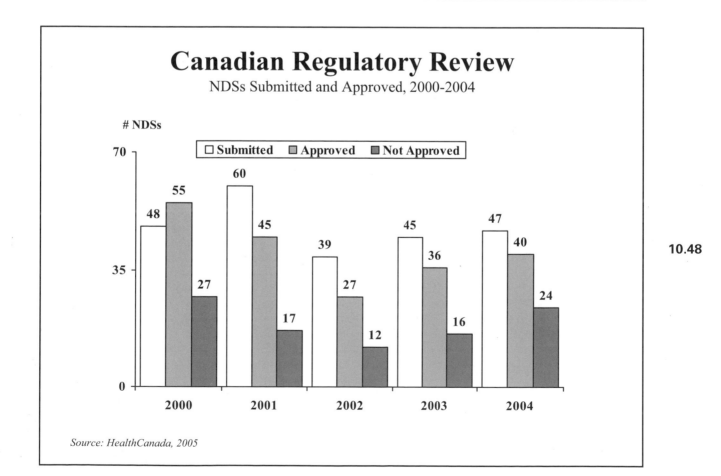

NDSs

□ Submitted   ▨ Approved   ■ Not Approved

- 2000: 48, 55, 27
- 2001: 60, 45, 17
- 2002: 39, 27, 12
- 2003: 45, 36, 16
- 2004: 47, 40, 24

Source: HealthCanada, 2005

10.48

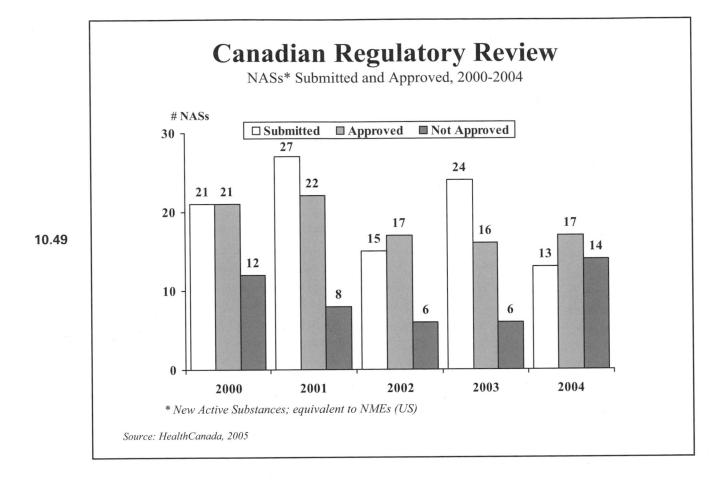

Canadian Regulatory Review
NASs* Submitted and Approved, 2000-2004

10.49

* New Active Substances; equivalent to NMEs (US)

Source: HealthCanada, 2005

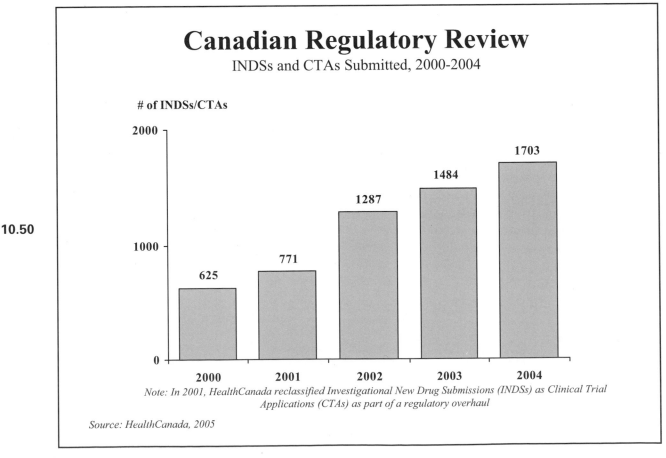

Canadian Regulatory Review
INDSs and CTAs Submitted, 2000-2004

10.50

Note: In 2001, HealthCanada reclassified Investigational New Drug Submissions (INDSs) as Clinical Trial Applications (CTAs) as part of a regulatory overhaul

Source: HealthCanada, 2005

Canadian Regulatory Review

CTAs Submitted by Phase, 2002-2004

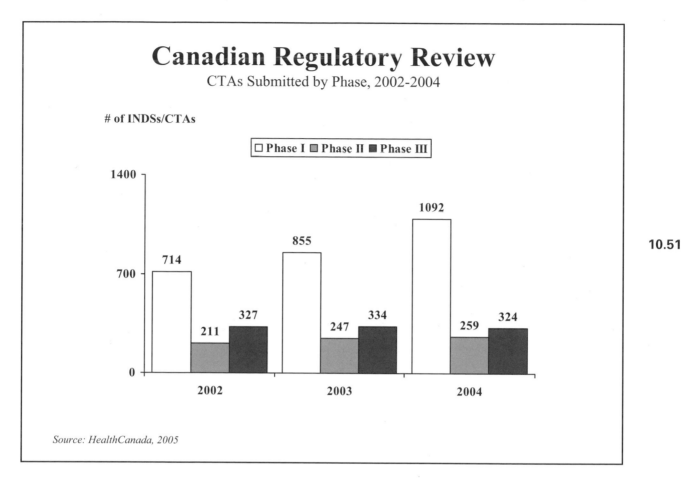

10.51

Source: HealthCanada, 2005

Canadian Regulatory Review

Priority Review Submissions Approved, 2000-2004

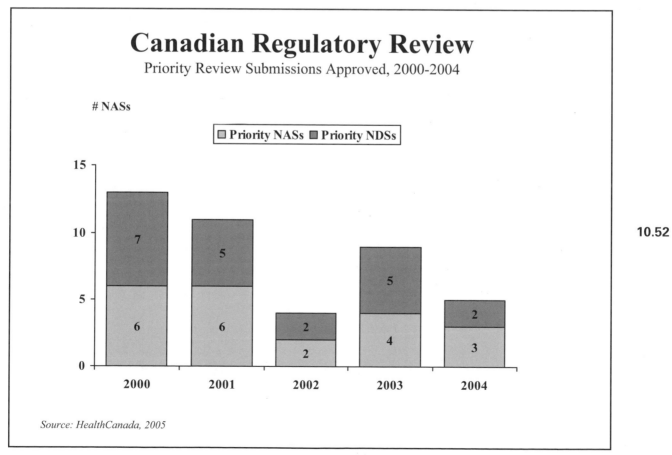

10.52

Source: HealthCanada, 2005

10.53

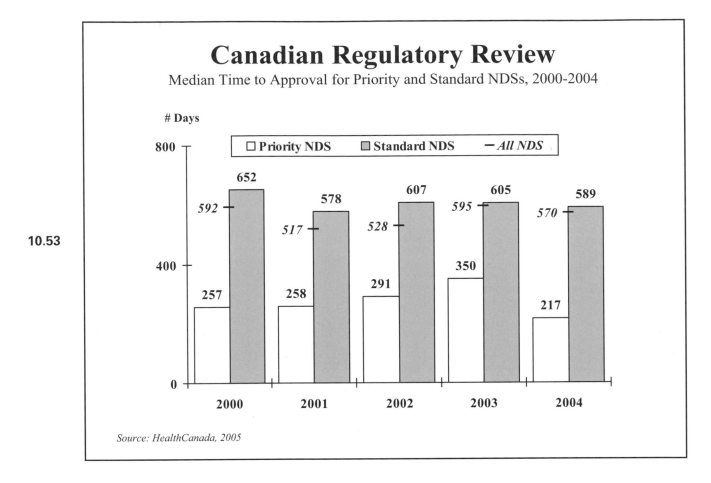

Canadian Regulatory Review
Median Time to Approval for Priority and Standard NDSs, 2000-2004

Source: HealthCanada, 2005

10.54

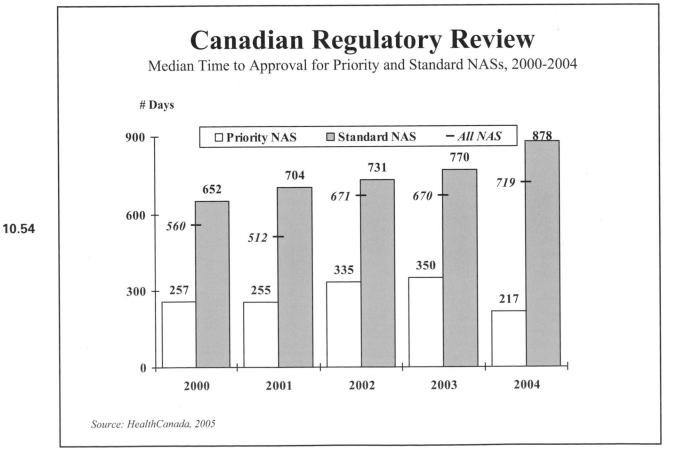

Canadian Regulatory Review
Median Time to Approval for Priority and Standard NASs, 2000-2004

Source: HealthCanada, 2005

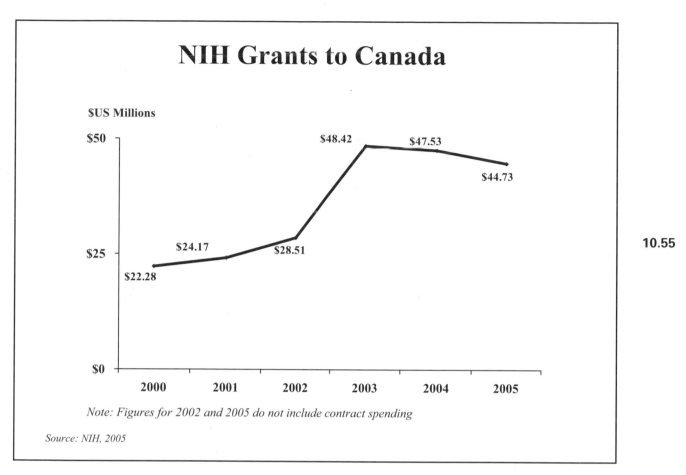

NIH Grants to Canada

$US Millions

$50

$48.42

$47.53

$44.73

$25

$24.17

$28.51

$22.28

$0

2000   2001   2002   2003   2004   2005

Note: Figures for 2002 and 2005 do not include contract spending

Source: NIH, 2005

10.55

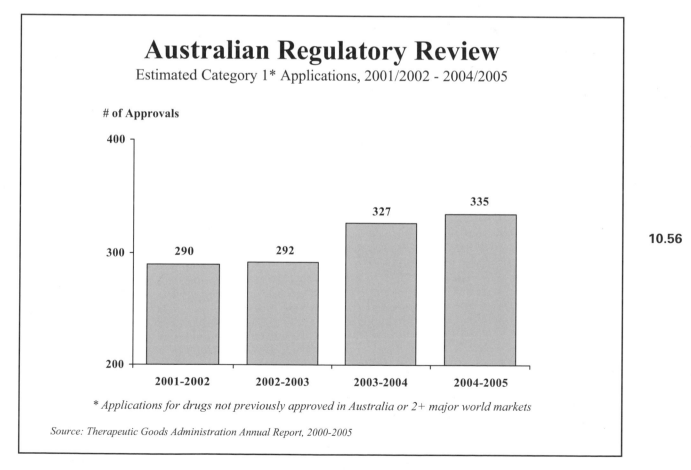

Australian Regulatory Review
Estimated Category 1* Applications, 2001/2002 - 2004/2005

# of Approvals

400

335

327

300

290   292

200

2001-2002   2002-2003   2003-2004   2004-2005

* Applications for drugs not previously approved in Australia or 2+ major world markets

Source: Therapeutic Goods Administration Annual Report, 2000-2005

10.56

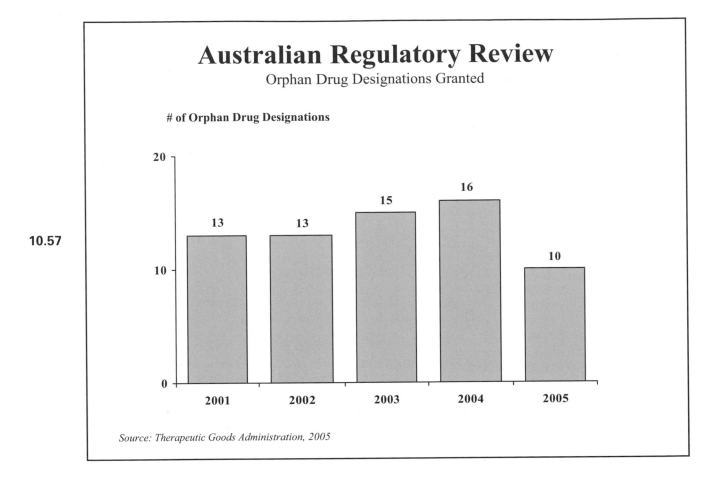

10.57

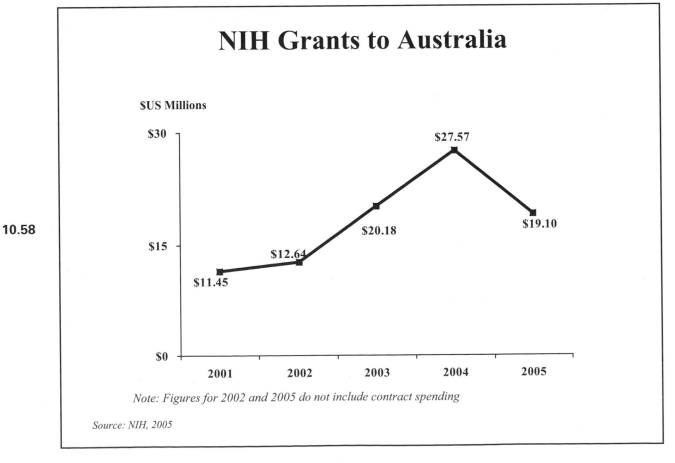

10.58

Regulatory Bodies For Selected EU Countries

Country	Regulatory Body	Abbr.
Austria	Bundesministerium für Gesundheit und Frauen	BMGF
Belgium	Directoraat generaal Geneesmiddelen	
Czech Republic	Státní ústav pro kontrolu léčiv (State Institute for Drug Control)	SUKL
Denmark	Lægemiddelstyrelsen (Danish Medicines Agency)	DMA
Estonia	Ravimiamet (State Agency of Medicines)	SAM
Finland	Lääkelaitos (National Agency for Medicines)	NAM
France	Agence française de sécurité sanitaire des produits de santé	AFSSaPS
Germany	Bundesinstitut für Arzneimittel und Medizinprodukte	BfArM
Greece	National Organization for Medicine	EOF
Hungary	Országos Gyógyszerészeti Intézet (National Institute of Pharmacy)	OGYI
Ireland	Irish Medicines Board	IMB
Italy	Ministero della Salute	
Netherlands	Inspectie Voor de Dezondheidszorg (Dutch Health Care Inspectorate)	IGZ
Poland	Ministerstwa Zdrowia (Ministry of Health)	
Portugal	Instituto Nacional da Farmacia e do Medicamento	INFARMED
Spain	Agencia Española del Medicamento (Spanish Medicines Agency)	AEM
Sweden	Läkemedelsverket (Medical Products Agency)	MPA
UK	Medicines and Healthcare products Regulatory Agency	MHRA

Source: Thomson CenterWatch Analysis 2005

10.59

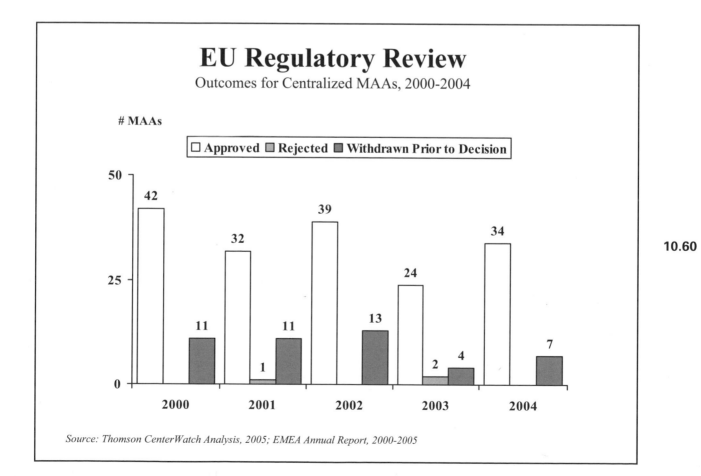

EU Regulatory Review
Outcomes for Centralized MAAs, 2000-2004

MAAs

☐ Approved ☐ Rejected ■ Withdrawn Prior to Decision

Source: Thomson CenterWatch Analysis, 2005; EMEA Annual Report, 2000-2005

10.60

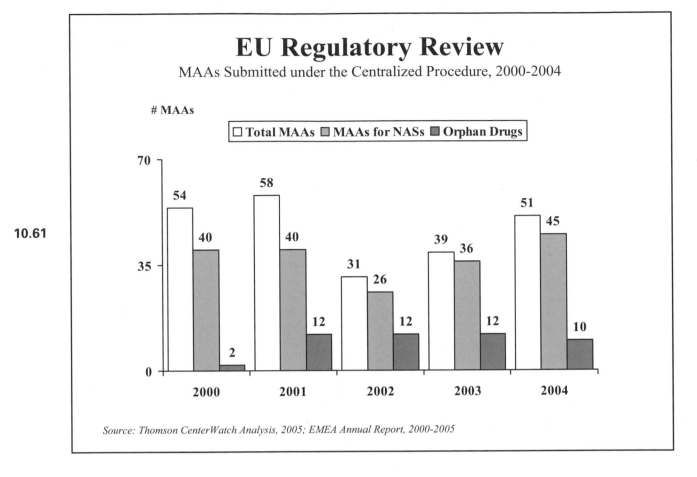

EU Regulatory Review

MAAs Submitted under the Centralized Procedure, 2000-2004

MAAs

☐ Total MAAs ▨ MAAs for NASs ■ Orphan Drugs

10.61

Source: Thomson CenterWatch Analysis, 2005; EMEA Annual Report, 2000-2005

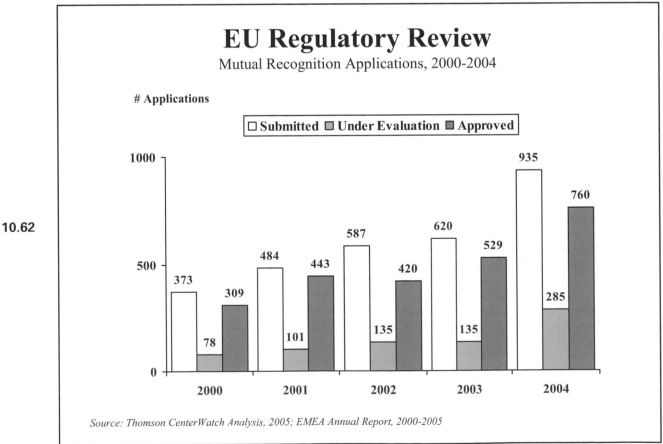

EU Regulatory Review

Mutual Recognition Applications, 2000-2004

Applications

☐ Submitted ▨ Under Evaluation ■ Approved

10.62

Source: Thomson CenterWatch Analysis, 2005; EMEA Annual Report, 2000-2005

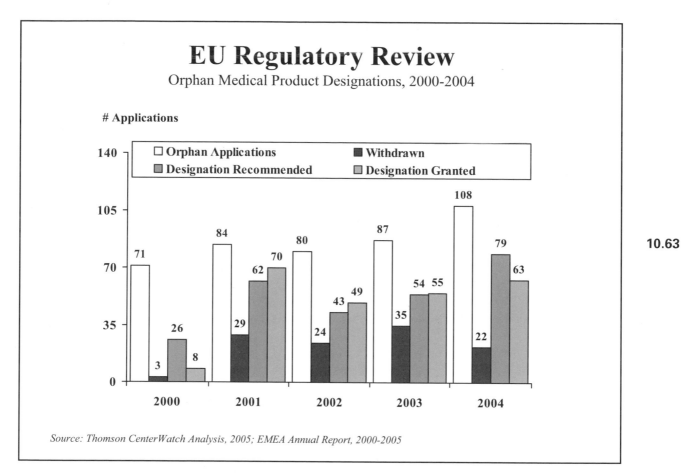

EU Regulatory Review
Orphan Medical Product Designations, 2000-2004

Applications

Legend:
- □ Orphan Applications
- ■ Withdrawn
- ■ Designation Recommended
- □ Designation Granted

Source: Thomson CenterWatch Analysis, 2005; EMEA Annual Report, 2000-2005

10.63

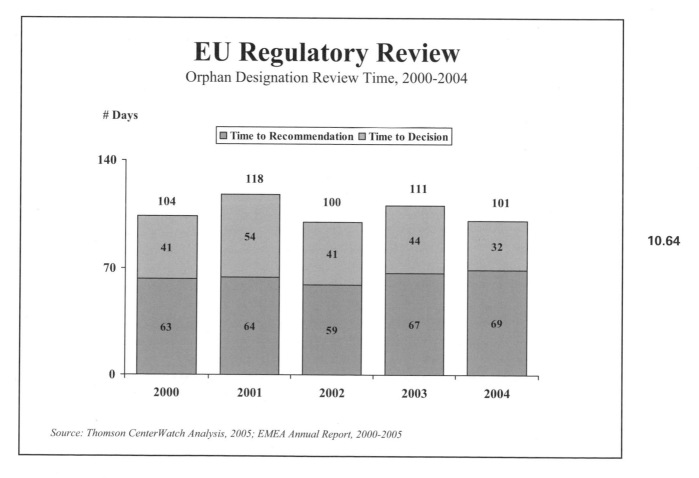

EU Regulatory Review
Orphan Designation Review Time, 2000-2004

Days

Legend:
- ■ Time to Recommendation
- □ Time to Decision

Source: Thomson CenterWatch Analysis, 2005; EMEA Annual Report, 2000-2005

10.64

10.65

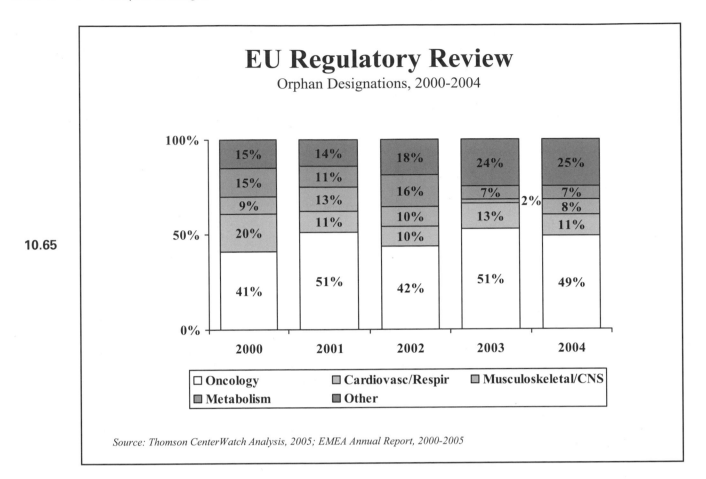

EU Regulatory Review
Orphan Designations, 2000-2004

Source: Thomson CenterWatch Analysis, 2005; EMEA Annual Report, 2000-2005

10.66

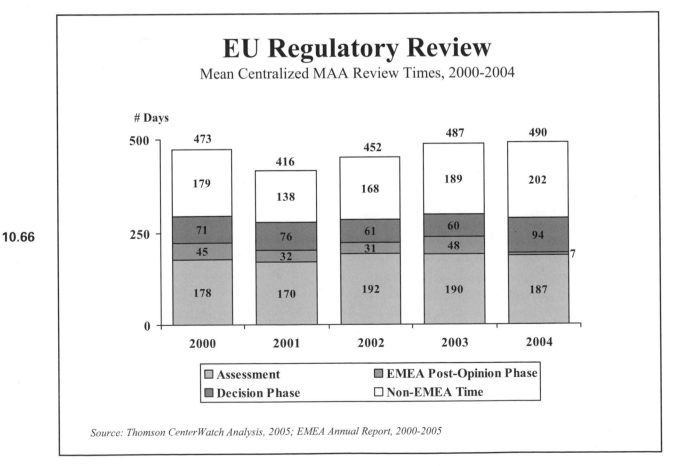

EU Regulatory Review
Mean Centralized MAA Review Times, 2000-2004

Source: Thomson CenterWatch Analysis, 2005; EMEA Annual Report, 2000-2005

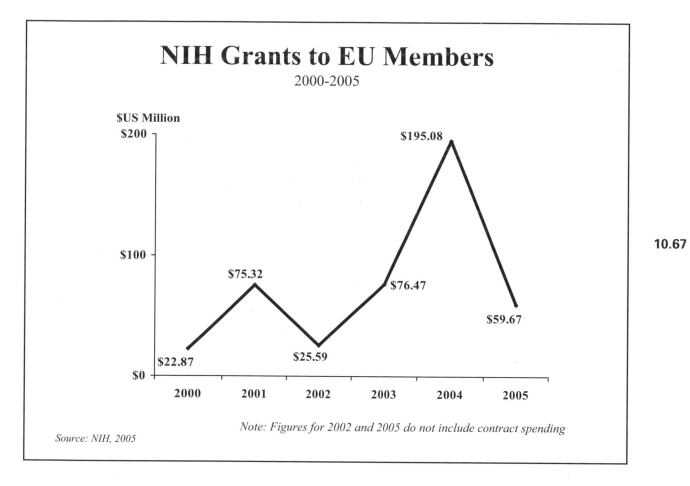

NIH Grants to EU Members
2000-2005

$US Million

$200 — $195.08

$100

$75.32 $76.47

$59.67

$22.87 $25.59

$0

2000 2001 2002 2003 2004 2005

Note: Figures for 2002 and 2005 do not include contract spending

Source: NIH, 2005

10.67

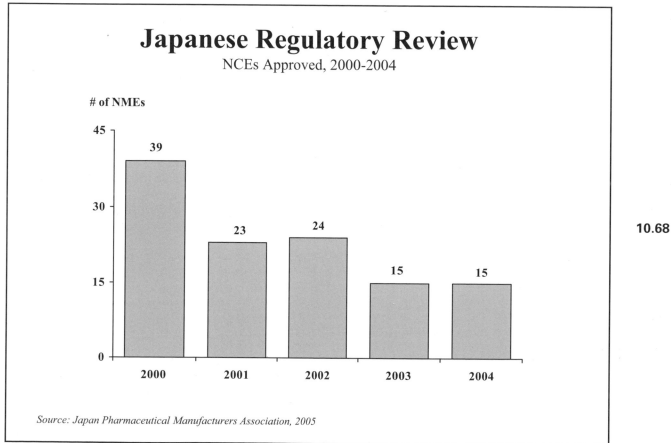

Japanese Regulatory Review
NCEs Approved, 2000-2004

of NMEs

45

39

30

23 24

15 15 15

0

2000 2001 2002 2003 2004

Source: Japan Pharmaceutical Manufacturers Association, 2005

10.68

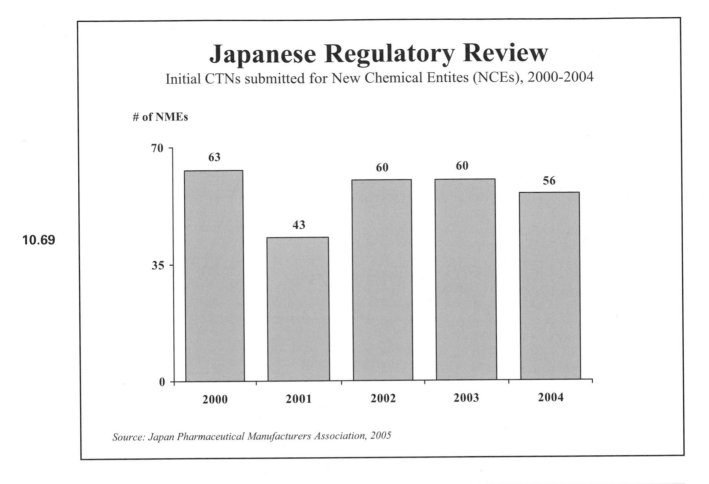

Japanese Regulatory Review

Initial CTNs submitted for New Chemical Entites (NCEs), 2000-2004

# of NMEs

Source: Japan Pharmaceutical Manufacturers Association, 2005

10.69

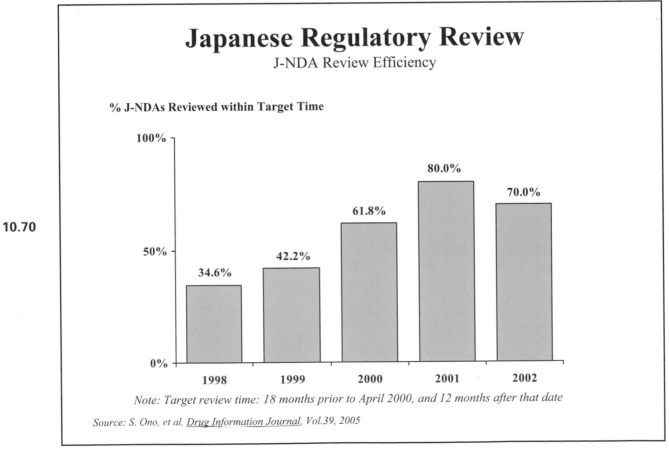

Japanese Regulatory Review

J-NDA Review Efficiency

% J-NDAs Reviewed within Target Time

Note: Target review time: 18 months prior to April 2000, and 12 months after that date

Source: S. Ono, et al. Drug Information Journal, Vol.39, 2005

10.70

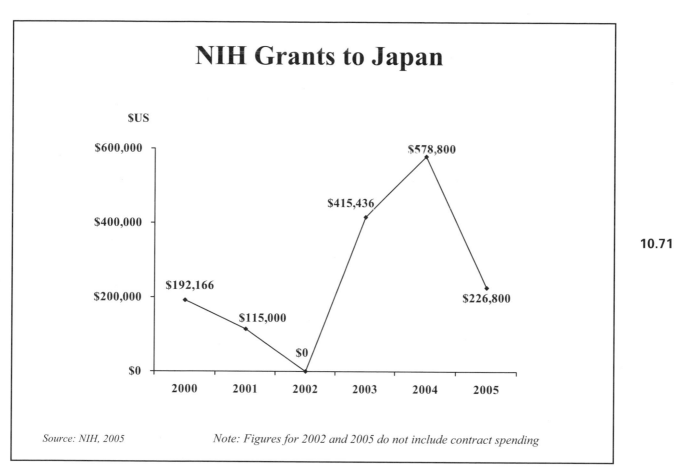

NIH Grants to Japan

$US

$600,000 ┤ $578,800

$400,000 ┤ $415,436

$200,000 ┤ $192,166

$0 ┤ $115,000 $0 $226,800

2000 2001 2002 2003 2004 2005

Source: NIH, 2005   *Note: Figures for 2002 and 2005 do not include contract spending*

10.71

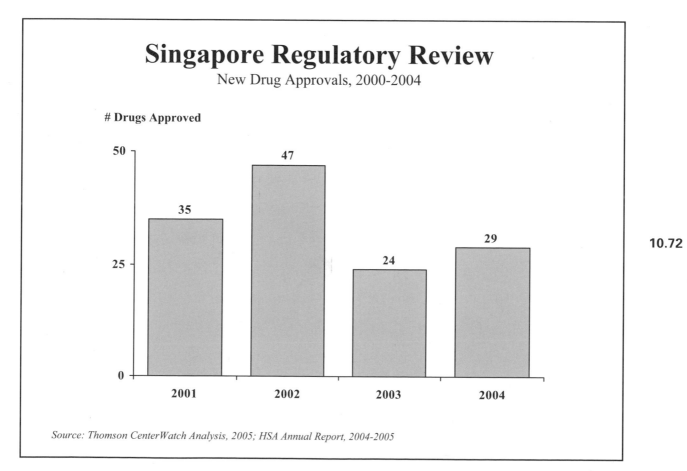

Singapore Regulatory Review
New Drug Approvals, 2000-2004

 # Drugs Approved

50 ┤   47

35

25 ┤   24   29

0 ┴ 2001   2002   2003   2004

Source: Thomson CenterWatch Analysis, 2005; HSA Annual Report, 2004-2005

10.72

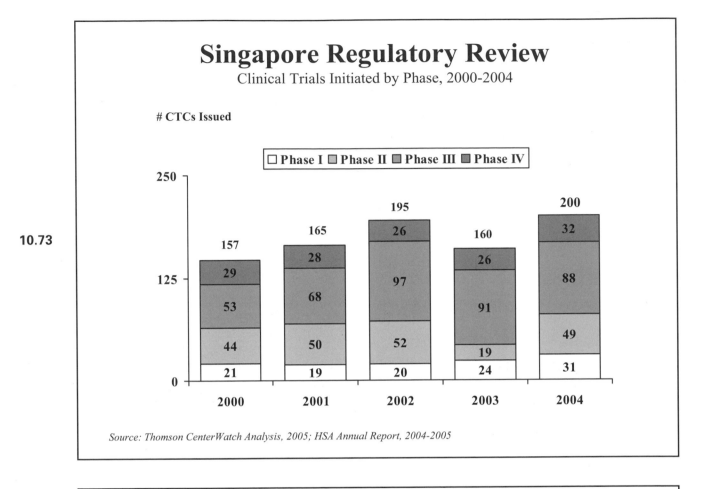

10.73

Singapore Regulatory Review
Clinical Trials Initiated by Phase, 2000-2004

Source: Thomson CenterWatch Analysis, 2005; HSA Annual Report, 2004-2005

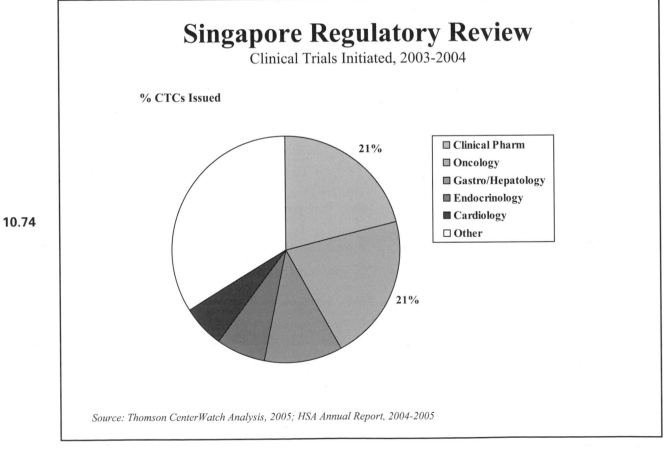

10.74

Singapore Regulatory Review
Clinical Trials Initiated, 2003-2004

Source: Thomson CenterWatch Analysis, 2005; HSA Annual Report, 2004-2005

INDEX

About Thomson CenterWatch

Thomson CenterWatch—a business of the Thomson Corporation—is a Boston-based publishing and information services company that focuses on the clinical trials industry. We provide a variety of publications and information services used by pharmaceutical and biotechnology companies, CROs, SMOs and investigative sites involved in the management and conduct of clinical trials. We are also a key part of Thomson Clinical Trial Solutions, a newly created group including Medstat, NexCura and New England IRB offering sponsors and CROs a streamlined solution for clinical trail planning, conducting and post-study needs.

Some of our top publications and services are described below. For a comprehensive listing and detailed information about our publications and services, please visit our web site at www.centerwatch.com. You can also contact us at (866) 219-3440 for subscription and order information.

22 Thomson Place · Boston, MA 02210
Phone (617) 856-5900 · Fax (617) 856-5901
www.centerwatch.com

CenterWatch Newsletters

The CenterWatch Monthly

Our flagship publication, *The CenterWatch Monthly* newsletter provides pharmaceutical and biotechnology companies, CROs, SMOs, academic institutions, research centers and the investment community with in-depth business news and insights, feature articles on trends and clinical research practices, original market intelligence and analysis, as well as grant lead information for investigative sites.

CWWeekly

This weekly newsletter, available as a fax or in electronic format, reports on the top stories and breaking news in the clinical trials industry. Each week the newsletter includes business headlines, industry briefs, financial information, market intelligence, drug pipeline news and clinical trial results.

Research Practitioner

Previously published by our sister company, Thomson Center for Clinical Research Practice (CCRP), *Research Practitioner* is a new addition to the CenterWatch portfolio. This bi-monthly journal presents the most pertinent and useful information on the conduct and oversight of clinical research. Each issue contains informative articles covering: regulatory developments and trends, issues in clinical research management, protocol design and implementation and ethical issues in human research.

JobWatch

This web-based resource at www.centerwatch.com, complemented by a PDF publication, provides comprehensive listings of career and educational opportunities in the clinical trials industry, including a searchable resume database service.

Companies use *JobWatch* regularly to identify qualified clinical research professionals and career and educational services.

Clinical Research Training Series

Becoming a Successful Clinical Research Investigator

This 'how-to' guidebook is the perfect introduction for any health professional considering a career in clinical research. Written by Dr. David Ginsberg and Norman Goldfarb, *Becoming a Successful Clinical Research Investigator* takes you through the process of determining whether clinical research is right for you to understanding the industry, setting up your own clinical research center and finding studies.

A Guide to Patient Recruitment and Retention

This 250+ page manual is designed to help clinical research professionals improve the effectiveness of their patient recruitment and retention efforts. Written by Diana Anderson, Ph.D., with contributions from 15 industry experts and thought leaders, this guide offers real world, practical recruitment and retention strategies, tactics and metrics. It is an invaluable resource for educating staff on patient recruitment, for managing recruitment initiatives for clinical trials, and for accelerating enrollment and retention efforts.

Protecting Study Volunteers in Research, Third Edition

In addition to addressing current and emerging issues that are critical to our system of human subject protection oversight, *Protecting Study Volunteers in Research* has been expanded to include a chapter on how to implement the HIPAA Privacy Rule in research. Written by Cynthia Dunn, M.D. of Western Institutional Review Board and Gary Chadwick, PharmD., M.P.H. of the University of Rochester, it is a suggested educational resource by NIH and FDA (source: NIH Notice OD-00-039, 2000, page 37841, Federal Registry 2003, page 47342) and is designed to help organizations provide the highest standards of safe and ethical treatment of study volunteers.

The CRC's Guide to Coordinating Clinical Research

Written by Karen E. Woodin, Ph.D., this guidebook was designed as a training resource for investigative site staff. It is filled with almost 400-pages of valuable information on the role and responsibilities of a clinical research coordinator (CRC) and explains in detail the research process from the site and CRC perspective. This training manual will teach readers to identify the regulations governing clinical research, discuss Good Clinical Practices (GCPs) and how to apply them in clinical trials, organize a clinical practice to manage clinical trials successfully to their completion and more.

The CRA's Guide to Monitoring Clinical Research

This 400-page book is an ideal resource for novice and experienced CRAs, as well as professionals interested in pursuing a career as study monitors. *The CRA's Guide covers* important topics along with updated regulations, guidelines and worksheets, including resources such as: 21 CFR Parts 50, 54, 56 & 312 Guidelines, various checklists (monitoring visit, site evaluation, informed consent) and a study documentation file verification log.

Standard Operating Procedures

Standard Operating Procedures for Good Clinical Practice at the Investigative Site

Standard Operating Procedures are critical to quality performance and the ethical conduct of clinical trials. Your SOPs are an indication of the level of professionalism at your investigative site. *Standard Operating Procedures for Good Clinical Practice at the Investigative Site* can be customized to meet the needs of your site. Each of its 184 pages can either be left as is, or altered to reflect the uniqueness of your research facility. Based upon the principles found in GCP Consolidated Guideline and the Code of Federal Regulations, it is written in an easy-to-read format that is clear, precise and pertinent to the day to day conduct of clinical research.

Policies and Standard Operating Procedures for the Institutional Review Board

Policies and Standard Operating Procedures for the Institutional Review Board is designed to be customized to fit the requirements of your IRB and reflect you institution's philosophy and standards. The template, which is based on the Code of Federal Regulations, guidance and ICH/GCP Consolidated Guideline, is in an easy-to-use format with content that is clear, precise, and pertinent to the day-to-day conduct of IRB activities. For any institutional IRB that is considering AAHRPP or Partnership for Human Research Protection (PHRP) accreditation, or simply strives to adhere to such standards, these SOPs are the most efficient and reliable way to achieve that level of compliance.

Standard Operating Procedures for Good Clinical Practice by Sponsors

Standard Operating Procedures for Good Clinical Practice by Sponsors are not only mandated by US federal regulation, they ensure reliable data and regulatory compliance. In addition, SOPs for GCP provides the framework of operational efficiency that ensures completing your drug or device clinical trials in budget and on schedule. Sponsor SOPs cover all the regulatory requirements for GCP, including: document control, FDA and NIH contacts and submissions, project management, monitoring visits and reports, human subject protection (IRB, consent) and PHI, data handling (CRF completion, electronic systems) and quality assurance (site audits, FDA inspections).

Online Directories and Sourcebooks

The Drugs in Clinical Trials Database

This database is a comprehensive online, searchable resource offering detailed profiles of new investigational treatments in phase I through III clinical trials. Updated daily, *The Drugs in Clinical Trials Database* provides information on more than 2,500 drugs for more than 800 indications worldwide in a well-organized and easy-to-reference format. Detailed profile information is provided for each drug along with a separate section on pediatric treatments. Search results may be downloaded to Excel for further sorting and analysis.

The eDirectory of the Clinical Trials Industry

Previously available as a printed directory, the *eDirectory* is a comprehensive, online, searchable and downloadable database featuring detailed contact and profile information on 2,200+ organizations involved in the clinical trials industry including pharmaceutical, biotech, CROs, SMOs, investigative sites and more. Company profiles can be searched by keyword, company name, city, state, phase focus, therapeutic specialties and services offered. Search results can be downloaded to an Excel spreadsheet for further sorting and analysis.

Research Center and Industry Provider Profile Pages

The CenterWatch web site (www.centerwatch.com) attracts tens of thousands of sponsor and CRO company representatives every month who are looking for experienced service providers and investigative sites to manage and conduct their clinical trials. No registration is required. Sponsors and CROs use this online directory free of charge. The CenterWatch web site offers all contract service providers—both CROs and investigative sites—the opportunity to present more information than any other Internet-based service available. This service is an ideal way to secure new contracts and clinical study grants.

CenterWatch Compilation Reports Series

These topic-specific reports provide comprehensive, in-depth features, original research and analyses and fact-based company/institution business and financial profiles. Reports are available on Site Management Organizations, Academic Medical Centers, Contract Research Organizations, and Investigative Sites. Spanning years of in-depth coverage and analyses, these reports provide valuable insights into company strategies, market dynamics and successful business practices. Ideal for business planning and for market intelligence/market research activities.

Drug Intelligence & Market Research Services

Thomson CenterWatch provides a wide range of quantitative and qualitative market intelligence services focusing on all aspects of the clinical trials industry. Our years of experience and unmatched perspective enable us to create unique research services individually tailored to our customers' needs and budget. Our *Drug Intelligence Services* provide fast, accurate, comprehensive reports on the status of drugs in clinical development through custom pipelines, metrics and statistical analyses. Our custom drug reports will help you identify business development opportunities, track competitors, size potential markets, and identify likely approval candidates. Our *Market Research Services* can be customized to meet your deadlines, budget and level of detail or analysis. With our unique perspective and resources, we are positioned to inform you of the latest trends and challenges in the clinical trials industry. In areas from outsourcing, globalization, and EDC to patient enrollment and physicians' needs, we can provide your organization with the information and analysis it requires to make business decisions more effectively.

TrialWatch Site-Identification Service

Several hundred sponsor and CRO companies use the *TrialWatch* service to identify prospective investigative sites to conduct their upcoming clinical trials. Every month, companies post bulletins of their phase I–IV development programs that are actively seeking clinical investigators. These bulletins are included in *The CenterWatch Monthly*—our flagship monthly publication that reaches as many as 25,000 experienced investigators every month. Use of the *TrialWatch* service is FREE.

Content License Services

CenterWatch offers both database content and static text under license. All CenterWatch content can be seamlessly integrated into your company Internet, Intranet or Extranet web site(s) with or without frames. Our database offerings include: *The Clinical Trials Listing Service*™, *Clinical Trial Results, Drugs in the Pipeline, Newly Approved Drugs,* and *The eDirectory of the Clinical Trials Industry.* Our static text offerings include: an editorial feature on background information on clinical trials and a glossary of clinical trial terminology. Other content may be developed according to your needs.

Patient Education Resources

The CenterWatch Clinical Trials Listing Service™

The CenterWatch Clinical Trials Listing Service™, on www.centerwatch.com, provides the largest and most comprehensive listing of industry- and government-sponsored clinical trials on the Internet. Each month, the CenterWatch web site receives over 750,000 visitors, 75% of which are patients. *The CenterWatch Clinical Trials Listing Service*™ provides an international listing of more than 20,000 industry sponsored and thousands of government sponsored clinical trials.

Volunteering For a Clinical Trial: Your Guide to Participating in Research Studies

This easy-to-read, six-page patient education brochure is designed to give patients and their advocates consistent, professional and unbiased educational information about clinical research. The brochure is IRB-approved and can be distributed to potential study subjects in a variety of ways including direct mailings, displays in waiting rooms, or as handouts to guide discussions. The brochure can be customized with company logos and custom information.

A Word from Study Volunteers: Opinions and Experiences of Clinical Trial Participants

This straightforward and easy-to-read ten-page pamphlet reviews the results of a survey conducted among more than 1,200 clinical research volunteers. This brochure presents first-hand experiences from clinical trial volunteers. It offers valuable insights for individuals interested in participating in a clinical trial. The brochure can be customized with company logos and custom information.

Understanding the Informed Consent Process

Understanding the Informed Consent Process is an easy-to-read, eight-page brochure designed specifically for study volunteers. The brochure provides valuable information and facts about the informed consent process, and reviews the volunteer's "Bill of Rights."